Behavioral Economics and Its Applications

Behavioral Economics and Its Applications

Peter Diamond

Hannu Vartiainen

Editors

PRINCETON UNIVERSITY PRESS

PRINCETON AND OXFORD

Published by Princeton University Press,
41 William Street, Princeton, New Jersey 08540

In the United Kingdom: Princeton University Press,
3 Market Place, Woodstock, Oxfordshire OX20 1SY

ISBN-13: 978-0-691-12284-7 (alk. paper)
ISBN-10: 0-691-12284-9 (alk. paper)

Library of Congress Control Number: 2006936337

A catalogue record for this book is available from the British Library

This book is based on the Yrjö Jahnsson Foundation 50th Anniversary
Conference held on June 22–23, 2004, in Espoo, Finland

This book has been composed in Times

Typeset by T&T Productions Ltd, London

Printed on acid-free paper ∞

pup.princeton.edu

Printed in the United States of America

10 9 8 7 6 5 4 3

Contents

Foreword

The Yrjö Jahnsson Foundation was established in 1954. Mrs. Hilma Jahnsson, the spouse of the deceased professor of economics Yrjö Jahnsson, donated a generous amount of their joint estate as initial capital for the foundation. The purpose of the foundation is to promote Finnish research in economics, medicine, and health economics, and to maintain and support Finnish educational and research facilities in these fields.

International contacts are essential to the foundation, and the Finnish economics community has benefited from lectures and seminars by a long list of internationally renowned economists. Since 1963 the foundation has arranged the Yrjö Jahnsson Lectures in Economics, one of the most distinguished scholarly lecture series in this field. The well-known Yrjö Jahnsson Award in Economics is given every two years to a young economist who has made an important contribution to economics in Europe. The foundation organizes a high-profile conference to celebrate each decennial anniversary.

This volume has its basis in an international conference held in Helsinki on June 22–23, 2004 to celebrate the 50th anniversary of the Foundation. As the title indicates, the aim of the conference was to discuss the role of behavioral economics in applied fields. It is important to understand how psychologically plausible features of human behavior affect—and should affect—the design and working of economic institutions. However, it is equally important to get feedback from the applied arena to see which behavioral tendencies really matter, and to see how the framework should be developed further.

I am grateful to Professor Peter Diamond of the Massachusetts Institute of Technology, who acted as the program chairman. He did a marvelous job in choosing the set of topics and speakers. I also thank Professor Bengt Holmström, also of the Massachusetts Institute of Technology, whose input in the initial phase of the conference was very important. I am grateful to Professor Seppo Honkapohja, University of Cambridge, U.K., for helping us to shape the conference and this volume through his experience and connections. Finally, I thank all the speakers and commentators, and the Scientific Director of the foundation, Dr. Hannu Vartiainen, for making the conference such a successful event.

TIMO LAATUNEN
Chairman of the Board

List of Contributors

Ian Ayres
Yale Law School

Ian Ayres is the William K. Townsend Professor at Yale Law School. He has published eight books and hundreds of articles on a wide variety of topics and is a regular contributor to public radio's Marketplace and a columnist for Forbes.

B. Douglas Bernheim
Stanford University

B. Douglas Bernheim is the Edward Ames Edmonds Professor of Economics at Stanford University. He has published extensively in public economics, political economy, behavioral economics, industrial organization, financial economics, game theory, and contract theory. He is a Fellow of the American Academy of Arts and Sciences, a Fellow of the Econometric Society, a recipient of a John Simon Guggenheim Memorial Foundation Fellowship, an Alfred P. Sloan Foundation Research Fellowship, and an NBER–Olin Research Fellowship. He has served as the Director of the Stanford Institute for Theoretical Economics, and as Co-Editor of the *American Economic Review*.

Truman F. Bewley
Yale University

Truman F. Bewley received a PhD in economics in 1970 and a PhD in mathematics in 1971, both from the University of California, Berkeley. He is now the Alfred C. Cowles Professor of Economics at Yale University. He has contributed to general equilibrium theory and has written a book, *Why Wages Don't Fall During a Recession* (1999) based on over 300 interviews with businesspeople, labor leaders, and other decision makers important to the labor market.

Colin F. Camerer

California Institute of Technology

Colin F. Camerer is the Axline Professor of Business Economics at Caltech. He studies the behavioral economics of decisions, strategic thinking, and markets, using a combination of experimental methods and field data. His recent work explores the neural foundations of economics. He has edited or written four books, including *Behavioral Game Theory* (2003) and published more than 100 articles in journals and books. He is a Fellow of the Econometric Society and was 2005–6 President of the Society for Neuroeconomics.

Anne Case

Princeton University

Anne Case is a Professor of Economics and Public Affairs at Princeton University, where she serves as Director of the Research Program in Development Studies. Her recent research has focused on the two-way links between economic status and health status, both in the United States and in developing countries. She has published extensively on health and well-being in professional journals, and she is currently serving on the editorial boards of the *American Economic Review* and the *World Bank Economic Review*.

Michael D. Cohen

University of Michigan

Michael D. Cohen is the William D. Hamilton Collegiate Professor of Complex Systems, Information, and Public Policy at the University of Michigan. He has published numerous articles on organizational decision-making in journals such as *Rationality and Society* and *Nature*. He is the coauthor (with Robert Axelrod) of *Harnessing Complexity: Organizational Implications of a Scientific Frontier*. His empirical work includes field studies of decision processes and laboratory experiments showing the foundations of group routines in individual procedural memory. He has served as an external faculty member of the Santa Fe Institute and as a long-term consultant at the Xerox Palo Alto Research Center.

Peter Diamond

Massachusetts Institute of Technology

Peter Diamond is an Institute Professor and Professor of Economics at MIT, where he has taught since 1966. He has been President of the American Economic Association, of the Econometric Society, and of the National Academy of Social Insurance. He is a Fellow of the American Academy of Arts and Sciences and a Member of the National Academy of Sciences. He has written on behavioral economics, public finance, social insurance, uncertainty and search theories, and macroeconomics.

Christoph Engel
Max Planck Institute for Research on Collective Goods, Bonn

Christoph Engel received his Dr. Juris from Tübingen, and did his Habilitation in Hamburg. He held a Chair of Media and Communication Law at the University of Osnabrück, was the head the Max Planck Project Group on the Law of Common Goods, and has been the Director of Max Planck Institute for Research on Collective Goods in Bonn since 2003. His main research area is the behavioral analysis of legal issues. His recent publications include *Generating Predictability* (2005) and, with Gerd Gigerenzer, *Heuristics and the Law* (2006).

Richard G. Frank
Harvard Medical School

Richard G. Frank is the Margaret T. Morris Professor of Health Economics in the Department of Health Care Policy at Harvard Medical School. He is also a Research Associate with the National Bureau of Economic Research and serves on the Bio-behavioral Sciences Board of the Institute of Medicine. He advises several state mental health and substance abuse agencies, and serves as Co-Editor for the *Journal of Health Economics*. He is a recipient of numerous awards, including the Georgescu-Roegen Prize from the Southern Economic Association, the Carl A. Taube Award from the American Public Health Association, and the Emily Mumford Medal from Columbia University's Department of Psychiatry.

Jacob Glazer
Tel Aviv University and Boston University

Jacob Glazer is a Professor of Economics at Tel Aviv University and Boston University. He received his PhD from Northwestern University in 1986. His fields of interest are health economics, industrial organization, and economic theory.

Seppo Honkapohja
University of Cambridge

Seppo Honkapohja is Professor of International Macroeconomics at the University of Cambridge. He was formerly Professor of Economics at the University of Helsinki. His interests are in macroeconomics, especially in the modeling of learning and expectations, bounded rationality, and their implications for monetary and fiscal policy.

Christine Jolls
Yale Law School and National Bureau of Economic Research

Christine Jolls is Professor of Law at Yale Law School and co-director of the National Bureau of Economic Research Law and Economics Program. She trained as both a lawyer and an economist and has written widely on both behavioral law and economics and the economics of employment and contract law.

Botond Koszegi
Department of Economics, University of California, Berkeley

Botond Koszegi is Assistant Professor of Economics at the University of California, Berkeley. He obtained his PhD at the Massachusetts Institute of Technology in 2000. His research focuses on mathematical modeling of psychological issues relevant to economics, and especially on self-control problems, anticipatory emotions, and reference-dependent preferences.

Ulrike Malmendier
Stanford University

Ulrike Malmendier is an Assistant Professor of Finance at Stanford University and a Faculty Research Fellow at the National Bureau of Economic Research (NBER) and the Institute for the Study of Labor (IZA) in Bonn. She received a PhD from Harvard University and a PhD in Law from the University of Bonn. She is Associate Editor of the *Economic Journal* and the *Journal of Financial Intermediation*.

Sendhil Mullainathan
Harvard University

Sendhil Mullainathan, Professor of Economics at Harvard University, specializes in Behavioral Economics, Poverty, and Finance, and has been involved in integrating psychology into economics. He was a founding member of the Poverty Action Lab, and a Research Associate at the NBER. He is the recipient of numerous grants and fellowships, including the prestigious MacArthur Fellowship and received his PhD in Economics from Harvard.

Antonio Rangel
Stanford University

Antonio Rangel is an Assistant Professor at the Stanford University Department of Economics and the Director of the Stanford Neuroeconomics Lab. His research interests include neuroeconomics, psychology, and economics, and their applications to public policy.

Emmanuel Saez
University of California at Berkeley

Emmanuel Saez obtained his PhD at MIT. He is Professor of Economics at the University of California at Berkeley, Research Associate at the NBER, and Editor of the *Journal of Public Economics*. He works on issues of taxation, redistribution, and retirement savings.

Eldar Shafir
Princeton University

Eldar Shafir is Professor of Psychology and Public Affairs at the Department of Psychology and the Woodrow Wilson School of Public and International Affairs at Princeton University. He received his PhD in Cognitive Science from the Massachusetts Institute of Technology in 1988. His interests are in descriptive studies of decision-making and their implications for economics and rationality. Recent research has focused on decision-making in the context of poverty.

Sir Nicholas Stern
Her Majesty's Treasury

Sir Nicholas Stern is Second Permanent Secretary to Her Majesty's Treasury, Director of Policy and Research for the Prime Minister's Commission for Africa, and Head of the Government Economic Service. He is also former Professor of Economics at the London School of Economics and a former Chief Economist and Senior Vice President of the World Bank. His research and publications have focused on economic development and growth, economic theory, tax reform, public policy and the role of the state and economies in transition. He is the author of the *Stern Review on the Economics of Climate Change*. He received his DPhil from the University of Oxford.

Jean Tirole
University of Toulouse

Jean Tirole received his PhD in economics from MIT. He is Scientific Director of the Institut d'Economie Industrielle, University of Social Sciences, Toulouse. He has taught at MIT, where he now holds a position as a permanent visiting professor. He has published over 150 professional articles and eight books on industrial organization, regulation, game theory, banking and finance, psychology and economics, and macroeconomics. He received the Yrjö Jahnsson Award from the European Economic Association in 1993.

Hannu Vartiainen

Yrjö Jahnsson Foundation

Hannu Vartiainen is Scientific Director of the Yrjö Jahnsson Foundation, and Docent of the Helsinki School of Economics. He received his PhD from the University of Helsinki and works on game theory, social choice, and decision theory.

Timothy D. Wilson

University of Virginia

Timothy D. Wilson received his PhD from the University of Michigan in 1977. He is currently Sherrell J. Aston Professor of Psychology at the University of Virginia. He is the author of *Strangers to Ourselves: Discovering the Adaptive Unconscious* (2002).

Behavioral Economics and Its Applications

Introduction

By Peter Diamond and Hannu Vartiainen[1]

Over the last decade or so, behavioral economics has fundamentally changed the way economists conceptualize the world. Behavioral economics is an umbrella of approaches that seek to extend the standard economics framework to account for relevant features of human behavior that are absent in the standard economics framework.[2] Typically, this calls for borrowing from the neighboring social sciences, particularly from psychology and sociology. The emphasis is on well-documented empirical findings: at the core of behavioral economics is the conviction that making our model of an economic man more accurate will improve our understanding of economics, thereby making the discipline more useful.

It is natural for such an endeavor to begin as a subdiscipline—one that catalogs anomalies and explores alternative ways to model choice, with applications illustrating the workings of such models. A more ambitious role for behaviorally based insights is to effect how researchers in applied fields make both positive and normative analyses. By and large, this is the arena in which the usefulness of new ideas is eventually evaluated. In the long run, one expects the arguments, if useful, to be integrated into the mainstream literature.

An example of such development in the behavioral context is finance. Success of behavioral finance, a thriving area which has produced enough material to warrant a handbook treatment (Thaler 1993),[3] is partly explained by the fact that the conflict between the standard benchmark model and a rich supply of data is particularly clear. Accounting for behavioral tendencies fills a disturbing gap in understanding financial markets, and institutions therein.

While other applied fields have not gone nearly so far, there is no reason why behavioral ideas could not, and should not, be applied to other domains too. Indeed, behavioral tendencies concern human behavior in general and there is no reason to

---

[1]We are grateful to the participants of the conference for stimulating discussions. We owe special thanks to Emma Dain of T&T Productions Ltd, London, for devotedly copyediting this volume.

[2]For a survey on the development of the field as well as some landmark works, see Camerer et al. (2003).

[3]Behavioral macroeconomics has also received some survey discussion (Akerlof 2002).

tie the arguments to a particular field. It is hoped that this volume will contribute to the integration of behavioral insights into applied fields. The contributors to this volume take for granted the fact that behavioral ideas have an important future in economics and hope, through this book, to promote developments that will make good use of them. Our aim is not to engage in the debate between the standard modeling and behavioral approaches, but to move on to applications.

The chapters in this volume examine behavioral dimensions of six fields of economics (public economics, development, law and economics, health, wage determination, and organization economics) in which behavioral argumentation has proven to be useful but has not yet been integrated as a part of the established framework. We have left out finance as being beyond the phase where contributions such as the ones in this volume can shift a field.

Interest in behavioral economics has been stimulated by accumulating evidence that the standard model of consumer decision-making provides an inadequate positive description of human behavior for some questions. According to the evidence (and contrary to the standard economic model), individuals are bounded in many dimensions, in particular in their rationality, self-control and self-interest.

Bounded rationality[4] manifests itself in incomplete information processing ability. Individuals appeal to heuristics and rules of thumb when making their decisions. They make biased probability judgments and are often overconfident. Moreover, individuals tend to anchor to seemingly irrelevant information or to the status quo, and they are loss aversive. In general, they do not maximize expected utility (Kahneman and Tversky 1979).[5]

Incomplete self-control refers to the tendency of economic agents to make decisions that are in conflict with their long-term interest. Self-control problems may lead to addictive behavior, undersaving, or procrastination. As opposed to the neoclassical view, restricting the choice set can be beneficial for an agent with bounded willpower (see, for example, Laibson 1997).

Lack of self-interest refers to the idea that preferences have a social dimension. Individuals care, or act as if they care, about other individuals' well-being (see, for example, Kahneman et al. 1986). They are also reciprocal: they care about being treated fairly and want to treat others fairly if those others are themselves behaving fairly. As a result, agents are both nicer and (when they are not treated fairly) more spiteful than postulated by the neoclassical theory.[6]

Beyond this familiar trilogy of bases for deviations from the standard model, economists are exploring additional psychological and sociological factors that

---

[4]The term was coined by Herbert Simon (see Simon 1982).

[5]Rabin (1998) gives a survey on economics and psychology.

[6]Gilbert et al. (1998) is a good survey on social psychology.

shape economic decision-making. They are also examining decision processes to view and model the black box of human decision-making; very recent work in neuroeconomics focuses directly on the question of *how* decisions are made. This is an important development, since it may help to address the fundamental difficulty of constructing welfare criteria based on individual choices.

In addition to revised models of individual choice, alternative behavioral models of individual choice can help us to understand the functioning of economic institutions. On the normative side, behavioral modeling can help us to design better institutions. This can take place not only through better understanding of how the institutions work, but also through better understanding of individual needs and the concept of welfare.[7]

One cannot evaluate the ultimate goodness of a behavioral model of an economic man without seeing how useful the model is in structuring our thinking of general economics. Applicability requires that the models and stylized facts compound to an integrated theory that is flexible, adequately parsimonious, and permits us to construct testable hypotheses. This suggests enhancing communication between applications and the underlying theory. To develop the theory further it helps to have feedback from areas where the theory could be applied. Studying applications may give a sharper view of the behavioral tendencies that really matter.

The chapters in this volume describe both realized and potential opportunities for applications of behavioral economics. Each chapter includes updated versions of a presentation at the conference and the remarks of the discussants. The final chapter consists of a modified transcript of a round-table discussion. Summaries of the highlights of the general discussion have been prepared by Botond Koszegi and Emmanuel Saez.

This volume consists of the following chapters.

Douglas Bernheim and *Antonio Rangel* discuss emerging methods for normative policy analysis in behavioral economics, with a particular focus on issues in public economics. They argue against the view that a departure from the doctrine of revealed preference, which is unavoidable in the presence of bounded rationality, necessarily renders welfare analysis infeasible or entirely subjective. Instead, they argue that it is sometimes possible to replace revealed preference by other compelling normative principles. For example, if one knows enough about the nature of decision-making malfunctions, it may be possible to recover tastes by relying on a *selective* application of the revealed-preference principle. Accordingly, practicing behavioral economics requires one to modify, not abandon, the key methodological principles of modern

---

[7]As pointed out by a reviewer, with social- or institution-dependent preferences it is no longer obvious that methodological individualism is the most useful doctrine for the analysis. For discussion on how institutions could affect preferences, see Camerer and Malmendier (Chapter 7, this volume), and for the importance of the "portability" of the underlying model, see Tirole (Chapter 8, this volume).

economics. The chapter considers three areas: addiction, saving, and contributions for public goods. The discussants are *Nicholas Stern* and *Emmanuel Saez*.

Sendhil Mullainathan gives an overview of potential applications of behavioral ideas to economic development. He argues that the work in the behavioral literature on savings and bounded willpower can be translated into understanding savings institutions and behavior in developing countries. Additionally, the insights about self-control have some direct links to understanding education, and the behavioral approach also appears to add some insight to the large body of research on the diffusion of innovation. The question of how (and when) to evaluate the impact of development policies can also be better understood. Mullainathan speculates about specific areas where psychology could be useful in the future: poverty traps, conflict, social preferences, corruption, and research on the psychology of the poor. The discussant is *Anne Case*.

Christine Jolls discusses applications of behavioral economics to law and economics. She describes some of the central attributes of behavioral law and economics and outlines an emerging focus on prospects for "debiasing" individuals through legal structures. She argues that using the vehicle of "debiasing through law," behavioral law and economics may open up a new space for legal interventions that recognize human limitations and attempt to steer individuals away from mistakes without taking the steering wheel from the individual's own hands. Because, however, debiasing through law cannot be applied in every context, Jolls suggests that future work in behavioral law and economics should seek to refine and strengthen analyses on how to structure legal rules when debiasing is not feasible. The discussants are *Ian Ayres* and *Christoph Engel*.

Truman F. Bewley studies the origins of wage rigidity. He reports the implications of interviews with company managers and labor leaders in the northeast of the United States during the early 1990s when unemployment was high because of a recession. During this era, standard economic arguments would have predicted wage cuts, but they never came. Quite surprisingly, the primary resistance to wage reduction comes from upper management, not from employees. Bewley finds that the main reason for avoiding pay cuts is that they damage morale. Morale has three components. One is the identification with the firm and an internalization of its objectives. Another is trust in an implicit exchange with the firm and with other employees; employees know that aid given to the firm or to coworkers will eventually be reciprocated, even if it goes unacknowledged. The third component is a mood that is conducive to good work. The mood need not be a happy one; good morale is not equivalent to happiness or job satisfaction. Workers may be content, simply because they do nothing. Good morale has to do with a willingness voluntarily to make sacrifices for the company and for coworkers. Thus, this chapter is an example of the adaptation of an organization to the behavioral traits displayed by economic agents working in the organization. This issue in general, and not just in wage setting, is the focus of the chapter on organizations (Camerer and Malmendier, Chapter 7, this volume). The discussant is *Seppo Honkapohja*.

Richard Frank argues that the health sector is full of institutions and decision-making circumstances that involve friction in markets and cognitive errors by decision makers. Stress of decision-making, anxiety, professionalism, insurance coverage, and lack of information make decision-making in health-related questions particularly relevant for behavioral analysis. He concludes that at the heart of the matter is the doctor–patient relationship, where trust plays the key role. Indeed, the field has drawn heavily on nonstandard arguments put forward by Arrow (1963) and may be ripe for expansion using the wider range of behavioral insights now available. Frank also discusses normative issues. He argues that the demand functions in health-care markets cannot be given the standard normative interpretation and, hence, that they cannot be taken as the definite guideline for policy analysis. He expresses skepticism over whether the prevailing cornerstones of the U.S. health policy—to increase information and the degree of available choices—will improve the quality health production. The discussants are *Jacob Glazer* and *Botond Koszegi*.

Colin Camerer and *Ulrike Malmendier* analyze, on the one hand, how behavioral economics can be applied to organizations and, on the other, how behavioral analysis of individuals can be enriched by thinking about the economic questions associated with economic organizations. Biases in behavior within organizations give rise to the question of how organizations should be designed in order to repair these mistakes or to exploit them, or how firms organize around them if they represent genuine regret-free preferences rather than errors. A lot of psychology and sociology is involved when workers team up in an organization: social comparison, changes in identity, camaraderie, attribution and diffusion of credit and blame, and so forth. This kind of behavioral analysis has played a small role in behavioral economics in recent years but looms large when thinking about organizations. The authors lay down an agenda for further research. Moreover, the study of institutions can provide important feedback for the analysis of behaviorally bounded individuals. The discussant is *Michael Cohen*.

The wrap-up panel consisted of *Eldar Shafir, Jean Tirole, Tim Wilson,* and *Peter Diamond*. Their remarks and the following discussion are presented in the final chapter.

REFERENCES

Akerlof, G. 2002. Behavioral macroeconomics and macroeconomic behavior. *American Economics Review* 92:411–33.
Camerer, C., G. Loewenstein, and M. Rabin. 2003. *Advances in Behavioral Economics.* Princeton University Press.

Gilbert, D., S. Fiske, and G. Lindzey. 1998. *Handbook of Social Psychology*, 4th edn. McGraw-Hill.

Kahneman, D., and A. Tversky. 1979. Prospect theory: an analysis of decision under risk. *Econometrica* 47:263–91.

Kahneman, D., J. L. Knetsch, and R. H. Thaler. 1986. Fairness as a constraint on profit seeking. *American Economics Review* 76:728–41.

Laibson, D. 1997. Golden eggs and hyperbolic discounting. *Quarterly Journal of Economics* 112:443–78.

Rabin, M. 1998. Psychology and economics. *Journal of Economic Literature* 36:11–46.

Thaler, R. (ed.). 1993. *Advances in Behavioral Finance*. New York: Russell Sage Foundation.

Simon, H. 1982. *Models of Bounded Rationality*. MIT Press.

Behavioral Public Economics: Welfare and Policy Analysis with Nonstandard Decision-Makers

By B. Douglas Bernheim and Antonio Rangel[1]

2.1 INTRODUCTION

Public economics has positive and normative objectives; it aims both to describe the effects of public policies and to evaluate them. This agenda requires us to formulate models of human decision-making with two components: one describing choices, and the other describing well-being. Using the first component, we can forecast the effects of policy reforms on individuals' actions, as well as on prices and allocations. Using the second component, we can determine whether these changes benefit consumers or harm them.

Traditionally, economists have made no distinction between the behavioral and welfare components of economic models. Such a distinction has not been necessary because standard welfare analysis is grounded in the doctrine of revealed preference. That is, we infer what people want from what they choose. When evaluating policies, we attempt to act as each individual's proxy, extrapolating his or her likely policy choices from observed consumption choices in related situations.

Interest in behavioral economics has grown in recent years, stimulated largely by accumulating evidence that the standard model of consumer decision-making provides an inadequate positive description of human behavior. Scholars have begun to propose alternative models that incorporate insights from psychology and neuroscience. Some of the pertinent literature focuses on behaviors commonly considered "dysfunctional," such as addiction, obesity, risky sexual behavior, and crime. However, there is also considerable interest in alternative approaches to more standard economic problems involving, for example, saving, risk-taking, and charitable contributions.

[1] We thank Colin Camerer, Peter Diamond, Emmanuel Saez, and Nicholas Stern for useful comments. Antonio Rangel gratefully acknowledges financial support from the NSF (Grant No. SES-0134618) and SIEPR.

Behavioral economists have proposed a variety of models that raise difficult issues concerning welfare evaluation. No consensus concerning appropriate standards and criteria has yet emerged. Broadly speaking, there are two main schools of thought.

One school of thought insists on strict adherence to the doctrine of revealed preference for the purpose of economic policy evaluation. In this view, observed "anomalies" should be explained, when possible, by expanding the preference domain. Indeed, in the view of some economists, the only legitimate objective of behavioral economics is to identify preferences that robustly rationalize choices (Gul and Pesendorfer 2001, 2004a,b). This perspective maintains the tight correspondence between the behavioral and welfare components of economic models.

The second school of thought holds that behavioral economics can in principle justify modifying, relaxing, or even jettisoning the principle of revealed preference for the purpose of welfare analysis. A number of possibilities have been explored. If people make systematic mistakes in identifiable circumstances, it may be appropriate to apply the principle of revealed preference *selectively* rather than systematically. If an individual's choices reveal several distinct sets of mutually inconsistent preferences, then normative evaluation may require the adoption of a particular perspective. If choices do not reveal coherent preferences, then perhaps normative evaluations should emphasize other aspects of well-being, such as opportunities. To pursue any of these possibilities, one must formulate separate, and potentially divergent, positive and normative models.

Adopting alternatives to the principle of revealed preference allows economists to engage on issues that specialists in other fields, as well as the public at large, regard as central policy concerns. For example, they can meaningfully address the "self-destructive" behavior of addicts or make sense of the claim that Americans save "too little" for retirement.

However, there is also a danger. Revealed preference is an attractive political principle because it guards against abuse (albeit quite imperfectly in practice). Once we relax this doctrine, we potentially legitimize government condemnation of almost any chosen lifestyle on the grounds that it is contrary to a "natural" welfare criterion reflecting the individual's "true" interests. If we can classify, say, the consumption of an addictive substance as contrary to an individual's interests, what about choices involving literature, religion, or sexual orientation? If choices do not unambiguously reveal an individual's notions of good and bad, then "true preferences" become the subject of debate, and every "beneficial" restriction of personal choice becomes fair game.[2]

Given these dangers, if we are to relax the principle of revealed preference when evaluating public policy, it behooves us to set a high scientific threshold for reaching

---

[2]McCaffrey and Slemrod (2006) make a similar argument.

a determination, based on objective evidence, that a given problem calls for divergent positive and normative models. It is important to emphasize that any justification for modifying or replacing the principle of revealed preference must necessarily appeal to evidence other than observations of choice. After all, in the absence of additional assumptions, it is impossible to disprove the hypothesis that people prefer what they choose simply by examining their choices. As we argue in detail below, this is one respect in which direct evidence on the neural mechanisms of decision-making is beginning to prove valuable.

Unfortunately, behavioral economists have typically been somewhat cavalier in adopting normative criteria. For example, in the literature on quasi-hyperbolic discounting, it is now standard practice to adopt the "long-run" perspective ($\beta = 1$) for welfare analysis, rather than the perspective that governs "short-run" choices ($\beta < 1$). This approach has been criticized on the grounds that, according to the principle of revealed preference, the short-run perspective also has status as a welfare criterion. The arguments that have been offered in defense of the "long-run" perspective have not convinced skeptics that it is appropriate to attach absolutely no normative significance to short-run preferences. The foundations for welfare analysis therefore require closer attention.

This chapter has two goals. First, we discuss emerging methods for normative policy analysis in behavioral economics, as well as potentially fruitful lines of inquiry. We explicitly argue against the view that any departure from the doctrine of revealed preference renders welfare analysis either infeasible or entirely subjective. We argue instead that it is sometimes possible to replace revealed preference with other compelling normative principles. For example, if one knows enough about the nature of decision-making malfunctions, it may be possible to recover tastes by relying on a *selective* application of the revealed-preference principle. Accordingly, practicing behavioral economics requires us to modify, not abandon, the key methodological principles of modern economics (see Rabin (2002) for a related argument).

Second, we review a collection of applications of behavioral economics to the field of public economics. In preparing this selective review, we have intentionally favored depth over breadth in the hope of providing a substantive discussion of welfare issues and policy implications. We focus on three specific policy issues: saving, addiction, and public goods. While each literature is still in its infancy, we argue that behavioral economics has already provided fundamental insights concerning public policy in each of these domains.

The remainder of this chapter is organized as follows. Section 2.2 discusses alternative approaches to the problem of welfare. This section is an abbreviated version of Bernheim and Rangel (2005a), to which we refer the reader for additional details. Sections 2.3–2.5 survey applications to, respectively, saving, addictive substances, and public goods. Section 2.6 provides a brief discussion of the future of behavioral public economics.

2.2 CONCEPTUALIZING AND MEASURING WELFARE

Welfare analysis has two main components. First, one determines how policies affect the well-being of each individual. Second, one aggregates across individuals. As is well-known, the second step involves some thorny issues (e.g., those raised by Arrow's Impossibility Theorem). However, since these are common to both neo-classical and behavioral approaches, we will say no more about them. Instead, we will focus on the assessment of each individual's well-being.

There is widespread agreement that normative criteria should respect the principle of individual sovereignty, which holds that notions of good and bad for society should be rooted in the notions of good and bad held by the affected individuals. This principle instructs policy analysts to act as each individual's proxy when comparing alternative policies. It precludes the analyst from imposing his or her own value judgments. Our focus here is, in effect, on the meaning of the phrase, "acting as each individual's proxy."

In the neoclassical paradigm, the analyst attempts to determine which policy choice the individual would make, given the opportunity. This is obviously difficult, since the policy choices under consideration differ considerably from the private choices that people ordinarily make. The beauty and power of standard consumer theory resides in the fact that it allows us to extrapolate choices among public policy outcomes from observations of private choices.

One common interpretation of the neoclassical approach is that people have well-defined preference rankings, which the analyst discovers by examining evidence on choices (through the principle of revealed preference). These rankings are then taken as the basis for welfare evaluations. As detailed in Bernheim and Rangel (2005a), this interpretation rests on the following four assumptions.

Assumption 2.1 (coherent preferences). Each individual has coherent, well-behaved preferences.

Assumption 2.2 (preference domain). The domain of each individual's preference rankings is the set of lifetime state-contingent consumption paths.

Assumption 2.3 (fixed lifetime preferences). Each individual's ranking of life-time state-contingent consumption paths remains constant across time and states of nature.

Assumption 2.4 (no mistakes). Each individual always selects the most preferred alternative from the feasible set.

It is important to emphasize that Assumption 2.3 does not rule out the possibility that tastes vary over time or across states of nature. To illustrate, consider the following problem: choose either an immediate five-day vacation, or a ten-day vacation after a three month delay. Assumption 2.3 allows for the possibility that the preferred choice changes with age, or fluctuates randomly with mood. For example, if an individual is under stress, the immediate vacation may be more attractive. The assumption does *not*, however, allow for the possibility that, while in a relaxed mood, the individual would wish to prescribe for himself a different choice than he would actually make at other points in time while in an stressed mood. On the contrary, while in a relaxed mood, he should regard the decisions he makes at other points in time while in stressed moods as optimal. Though he is willing to make different trade-offs at different points in time and in different states of nature, his notion of a "life well-lived" remains fixed.

Another interpretation of the neoclassical approach, discussed at greater length in Bernheim and Rangel (2005a), holds that revealed preferences are merely constructs for systematizing information concerning choices. This view does not require one to take a position as to whether people actually have preferences, or whether revealed preferences coincide with "true" preferences. Rather, it posits that people act *as if* they optimize given particular preferences, and uses this representation to extrapolate choices among policy alternatives. According to this view, the neoclassical paradigm is only about choice.

Throughout the remainder of this section, we adopt the perspective that preferences are "real" objects. In our view, the concept of preference is something that we all understand in concrete terms. Even if we are limited to inferring others' preferences from their choices, this does not call the existence of preferences into question. After all, most of us believe we can learn much about our own preferences from introspection. None of us have ever chosen between spending two weeks on Maui and two years in prison, yet we know we would be happier with the first alternative; we do not need to infer this preference from an actual choice. From this perspective, the discovery of true preferences is a central objective of welfare economics.

One can think of the various approaches to welfare analysis that have appeared in the behavioral literature as efforts to grapple with the distinctive issues that arise when we relax each of the four assumptions listed above. We will consider each of them in turn.

2.2.1 *Relaxing the First Assumption (Coherent Preferences)*

Assumption 2.1 holds that people have well-defined, coherent preferences. If observed choices are highly context dependent, with significant decisions turning on minor and seemingly irrelevant aspects of framing (see, for example, Tversky and Kahneman 1986), then it may be appropriate to assume that people have poorly behaved or incoherent preferences (or possibly no preferences at all). In this case, how does one evaluate an individual's well-being?

One possibility is to abandon the principle that the welfare criterion used to evaluate public policy should be based on individual notions of good and bad *allocations*. Unlike the standard approach, this leads to a sharp separation between positive models describing choice and normative models describing welfare. One interesting example of this approach appears in Sugden (2004), who argues for a notion of welfare based on *opportunities*. Sugden formulates a rigorous welfare criterion along these lines, and proves a counterpart to the first welfare theorem.

There are many practical and philosophical reasons to consider welfare standards based on opportunities rather than allocations (see, for example, Cohen 1989; Sen 1992; Roemer 1998). This certainly simplifies some aspects of measurement, and it avoids the need to systematize behavioral observations by imposing untested assumptions. Yet we suspect that most economists will resist such a radical departure from the standard approach. Even if we acknowledge that opportunities are important, people also appear to care a great deal about allocations and subjective perceptions of well-being. And while there is *some* evidence of context dependence and incoherence, we doubt anyone would claim that preferences are *entirely* incoherent (e.g., one cannot induce the typical person to exchange two weeks at a resort in Maui for two years in prison by manipulating framing). An approach based *exclusively* on opportunities would appear to ignore this potentially valuable information.

2.2.2 *Relaxing the Second Assumption (Preference Domain)*

Some behavioral anomalies that defy explanation within the standard approach may become explicable if we expand the preference domain. Conceptually, this permits us to conduct welfare analysis by applying the principle of revealed preference, as in the standard approach (that is, we can use essentially the same model to describe choices and welfare). We discuss two examples.

The first example involves temptation and self-control. Motivating behavioral anomalies include evidence of apparent time-inconsistency and various forms of precommitment. Gul and Pesendorfer (2001) argue that it is possible to account for a range of otherwise puzzling behavioral observations if preferences are defined over both allocations and *choice sets* (see also Gul and Pesendorfer 2004a,b). If some choices feel tempting when they are available, and if this detracts from well-being, then an individual may prefer small choice sets to large ones. This provides a reason to constrain future alternatives *even when constraints have no impact on choices*. In the Gul–Pesendorfer framework, a desire to constrain future choices does not imply that preferences change over time. On the contrary, as in the standard framework, the individual applies the same set of lifetime preferences at every moment in time. Even though, at time t, he might wish to constrain his available options for time $s > t$, he nevertheless approves of the choice he would actually make at time s in the absence of this constraint (because he understands the significance of temptation). In this framework, if one imposes suitable structure on choice data, one can discover lifetime preferences over allocations and choice sets by applying the principle of revealed preference, and one can use these preferences to make welfare evaluations, just as in the standard approach.

The second example involves social preferences. Motivating behavioral anomalies include, among others, a tendency to give money away in settings where there is no room for reciprocity (see, for example, Camerer (2003) for a review of evidence on the dictator game), an apparent aversion to inequality (see, for example, Fehr and Schmidt 1999; Bolton and Ockenfels 2000), and a desire to conform to group norms (see Jones (1984) for a review of pertinent evidence). For the purpose of positive modeling, behavioral economists frequently assume that preferences are defined not only over an individual's own consumption bundle, but also over social outcomes, such as the consumption bundles of others. If one imposes suitable structure on choice data, one can once again discover these tastes by applying the principle of revealed preference. These preferences provide a foundation for normative evaluation (in other words, one again uses essentially the same model to describe choices and welfare).

2.2.3 Relaxing the Third Assumption (Fixed Lifetime Preferences)

The third assumption states that preferences over lifetime state-contingent consumption paths do not change over time or across states of nature. Behavioral anomalies motivating relaxation of this assumption include, again, evidence of apparent time-inconsistency and various forms of precommitment. From a positive perspective, a common modeling strategy involves endowing the individual with different well-behaved lifetime preferences at different points in time (Laibson 1997; O'Donoghue and Rabin 1999b, 2001); one could, of course, also allow lifetime preferences to vary across states of nature (Loewenstein 1996; Loewenstein and O'Donoghue 2004). Assuming we have measured these preferences properly, welfare analysis requires us, in effect, to adjudicate conflicts among them. The problem is analogous to welfare aggregation involving many individuals; here, we aggregate over multiple "selves."

One branch of the literature exploits this analogy. Effectively, it envisions person A at time t as the "child" of person A at time $t-1$. It then applies standard multi-person welfare principles. One possibility is to apply the Pareto criterion (see Phelps and Pollack (1968), Laibson (1997), or Bhattacharya and Lakdawalla (2004) for recent examples). The main problem with this approach is that the criterion is not very discerning. As a result, it is often impossible to rank interesting classes of policies. One usually ends up being able to offer policy makers little in the way of clear guidance. A second possibility is to aggregate preferences through the application of some welfare function. As in problems with multiple consumers, one can write down a class of well-behaved aggregators (i.e., the analog of Samuelson–Bergson social welfare functions) and attempt to derive general results. However, unless one has a basis for making specific assumptions about the aggregator, this approach fails to sharpen the prescriptions generated from application of the Pareto criterion. Alternatively, one could in principle provide the policy maker with a mapping from properties of the aggregator (e.g., welfare weights) to prescriptions.

A second branch of the literature makes welfare evaluations based on some reasonably stable component of preferences. For example, O'Donoghue and Rabin (1999b) argue for the application of a "long-run" welfare criterion ($\beta = 1$) in models with quasi-hyperbolic discounting. In Bernheim and Rangel (2005a), we provide a formal justification of this criterion based on aggregation principles. In particular, we demonstrate that if the consumer's horizon is sufficiently long, and if the policy analyst applies any member of a large class of well-behaved aggregators, the resulting welfare criterion is "close" to long-run preferences. The intuition for this result is that the consumer judges trade-offs between period t and $t + 1$ by exactly the same criteria in all periods but one, and the influence of any one "self" must decline to zero as the number of selves becomes large.

One can make a similar point concerning states of nature. To illustrate, consider an individual who lives in continuous time. Choices are essentially instantaneous but have long-lasting consequences (as an example, think of drug use). The individual's mental state is either "cold," which corresponds to one set of lifetime preferences, or "hot," which corresponds to another. Normally, the individual operates in a cold mode. At each moment, there is some chance that he enters the hot state, which has a fixed duration of ε. Suppose we model the arrival of the hot state as a failure time process, with a fixed hazard parameter. As ε approaches zero, the fraction of time spent in the cold state converges to unity. Accordingly, if we aggregate preferences according to the frequency with which they prevail, we end up using the cold preferences for normative analysis. Even so, cold preferences do not describe behavior in this limit. Since hot states can create "momentary lapses" with long-lasting effects, the appropriate positive and normative models diverge. See Bernheim and Rangel (2005a) for a formal treatment.

2.2.4 *Relaxing the Fourth Assumption (No Mistakes)*

Assumption 2.4 holds that choice and preferences do not diverge. Gul and Pesendor-fer (2004a) defend this assumption as follows:

> Revealed-preference theory defines the interest of people to be what they do. Since there is no objective standard of self-interested behavior it is unclear what it would mean for an agent to act against his self-interest.

Yet there are clearly situations where virtually everyone would agree that divergence does occur—where a choice is obviously not in someone's interest. There are also situations in which most would agree that public policy should recognize these divergences.

Consider the following example. American visitors in London suffer numerous injuries and fatalities because they often look only to the left before stepping into streets, even though they know traffic approaches from the right. This is a systematic pattern; one cannot dismiss it as an isolated incident. A literal application of the revealed preference compels us to conclude either that these people simply have a very strong preference to look left, or that they are masochistic. If we use these revealed preferences for welfare analysis, there is no legitimate basis for preventing someone from stepping in front of a truck. And yet it is safe to say that, after recognizing the purpose of the intervention, anyone would be grateful. The pedestrian's objective—to cross the street safely—is clear, and the decision is plainly a mistake.

As another example, consider the treatment of children. Few economists would apply notions of consumer sovereignty and revealed preference to evaluate the welfare of a child. We acknowledge that children do not know what is best, and that their actions often fail to reflect valid preferences, probably because they give insufficient weight to consequences. Policies prohibiting the sale of cigarettes and alcohol to minors are therefore relatively uncontroversial. And yet it is difficult to justify, objectively, the sense in which the revealed preferences of an irresponsible nineteen-year-old are legitimate, whereas those of a fourteen-year-old are not. While turning eighteen has profound legal significance, it does not discontinuously change the mechanics of decision-making.

There are other contexts for which revealed preference seems untenable as a guiding principle for public policy evaluation. For example, when people have sufficiently severe diagnosed psychiatric disorders, the state can and should step in to protect them. Eating disorders, while not quite as extreme, provide another illustration. For the purpose of public policy, we probably should not proceed on the assumption that an anorexic's refusal to eat is just an expression of valid preferences. On the contrary, we should and generally do regard this as dysfunctional. These examples are instructive because they suggest that, in some circumstances, it is reasonable to use evidence of brain process malfunctions—something other than choice data—to trump the principle of revealed preference. In these situations, denying the possibility of mistakes while rigidly adhering to the principle of revealed preference guarantees the use of an improper welfare criterion.

So far, we have confined our discussion to "dysfunctional" choices. More generally, almost any behavioral anomaly motivating some relaxation of the first three assumptions can also motivate relaxation of the fourth. For example, evidence of time-inconsistent present-bias may reflect a systematic tendency to "over consume." Likewise, people may make precommitments to prevent themselves from repeating a pattern of mistakes.

A natural analytic strategy involves endowing the individual with well-behaved lifetime preferences, while simultaneously specifying a decision process (or decision criterion) that does not necessarily involve selecting the maximal element in the preference ordering. To conduct positive analysis, one employs a model of the decision process (or criterion). To conduct normative analysis, one uses a model of lifetime preferences. In contrast to the standard approach, these positive and normative models potentially diverge.

Our model of addiction (Bernheim and Rangel 2004), discussed in greater detail below, exemplifies this approach. We assume that people attempt to optimize given their true preferences, but randomly encounter conditions that trigger systematic mistakes, the likelihood of which evolves with previous substance use. One can also interpret the familiar model of quasi-hyperbolic discounting along similar lines (indeed, many of those who advocate this model favor this interpretation). In this interpretation, present-biased behavior is a mistake that results from the decision-making processes' tendency to place too much weight on immediate rewards relative to future rewards.[3]

In justifying and implementing this approach, we encounter two critical and difficult issues. First, how do we know that choices and preferences diverge? That is, what is the basis for overturning the principle of revealed preference? Second, if we find compelling evidence of divergence, how do we identify preferences empirically? Both questions are addressed in the literature, though not in a single paper.

Criteria for Overturning Revealed Preferences. With respect to the first issue, it is important to acknowledge that, strictly speaking, it is impossible to overturn the principle of revealed preference using only observations of choices. While choice experiments can overturn specific structural assumptions, overturning the principle itself necessarily requires other types of evidence. It is always possible to rationalize choice data by assuming that tastes are sufficiently context-specific.

---

[3]McClure et al. (2004) present evidence that potentially supports this interpretation.

One promising approach is to use evidence from neuroscience and psychology on the neural processes at work in decision-making. For example, if it is possible to isolate a process that provides *inputs* for decision-making, and to show either that this process has substantive limitations, or that it malfunctions under identifiable circumstances, then the evidence may provide a foundation both for asserting the existence of errors, and for a particular reduced-form model of the error-producing mechanism. In this regard, brain processes of particular interest include those involved in anticipating and evaluating the outcomes of different choices, remembering pertinent information (memory), and attending to relevant data and options (attention). An example of this approach appears in Bernheim and Rangel (2004), where we argue that addictive substances interfere with the proper operation of an automatic neural forecasting system, thereby skewing decisions. We elaborate on this example in Section 2.4.5, below.

Strategies for Identifying Preferences. With respect to the second issue, it may be possible in a given instance to identify preferences by interpreting the available data through the lens of structural modeling. This approach requires one to formulate two tightly parameterized models: one for preferences, and one for choices. Ideally, it should be possible to justify the major structural assumptions of the decision-making model through the type of neurological and psychological evidence used to establish the existence of a discrepancy between preferences and choices.

As long as true preferences *influence* choices, even if the individual does not optimize, there will be some relationship between the parameters of the positive and normative models, and this will be useful for purposes of identification. Indeed, for the two examples mentioned so far (stochastic mistakes, as in Bernheim and Rangel (2004, 2005b), and quasi-hyperbolic discounting, as in Laibson (1997) and O'Donoghue and Rabin (1999b, 2001)), the parameters of the normative model are a *subset* of the parameters of the positive model (certain parameters describe true preferences, and others describe discrepancies between choices and preferences). Consequently, by estimating the positive model, one can recover preferences under the maintained hypothesis that the structural assumptions are correct.

Ideally, the assumed structure should subsume the possibility that there is no discrepancy between preferences and choices, so that it is possible to test this hypothesis. Both of the examples considered above satisfy this requirement.

Identification of Preferences through Choice Data. As long as the parameters of the normative model are a subset of the parameters of the positive model, one can in principle estimate these parameters using data on choices, and nothing else. For example, Laibson et al. (forthcoming) use consumption data to parameterize a model with quasi-hyperbolic discounting. This in turn implies that it is

17

possible to test the hypothesis of no mistakes (e.g., $\beta = 1$ in the context of quasi-hyperbolic discounting) without considering anything other than choices. This statement seems inconsistent with the principle that it is impossible to falsify the principle of revealed preference with choice data alone. The explanation for this apparent inconsistency is that one tests the hypothesis of no mistakes jointly with the assumptions of the structural model. Even if this joint hypothesis is rejected, there is some other structural model for which the hypothesis of no mistakes would not be rejected. When interpreting the results, one therefore necessarily relies on the nonchoice evidence used to justify the assumed structure. Accordingly, the reliability and strength of this nonchoice evidence limits the force of one's conclusions.

The observations in the preceding paragraph remain valid even if one uses data on nonstandard types of choices, such as decisions made in advance of consequences, precommitments, and expenditures on self-control. For any given structural decision-making model, this type of evidence may prove extremely useful from the perspective of estimating parameters precisely and convincingly, and it may allow one to reject the hypothesis of no mistakes for a much broader class of preferences (e.g., any preference for which the decision maker would exhibit time-consistent behavior). However, stepping outside of the assumed structure, there will always be other formulations of preferences that can explain the choice data without assuming a divergence between preferences and decisions. Of course, any such formulation will necessarily diverge from the standard model (as in Gul and Pesendorfer 2001), and, in any given case, rationalization of the data may require strange assumptions about preferences.

It is worth emphasizing that the estimation of separate positive and normative models does not require us to abandon the principle of revealed preference completely. Instead, one implicitly invokes a principle of *selectively* revealed preference. Depending on the structural model, identifiable decisions (e.g., in the context of quasi-hyperbolic discounting, choices well in advance of consequences) may, by assumption, reveal preferences with certainty, or there may be uncertainty as to whether a given decision conforms to preferences (as in models with stochastic mistakes). In the latter case, one can model this uncertainty explicitly, proceeding, for example, as in the literature on switching regimes.

Identification of Preferences through Both Choice and Nonchoice Data. Another largely unexplored possibility would involve the use of both choice and nonchoice data in structural estimation. Data of potential interest could include self-reported information about preferences and/or well-being, as well as measures of physical states such as arousal and stress.

These additional data could facilitate more precise and reliable estimation of key structural parameters. One might, for example, use self-reported data on preferences along with choice data to estimate the parameters of a normative model. In principle, the normative model could even include parameters that do not appear in the positive model. Likewise, nonchoice data may prove useful in identifying circumstances in which choices reliably reflect preferences, and those in which they do not. If, for example, there is reason to believe that people are more prone to make mistakes when they are under stress, data on cortisol levels might help to identify choices that reveal preferences more reliably.

The use of nonchoice data raises several concerns. First, one can interpret the data through the lens of structural modeling only if one is willing to make additional assumptions, for example, about how the nonchoice data relate to decision-making processes. Advocates of the revealed-preference approach view these assumptions with considerable suspicion (Gul and Pesendorfer 2001, 2004a,b). However, an emerging theme in behavioral economics is that it is possible to justify, defend, and test these assumptions through the careful use of data from psychology and neuroscience. Furthermore, in practice the revealed-preference approach relies on assumptions that are not directly supported by choice data (e.g., structural estimation *always* entails untested restrictions on the form of preferences) and people have different opinions as to which of these assumptions are most "reasonable" in a given instance. To the extent that we judge an assumption as reasonable based on evidence not involving choice, it behooves us to make the basis of our inference explicit, regardless of whether we follow the standard approach or a behavioral alternative. One cannot claim an advantage for the standard approach simply by sweeping the implicit reliance on nonchoice evidence under the rug, or by theorizing about an idealized procedure that is impossible to follow in practice (see Bernheim and Rangel (2005a) and Koszegi (2002) for elaborations of this point).

Second, economists generally view nonchoice data as significantly less reliable and considerably more ambiguous than information on choices. In part, this view is justified by evidence indicating that certain types of self-reported data are unreliable (Diamond and Hausman 1994; Schwarz and Strack 1999). In our view, this deficiency is exaggerated, particularly with regard to evidence concerning limitations and malfunctions of specific brain processes involving forecasting, memory, and attention (as discussed above). There is every reason to believe that the quality of this and other nonchoice evidence, as well as our ability to interpret it, will improve with time. Furthermore, given the potential value of nonchoice data, concerns about the quality of this information should motivate the development of better procedures for acquiring and interpreting it, rather than a policy of ignoring it on "conceptual" grounds.

We conclude this section by acknowledging two further concerns. First, the feasibility and value of the empirical approach to measuring welfare discussed in this section has yet to be established through a series of persuasive applications. Only a few studies (discussed below) have made a start in this direction. There are many unresolved issues, e.g., those concerning how to elicit and use data on self-reported preferences. Nevertheless, at a conceptual level, it does appear that one can meaningfully conduct empirical welfare analysis allowing for some types of divergences between preferences and choices.

Second, there are significant political dangers associated with the research agenda described in this section. As we mentioned in Section 2.1, revealed preference is an attractive political principle because it prevents critics of any particular choice (e.g., concerning literature, sexual orientation, or religion) from condemning it on the grounds that it is contrary to a "natural" welfare criterion reflecting the individual's "true" interests. While we do not condone casual departures from this principle, we do think it is possible to insist on a high standard of proof, based on scientific evidence. In classifying certain behavioral patterns, such as psychoses, eating disorders, and addiction, as mental illnesses, the medical profession has grappled with essentially the same issues. While there have certainly been some dubious decisions (e.g., the classification, until relatively recently, of homosexuality as a psychiatric disorder), the process has, on the whole, reflected the balanced application of sound scientific principles.

2.3 SAVING

For more than fifty years, the framework of intertemporal utility maximization has dominated economists' thinking about personal saving. This framework traces its roots to Fisher (1930), and lies at the heart of the Life-Cycle Hypothesis articulated by Modigliani and Brumberg (1954). In recent years it has become controversial, and an increasing number of economists have expressed doubts concerning its general validity. Many have turned to new approaches.

In this section, we survey some of the pertinent empirical evidence motivating the growing interest in alternatives to the standard model, describe some leading behavioral models, and explore some of their key policy implications. Our objective is to cover central themes. Given the size and rapid growth of this literature, we make no attempt to be comprehensive. Also, in describing competing models of saving, we focus on basic formulations, and ignore complications arising from liquidity constraints, intertemporal complementarities, and uncertainty about length of life and market parameters.

2.3.1   *The Policy Issues*

The last few decades have witnessed sharp declines in rates of saving for many developed countries. For example, according to statistics from the National Income and Product Accounts (NIPA), the rate of net national saving for the United States dropped from 8.3% of net national product in 1980 to 1.8% in 2003. Low rates of saving have created widespread concern over investment, growth, the balance of payments, and the financial security of individual households. As a result, policy-makers worldwide have become increasingly interested in developing strategies for stimulating thrift.

Public policies affecting private saving are highly contentious. In the United States, policy makers are currently debating a variety of critical questions. Should the United States partly replace its traditional social security system with individual savings accounts? If so, how should we structure the new system? Should the government impose more stringent regulations on defined-contribution pension plans, which appear to be replacing defined-benefit plans at a steady rate? Should we create or expand tax-deferred savings accounts for special needs, such as medical care and education? Or should we consider more fundamental tax reform that would reduce or eliminate the tax burden on capital income across the board?

To answer these and other critical questions, public economists require a theory of personal financial decision-making that can explain observed behavior and generate credible out-of-sample predictions. It must also provide clear answers to normative questions, such as whether people save enough for retirement, and whether they invest their savings wisely.

2.3.2   *The Neoclassical Perspective on Saving*

We begin by reviewing a simple version of the standard model. An individual lives for $T + 1$ periods. In each period $t = 0, \ldots, T$, he consumes c_t units of an aggregate consumption good. His preferences are defined over consumption bundles of the form $c = (c_0, \ldots, c_T)$. We assume that it is possible to represent these preferences with a separable utility function of the form

$$U(c_1, \ldots, c_T) = \sum_{t=0}^{T} \delta^t u(c_t),$$

where δ is a constant rate of time preference. The individual selects a consumption bundle from some feasible set, which reflects the distribution of earnings over time, interest rates, liquidity constraints, and the like. In practice, he chooses each element of c sequentially, rather than selecting the entire bundle at time 0. However, as time passes, he continues to apply the same lifetime preferences. This means that, as of time s, he evaluates continuation bundles, $(c_s, \ldots, c_T)$, according to the utility function

$$U_s(c_s, \ldots, c_T) = A \sum_{t=s}^{T} \delta^{t-s} u(c_t) + B,$$

where $A = \delta^s$ and $B = \sum_{t=0}^{s-1} \delta^t u(c_t)$.

When writing down this model, economists usually follow the convention of renormalizing utility so that $A = 1$ and $B = 0$ in every period. This normalization obscures the fact that the individual has the same lifetime preferences at every moment in time. Since lifetime preferences are fixed, the appropriate welfare standard is unambiguous. Behavior is dynamically consistent in the sense that, fixing $(c_0, \ldots, c_{t-1})$, he would choose the same continuation bundle, $(c_t, \ldots, c_T)$, regardless of whether he made the decision in period t or in some prior period. Accordingly, the individual behaves exactly as he would if he chose the entire bundle at time 0, which rules out any demand for precommitment.

The literature pertaining to the standard model is vast, and we make no attempt to review it here. However, in keeping with our objectives, it is important to summarize some of the key implications for public policy. The neoclassical approach assumes that people make appropriate decisions, provided they are well informed. If the government can provide relevant information more effectively and efficiently than private markets, educational policies are potentially beneficial. Assuming that information is not an issue, there is no role for government in the absence of pre-existing distortions. It may be appropriate for the government to tax or subsidize capital income as part of a second-best policy in the presence of revenue requirements, to ensure an adequate level of competition in financial markets, to minimize fraud, and to alleviate adverse selection problems. However, under the standard view, there is nothing wrong with the choices people make, given the constraints they face. Reasons for government intervention involve market failures, not individual decision-making failures.

In practice, policy makers worry that people are not saving enough for their own security and future well-being. This is part of the motivation for proposals involving subsidized saving and/or mandatory accumulation. The standard model does not, however, recognize the legitimacy of this concern (except insofar as it results from a market failure). Under this view, saying that someone saves "too little" is comparable to asserting that he or she does not listen to enough classical music: thrift is simply a matter of taste (Lazear 1994). In contrast, if households potentially make systematic mistakes, the adequacy of saving becomes a well-posed and important empirical issue.

In the ensuing sections, we review some of the evidence that calls the legitimacy of the standard approach into question, and we explore the implications of several emerging alternatives.

2.3.3 *Some Problematic Observations*

In some respects, saving behavior conforms reasonably well to the predictions of the Life-Cycle Hypothesis. For example, most people tend to accumulate wealth, broadly defined to include things like pension and social security entitlements, over the course of their working lives, and use either some or all of it to finance consumption after retirement. Yet there are also sound reasons to question the general applicability of this model and to examine alternatives. Here we list a number of problematic patterns identified in the literature. While it may be possible to account for some of these within the context of the Life-Cycle framework, collectively they pose a serious challenge to this approach.

Changes in Consumption Near Retirement.   The standard framework implies that people should smooth consumption, avoiding sudden and predictable changes in living standard. Yet a variety of studies have found that consumption declines sharply at retirement, when households experience a predictable decline in disposable income (Hammermesh 1984; Mariger 1987; Hausman and Paquette 1987; Robb and Burbidge 1989; Banks et al. 1998; Bernheim et al. 2001a). The decline in consumption is strongly correlated with accumulated wealth; those who accumulate less experience larger declines (Bernheim et al. 2001b).

One can try to account for this pattern within the standard model in several ways. First, retirement may be associated with a decline in work-related expenses and/or consumption goods that are substitutes for leisure. If these effects are anticipated, and if their magnitudes vary across the population, then people who plan for larger spending cuts after retirement will intentionally accumulate less wealth. Yet the evidence does not support this interpretation, as the effect is equally strong for categories of spending that would appear complementary to leisure and unrelated to work (Bernheim et al. 2001b). Second, for those who stop working earlier than expected (e.g., due to disability), retirement reflects "bad news," to which consumption must adjust. Moreover, these same individuals find themselves with less-than-average wealth at retirement. However, even when the effects of unexpected retirement are removed through statistical procedures, one still observes both a decline in consumption at retirement, and a strong correlation between the size of this effect and accumulated wealth.

Notably, the sharp drop in consumption at retirement is also larger for households with lower rates of income replacement from social security and pension plans

(Bernheim et al. 2001a). Once again, this pattern is observed even when the effects of unexpected retirement are removed. Since income replacement rates are easily anticipated, and since this variable is not likely to be strongly correlated with work-related expenses or a preference for leisure substitutes, standard theory is hard-pressed to account for the evidence.

This evidence would appear to indicate that people reduce consumption at retirement because they are surprised, either by the decline in their disposable income or by the inadequacy of their accumulated wealth. Yet other evidence suggests that the decline in consumption at retirement is anticipated (Hurd and Rohwedder 2003). The explanation for this apparent puzzle remains an open question.

Self-Reported Mistakes. Several studies document large gaps between self-reported behavior and self-reported plans and/or preferences. A large fraction of the population reports saving too little (that is, significantly less than planned, or less than appropriate) for retirement (Bernheim 1995; Farkas and Johnson 1997; Choi et al. 2004, 2006). The reported gap is quite large, and few people report saving too much. Of those who express an intention to increase their saving, only a small fraction follow through (Choi et al. 2004, 2006). Taking these self-reports literally, one would conclude that pro-saving policies are potentially welfare-improving.

Skeptics counter that people are inclined to report "ideal" or "virtuous" behavior in answer to questions about plans or preferences; they might well also report that they watch too much television. This is a serious concern. However, the finding appears to be robust across samples, contexts, and phrasing of the pertinent questions. While the evidence is imperfect, in our view it should not be dismissed.

Others minimize the significance of the self-reported savings gap on the grounds that carefully calibrated life-cycle models can replicate data on wealth accumulation (see, for example, Scholz et al. 2004). We find this line of argument unconvincing. At most, it supports an "as-if" interpretation of the life-cycle model. This does not rule out the possibility that people actually do make mistakes. Within the standard framework, one can rationalize a systematic tendency to consume too much as impatience—that is, a low value of δ. However, if overconsumption is indeed a mistake, then the true value of δ is higher than the as-if value, and this rationalization leads to an inappropriate welfare criterion. In addition, the models used to "explain" the level and distribution of wealth have other counterfactual implications (e.g., they produce no decline in consumption at retirement).

Limited Planning Skills. Most people are poorly equipped to engage in life-cycle planning without assistance. Collectively, existing studies paint a rather bleak picture of economic and financial literacy (see, for example, Walstad and Soper 1988; Walstad and Larsen 1992; O'Neill 1993; Consumer Federation of America and the American Express Company 1991; Bernheim 1998). For example, only 20% of adults can determine correct change using prices from a menu, and many have trouble determining whether a mortgage rate of 8.6% is better or worse than $8\frac{3}{4}$%. People tend to underestimate the power of compound interest, and many poorly understand common financial instruments.

In principle, financially illiterate individuals could seek guidance from experts. In practice, somewhere in the neighborhood of 60% of virtually every population subgroup relies primarily on parents, relatives, friends, and personal judgment. People with less education are actually *more* likely to rely on their own judgment. Only a minority consults financial professionals or print media (Bernheim 1998). Moreover, in some cases, financial professionals rely on simple rules of thumb (Doyle and Johnson 1991), and even their relatively sophisticated tools conflict in some ways with sound life-cycle planning principles (Bernheim et al. 2002).

Financial literacy is strongly related to behavior. Those who are less financially literate also tend to save less (Bernheim 1998). Moreover, measures designed to address financial illiteracy appear to have significant effects on choices. Policies mandating financial education for high school students result in higher asset accumulation once exposed students reach adulthood (Bernheim et al. 2001a). Likewise, financial education in the workplace increases participation in employee-directed pension plans and stimulates saving (see Bernheim and Garrett 2003; Bayer et al. 1996; Duflo and Saez 2003).

Failure to Formulate Sophisticated Plans. Under an "as-if" interpretation, the standard model implies nothing about the process by which an individual arrives at consumption and saving decisions. Yet it is difficult to see how someone would formulate coherent life-cycle choices without extensive and deliberate planning. In practice, many people report spending little if any effort formulating long-range financial plans; moreover, those who fail to plan tend to save less (see Bernheim 1994; Lusardi 2000, 2003; Ameriks et al. 2003).

When they exist, financial plans tend to be relatively unsophisticated. Many people establish saving targets, and in most cases think of these targets as percentages of income. However, the targets appear to reflect rough rules of thumb: in the vast majority of cases, they are integer multiples of 5%, and they vary neither with stated expectations about earnings growth nor with age (Bernheim 1994).

In addition, important financial decisions often appear to turn on arguably irrelevant considerations. People are significantly more likely to make tax-deductible Individual Retirement Arrangement (IRA) contributions if they owe the Internal Revenue Service money at the end of the tax year (Feenberg and Skinner 1989).[4]

---

[4]Gravelle (1991) attributes this to spurious correlations with income, tax filing status, and/or asset holdings, but the pattern is apparent even when Feenberg and Skinner include plausible controls for these factors.

There is a striking tendency for a household to make an IRA contribution equal to the single-person limit, even when they are eligible to contribute more (Feenberg and Skinner 1989; Engen et al. 1994). And IRA participation rates rose sharply when the system was expanded in 1982, *even among groups that had been eligible prior to the expansion*, and fell sharply once the system was scaled back in 1986, *even among groups that remained eligible* (Long 1990; Venti and Wise 1992).

The Importance of Default Options.   We use the term "default option" to signify the outcome resulting from inaction. For a neoclassical consumer, choices depend only on preferences and constraints. Consequently, in the absence of significant transaction costs, default options should be inconsequential. Yet, in the context of decisions concerning saving and investment, they appear to matter a great deal.

With respect to 401(k) plans, there is considerable evidence that default options affect participation rates, contribution rates, and portfolios (Madrian and Shea 2001; Choi et al. 2004). Also, automatic cash distributions for terminated employees with small balances reduce retirement account balances, even though these employees are free to roll their funds into an IRA (Choi et al. 2004).[5] Effects of defaults on portfolio allocation have also been documented in the context of the recent privatization of social security in Sweden. The dissemination of information about investment alternatives appears to counter this effect (Cronqvist and Thaler 2004).

In the standard framework, defaults can matter if other choices are associated with significant transaction costs. Yet in the contexts described above, transactions costs are presumably quite low. Alternatively, the effect of a default option may be related to the costs of decision-making. In pressing this explanation, one must explain why these costs favor the default option over other alternatives (e.g., the simplest or most transparent choices). One possibility is that people believe the default conveys information about the wisdom of a particular choice. This may be a plausible assumption in the context of portfolio allocation within 401(k) plans, where the employer has a fiduciary responsibility to its employees in its role as plan sponsor. In any case, even if default options are viewed as informative, their strong effects tell us that people regularly make significant decisions concerning saving on the basis of precious little information.

Inefficient Choices.   In the standard framework, consumers always choose alternatives on the efficient frontiers of their constraint sets. When evaluating evidence pertaining to this implication, it would be unfair to interpret it too literally. In some instances (e.g., failure to engage in sophisticated tax arbitrage), squeezing out the last dime involves complex arrangements and potentially high transaction costs,

---

[5]Choi et al. (2004) also contains a discussion of the "optimal defaults."

so the appearance of inefficiency may be illusory. However, in some cases, people select alternatives far from the efficient frontiers of their choice sets in settings in which superior alternatives are clearly available. Examples include failures to take advantage of low-interest loans available through life insurance policies (Warshawsky 1987), naive diversification strategies (Bernartzi and Thaler 2001), the tendency to invest 401(k) balances heavily in the stock of one's employer (Holden et al. 2001; Bernartzi 2001), the proclivity to maintain substantial balances on high-interest credit cards (Laibson et al. 2003, 2006; Gross and Souleles 2002), and the inclination to delay IRA contributions until the end of the tax year (Summers 1986).

2.3.4 *Insights from Psychology*

A number of the empirical puzzles described in the previous section may be related to problems involving the exercise of self-control. There is a sizable and rapidly growing literature in psychology and neuroscience concerning the properties, development, and limitations of self-control processes. In this section we provide a brief introduction to this literature by summarizing some of the evidence most relevant for savings. See Frederick et al. (2002) and Loewenstein et al. (2003b) for more comprehensive reviews of the literature.

Evidence of Dynamically Inconsistent Choice. Saving reflects a decision to accept a lower level of consumption in one period in exchange for a higher level of consumption in another. The standard model assumes that the individual evaluates a trade-off involving consumption at two future fixed points in time, say s and t (with $s < t$), precisely the same way at every moment r. Yet a large body of evidence finds that this evaluation in fact depends on the proximity of r to s. In particular, when s is sufficiently proximate, people tend to favor consumption in the closer period s.

The direct evidence for this proposition is experimental. The typical experiment involves two treatments. In the first, subjects are offered a small prize in s days, or a large prize in t days. In the second, they are offered the same small prize in $s + d$ days, or the same large prize in $t + d$ days, for some $d > 0$ (where we interpret d as "delay"). When $s = 0$ (that is, the subject decides between an immediate reward and a delayed one in the first treatment), a significantly larger fraction of subjects choose the small prize in the first treatment than in the second (see, for example, Ainslie and Haendel (1983), or, for a recent review of the evidence, Frederick et al. (2002)). For relatively small values of s (on the order of seven days), this differential disappears (Coller et al. 2003).

The simple experiment described in the previous paragraph potentially suffers from a variety of confounds. An immediate reward is usually distinguished by more than just its immediacy. Arguably, it is less risky (that is, less likely to be forgotten by the subject or neglected by the experimenter), and it involves lower transaction costs. However, the discrepancy between the two treatments persists even when reasonable steps are taken to eliminate these confounds. Another concern is that, with state-contingent utility, evaluations of trade-offs may depend on "moods." For an immediate reward, mood is known, while for a future reward it is not. Under appropriate (if somewhat special) assumptions, this can account for the observed pattern (Fernandez-Villaverde and Mukherji 2002).

Notably, similar results are obtained regardless of whether the reward consists of money or a consumption good. This is surprising in that, for a wide range of standard and nonstandard behavioral theories, the best choice with monetary rewards involves the maximization of present discounted value (at least in the absence of binding liquidity constraints), which means it should not vary with d.

Precommitment. People who understand that their behavior is dynamically inconsistent might want to exercise self-control through the use of precommitment devices. There is evidence that this occurs in practice. For example, Ariely and Wertenbroch (2002) study a field experiment in which students are allowed to self-impose deadlines on assignments. They find that many subjects choose these constraints. Wertenbroch (1998) discusses suggestive evidence that people attempt to control their consumption of "tempting" foods by purchasing small packages, even when the unit price is lower for larger packages.

The Role of Cues and Cognitive Processes in Self-Control. In an influential study, Shiv and Fedorikhin (1999) show that cognitive load can affect self-control. Subjects are given a number to memorize, and are asked to report it in another room. In some cases the number has two digits, and in others it has seven. Before reporting the number, they are asked to choose between two deserts, chocolate cake and fruit salad, which are physically present. Individuals in the seven-digit treatment are roughly 50% more likely to choose the chocolate cake. This suggests that self-control requires cognitive effort, and that this becomes more difficult when cognition is engaged in other tasks.

Shiv and Fedorikhin (1999) also consider a variation of this experiment in which the deserts are not physically present; instead, subjects are shown pictures. The differential in choices between the two treatments disappears. This suggests that cues can impair self-control. To account for this effect, psychologists hypothesize that self-control is difficult when the individuals enter strong "visceral states," and that the real items are more likely than pictures to trigger such states.

These findings are consistent with the work of Mischel and coauthors, which shows that self-control is affected by the deployment of attention and the presence of cues (see Mischel 1974; Mischel and Moore 1973; Mischel et al. 1992; Metcalfe and Mischel 1999). In a typical experiment, a subject (often a child) is placed in a room and is offered a choice between an inferior and a superior prize (one or two pieces of candy). Subjects can obtain the inferior prize at any time by calling the experimenter, but must wait until he returns to obtain the superior prize. In practice, the child's ability to wait depends crucially on whether the inferior prize is visible. Merely covering the object significantly enhances self-control.

More generally, in Mischel's experiments, the deployment of attention emerges as a key determinant of self-control. Any stimulus that focuses attention on the "tempting" features of the inferior prize increases the likelihood that the children will select it. Children are significantly more likely to wait if they are advised to distract themselves by thinking about something else, or if they are provided with a toy, even when children in a control group show no interest in the toy.

Discussion. The evidence suggests that exercising self-control is sometimes difficult. The amount of effort devoted to imposing self-control appears to depend on a variety of environmental and contextual factors that are arguably unrelated to true preferences. Accordingly, lapses in self-control are potentially associated with divergences between choices and true preferences (i.e., mistakes). Moreover, one expects such lapses to arise probabilistically, as the result of chance encounters with cues and stimuli outside the individual's control.

The models of decision-making described in the next two sections attempt to capture these ideas in different ways. They make different assumptions about the nature of the processes responsible for the mistakes associated with self-control lapses, and they employ different reduced-form representations of these processes.

2.3.5 *Models of Saving with Quasi-Hyperbolic Discounting*

Laibson (1997), building on previous work by Strotz (1955/56), Phelps and Pollack (1968), and Akerlof (1991), proposes a model of saving intended to capture some of the self-control problems described in Sections 2.4.3 and 2.3.5. This framework is widely known as "quasi-hyperbolic" or "(β, δ)" discounting.[6] From a positive perspective, individuals behave as if they optimize subject to lifetime preferences that change with time. In particular, in each period t, the decision maker acts as if he picks the feasible consumption path that maximizes a utility function of the form

$$u(c_t) + \beta \left[\sum_{k=t+1}^{T} \delta^{k-t} u(c_k) \right].$$

This formulation differs from the standard model in only one respect: it includes an additional discount factor, $\beta > 0$, which is applied to the utility associated with

---

[6]See O'Donoghue and Rabin (1999a,b) for other early influential variations of the (β, δ)-model.

all future consumption. The parameter β is meant to represent the degree of *present bias*, or *myopia*. The standard model corresponds to the special case where $\beta = 1$. With $\beta < 1$, the present is given special status relative to all other time periods, and this creates a powerful tendency to consume immediately.

As long as $\beta \neq 1$ this model gives rise to dynamically inconsistent behavior. With $\beta < 1$, the individual always wishes to consume more in the current period than he would have chosen for himself at any point in the past. This complicates positive analysis. One can no longer characterize the individual's behavior by solving a single optimization problem. Instead, the model gives rise to a game played between "multiple selves." The literature solves this game under three different assumptions about the accuracy of the decision maker's expectations concerning his own future behavior.

A naive individual acts as if his future selves will be willing to follow through on his current plans. In this case, one determines behavior by solving a sequence of optimization problems. In each period, the naive self divides his resources between current consumption and saving, anticipating that he will use his wealth to finance his desired consumption path for the rest of his life. He never actually follows this plan because, in the next period, he again attaches disproportionate weight to the present. The naive individual does not understand his self-control problem, and makes no attempt to manage it.

A sophisticated decision maker perfectly anticipates his future actions. In particular, he knows that, given the opportunity in any future period, he will consume a larger fraction of his resources than he would like. Under this assumption, one determines behavior by solving for the subgame perfect equilibria of the dynamic game played between multiple selves. Frequently, this setting gives rise to multiple equilibria, which means behavior is indeterminate unless one applies a selection criterion or refinement (Laibson 1994; Krusell and Smith 2003; Bernheim et al. 1999). In contrast to naive decision makers, a sophisticated decision maker understands his self-control problem perfectly, and may attempt to manage anticipated lapses of self-control by limiting future choices.

Finally, a partially sophisticated decision maker understands that he will have a self-control problem in the future, but underestimates its magnitude. O'Donoghue and Rabin (1999b, 2001) parameterize the degree of sophistication to create a continuum between the two extreme cases of complete naïveté and perfect sophistication. (See their papers for details, as well as for further discussion of the relationships between these assumptions.)

There has been much confusion in the literature concerning interpretations of the (β, δ)-model. This confusion reflects the fact that the positive model described above is consistent with at least two distinct approaches to the formulation of a normative model. One approach follows the agenda outlined in Section 2.2.3: think of person A at time t as the "child" of person A at time $t-1$, and then apply standard multi-person welfare principles. The second approach follows the agenda outlined in Section 2.2.4: assume the individual has stable lifetime preferences, and interpret the reduced-form parameter β as measuring the tendency to make present-biased mistakes. With few exceptions, the leading advocates of the (β, δ)-model endorse the second approach.[7] Typically, they assume that true preferences correspond to a standard intertemporal utility function with exponential discounting at the rate δ ("long-run" preferences).[8] Yet much of the profession continues to think of the (β, δ)-model literally as one with "multiple selves," which is in keeping with the first approach, but not the second.

Several papers have estimated (or calibrated) (β, δ)-models using data on consumption and saving. In principle, this permits one to test the hypothesis that $\beta = 1$. Under the second approach to normative analysis described in the preceding paragraph, it also allows one to recover true preferences, and to conduct welfare analysis.

Angeletos et al. (2001) simulate a ninety-period life-cycle model with uncertain labor income, probabilistic death, constant discount factors, additively separable preferences, and three types of assets: riskless bonds, credit card borrowing, and an illiquid asset resembling housing wealth. They calibrate the model to match the median level of wealth near retirement assuming $\beta = 1$, and again assuming $\beta = 0.7$. They then compare the model's ability to track data from the Panel Study of Income Dynamics (PSID) under these two different assumptions. Both versions generate similar consumption patterns, except that borrowing is higher earlier in life and consumption is higher later in life with quasi-hyperbolic discounting. However, with $\beta = 0.7$, the model performs substantially better in tracking credit card balances, the share of wealth held in liquid form, the marginal propensity to consume out of anticipated income, and the discontinuity in consumption at retirement.

Laibson et al. (forthcoming) develop and estimate a similar model with stochastic labor income, liquidity constraints, child and adult dependents, liquid and illiquid assets, and revolving credit. They use the "method of simulated moments" to estimate many of the parameters of the model based on data from the Survey of Consumer Finances. They formally reject the standard exponential model in favor of quasi-hyperbolic discounting. According to their estimates, the short-run annualized discount rate is 40%, while the long-run annualized discount rate is only 4%. Their rejection of exponential discounting is driven by the observation that high levels of credit card borrowing coexist with significant wealth accumulation. Paserman (2002) uses labor market data on unemployment durations and market wages to

---

[7]This statement is based in large part on personal conversations. Much of the literature is not explicit on this point.

[8]As discussed in Section 2.2.3, one can justify the same welfare criterion under the first approach.

estimate a related model. He finds a long-run discount rate of 0.1% and a short-term discount rate of 10–60%. Fang and Silverman (2002) conduct a similar exercise using welfare participation data.

These studies exemplify the approach to empirical Behavioral Public Economics described in Section 2.2.4. They demonstrate the feasibility of this approach, and provide important evidence in support of a behavioral approach to savings policy. However, much additional empirical work is required to establish the stability, robustness, and scope of these findings.

It is important to emphasize that, while this collection of empirical papers provides evidence against the standard model, they do not allow one to conclude that the (β, δ)-model outperforms other behavioral alternatives, such as those discussed in the ensuing sections. The patterns in the data that produce estimates of $\beta < 1$ could result from other processes that generate excessive consumption. To our knowledge, no one has yet undertaken empirical comparisons of alternative behavioral models.

The policy implications of the (β, δ)-model are dramatically different from those of the standard model. Since many individuals choose suboptimally low levels of saving, there may be welfare-improving policy interventions *even in the absence of capital market failures*. First, mandatory savings programs may be welfare-enhancing, provided that they are large enough to crowd out private savings (in the form of liquid assets) at some point during the life cycle (Imrohoroglu et al. 2003). See Feldstein (1985) for a characterization the optimal level of social security benefits in an overlapping generations economy with two-period lifetimes and heterogeneous self-control problems, and Diamond and Koszegi (2003) for an analysis of social security with quasi-hyperbolic discounting and endogenous retirement.[9] Third, as long as the population includes some individuals with self-control problems, and assuming the social welfare function is continuous and concave, a small subsidy for saving financed with lump-sum taxes is welfare-improving. Intuitively, since individuals with self-control problems save too little, the subsidy produces a first-order improvement in their well-being, and has only a second-order effect on the welfare of those without self-control problems. (For a discussion of optimal taxation in the (β, δ)-model, see O'Donoghue and Rabin (2005) and Krusell et al. (2000, 2002).) Finally, introducing restrictions on the availability of credit, for example, by regulating the distribution of revolving credit-lines and mandating credit ceilings, can significantly enhance the well-being of those with self-control problems.

2.3.6 *Models of Savings with Cue-Triggered Mistakes*

Bernheim and Rangel (2005b) propose an alternative model of savings in which individuals make stochastic mistakes. As in the standard model, true preferences

---

[9]Feldstein does not use the (β, δ)-language, but his model is a special case of this framework.

correspond to an additively separable function with exponential discounting. The individual makes decisions in two distinct modes. With probability p_t, decision processes function properly, and he optimizes as in the standard model. With probability $1 - p_t$, decision processes are faulty (implicitly because an environmental cue triggers a lapse of self-control), and he consumes excessively. He can influence the probability of encountering cues that trigger the faulty decision mode through choices of activities (for example, whether to shop at expensive stores).

In the functional mode, the decision maker is sophisticated about his self-control problem: he selects the optimal level of current consumption recognizing the probabilities and consequences of entering the faulty mode in the future, as well as the manner in which his actions affect the distribution of future decision modes. In the faulty mode, he "binges." This response is mechanical, reflecting simple impulses. In the simplest versions of the model, the size of the binge is proportional either to intended consumption (e.g., because he has chosen to shop in an expensive store), or to remaining lifetime resources (where the factor of proportionality is sufficiently large to ensure that the binge exceeds intended consumption). In either case, the size of the binge is constrained by his available liquid resources.

The model has two straightforward implications. First, precommitment technologies are valuable because they can reduce the size of a mistake when the faulty mode is triggered. Second, the consumer can actively manage his self-control problem, for example, by choosing activities that reduce the likelihood of encountering cues that trigger binges. If the size of the binge is related to intended consumption, he can also reduce the size of mistakes, when they occur, by planning to consume less (e.g., lapses are less costly if he shops at less expensive stores).

Other implications of the model are less immediate. While an increase in the probability or size of a binge always reduces welfare, it can either increase or decrease the level of saving (depending on parameter values). Additional saving becomes more attractive because it allows the individual to self-insure against future mistakes. However, it also becomes less attractive because it leads to greater waste. The net effect on savings depends on the balance of these two forces.

The model also predicts the existence of low-asset traps. For an individual with few assets, the size of a binge is constrained by liquid resources. If he saves an additional dollar and then experiences a binge, the entire dollar is wasted. For an individual with substantial wealth, the size of a binge is ordinarily not constrained by liquid resources. If he saves an additional dollar and then experiences a binge, only a fraction of the dollar is wasted. Consequently, saving is relatively less attractive when wealth is low.

With respect to durable consumption goods, the implications of this model potentially differ from those of the (β, δ)-framework. The (β, δ)-model envisions present-bias with respect to consumption flows. Consequently, it cannot explain excessive consumption of durable goods with long lives, for which the bulk of consumption occurs in the future. In contrast, since an individual may act impulsively with respect to both present and future consumption, a model with stochastic cue-conditioned decision modes can easily generate excessive consumption of durable goods. Accordingly, this model potentially justifies cooling-off periods for automobile purchases, whereas the (β, δ)-model does not.

Many of the policy implications of this model parallel those in the (β, δ)-framework. Even in the absence of capital market imperfections, government intervention is potentially welfare-improving. The introduction of mandatory savings can enhance the well-being of those with self-control problems, but only if the program is large enough to crowd out all liquid assets at some point during the life-cycle, in some state of nature. Regulations that restrict the availability of credit are also potentially beneficial.

There are, however, important differences between the two models. Perhaps most notably, whereas optimal policy in the (β, δ)-model entails subsidized savings, in this model either taxation or subsidization of saving may be optimal. To understand why, note that there are two key differences between the models. First, in the (β, δ)-model consumers *always* make present-biased mistakes, while in this model mistakes are stochastic. This means that social insurance considerations come into play. To partially insure the consumer against bad realizations, the government should give him money when random events reduce his wealth, and take money away when random events increase his wealth. In this context, the random event that potentially reduces his wealth is a cue-triggered binge. A capital income tax (coupled with a lump-sum subsidy) supplements the individual's wealth when he experiences a binge (because his saving is low), and reduces his wealth when he does not binge (because his saving is high). Second, in the (β, δ)-model, the decision maker responds to future economic incentives even while making mistakes, whereas this model assumes that errors result from a mechanical and largely inflexible impulses. Accordingly, taxation directly reduces the magnitude of decision errors in the (β, δ)-framework, but has a limited effect on binges in this model.[10]

In models with cue-triggered binges, there is also a natural role for cognitive policies such as the regulation of advertising and marketing. If advertising increases the likelihood and size of mistakes by proliferating cues, restrictions on advertisements are potentially welfare-improving, particularly if their information content is small. However, for the reasons discussed above, the impact of such restrictions on the level of saving is ambiguous. One could incorporate the same forces in the (β, δ)-model

---

[10]It is worth mentioning that the (β, δ) model also fails to explain an important general fact about present-bias: the phenomenon persists even in experiments in which participants are rewarded in dollars, rather than with rewards experienced at fixed points in time. Even a (β, δ)-discounter should always maximize the present discounted value of resources.

by assuming that advertising reduces the value of β. In contrast to the current model, this would necessarily reduce saving (provided the consumer's horizon is finite).

One can also rationalize framing effects in this model by assuming that the probability of entering the faulty mode depends on cues embedded in the presentation of a decision problem. It may then be possible to design savings plans that increase thrift without providing new information or changing budget constraints, as claimed by Thaler and Shefrin (1981).

The model of savings described in this section is closely related to the process-malfunction theory of addiction discussed in Section 2.4.5. Since we advocate the use of reduced-form models of decision-making justified by evidence on underlying psychological and neural processes, we end this section with a disclaimer. In the context of addiction, the hypothesis that people make cue-triggered mistakes has a solid foundation in neuroscience. In the context of saving, the foundations are less solid. As emphasized in Section 2.4.4, it is known that self-control plays a critical role in determining saving, and a significant body of evidence suggests that cues influence the ability to impose self-control. However, it is difficult to draw a clear distinction between a lapse of self-control and, say, a temporary (and possibly cue-triggered) state of impatience. Our understanding of the neurobiology of self-control, and how it relates to intertemporal choice, is still preliminary.

2.3.7 *Models of Savings with Nonstandard Preferences*

Gul and Pesendorfer (2004a,b) propose an alternative model to account for the role of self-control in determining saving. In contrast to the approaches discussed in the preceding sections, they adhere to the principle of revealed preference, thereby excluding the possibility that lapses of self-control involve mistakes. According to their model, the consumer acts as if he maximizes an intertemporal utility function of the following form:

$$U(c_1, \ldots, c_T; B_1, \ldots, B_T) = \sum_{t=0}^{T} \delta^t u(c_t, B_t),$$

where B_t denotes the budget set in period t. The inclusion of B_t as an argument of u differentiates this framework from the standard approach. The budget constraint enters preferences in a specific way:

$$u(c_t, B_t) = v(c_t) - \left[\max_{c \in B_t} \tau(c) - \tau(c_t) \right],$$

where $v(\cdot)$, the flow of utility of consumption, and $\tau(\cdot)$, the level of temptation associated with a given option, are increasing concave functions satisfying the usual properties. The second term (in brackets) reflects the unpleasant sensation of temptation experienced by the consumer when he fails to select the most tempting alternative in his budget set.

To understand how the model works, it is useful to consider a simple consumption-saving problem with two periods, no discounting, and zero interest. Let R denote the amount of resources available to the individual in period 1, and let $s = R - c_1$ denote the level of saving. The period 2 value function is given by

$$V_2(s) = v(s) = \left[\max_{c \in [0,s]} \tau(c) - \tau(s) \right] = v(s).$$

That is, since the individual spends all his resources in the second period, he does not experience unpleasant temptation. Using this expression, we can write lifetime utility as a function of first-period saving:

$$V_1(s) = v(R - s) - \left[\max_{t \in [0,R]} \tau(R - t) - \tau(R - s) \right] + V_2(s)$$

$$= v(R - s) - [\tau(R) - \tau(R - s)] + v(s).$$

In the absence of temptation, the individual would simply maximize $v(R - s) + v(s)$. At an interior solution, this requires $v'(R - s) = v'(s)$. The introduction of temptation increases the cost of savings by $\tau'(R - s)$, which causes saving to fall.

Several properties of the model are worth highlighting. First, the presence of temptation can decrease well-being even if does not affect behavior. In this sense, self-control is costly. Second, the individual is always (weakly) better off when a planner removes all discretion and forces him to consume the allocation that would be optimal in the absence of temptation. Third, the individual experiences temptation with respect to current choices, but not with respect to future choices. (He is not, for example, tempted to purchase a sports car delivered with some lag.) As a result, in the absence of uncertainty, an individual who has the ability to fix his choices one period in advance can achieve the first-best (except in the first period). Fourth, as in the standard model, choices are dynamically consistent.

Gul and Pesendorfer's model can be interpreted as a reduced form representation of the process that generates the costs associated with temptation and the exercise of self-control. A closely related model, pioneered by Thaler and Shefrin (1981) and recently revisited by Fudenberg and Levine (2005), makes the sources of these costs more explicit. Preferences are given by an intertemporal utility function of the form

$$U(c_1, \ldots, c_T; a_1, \ldots, a_T) = \sum_{t=0}^{T} \delta^t u(c_t, a_t),$$

where a_t measures the intensity with which the individual deploys self-control in period t. The consumer chooses a_t at the outset of each period with the object of

maximizing intertemporal utility; he then chooses c_t myopically, based on immediate benefits. The imposition of self-control is costly in the sense that $\partial u / \partial a < 0$,
but it leads to lower consumption.

As shown by Benabou and Pycia (2002), Loewenstein and O'Donoghue (2004),
and Fudenberg and Levine (2005), this framework is equivalent over consumption-
saving choices to Gul and Pesendorfer's theory of temptation. See also Loewenstein
and O'Donoghue (2004) for an insightful discussion of the relationship between
this class of models and the (β, δ)-framework.

Gul and Pesendorfer (2004a,b) emphasize that their approach is conceptually
consistent with the method of revealed preference. Supposedly, this eliminates the
need for nonchoice data, and prevents the policy analyst from imposing his or her
own judgments when evaluating welfare. We disagree. Practical implementation
of the revealed-preference methodology requires the analyst to make assumptions
about the data generating process (e.g., about functional forms, or similarities across
individuals). There are always untested assumptions, which the analyst selects based
on other information, instinct, introspection, or fuzzy notions of "reasonableness."
We believe it is fair to say that these assumptions are not chosen exclusively on the
basis of choice data. Moreover, as all veterans of empirical policy debates are aware,
the analyst's judgments about untested assumptions translate directly into judgments
about welfare. There are also theoretical considerations, which we discuss at length
in Bernheim and Rangel (2005b). Assuming one restricts one's attention to data on
choices over allocations and constraint sets, both the standard theory and Gul and
Pesendorfer's model are observationally equivalent to other models with different
welfare implications. Hence, the analyst's judgment, expressed through axioms and
assumptions, is unavoidable.

What are the novel policy implications of the temptation model? First, mandatory
savings programs can improve welfare *even if they do not increase savings*. This
follows from the fact that any limit on consumption reduces temptation. In contrast
to models with (β, δ)-discounting and cue-triggered mistakes, a small program of
mandatory saving can enhance welfare even if people still retain positive liquid
assets in all time periods and states of nature. Second, unlike models with (β, δ)-
discounting and cue-triggered mistakes, there is no role for corrective taxation. (See
Krusell et al. (2001) for further results and discussion.)

2.3.8 *Discussion*

Economists have only recently begun to study saving using tools from behavioral
economics. Even so, the models described in this section have already provided
valuable insights.

We conclude this section with a brief description of some important open questions.

The models described in this survey provide an explanation for some of the patterns described in Sections 2.3 and 2.4, including time inconsistency, self-reported mistakes, and some types of inefficient financial choices. However, it is not clear that they can adequately account for other patterns, such as the discontinuity of consumption near retirement, the role of default options, the failure to plan, and the use of rough rules of thumb. None provides a fully satisfactory explanation for the success of the Saving for Tomorrow Savings Plan designed by Thaler and Benartzi (2004), which relies on framing effects instead of changes in budget constraints. Nor do they incorporate limitations on financial skills. In focusing on self-control problems, they ignore issues associated with the complexity of financial decision-making.

Likewise, the theoretical work described in the previous sections has formalized only a few of the behavioral channels through which public policy could affect choices and welfare. It is important to study other behavioral mechanisms with the same level of rigor. Interesting possibilities include the following.

The Role of Financial Professionals.   Many people rely on advice from financial professionals. One can therefore potentially learn about behavior by studying the methods used to generate this advice (see, for example, Bernheim et al. 2002). For example, the most common retirement planning technique involves setting some fixed target for retirement (usually derived from an arbitrary earnings replacement rate) and computing the annual inflation-adjusted contribution to savings sufficient to achieve this target (see Doyle and Johnson 1991). This generates a negative interest elasticity of saving because higher rates of return make it easier to accumulate the resources required to reach the target.

Social Influences.   When saving incentives are in place, boundedly rational individuals may be more likely to learn that others regard the benefits of saving as important. For example, the availability of a 401(k) in an employment setting may stimulate conversations about contributions and investments, and thereby produce "peer group" influences involving both demonstration and competition (see, for example, Duflo and Saez 2002, 2003). The very existence of a pro-saving policy may indicate that "authorities" perceive the need for greater thrift, or endorse a particular level of saving (e.g., the contribution limit).

Keeping Score.   By segmenting retirement saving from other forms of saving, certain kinds of tax-favored accounts may make it easier to monitor progress towards long-term objectives. Information on total accumulated balances is usually provided automatically, or is readily available. This gives individuals a convenient yardstick for measuring the adequacy or inadequacy of their thrift. This may have the effect of making the costs of short-sightedness more explicit. It could also help people to formulate goals and simple behavioral rules. According to Thaler and Shefrin (1981): "[s]imply keeping track seems to act as a tax on any behavior which the planner views as deviant."

Intrinsic Motivation. Scitovsky (1976) has raised the possibility that some individuals may view saving as a virtuous activity in and of itself, without any explicit contemplation of future consequences (see also Katona 1975). Pro-saving policies may promote this outlook by reinforcing the notion that, as something worthy of encouragement, saving is intrinsically rewarding and immediately gratifying.

Intrinsic Gratification from Tax Avoidance. We have noted that people are more likely to contribute to IRAs if they owe money at the end of the tax year. This suggests that immediate tax avoidance is intrinsically gratifying. If so, "front-loaded" plans, wherein contributions are deductible and withdrawals are fully taxable, may be more effective in stimulating saving than "back-loaded" plans, wherein contributions are not deductible and withdrawals of *principal* are not taxable.

Mental Accounting. Thaler and Shefrin (1981) and Prelec and Loewenstein (1998) argue that people exercise self-control by separating resources into "mental accounts," each associated with a different objective. IRAs and 401(k)s may reinforce the discipline of mental accounting by earmarking certain resources for retirement, particularly in the presence of penalties for early withdrawal.

Education and Promotion. The existence of tax-deferred savings accounts may stimulate promotional activities and advertisements by financial services firms. Policies that favor the development of employee-directed pensions (like the 401(k)) may encourage employers to provide retirement education. While advertising and education appear to affect financial decisions, the precise mechanisms are poorly understood.

These types of considerations potentially have important implications for critical policy questions, such as the choice between broad-based policies for promoting saving (e.g., consumption taxation) and more targeted strategies (e.g., IRAs). From a behavioral perspective, narrow measures can focus attention on a single issue (such as the adequacy of saving for retirement), expose individuals to information concerning the importance of saving, provide a natural context for the development and enforcement of private rules, and promote the growth of pro-saving institutions. Contribution limits may actually stimulate saving if they validate specific targets, provide natural focal points for the formation of private rules, or make it easier to monitor compliance with these rules.

2.4 ADDICTION

Although more than four million chemical compounds have been cataloged to date, only a few score are classified as addictive by clinical consensus (Gardner and David 1999). These include alcohol, barbiturates, amphetamines, cocaine, caffeine and related methylxanthine stimulants, cannabis, hallucinogens, nicotine, opioids, dissociative anesthetics, and volatile solvents. There is also some debate as to whether other substances, such as fats and sugars, or activities, such as shopping, shoplifting, sex, television viewing, and internet use, are clinically addictive. These substances and activities pose challenges both for public policy, and for standard economic analysis.

This section reviews the distinctive behavioral patterns associated with the consumption of addictive substances, describes the neuroscientific foundations of addiction, summarizes several competing economic models, and reviews their policy implications.

2.4.1 *The Policy Issues*

The consumption of addictive substances raises important social issues affecting members of all socioeconomic strata, and citizens of virtually every nation. Readily available statistics for the United States illustrate the scope of the phenomenon.[11] Estimates for 1999 place total expenditures on tobacco products, alcoholic beverages, cocaine, heroin, marijuana, and methamphetamines at more than $150 billion. During a single month in 1999, more than 57 million individuals smoked at least one cigarette, more than 41 million engaged in binge drinking (involving five or more drinks on one occasion), and roughly 12 million used marijuana. In 1998, slightly more than 5 million Americans qualified as "hard-core" chronic drug users. Roughly 4.6 million persons in the workforce met the criterion for a diagnosis of drug dependence and 24.5 million had a history of clinical alcohol dependence. In 1998, additional social costs resulting from health-care expenditures, loss of life, impaired productivity, motor vehicle accidents, crime, law enforcement, and welfare totaled $185 billion for alcohol and $143 billion for other addictive substances. Smoking killed roughly 418,000 people in 1990, alcohol accounted for 107,400 deaths in

---

[11]The statistics in this paragraph were obtained from the following sources: Office of National Drug Control Policy (2001a,b); United States Census Bureau (2001); National Institute on Drug Abuse (1998); National Institute on Alcohol Abuse and Alcoholism (2001); Center for Disease Control (1993). There is, of course, disagreement as to many of the reported figures.

1992, and drug use resulted in 19,277 deaths during 1998. Alcohol abuse contributed to 25–30% of violent crimes.

Even within jurisdictions, public policy toward various addictive substances is far from uniform, despite the commonalities suggested by their shared clinical classification. Policies range from laissez faire to taxation, subsidization (e.g., of rehabilitation programs), regulated dispensation, criminalization, product liability, and public health campaigns. Each alternative policy approach has passionate advocates and detractors.

Despite sharp disagreements about the ideal treatment of addictive substances, there is reasonably widespread agreement that most existing policies work poorly. The United States's "War on Drugs" is, for example, often labeled a "failed policy." Use of banned substances remains widespread, and the resulting health costs are high. Prohibitions on certain substances, like marijuana, lack credibility among younger Americans, who fail to see why alcohol is singled out as socially acceptable. While the incidence of criminal activity among drug addicts is relatively high, it is important to acknowledge that drug-related crime is, to a significant extent, a consequence of current policy, rather than a justification for it. Criminalization promotes black markets, fosters organized crime, enriches criminals, and contributes to a culture of violence. As a result, more than 625,000 citizens were incarcerated for drug-related offenses during 1999. These people were disproportionately poor, black, and among society's most economically vulnerable members.

While existing policies have serious drawbacks, alternatives are also potentially problematic. For example, the high incidence of alcohol abuse and smoking, along with the attendant social costs, at a minimum raise serious concerns about the potential consequences of across-the-board legalization. The apparent intractability of social problems related to addiction underscores the importance of creatively and openly rethinking policy strategies.

2.4.2 The Neoclassical Perspective on Addiction

Prior to the 1990s, neurological theories of addiction were based on the "pleasure principle." It was widely believed that people start using drugs to achieve a pleasurable "high," and continue using them despite a deterioration of the high (a phenomenon known as "tolerance") to avoid unpleasant feelings associated with cravings and withdrawal. These hedonic properties are easily incorporated into standard models of consumer choice. Early work in this tradition includes papers by Stigler and Becker (1977), Iannacone (1986), and Becker and Murphy (1988). The last of these is widely viewed as the definitive articulation of the neoclassical perspective on addictive behavior, also known as the theory of "rational addiction."

In Becker and Murphy's model, the individual's well-being depends on consumption of an addictive good, consumption of a nonaddictive good, and a state variable summarizing past consumption of the addictive good. This addictive state rises with use of the substance and falls with abstinence. To model tolerance, one assumes that utility declines as the addictive state rises. To model the effects of cravings and the pain of withdrawal on the inclination to use a substance, one assumes that the marginal utility of the addictive good rises with the addictive state. This assumption is necessary (but not sufficient) to generate a property known as "adjacent complementarity," which means that greater current consumption leads to greater consumption in the future. According to Becker and Murphy, this is the distinguishing feature of an addictive substance.

Becker and Murphy's model generates a variety of interesting positive results regarding the use of addictive substances. For example, with appropriate parameterizations, the model generates behavior that is consistent with aspects of bingeing cycles and abrupt withdrawals. It distinguishes between conditions that lead to certain behaviors that they associate with addiction, and conditions that do not. It also predicts that an anticipated *future* increase in the price of an addictive substance leads to an immediate decrease in drug use (see Gruber and Koszegi (2001) and Chaloupka and Warner (2001) for a review of supporting evidence).

From a normative perspective, the theory of rational addiction makes no distinction between addictive substances and other goods. Accordingly, the standard welfare theorems apply. It follows that government intervention is justified only if markets for addictive substances function imperfectly. There are two main concerns in this regard. First, if people are either poorly informed or misinformed about the effects of addictive substances, they may make poor decisions. As long as the government can provide relevant information more effectively and efficiently than private markets, educational policies (e.g., public health campaigns) are potentially beneficial. Second, the consumption of addictive substances may generate externalities. For example, driving under the influence leads to accidents, addicts commit crimes to support their habits, and addiction can be devastating to family members. The standard policy prescription for externalities involves a Pigouvian tax per unit of the substance equal to the marginal external damage that it imposes on others.

Since the publication of Becker and Murphy's paper, others have extended the theory of rational addiction in a variety of ways, mainly to account for other observed features of addictive behavior. For example, in Orphanides and Zervos (1995,1998), different people have different susceptibilities to addiction, which they discover through experimentation. The paper shows that a highly susceptible individual can control his addictive tendencies if he discovers his susceptibility quickly, but not if he discovers it slowly. The authors briefly discuss a few policy implications. Clearly, consumers benefit from accurate information concerning the distribution of susceptibilities. Moreover, since people are uncertain about their addictive suscepti-bilities, imperfections in private markets for rehabilitation insurance can leave them with residual risk, which potentially creates a role for government as a provider of social insurance. Other contributions include (but are not limited to) Dockner and Feichtinger (1993), who show how the theory of rational addiction can account for cyclical consumption patterns, and Orphanides and Zervos (1998), who intro-duce impulsiveness by allowing the consumer's discount rate to depend (in a time-consistent way) on use.

2.4.3 *Some Problematic Empirical Observations*

In some ways, consumption patterns for addictive substances are no different than for other goods. A number of studies have shown that aggregate drug use responds both to prices and to information about the effects of addictive substances. For example, an aggressive U.S. public health campaign is widely credited with reductions in smoking rates. There is also evidence that users engage in sophisticated forward-looking deliberation, reducing current consumption in response to anticipated price increases.[12] What, then, makes addiction a distinctive phenomenon? Bernheim and Rangel (2004) list five important behavioral patterns distilled from the extensive body of research on addiction in neuroscience, psychology, and clinical practice.

Unsuccessful Attempts to Quit. Addicts often express a desire to stop using a sub-stance permanently and unconditionally but are unable to follow through. Short-term abstention is common, while long-term recidivism rates are high. For example, dur-ing 2000, 70% of current smokers expressed a desire to quit completely and 41% stopped smoking for at least one day in an attempt to quit, but only 4.7% success-fully abstained for more than three months (see Trosclair et al. 2002; Goldstein 2001; Hser et al. 1993; Harris 1993; O'Brien 1997). This pattern is particularly striking because regular users experience painful withdrawal symptoms when they first attempt to quit, and these symptoms decline over time with successful absten-tion. Thus, recidivism often occurs after users have borne the most significant costs of quitting, sometimes following years of determined abstention.

Cue-Triggered Recidivism. Recidivism rates are especially high when addicts are exposed to cues related to past drug consumption. Long-term usage is consider-ably lower among those who experience significant changes of environment (see Goldstein 2001; Goldstein and Kalant 1990; O'Brien 1976, 1997; Hser et al. 1993,

---

[12] See Chaloupka and Warner (2001), MacCoun and Reuter (2001), and Gruber and Koszegi (2001) for a review of the evidence.

2001).[13] Treatment programs often advise recovering addicts to move to new locations and to avoid the places where previous consumption took place. Stress and "priming" (exposure to a small taste of the substance) have also been shown to trigger recidivism (see Goldstein 2001; Robinson and Berridge 2003).

Self-Described Mistakes. Addicts often describe past use as a mistake in a very strong sense: they think that they would have been better off in the past as well as the present had they acted differently. They recognize that they are likely to make similar errors in the future, and that this will undermine their desire to abstain. When they succumb to cravings, they sometimes characterize choices as mistakes even while in the act of consumption. It is instructive that the twelve-step program of Alcoholics Anonymous begins: "We admit we are powerless over alcohol—that our lives have become unmanageable."

As an example, Goldstein (2001, p. 249) describes an addict who had been

> ... suddenly overwhelmed by an irresistible craving, and he had rushed out of his house to find some heroin... it was as though he were driven by some external force he was powerless to resist, *even though he knew while it was happening that it was a disastrous course of action for him* [our italics].

Self-Control through Precommitment. Recovering users often manage their tendency to make mistakes by voluntarily removing or degrading future options. They voluntarily admit themselves into "lock-up" rehabilitation facilities, often not in order to avoid cravings but precisely because they expect to experience cravings and wish to control their actions. They also consume medications that either generate unpleasant side effects, or reduce pleasurable sensations, if the substance is consumed subsequently.[14] Severe addicts sometimes enlist others to assist with physical confinement to assure abstinence through the withdrawal process.

Self-Control through Behavioral and Cognitive Therapy. Recovering addicts attempt to minimize the probability of relapse through behavioral and cognitive

---

[13]Robins (1993) and Robins et al. (1974) found that Vietnam veterans who were addicted to heroin and/or opium at the end of the war experienced much lower relapse rates than other young male addicts during the same period. A plausible explanation is that veterans encountered fewer environmental triggers (familiar circumstances associated with drug use) upon returning to the United States.

[14]Disulfiram interferes with the liver's ability to metabolize alcohol; as a result, ingestion of alcohol produces a highly unpleasant physical reaction for a period of time. Methadone, an agonist, activates the same opioid receptors as heroin, and thus produces a mild high, but has a slow onset and a long-lasting effect, and it reduces the high produced by heroin. Naltrexone, an antagonist, blocks specific brain receptors, and thereby diminishes the high produced by opioids. All of these treatments reduce the frequency of relapse (see O'Brien 1997; Goldstein 2001).

therapies. Successful behavioral therapies teach cue-avoidance, often by encouraging the adoption of new lifestyles and the development of new interests. Successful cognitive therapies teach cue-management, which entails refocusing attention on alternative consequences and objectives, often with the assistance of a mentor or trusted friend or through a meditative activity such as prayer. Notably, these therapeutic strategies affect addict's choices without providing new information.[15]

The clinical definition of addiction makes reference to some of these patterns. Substance addiction is said to occur when, after significant exposure, users find themselves engaging in compulsive, repeated, and unwanted use despite clearly harmful consequences, and often despite a strong desire to quit unconditionally (see DSM-IV 1994).

From the perspective of traditional economic analysis, each of the patterns listed above is at least somewhat puzzling. The rational consumers of economic textbooks have no trouble following through on plans, and therefore should manifest neither of the first two patterns. Contrary to the third pattern, rational consumers always choose what they want, so, armed with good information, they cannot make systematic mistakes. The notion that someone might be powerless over a consumption good is an anathema to a neoclassical economist. The standard theory of consumer behavior embraces the principle that expanding or improving the set of available alternatives necessarily makes an individual better off, so precommitments can only be counterproductive, contrary to the fourth pattern. Finally, since in the standard model individuals never make mistakes, there is no role for expenditures on self-control.

Creative extensions of the basic model may provide rationalizations for some of these patterns without overturning the basic paradigm. For example, Laibson (2001) has proposed a variant of the Becker–Murphy framework in which preferences become state-contingent with experience, and which can in principle account for cue management and avoidance. Even so, the five patterns described above collectively pose a serious challenge to neoclassical perspective, and provide motivation for economists to think "outside the box."

2.4.4 *Recent Insights from the Neuroscience of Addiction*

Over the last ten years, a new scientific consensus has begun to emerge concerning the nature of addiction. It now appears that addiction does not result primarily from the pleasurable effects of substances on the hedonic system. Instead, the new view

---

[15]Goldstein (2001) reports that there is a shared impression among the professional community that twelve-step programs such as Alcoholics Anonymous (p. 149) "are effective for many (if not most) alcohol addicts." However, given the nature of these programs, objective performance tests are not available. The Alcoholics Anonymous treatment philosophy is based on "keeping it simple by putting the focus on not drinking, on attending meetings, and on reaching out to other alcoholics."

of addiction holds that certain substances interfere with the proper operation of a neural system that plays an important role in learning. This is not to say that pleasure is unimportant. However, the key feature of addiction appears to be the fact that addictive substances cause a specific learning process to malfunction.

Figure 2.1 shows, at a high level of abstraction, how the brain normally makes decisions about standard consumption goods. Our senses provide us with information about environmental conditions. We process this information, along with information about our internal states—things like hunger, fatigue, and so forth—and this results in a decision. The decision is followed by experience, including rewards. The experienced relationship between environmental conditions, decisions, and rewards induces learning, which normally improves the quality of future decisions.

On left-hand side of this diagram, we have broken out an important component of the decision-making system, which we have labeled the "basic forecasting mechanism." This is a hard-wired system for measuring correlations between conditions, decisions, and short-term rewards. It does not involve higher reasoning; in fact, it is present in lower life forms as well as humans. For nonaddictive substances, the basic forecasting mechanism learns with experience to construct an accurate forecast of the subsequent hedonic experiences.

It is worth emphasizing that the brain appears to have a variety of mechanisms for forecasting the possible consequences of decisions. Some involve higher cognition (represented on the right-hand side of the diagram); for example, we sometimes develop causal models of the world and reason out the implications of our actions. Some, like the basic forecasting mechanism, are more mechanical.

Both types of forecasting mechanisms play a role in decision-making. Sometimes we act based on the "gut reactions" generated by the basic forecasting mechanism. Sometimes higher cognition overrides a gut reaction. This is how the brain works. Each process has its advantages and disadvantages. The basic forecasting mechanism is very fast, but it is inflexible and unsophisticated. Higher cognition is flexible and sophisticated, but comparatively slow. When we have to make decisions quickly, we rely on our gut reactions. When there is no time pressure, we take the time to think things through. A balance between these systems emerged through evolution as nature's compromise. Consequently, the mere fact that we rely in some instances on impulses and gut reactions rather than reasoned deliberation does not mean that our choices are irrational or dysfunctional. For nonaddictive substances, these mechanisms, operating in parallel, typically produce reasonable decisions.

Figure 2.2 shows how addictive substances interfere with the proper operation of these decision-making processes. In a nutshell, the problem with the addictive substances is that they act *directly* on the learning process underlying the basic forecasting mechanism, short circuiting the neurological process by which

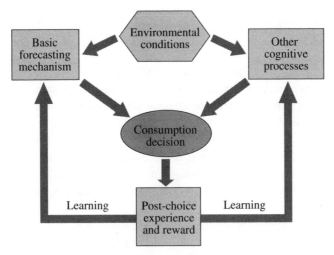

Figure 2.1. Decision processes for standard consumption goods.

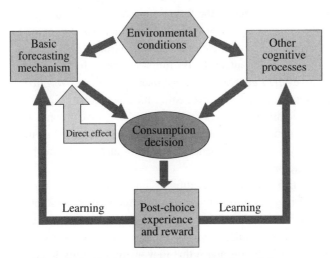

Figure 2.2. Decision processes for addictive substances.

this mechanism discovers correlations between environmental conditions, decisions, and rewards. As a result, the mechanism massively overstates the correlation between drug use and actual experienced pleasure. Loosely speaking, drugs fool a subconscious, hard-wired brain process into anticipating an exaggerated level of pleasure. An addict can try to compensate for this effect by exercising cognitive control, but he cannot consciously correct the malfunction of the basic forecasting mechanism.

More specifically, the available neurological evidence supports four specific hypotheses that justify the new view of addictive substances (see Bernheim and Rangel (2004) for a more detailed discussion).

First, the mesolimbic dopamine system (MDS) serves, at least in part, as a basic forecasting mechanism which, with experience, learns to produce a response to situations and opportunities, the magnitude of which constitutes a forecast of near-term pleasure (see Schultz et al. 1997; Schultz 1998, 2000).

Second, MDS forecasting does not appear to directly produce or reflect the experience of pleasure. Indeed, the human brain appears to contain a separate hedonic system that is responsible for producing sensations of "well-being" (see Berridge 1996, 1999; Berridge and Robinson 1998, 2003; Robinson and Berridge 1993, 2000, 2003).

Third, MDS-generated forecasts directly influence choices (see Berridge and Robinson 1998, 2003; Robinson and Berridge 1993, 2000, 2003). In an organism with a sufficiently developed frontal cortex, higher cognitive mechanisms can override impulses resulting from MDS forecasts, for example, by identifying alternative courses of action or projecting the future consequences of choices. The outcome depends on the intensity of the MDS forecast and on the ability of the frontal cortex to engage the necessary cognitive operations. A strong MDS forecast can impair this ability by influencing attention to stimuli, cognitive focus, and memory. Thus, a more attractive MDS-generated forecast makes cognitive override less likely.

We emphasize that the basic forecasting mechanism and higher cognitive processes are not two different sets of "preferences" or "selves" competing for control of decisions. Hedonic experiences are generated separately, and an individual maximizes the quality of these experiences by appropriately deploying both forecasting processes to anticipate outcomes.

Fourth, addictive substances act directly on the basic forecasting mechanism, disrupting its ability to construct accurate hedonic forecasts and exaggerating the anticipated hedonic benefits of consumption. Although addictive substances differ considerably in their chemical and psychological properties, there is a large and growing consensus in neuroscience that they share an ability to activate the firing of dopamine into the nucleus accumbens with much greater intensity and persistence than other substances. They do this either by activating the MDS directly, or by activating other networks that have a similar effect (see Nestler and Malenka 2004; Hyman and Malenka 2001; Nestler 2001; Wickelgren 1997; Robinson and Berridge 2003). For nonaddictive substances, the MDS learns to assign a hedonic forecast that bears some normal relation to the subsequent hedonic experience. For addictive substances, consumption activates dopamine firing directly, so the MDS learns to assign a hedonic forecast that is out of proportion to the subsequent hedonic experience. This not only creates a strong (and misleading) impulse to seek and use the substance, but also undermines the potential for cognitive override. Cognitive override still occurs, but in a limited range of circumstances.

The preceding discussion implies that, in some circumstances, drug use can literally be a mistake, in the sense that the brain is fooled into making a choice. It does not, however, imply that drug use is always a mistake. Even if the integrity of the basic forecasting mechanism is compromised, higher cognition can still either agree with it or override it. In different people, brain chemistry appears to strike different balances between these mechanisms. This may explain why some people become addicts, while others use repeatedly without becoming addicted. Use can be rational in some instances and irrational in others. It is important to bear this point in mind when evaluating public policy alternatives.

In emphasizing the effects of addictive substances on decision processes, we do not mean to discount the significance of their hedonic effects. The typical user is initially drawn to an addictive substance because it produces a hedonic "high." Over time, regular use leads to hedonic and physical tolerance. That is, the drug loses its ability to produce a high unless the user abstains for a while, and any attempt to discontinue the drug may have unpleasant side effects (withdrawal). Cue-conditioned "cravings" may have hedonic implications as well as nonhedonic causes. All of these effects are clearly important. However, there is an emerging consensus in neuroscience and psychology that decision-process effects, rather than hedonic effects, provide the key to understanding addictive behavior (see Wise 1989; Robbins and Everitt 1999; Di Chiara 1999; Kelley 1999; Nestler and Malenka 2004; Hyman and Malenka 2001; Berridge and Robinson 2003; Robinson and Berridge 2000; Redish 2004).

2.4.5 *Modeling Addiction as a Decision-Process Malfunction*

Bernheim and Rangel (2004) present a theory of addiction that departs from Assumption 2.4 discussed in Section 2.2 (i.e., choices are always aligned with preferences). The theory is based on the following three main premises:

(i) use among addicts is sometimes a mistake, in the sense that actions diverge from preferences, and sometimes rational;

(ii) experience with an addictive substance sensitizes an individual to environmental cues that trigger mistaken usage;

(iii) addicts understand their susceptibility to cue-triggered mistakes and attempt to manage the process with some degree of sophistication.

The first two premises are justified by the body of research described in Section 2.3.4, which shows that, after repeated exposure to an addictive substance, the brain tends to make skewed hedonic forecasts upon encountering environmental cues that are associated with past substance use. The third premise is justified by behavioral evidence indicating that users are often surprisingly sophisticated and forward-looking. For example, they reduce current consumption in response to expected future price increases (Gruber and Koszegi 2001). Some also enter detox not because they intend to remain sober, but rather because they want to increase the intensity of the next high.

A Summary of the Model. The formal model in Bernheim and Rangel (2004) envisions an individual who makes a sequence of decisions regarding lifestyle, the use of an addictive substance, and the consumption of nonaddictive substances. It assumes that, at any point in time, the individual operates in one of two modes: a "cold" mode, in which properly functioning decision-making processes lead to the selection of his most preferred alternative, and a dysfunctional "hot" mode, in which decisions and preferences may diverge (because he responds to distorted MDS-generated forecasts).[16] The hot mode is transient, but always results in use of the substance. The likelihood of entering the hot mode at any moment depends on the individual's history of substance use, his chosen lifestyle (e.g., partying exposes the individual to more intense substance-related cues), and random events (e.g., the frequency and intensity of recently encountered environmental cues to which he has been sensitized through prior use).

The history of use is summarized through the notion of an addictive state. Use moves the individual to a higher addictive state, and abstention moves him to a lower addictive state. An increase in the addictive state raises the likelihood of entering the hot mode at any moment (e.g., because it implies increased sensitivity to randomly occurring environmental cues). Higher addictive states are also associated with lower baseline well-being (e.g., due to deteriorating health), lower financial resources (due to decreased productivity, absenteeism, and out-of-pocket medical expenses), and possibly a greater "boost" from consuming the addictive substance.

By varying assumptions about the properties of the substance in question, the model can replicate a wide range of observed behaviors. In particular, it can account for each of the patterns discussed in Section 2.4.3 (see Bernheim and Rangel (2004) for details and Bernheim and Rangel (forthcoming) for simulations of the model).

---

[16]Our analysis is related to work by Loewenstein (1996, 1999), who considers simple models in which an individual can operate either in a hot or cold decision-making mode. Notably, Loewenstein's approach relaxes the assumption of fixed life-time preferences. He assumes that behavior in the hot mode reflects the application of a "false" utility function, rather than a breakdown of the processes by which a utility function is maximized. He also argues, contrary to our findings, that imperfect self-understanding is necessary for addiction-like behaviors.

Policy Implications. This theory admits two classes of rationales for government intervention. First, as in the theory of rational addiction, intervention may be justified to correct market failures involving addictive substances (i.e., the government can address externalities, misinformation, and ignorance). Second, policies may also affect the frequency and consequences of mistakes. This consideration gives rise to a number of nonstandard policy implications.

Limitations of Informational Policy. In practice, public education campaigns (such as the U.S. anti-smoking and anti-drug initiatives) have achieved mixed results. The process-malfunction theory of addiction highlights a fundamental limitation of informational policy: contrary to standard theory, one cannot assume that even a highly knowledgeable addict always makes informed choices. Information about the consequences of substance abuse may affect initial experimentation with drugs, but cannot alter the neurological mechanisms through which addictive substances subvert deliberative decision-making.

Counterproductive Disincentives. Policies such as "sin taxes" and criminalization strive to discourage use by making substances costly. As we have noted, this is potentially justifiable on the grounds that use generates negative externalities. In the context of the theory described in this section, even higher taxes (whether implicit or explicit) might be justified if they reduce excessive use in "hot" decision states. Unfortunately, it is likely that compulsive use of addictive substances is much less sensitive to costs and consequences than is deliberative use. Consequently, imposing costs in excess of external diseconomies is likely to distort cold-state choices detrimentally, without significantly reducing problematic hot-state usage. Indeed, policies that impose high costs on use may thwart social insurance objectives by exacerbating the consequences of uninsurable risks associated with the use of addictive substances.[17] Accordingly, the optimal rate of taxation for addictive substances may be significantly *lower* than that implied by externalities (see Bernheim and Rangel (forthcoming) for simulation results).[18]

Supply Disruption. Standard reasoning suggests that taxation is preferable to criminalization. Both impose costs, but taxes generate revenues, while criminalization dissipates social resources. In the context of the theory discussed in this section, criminalization offers an offsetting benefit: it disrupts supply, making it particularly difficult for users to obtain a banned substance on short notice. The effect on use is likely to be larger in hot states, when people act impulsively, than in cold states,

---

[17] In practice, addicts often suffer severe economic deprivation, turning to crime and prostitution for support. High substance costs aggravate these consequences.

[18] As shown in Bernheim and Rangel (2004), this result depends on usage patterns.

when people plan deliberatively. This is exactly what one would hope to achieve, and precisely opposite the effect of a tax. To put it somewhat differently, criminalization may help some addicts impose self-control, without (as a practical matter) preventing deliberate use. There is, however, an associated disadvantage: while in the hot state, addicts may engage in costly and potentially dangerous search activity.

Harm Reduction. If addiction results in significant part from randomly occurring mistakes, various interventions can serve social insurance objectives by ameliorating some of its worst consequences. For instance, subsidization of rehabilitation centers and treatment programs (particularly for the indigent) can moderate the financial impact of addiction and promote recovery. Likewise, the free distribution of clean needles can moderate the incidence of diseases among heroin addicts. In some cases, it may even be beneficial to make substances available to severe addicts at low cost.[19] As is usually the case, one must trade off the benefits from insurance against incentive effects: by moderating consequences, harm-reducing policies could in principle encourage casual use and experimentation.

Policies Affecting Cues. Since environmental cues frequently trigger addictive behaviors, public policy can also influence use by changing the cues that people normally encounter. One approach involves the elimination of problematic cues. For example, advertising and marketing restrictions of the type imposed on sellers of tobacco and alcohol suppress one possible artificial trigger for compulsive use. Since one person's decision to smoke may trigger another's, confining use to designated areas may reduce unintended use. A second approach involves the creation of counter-cues. For example, Brazil and Canada require every pack of cigarettes to display a prominent, viscerally charged image depicting some deleterious consequences of smoking, such as lung disease and neonatal morbidity. In principle, a sufficiently strong counter-cue could trigger thought processes that induce users to resist cravings, even though the same information is ineffective when offered in a less provocative format. Policies that eliminate problematic cues or promote counter-cues are potentially beneficial because they combat compulsive use, while imposing minimal inconvenience and restrictions on deliberate rational users.

Facilitation of Self-Control. The process-malfunction theory of addiction places a high value on policies that provide better opportunities for self-regulation without making particular choices compulsory. This could potentially help those who are vulnerable to compulsive use, without encroaching on the freedoms of those who would deliberately choose to use. Laws that limit the sale of a substance to

---

[19]For example, Swiss policy makes heroin available at low cost to severe addicts.

particular times, places, and circumstances frequently provide limited opportunities along these lines (see, for example, Ornstein and Hanssens 1985; Norstrom and Skog 2005; Tigerstedt and Sutton 2000). Well-designed policies could in principle accomplish this objective more effectively. For example, a number of U.S. states have enacted laws allowing problem gamblers to voluntarily ban themselves from casinos (Yerak 2001). Alternatively, if a substance is available only by prescription, and if prescription orders are filled on a "next day" basis, then deliberate forward-looking planning becomes a prerequisite for availability. Recovering heroin addicts could self-regulate problematic compulsive use by carefully choosing when, and when not, to file requests for refills.

2.4.6 *Modeling Addiction with Quasi-Hyperbolic Discounting*

One important line of work modifies Becker and Murphy's model of "rational addiction" by adding quasi-hyperbolic (β, δ)-discounting (see Gruber and Koszegi 2001, 2004; O'Donoghue and Rabin 2001).[20] In contrast to the theory of rational addiction, the consumer acts as if he attaches disproportionate importance $(1/\beta)$ to current well-being when making decisions about current consumption.

Gruber and Koszegi use this model to compute optimal cigarette taxes. When evaluating individual welfare, they assume that true preferences correspond to standard exponential discounting. Implicitly, they adopt the interpretation of quasi-hyperbolic discounting discussed in Section 2.4.4: true preferences are standard, but the decision-making process leads individuals to make present-biased mistakes, which the (β, δ)-model captures in reduced form.

In principle, one could defend this interpretation with reference to the evidence described in Section 2.4. Unfortunately, the model does not fit these facts in two important respects. First, the evidence indicates that mistakes are domain-specific. In contrast, the proclivity to make present-biased mistakes in the (β, δ)-model cuts across all domains. Second, the evidence indicates that mistakes are triggered by intermittent environmental cues. In contrast, the decision maker *always* suffers from present-bias in Gruber and Koszegi's framework.

One could, of course, formulate a variant of Gruber and Koszegi's model with narrow-domain, cue-triggered present-bias. The resulting model would be a close cousin of the process-malfunction theory of addiction discussed in the previous section. However, one significant difference would remain. In the (β, δ)-framework with the proposed modifications, the decision maker would remain sophisticated, forward-looking, and responsive to economic incentives even when suffering from

---

[20]In an earlier related paper, Winston (1980) modeled addiction by assuming that lifetime preferences vary with states of nature.

present-bias. In contrast, the process-malfunction theory holds that mistakes result from simple impulses generated by a hard-wired process that encompasses a limited range of consequences.

In some respects, the policy implications of this approach are similar to those discussed in the preceding section. Informational policy alone is limited because it cannot address the causes of present-bias. Supply disruption is potentially beneficial, as are policies that facilitate the exercise of self-control.

In other respects, the policy implications described by Gruber and Koszegi differ sharply from those discussed in the preceding section. Most notably, the (β, δ)-framework provides a rationale for "sin taxes" (see also O'Donoghue and Rabin 2005). When making decisions, the consumer always puts too little weight on future consequences, including those resulting from adjacent complementarities. The government can address these "internalities" (externalities imposed on future selves) by imposing a Pigouvian tax on current consumption. Accordingly, the rate of taxation for addictive substances should be higher than that justified by marginal externalities. For example, according to Gruber and Koszegi's simulations, the optimal tax on each pack of cigarettes is at least a dollar higher than would be justified by externalities alone.

Why do the models of Bernheim and Rangel and Gruber and Koszegi lead to sharply differing conclusions concerning substance taxation? The answer lies in two of the issues discussed above. First, Gruber and Koszegi assume that consumers *always* make present-biased mistakes, while Bernheim and Rangel assume that mistakes occur only in the presence of intermittent environmental cues. Accordingly, social insurance can enhance the consumer's well-being in Bernheim and Rangel, but not in Gruber and Koszegi. In other words, Gruber and Koszegi's assumptions eliminate the factor that argues *against* high tax burdens in Bernheim and Rangel's model. Second, Gruber and Koszegi assume that the decision maker remains sophisticated, forward-looking, and responsive to economic incentives even while committing errors, whereas Bernheim and Rangel assume that errors result from a mechanical and largely inflexible process. Accordingly, taxation directly reduces decision errors in Gruber and Koszegi, but has a limited effect along these lines in Bernheim and Rangel.

2.4.7 *Modeling Addiction with Temptation Preferences*

Gul and Pesendorfer (forthcoming) propose a model of addiction based on the temptation preferences discussed in Section 2.3.5. Following their earlier work on temptation (Gul and Pesendorfer 2001), they assume that the consumer's preferences are defined both over consumption bundles and over the sets from which these bundles are chosen. In each period of life, the consumer divides his resources between two goods, one of which is addictive, with the object of maximizing an intertemporal utility function. This function is standard in all respects, except that it is modified to include, for each period, a penalty representing net temptation from the most tempting unchosen alternative in the choice set. Even though the consumer applies the same lifetime preferences at every moment in time and makes no mistakes, precommitments are still potentially valuable because they reduce the unpleasant feelings associated with the temptation to consume addictive substances.

Gul and Pesendorfer's model invokes a number of important assumptions. The following three deserve emphasis. First, the level of temptation associated with an alternative depends only on the level of the addictive good, and not at all on the level of the nonaddictive good. Second, recent consumption of the addictive substance increases the weight given to temptation, but does not enter the "standard" portion of the utility function. According to this assumption, as long as an individual is forced to abstain from the addictive substance, his experienced well-being is unrelated to his past consumption. As a result, this assumption is in sharp conflict with evidence on cravings and withdrawal. Third, the consumer only experiences temptation with respect to current choices. For example, when deciding whether to enter rehabilitation for the next period, he is not tempted by the prospect of future drug use.

In the Gul–Pesendorfer model, private markets tend to work poorly relative to the first-best. Markets provide people with choices, and choices create costly temptation. Unless it is possible to irrevocably lock in all choices in advance, a consumer is typically happier with the first-best consumption trajectory when someone else chooses it for him, than when he chooses it himself in "real time" (it is first-best in the first instance, but not in the second).

Even though the laissez faire solution is inefficient, the optimal rate of taxation or subsidization for an addictive good is zero. The same result holds in standard models of commodity taxation (when the government has no revenue requirement), for essentially the same reasons. However, we conjecture that this is a knife-edge case, driven by the first assumption mentioned above. It would appear that if, contrary to the assumption, temptation depends, at least to some extent, on immediate rewards from the nonaddictive good (in addition to consumption of the addictive substance), the optimal rate of sin taxation is strictly positive.[21]

---

[21] Holding the consumption level for the addictive substance fixed (Winston 1980), an increase in the rate of sin taxation reduces the consumption level of the nonaddictive good, rendering the alternative less attractive. Since the size of this effect is proportional to the quantity of the addictive substance, taxation presumably reduces the "temptation gap" between alternatives with low and high levels of addictive consumption. Furthermore, this is a first-order effect. Accordingly, one suspects, intuitively, that a small positive tax is welfare-enhancing. We have not yet attempted to verify this conjecture formally.

Other policy implications resemble those discussed in previous sections. Informational policy alone is limited because it cannot address the causes of temptation. Supply disruption is potentially beneficial because it removes tempting alternatives. Policies that facilitate self-control can also enhance welfare by allowing consumers to eliminate alternatives that would otherwise prove tempting in the future.

2.4.8 *Looking Ahead*

The case of addiction exemplifies the potential for improving policy analysis through the integration of psychology, neuroscience, and economics. Though progress is evident, much work remains. We close this section with a brief discussion of some important open questions.

Estimation and Testing of Competing Behavioral Models.   Almost all of the existing empirical work on addictive behavior is either atheoretical (i.e., it documents factual patterns) or based on the framework of rational addiction. So far, research on behavioral alternatives has been almost exclusively theoretical. It is important to explore the feasibility of estimating parsimonious structural versions of the various competing behavioral models, using both choice data and a combination of choice and nonchoice data. Insights from ongoing research in neuroscience should be exploited to develop procedures for acquiring and using new types of pertinent nonchoice data (e.g., on physical states). Future research should compare the performance of the models in explaining observed behavior, and examine testable implications that distinguish between them. Empirical research can potentially shed light on the relative importance of the various forces at work in these models.

Imperfect Foresight.   Most of the economic literature on addiction assumes that people perfectly understand the benefits and costs of substance use, including its effects on future tastes and decision-making processes. The evidence suggests that this extreme assumption is unrealistic. For example, in a study of high-school seniors who smoked cigarettes, 56% predicted that they would not be smoking in five years, but in fact only 31% were able to quit (United States Department of Health and Human Services 1994).

Under the assumption that decision makers are completely or partially naive, models with quasi-hyperbolic discounting incorporate imperfect self-understanding. While this represents a step in the right direction, further work is clearly needed. Models of naive behavior should draw on new and existing empirical research concerning the nature of unsophisticated decision-making. They should allow for the possibility that people lack perfect foresight not only with respect to their own future tastes and choices, but also with respect to other consequences, such as health effects.

They should also introduce the possibility that people learn about their self-control problems with experience.

The literature on "projection bias" (see, for example, Loewenstein et al. 2003a) illustrates the potential to discover important regularities concerning the structure of naive decision-making through empirical research. This phrase refers to the tendency for people to assume that their future likes and dislikes will be more similar to their current likes and dislikes than is actually the case.[22] Loewenstein et al. (2003a) briefly and informally discuss several provocative implications for addiction. Victims of projection bias are more likely to become addicted against their interests because they underestimate both the effects of habit formation and the degree to which current consumption has negative consequences for future health. Once addicted, they are more likely to try to quit when they are not experiencing cravings, because they underestimate future cravings. Conditional on attempting to quit, they are also more likely to "fall off the wagon" because, upon experiencing cravings, they overestimate the difficulty of continued abstention in the future.

Differences across Substances and Populations. It is important to emphasize that there is no single combination of policies that is ideal for all addictive substances. For example, while alcohol and crack cocaine are both addictive, public policy should (and does) treat them differently. A number of factors affect the relative desirability of the various policy alternatives, including (but not limited to) the typical individual's susceptibility to addiction, the responsiveness of compulsive and deliberative use to prices and other incentives, and the magnitude of the externalities imposed on third parties. It is also important to stress that the ideal policy regime for any particular substance may evolve over time as our ability to treat, control, and/or predict addiction develops. Ideally, economists should attempt to estimate parametric behavioral models for a wide range of substances and populations, and to use these estimates as a basis for determining the best policy for each substance.

2.5 PUBLIC GOODS

In this section, we review the contributions of behavioral public economics to our understanding of public goods. As in previous sections, we identify the key policy issues, summarize the standard approach, and discuss empirical evidence that calls this approach into question. We then review the leading behavioral alternative and discuss its implications.

---

[22]Projection bias does *not* imply that *lifetime* preferences vary from one point in time to another. On the contrary, an otherwise standard consumer suffering from projection bias wants future tastes to govern future choices. However, he makes decisions based on biased forecasts of future tastes.

2.5.1 The Policy Problem

A large number and wide variety of public policy issues—from the environment to school finance, and from the war on poverty to the financing of basic research—involve the provision of public goods. Funding for these goods flows from both public and private sources. At the community level, philanthropic activities in the United States address a large class of socially valuable activities, from assisting the poor to financing cultural events. Andreoni (2006) reports that, for the United States, contributions to the philanthropic sector totaled 240.3 billion dollars in 2003; moreover, in 1997, roughly 45,000 charitable, religious, and other non-for-profit organizations were registered with the government.[23] Voluntarily provided public goods also play important roles in smaller groups, such as families.

In each of these domains, public goods give rise to a common problem: how can the group best overcome free riding and provide funding at an appropriate level? Should the group provide its members with incentives to contribute (e.g., tax breaks)? Should it require mandatory contributions (e.g., through taxes)? Is it best to have a hybrid system that draws on both public and private contributions?

To answer these questions, economists require a theory of public goods that explains observed patterns of voluntary giving. The theory must explain why people give, how they select the causes to which they contribute, and how their contributions respond to economic variables, government policies, and the behavior of others. It should also account for the existence of philanthropic organizations, and explain how the activities of these entities respond to government policy.

2.5.2 The Neoclassical Perspective on Public Goods

The standard model of public goods assumes that each member of a group of N individuals has true preferences over consumption of private goods (denoted by x^i) and public goods (denoted by G). These preferences are represented by a utility function $U^i(x^i, G)$. For expositional simplicity, we focus here on a simple model with only one private good and one public good, where one unit of the private good is required to produce each unit of the public good, and where each individual i is endowed with w^i units of the private good. All of the results described below generalize to more complicated settings. Each individual contributes an amount g^i to the public good. In addition, individual i pays a lump-sum tax, T^i, and the government contributes all revenues to the public good. Consequently, $G = (g^1 + T^1) + \cdots + (g^N + T^N)$. Individuals simultaneously select their contributions after learning the values of the

---

[23]The sources of these funds are as follows: 76.3% came from individuals, 11.2% came from foundations, 7.5% from bequests, and the remaining 5.1% was by corporations; the numbers have been rounded up.

lump-sum taxes. Behavior is governed by Nash equilibrium. Let g^{i*} denote the equilibrium level of contributions, and $G^* = g^{1*} + \cdots + g^{N*}$ denote the equilibrium level of public goods.

It is useful to highlight the key assumptions built into this framework. First, individuals only care about their consumption of private and public goods. They do not benefit *directly* from making contributions, nor do they care about others' consumption or well-being. Second, individuals do not care about the *process* through which allocations are determined. For example, they are indifferent between public and private provision as long as the level of private consumption and public good provision is the same in both instances. Notice also that, in this simple model, there is no obvious role for charitable fund-raising. For example, since people are fully informed about the public good, there is no reason for charities to disseminate information.

This model has featured prominently in several important strands of the literature. These include work on optimal tax and regulatory policy in the presence of externalities, the design of efficient mechanisms for public goods problems, and political economy models of public goods provision. From a positive perspective, the model has a number of sharp, testable implications, including the following (see Bergstrom et al. (1986) and Andreoni (1988) for details).

Extreme Income Elasticities. If individuals have identical preferences, there exists an endowment level w^* such that only those with an endowment larger than w^* contribute, and $g^{i*} = w^i - w^*$ otherwise. The result extends to the case of heterogeneous tastes as long as each taste-type is represented across the income distribution. It follows that the marginal propensity to contribute to the public good is exactly unity (measured in the cross-section, controlling for individual characteristics) for those with sufficiently high resources,[24] and exactly zero for the rest of the population. It also follows that all contributors (of the same type) consume the same amount of private goods.

Only the Wealthy Contribute. In large groups only the very upper tail of the income distribution contributes to the public good. Furthermore, as the population grows (fixing the distribution of wealth), contributors account for a smaller fraction of the population. As a result, the effect of population size on total contributions converges to zero for sufficiently large populations. Unless the group is small, the level of public goods depends only on the wealth of the very rich: changes in wealth for the rest of the population have no impact on total provision.

---

[24]In response to an exogenous increase in resources (as opposed to cross-sectional variation), a contributor will increase private consumption. However, if the number of contributors is large, the recipient's marginal propensity to consume the private good is approximately zero.

Neutrality of Public Provision. Public provision of public goods financed through lump-sum taxation is neutral as long as no individual pays a lump-sum tax greater than the contribution he would make in the absence of government intervention. In this case, public contributions fully crowd out private contributions. While the conditions required for neutrality seem stark, the result generalizes to other environments. For example, Bernheim (1986) and Andreoni (1988) have shown that the total level of the public goods is invariant, or approximately invariant, with respect to public provision financed by distortionary taxes, and with respect to subsidized giving. These results build on earlier work by Warr (1982) and Roberts (1984).

Contributions from External Sources (Almost) Fully Crowd Out Internal Funding. In a large economy, exogenous contributions to the public good (made by someone outside the group, say a higher level of government) have a negligible impact on the level of provision. In other words, external funding almost fully crowds out private contributions. It follows, for example, that contributions from a higher level of government to a local charity cannot measurably increase total funding, assuming that the number of contributors is reasonably large.

Neutrality of Redistribution. Redistributing wealth among contributors has no effect on the total level of contributions. In contrast, redistributing wealth from the group of contributors to the group of noncontributors decreases the total level of the public good.

These results are valuable because they provide stark and robust testable implications of the standard model. How well do they match the data?

2.5.3 Some Problematic Observations

One of the most influential empirical tests of the standard model is Kingma (1989). In contrast to the bulk of the literature that preceded it, this chapter studies contributions to a *particular* public good—the operation of public radio stations—rather than aggregate contributions. The narrow focus is desirable because, when analyzing aggregates, it is difficult to harmonize the scope of data pertaining to public and private contributions. Moreover, a high rate of giving in the aggregate may mask low rates of giving to individual causes. The paper uses a unique cross-sectional dataset on the funding sources and member contributions to sixty-six public radio stations across the United States serving nonoverlapping markets. It has two main findings. First, about half of the subjects in the sample (who were recruited for a study of listening habits) contribute positive amounts. The average contribution given was $45. Contributors were wealthier and more educated on average, but not by a significant amount. This finding stands in sharp contrast to the first two implications from the previous section. Second, a $10,000 increase in "exogenous" public contributions to the station (that is, contributions financed by federal taxes rather than taxes on local members) reduces private contributions by $1,350 for a typical station with 9,000 members. This contradicts the fourth implication.

Kingma's first finding is consistent with patterns observed in the aggregate data. For example, Andreoni (2006) reports that, in 1995, 68.5% of all households gave to charity, and the average gift amount was $1,081. Even relatively poor households gave almost 5% of their incomes, on average, to charity; as a fraction of income, households in upper-income brackets actually gave less.

Kingma's second finding is also roughly consistent with other studies based on aggregate data. For example, Abrams and Schmitz (1978a,b) and Clotfelter (1985) find that public transfers to the 'non-for-profit' sector crowd out private giving at the rate of 5–28 cents on the dollar.

The first four implications listed in the previous section have also been tested in the laboratory. Isaac and Walker (1988) study the effect of group size in linear public-good experiments. Subjects play repeatedly with either three or nine other participants. In each round they receive an endowment of tokens and decide how many tokens to contribute to the public good. Tokens are valuable because they are exchangeable for cash at the end of the experiment. Each token contributed to the public good yields either 0.3 or 0.7 tokens for everyone in the group, including the contributor. Since each token contributed entails a net loss, the standard model predicts that it is a dominant strategy for every subject to contribute nothing. As in many other experiments in this literature, subjects initially contribute roughly 50% of tokens on average, but this figure falls as the experiment is repeated. Neither average individual contributions nor the fraction of subjects contributing a positive amount decline with group size. These findings contradict the second implication above.

Andreoni (1993) studies a variant of the previous experiment in which payoffs vary nonlinearly with the number of tokens. This generates a Nash equilibrium with strictly positive contributions. He tests the neutrality of public provision (the third implication) by comparing behavior in two closely related treatments. In each case, subjects choose how many tokens to contribute and are given a two-dimensional table that describes how their payoffs change as a function of their contribution and the aggregate contributions of others. In one treatment, they are, in effect, required to contribute at least two tokens; in the other treatment, they are not required to contribute anything.[25] Andreoni's results imply that public contributions crowd out

---

[25] Given the importance of framing effects in social exchange experiments, it is noteworthy that the minimum contribution level is imposed by restating the payoffs associated with a given contribution profile, rather than by retaining the same payoff mapping and restricting choices.

private contributions at the rate of 71 cents on the dollar. While this rate of crowding-out is high in comparison with other estimates in the literature, it is still inconsistent with the third implication.

These papers, together with a growing body of related evidence (see Ledyard (1995) and Camerer (2003) for reviews), have led many economists to reject the standard model, and to search for superior alternatives. The rest of this section reviews the state of the literature and summarizes its implications for public economics.

2.5.4 *Models Involving "Warm Glow"*

To account for the evidence described in the preceding section, Andreoni (1989, 1990) proposed a "warm-glow" model of public good contributions, which builds on ideas in papers by Blinder (1974), Becker (1974), Cornes and Sandler (1984) and Steinberg (1987). His approach entails a straightforward modification of the standard model: individuals are assumed to behave as if they maximize a utility function of the form $U^i(x^i, g^i, G)$ instead of $U^i(x^i, G)$. In this formulation, each individual cares *directly* about the amount he contributes to the public good, in addition to his consumption of the private and public goods.

This modification overturns each of the implications discussed in the preceding section, and leads to more sensible policy implications. For example, as the size of the population increases, choosing a contribution level becomes more and more like picking the level of consumption for any conventional good. In the limit, the contributor simply weighs the relative merits of spending money on two different private goods, x^i and g^i; the effect on his well-being through G becomes negligible. Accordingly, the model can produce sensible income elasticities and high rates of charitable giving throughout the income distribution. The level of the public good is responsive to changes in the income distribution, public provision increases funding levels whether financed by taxes on group members or by external sources, and redistributions among contributors are nonneutral. In fact, in the warm-glow model, the optimal tax treatment of charitable contributions qualitatively resembles the U.S. tax code (Diamond 2006). In short, the implications of the warm-glow model are more consistent than the standard framework both with the empirical findings described in the previous section, and from the perspective of policy makers.

In contrast to some of the work on addiction or saving summarized in the previous two sections, the literature on warm-glow giving has had little to say about the mechanisms responsible for generating departures from the standard framework. While it is plainly appropriate to think of the model as a reduced form representation of a more complex underlying process, the nature of this process is largely unexplained.

A partial list of possible warm-glow mechanisms includes the following. First, people may experience positive emotions (e.g., pride) when they conform to or exceed certain standards of "virtuous" behavior, or negative emotions (e.g., guilt) when they fall short of these standards. Second, they may be concerned about the inferences that others draw from their actions (for example, whether they are generous or public-spirited), and this may increase their willingness to contribute (Harbaugh 1998; Shang and Croson 2005). Third, upon forming a group, people may contribute to establish a norm of positive reciprocity, thereby promoting future cooperation. Fourth, when it is possible for group members to inflict harm on each other, giving may rise in response to implicit or explicit threats (negative reciprocity) that become credible as a result of emotional responses, such as anger (Fehr and Gächter 2000, 2002; Fehr and Fischbacher 2003, 2004; Sefton et al. 2002; Masclet et al. 2003).

One of the main themes of this chapter is that a good understanding of pertinent psychological and neural processes is often helpful in formulating reduced-form models that can faithfully reproduce observed patterns and reliably predict behavior out of sample, as well as in justifying specific normative criteria. Unfortunately, in the context of warm-glow giving and public goods, these processes are not yet well understood. The warm-glow model remains a "black box," and one can interpret it as a reduced form for a variety of mechanisms with starkly differing welfare implications. Diamond (2006) argues that, given the limited state of knowledge concerning processes, measures of social welfare should exclude the apparent benefits from the warm glow. He advocates using the warm-glow model for positive purposes (that is, to describe behavior), but favors the standard model for evaluating welfare. Andreoni (2006) expresses a similar view, and in addition argues that economists are unlikely to shed much light on the nature of the true preferences that give rise to warm-glow behavior. While we are more sanguine about the prospects for meaningful progress, we agree that economists do not yet understand warm-glow mechanisms sufficiently well to resolve important questions about positive and normative analysis.

One concern is that apparent warm-glow behavior may sometimes reflect a divergence between choices and true preferences. In some instances, people may give because they derive pleasure from the act. For example, giving to a worthy cause may make them feel proud to have taken constructive action, or it may assuage their guilt. In such cases, revealed preference provides a reasonable basis for welfare evaluation (subject to the further qualifications discussed below). However, in other situations, exposure to an emotionally manipulative message may precipitate giving by triggering a short-lived emotional reaction such as shame, and people may experience remorse shortly thereafter (see Loewenstein (1996) and Loewenstein and O'Donoghue (2004) for other interesting examples of this type of phenomenon). Different implications for welfare follow depending on whether the individual, when in a normal state of mind, wishes to limit his ability to give upon encountering an emotional trigger. If behavior is dynamically consistent, it may be appropriate to adopt a state-contingent version of the warm-glow model for both positive and normative analysis. However, if behavior is dynamically inconsistent, it may be appropriate to discount the "revealed" impact of giving on transient perceptions of well-being (e.g., for the reasons discussed at the end of Section 2.3).

A second concern is that warm-glow effects appear to be context dependent. Experiments have shown that the amount of giving depends on framing, the identity of the group, the emotional state of the subjects, and the history of play. Here we mention two examples. First, Andreoni (1995) finds that a change in the phrasing of instructions can have a sizable effect on contributions, even when strategy sets and payoffs are unchanged. Second, Isaac and Walker (1988) (and dozens of subsequent studies) find that the level of contributions decreases with repetition in both small and large groups.[26] Furthermore, the rate of decline depends on the behavior of others: subjects are more likely to stop acting cooperatively if others behave selfishly (see Ledyard (1995) and Camerer (2003) for surveys of the literature).

This concern is relevant for policy analysis. The appropriate reduced-form representation of warm-glow giving may vary from one set of policies and institutions to another. The practice of forecasting the behavioral effects of a policy change based on fixed warm-glow parameters is therefore vulnerable to the Lucas critique. For example, if people experience less pride when making contributions in the presence of economic incentives, subsidization of contributions will stimulate less giving than anticipated, and could even reduce it. Alternatively, people may become less resistant to taxation if they are regularly supplied with more concrete and visual evidence of the benefits derived from public expenditures. Public relation campaigns that show "your tax dollars at work" are, in effect, intended to foster a warm glow.

One could, of course, modify the warm-glow model to account for context dependence by linking the taste for giving to features of the environment in just the right way. However, this solution is conceptually unsatisfactory. One cannot usefully explain a phenomenon by selecting ad hoc preferences that rationalize choices ex post (Stigler and Becker 1977). If every context is potentially associated with a different mode of behavior, out-of-sample prediction is impossible. To anticipate the positive effects of policy changes, one therefore needs a broad theory that accounts for the relevance of context. This requires us to open the black box.

Since the warm-glow mechanism may differ from one context to another, a deeper understanding of context dependence is also essential for welfare analysis. To illustrate the problem, consider the following hypothetical example. How should we evaluate a policy that replaces private contributions to a public good with tax-financed

---

[26]Palfrey and Prisbrey (1997) argue that the implied decline in the warm-glow taste parameter may in part reflect falling rates of decision errors. To our knowledge, there is no evidence that distinguishes between the hypothesis that tastes evolve with repetition and the possibility that error rates decline. However, errors do not appear to explain many other findings in this literature.

contributions, without changing either the total amount obtained from any individual or the overall level of funding? Are people worse off because they lose the beneficial warm glow associated with giving? Are they better off because public funding relieves them of guilt? Or are they equally well-off because they experience the same warm glow from giving voluntarily and from paying their taxes? While it may be difficult to resolve this issue, we are optimistic about the prospects for progress through further research involving a combination of psychology, neuroscience, and experimental economics.

Despite these concerns, the theoretical and empirical literatures concerning warm-glow giving have already contributed significantly to our understanding of public goods, and have changed the way many public economists think about related policies. We can now say with some confidence that people act *as if* they care about the levels of their own contributions. We know that the intensity of this effect depends on context. While we lack a good theory of context dependence, we have a good set of empirical regularities from which to build. We have good reason to believe that people feel differently about public and private contributions. We have both direct and indirect evidence that public contributions crowd out private contributions at a rate significantly less than dollar-for-dollar. Accordingly, even low levels of public contributions can significantly raise total funding. There is strong evidence that people give more when institutions activate psychological mechanisms, such as concerns about reciprocity and fairness, that play central roles in giving. From a policy perspective, this suggests that relatively inexpensive strategies involving advertising and the promotion of community leadership may deserve greater emphasis.

2.5.5 *Looking Ahead*

Given the crucial role that public goods and externalities play in many important policy problems, one of the main challenges ahead for public economics is to build and test better models of public goods, and to apply them to basic questions in public finance, political economy, and mechanism design. We are still far from a satisfactory model of public goods that can become a new workhorse for economic applications across the board. However, based on the rapidly growing body of evidence concerning the psychological and neural processes at work, including research on the neural basis of empathy, punishment, and cooperation (see de Quervain et al. 2004; McCabe et al. 2001; Singer et al. 2004; Rilling et al. 2002, 2004), we are optimistic that such a framework is on the horizon. Given the number of likely forces at work (reciprocity, social norms, social emotions, social signaling, and so forth) it seems likely that a relatively complex and multifaceted approach is needed. Yet it is also likely that the discovery of new organizing principles will permit useful simplifications that render the problem more tractable.

In focusing here on individual behavior, we have largely neglected the role of philanthropic organizations. As Andreoni (2006) convincingly argues, it is also essential to understand the behavior of the philanthropic sector. A growing body of evidence shows that charities significantly stimulate giving, and that their activities respond both to government policy and to the behavior of other non-for-profit institutions. For example, Andreoni and Payne (2003) show that government grants to charities reduce fund-raising activities; Andreoni and Petrie (2004) document the role of charities in disseminating information; Harbaugh (1998) provides evidence that charities exploit social signaling in their fund-raising campaigns. For reviews of the economics of philanthropy, see Andreoni (2006) and Rose-Ackerman (1996).

2.6 THE ROAD AHEAD

In our view, behavioral public economics has enormous potential, and has already demonstrated its value by making important contributions to critical policy discussions. We have emphasized that the behavioral perspective does not preclude coherent normative analysis. Indeed, in many cases, it is possible to modify and extend the tools of empirical welfare analysis without abandoning familiar methodological principles. We have also reviewed recent behavioral work concerning policies affecting saving, addiction, and public goods. Each of these literatures offers novel and important insights, as well as the potential for groundbreaking innovation.

The goal of this final section is to briefly highlight some critical directions for future research.

Better Models. While the current generation of behavioral models improves the explanatory power of economic theory, many behavioral patterns remain unexplained. Among other things, recent research has deemphasized considerations for which satisfactory and tractable formal models are not yet available, such as framing effects, the adoption of rules of thumb, and other responses to environmental complexity. To study the policy implications of these phenomena, better models are required. For example, we need theories that explain how people adopt rules of thumb, and how they adapt these rules to new environments.

New Types and Sources of Data. With sufficiently restrictive structural assumptions, it is possible to estimate positive and normative behavioral models using data only on choices. The use of nonchoice data would potentially allow economists to estimate these models more reliably, and to formulate more discriminating and robust tests of competing alternatives.

Future research should examine the possibility of measuring preferences directly, instead of inferring them from choices. Self-reporting is a natural source of information about tastes. In practice, there are several problems with self-reported preferences. First, when choices are not involved, questions about preferences are inherently hypothetical. There is some reason to believe that people do not give reliable answers to hypothetical questions (see, for example, List (2001) and the references therein). For example, unless there is something at stake, they may not take these questions seriously. Second, true preferences may conflict with social and moral norms, leading subjects to either rationalize or report false preferences. Third, people may make mistakes in assessing their own preferences. For example, a sizable body of literature has documented systematic errors in affective forecasting (see Loewenstein and Schkade (1999) for a review). Fourth, context may affect an individual's ability to cognitively access his true preferences.

Despite considerable evidence that self-reporting is susceptible to these problems (see Schwartz and Strack (1999) for a review), there is cause for optimism. For the most part, the object of this body of work has been to identify experimental manipulations that lead to nonsensical self-reports. While this demonstrates that there are important pitfalls associated with the direct elicitation of preferences, it does not prove that this approach is worthless. As far as we know, there has been no systematic attempt to design elicitation protocols that are stable and resistant to manipulation.

Many other types of data merit consideration. Even without eliciting complete preferences, one can potentially learn whether an individual regards a particular choice as a mistake, whether his choices correspond to his intentions, or whether he systematically fails to follow through on plans (see, for example, Choi et al. 2004, 2006; Bernheim 1995). One can also elicit information about expectations and make comparisons with realizations (see, for example, Bernheim 1988, 1989; Hurd and McGarry 2002; Loewenstein et al. 2003a). Obviously, information along these lines raises many of the same concerns as self-reported preferences. Finally, economists have only just started to tap data on physical states, brain activity, and the like. While the value of neuroeconomic data remains largely unproven, the potential payoffs are high, and the possibilities are worth exploring.

Difficult Issues in Welfare Economics. The nascent field of "behavioral welfare economics" is far from settled. Many thorny issues remain. The following hypothetical problem illustrates one challenging issue. An individual is presented with a choice between two options, A and B. He is indifferent between them. However, his preferences change as a result of his choice. If he chooses A, he prefers B (call this the "A self"). If he chooses B, he prefers A (call this the "B self"). Suppose he chooses A. Since only the initial self and the A self actually exist, it seems natural to place no weight on the preferences of the B self. But if we place any weight on the A self, B is the welfare optimum. Of course, if we enforce this choice through public policy, the A self vanishes and the B self materializes, in which case A is

67

the welfare optimum. Is there a coherent way to resolve this ambiguity? See Bernheim and Rangel (2005a) for a more systematic treatment of welfare economics in behavioral settings.

Nonstandard Policies.   In the standard model, public policy affects behavior only through its effect on information and budget constraints. A growing body of literature, partially reviewed in the previous three sections, suggests that policy can also have powerful effects on behavior through other channels. For example, it can provide or suppress cues, and it can alter the way decision problems are framed. If economists can develop reliable formal models of these effects, it should be possible to study the optimal design of unconventional economic policies (e.g., restrictions on advertising, warning labels, and clever manipulations of framing effects as in Thaler and Benartzi's (2004) Saving for Tomorrow Savings Plan) with the same rigor as traditional tax and expenditure policy.

New Applications.   The interesting collection of papers in this volume show that, as time passes, economists are applying behavioral economics to an increasingly wide range of economic problems. No doubt this trend will continue within the field of public economics. Many of the tools described in this chapter should prove useful in understanding issues pertaining to poverty, crime, corruption, and other important topics.

REFERENCES

Abrams, B. A., and M. A. Schmitz. 1978a. The "crowding-out" effect of government transfers on private charitable contributions. *Public Choice* 33:29–39.
——. 1978b. The "crowding-out" effect of government transfers on private charitable contributions: cross-sectional evidence. *National Tax Journal* 37:563–68.
Ainslie, G., and V. Haendel. 1983. The motives of the will. In *Etiologic Aspects of Alcohol and Drug Abuse* (ed. E. Gotteheil et al.). Springfield, IL: Thomas.
Akerlof, G. 1991. Procrastination and obedience. *American Economic Review* 81:1–19.
Ameriks, J., A. Caplin, and J. Leahy. 2003. Wealth accumulation and the propensity to plan. *Quarterly Journal of Economics* 118:1007–47.
Andreoni, J. 1988. Privately provided public goods in a large economy: the limits of altruism. *Journal of Public Economics* 35:57–73.
——. 1989. Giving with impure altruism: applications to charity and Ricardian equivalence. *Journal of Political Economy* 97:1147–58.
——. 1990. Impure altruism and donations to public goods: a theory of warm glow giving. *Economic Journal* 100:464–77.
——. 1993. An experimental test of the public-goods crowding-out hypothesis. *American Economic Review* 83:1317–27.
——. 1995. Warm-glow versus cold-pickle: the effects of positive and negative framing on cooperation experiments. *Quarterly Journal of Economics* 110:2–21.

Andreoni, J. 1998. Towards a theory of charitable fund-raising. *Journal of Political Economy* 106:1186–1213.

——. 2006. Philanthropy. In *Handbook of the Economics of Giving, Altruism, and Reciprocity* (ed. L. A. Gerard-Vared, S.-C. Kolm, and J. M. Ythier), Volume 2, Chapter 18. Elsevier.

Andreoni, J., and A. Payne. 2003. Do government grants to private charities crowd out giving or fund-raising? *American Economic Review* 93:792–812.

Andreoni, J., and R. Petrie. 2004. Public goods experiments without confidentiality: a glimpse into fund-raising. *Journal of Public Economics* 88:1605–23.

Angeletos, G.-M., D. Laibson, A. Repetto, J. Tobacman, and S. Weinberg. 2001. The hyperbolic consumption model: calibration, simulation, and empirical evaluation. *Journal of Economic Perspectives* 15(3):47–68.

Ariely, D., and K. Wertenbroch. 2002. Procrastination, deadlines and performance: self-control by precommitment. *Psychological Science* 13(3):219–24.

Banks, J., R. Blundell, and S. Tanner. 1998. Is there a retirement-savings puzzle? *American Economic Review* 88:769–88.

Bayer, P. J., B. D. Bernheim, and J. K. Scholz. 1996. The effects of financial education in the workplace: evidence from a survey of employers. Mimeo, Stanford University.

Becker, G. 1974. A theory of social interactions. *Journal of Political Economy* 82:1063–93.

Becker, G., and K. Murphy. 1988. A theory of rational addiction. *Journal of Political Economy* 96:675–700.

Benabou, R., and M. Pycia. 2002. Dynamic inconsistency and self-control. *Economics Letters* 77:419–24.

Bergstrom, T., L. Blume, and H. Varian. 1986. On the private provision of public goods. *Journal of Public Economics* 29:25–49.

Bernartzi, S. 2001. Excessive extrapolation and the allocation of 401(k) accounts to company stock. *Journal of Finance* 56:1747–64.

Bernartzi, S., and R. H. Thaler. 2001. Naïve diversification strategies in defined contribution savings plans. *American Economic Review* 91:71–98.

Bernheim, B. D. 1986. On the voluntary and involuntary provision of public goods. *American Economic Review* 76:789–93.

——. 1988. Social security benefits: an empirical study of expectations and realizations. In *Issues in Contemporary Retirement* (ed. E. Lazear and R. Ricardo-Campbell), pp. 312–45. Stanford, CA: Hoover Institution Press.

——. 1989. The timing of retirement: a comparison of expectations and realizations. In *The Economics of Aging* (ed. D. Wise), pp. 335–55. NBER and University of Chicago Press.

——. 1994. Personal saving, information, and economic literacy: new directions for public policy. In *Tax Policy for Economic Growth in the 1990s*, pp. 53–78. Washington, DC: American Council for Capital Formation.

——. 1995. Do households appreciate their financial vulnerabilities? An analysis of actions, perceptions, and public policy. In *Tax Policy for Economic Growth in the 1990s*, pp. 1–30. Washington, DC: American Council for Capital Formation.

——. 1998. Financial illiteracy, education, and retirement saving. In *Living with Defined Contribution Pensions* (ed. O. S. Mitchell and S. J. Schieber), pp. 38–68. University of Pennsylvania Press.

Bernheim, B. D., and D. M. Garrett. 2003. The effects of financial education in the workplace: evidence from a survey of households. *Journal of Public Economics* 87:1487–519.

Bernheim, B. D., and A. Rangel. 2004. Addiction and cue-triggered decision processes. *American Economic Review* 94:1558–90.

———. 2005a. Behavioral welfare economics. Manuscript.

———. 2005b. Savings and cue-triggered decision processes. Manuscript.

———. Forthcoming. From neuroscience to public policy: a new economic view of addiction. *Swedish Economic Policy Review*.

Bernheim, B. D., D. Ray, and S. Yeltekin. 1999. Self-control, saving, and the low asset trap. Mimeo, Stanford University.

Bernheim, B. D., D. M. Garrett, and D. Maki. 2001a. Education and saving: the long-term effects of high school financial curriculum mandates. *Journal of Public Economics* 80:435–65.

Bernheim, B. D., J. Skinner, and S. Weinberg. 2001b. What accounts for the variation in retirement wealth among U.S. households? *American Economic Review* 91:832–57.

Bernheim, B. D., L. Forni, J. Gokhale, and L. Kotlikoff. 2002. An economic approach to setting retirement saving goals. In *Innovations in Financing Retirement* (ed. O. Mitchell, Z. Bodie, B. Hammond, and S. Zeldes), pp. 77–105. University of Pennsylvania Press.

Berridge, K. 1996. Food reward: brain substrates of wanting and liking. *Neuroscience and Biobehavioral Reviews* 20:1–25.

———. 1999. Pleasure, pain, desire, and dread: hidden core processes of emotion. In *Well-Being: The Foundations of Hedonic Psychology* (ed. D. Kaheman, E. Diener, and N. Schwarz), pp. 525–57. New York: Russell Sage Foundation.

Berridge, K., and T. Robinson. 1998. What is the role of dopamine in reward: hedonic impact, reward learning, or incentive salience? *Brain Research Review* 28:309–69.

———. 2003. Parsing reward. *Trends in Neuroscience* 26:507–13.

Bhattacharya, J., and D. Lakdawalla. 2004. Time-inconsistency and welfare. Mimeo, Stanford University.

Blinder, A. S. 1974. *Toward an Economic Theory of Income Distribution*. MIT Press.

Bolton, G. E., and A. Ockenfels. 2000. ERC: a theory of equity, reciprocity, and competition. *American Economic Review* 20:166–93.

Camerer, C. F. 2003. *Behavioral Game Theory: Experiments in Strategic Interaction*. Princeton University Press.

Center for Disease Control. 1993. Smoking-attributable mortality and years of potential life lost: United States, 1990. *Morbidity and Mortality Weekly Report* 42:645–48.

Chaloupka, F., and K. Warner. 2001. The economics of smoking. In *Handbook of Health Economics* (ed. J. Newhouse and D. Cutler). Amsterdam: North-Holland.

Choi, J. J., D. Laibson, B. C. Madrian, and A. Metrick. 2004. Optimal defaults and active decisions. Manuscript.

———. 2006. Saving for retirement on the path of least resistance. In *Behavioral Public Finance: Toward a New Agenda* (ed. E. J. McCaffrey and J. Slemrod). New York: Russell Sage Foundation.

Clotfelter, C. 1985. *Federal Tax Policy and Charitable Giving*. University of Chicago Press.

Cohen, G. A. 1989. On the currency of egalitarianism justice. *Ethics* 99:906–44.

Coller, M., G. W. Harrison, and E. E. Rutström. 2003. Are discount rates constant? Reconciling theory and observation, Working Paper 3-31, Department of Economics, College of Business Administration, University of Central Florida.

Consumer Federation of America and the American Express Company. 1991. High School Competency Test: Report of Findings, Washington, DC.

Cornes, R., and T. Sandler. 1984. Easy riders, joint production and public goods. *Economic Journal* 94:580–98.

Cronqvist, H., and R. H. Thaler. 2004. Design choices in privatized social security systems: learning from the Swedish experience. *American Economic Review* 94:424–28.

de Quervain, D., U. Fischbacher, V. Treyer, M. Schellhammer, U. Schnyder, A. Buck, and E. Fehr. 2004. The neural basis of altruistic punishment. *Science* 305:1254–58.

Diamond, P. 2006. Optimal tax treatment of private contributions for public goods with and without warm-glow preferences. *Journal of Public Economics* 90:897–919.

Diamond, P., and J. Hausman. 1994. Contingent valuation: is some number better than no number? *Journal of Economic Perspectives* 8:45–64.

Diamond, P., and B. Koszegi. 2003. Quasi-hyperbolic discounting and retirement. *Journal of Public Economics* 87:1839–72.

Di Chiara, G. 1999. Drug addiction as dopamine-dependent associative learning disorder. *European Journal of Pharmacology* 375:13–30.

Dockner, E. J., and G. Feichtinger. 1993. Cyclical consumption patterns and rational addiction. *American Economic Review* 83:256–63.

Doyle Jr., R. J., and E. T. Johnson. 1991. *Readings in Wealth Accumulation Planning*, 4th edn. Bryn Mawr, PA: The American College.

DSM-IV. 1994. *Diagnostic and Statistical Manual of Mental Disorders*, 4th edn. Washington, DC: American Psychiatric Association.

Duflo, E., and E. Saez. 2002. Participation and investment decisions in a retirement plan: the influence of colleagues' choices. *Journal of Public Economics* 85:121–48.

———. 2003. The role of information and social interactions in retirement plans decisions: evidence from a randomized experiment. *Quarterly Journal of Economics* 118:815–42.

Engen, E. M., W. G. Gale, and J. K. Scholz. 1994. Do saving incentives work? *Brookings Papers on Economic Activity* 1:85–151.

Fang, H., and D. Silverman. 2002. Time-inconsistency and welfare program participation: evidence from the NLSY. Cowles Foundation Discussion Paper 1465, Yale University.

Farkas, S., and J. Johnson. 1997. *Miles to Go: A Status Report on Americans' Plans for Retirement*. New York: Public Agenda.

Feenberg, D. R., and J. Skinner. 1989. *Sources of IRA Saving*. Tax Policy and the Economy, Volume 17, pp. 25–46. MIT Press.

Fehr, E., and S. Gächter. 2000. Cooperation and punishment in public good experiments. *American Economic Review* 90:980–94.

———. 2002. Altruistic punishment in humans. *Nature* 415:137–40.

Fehr, E., and U. Fischbacher. 2003. The nature of human altruism. *Nature* 425:785–89.

———. 2004. Social norms and human cooperation. *Trends in Cognitive Sciences* 8:185–90.

Fehr, E., and K. M. Schmidt. 1999. A theory of fairness, competition, and cooperation. *Quarterly Journal of Economics* 114:817–68.

Feldstein, M. 1985. The optimal level of social security benefits. *Quarterly Journal of Economics* 100:303–20.

Fernandez-Villaverde, J., and A. Mukherji. 2002. Can we really observe hyperbolic discounting? Mimeo, University of Pennsylvania.

Fisher, I. 1930. *The Theory of Interest*. London: Macmillan.

Frederick, S., G. Loewenstein, and T. O'Donoghue. 2002. Time discounting and time preference: a critical review. *Journal of Economic Literature* 40:351–401.

Fudenberg, D., and D. K. Levine. 2005. A dual self-model of impulse control. UCLA Department of Economics Working Paper.

Gardner, E., and J. David. 1999. The neurobiology of chemical addiction. In *Getting Hooked: Rationality and Addiction* (ed. J. Elster and O.-J. Skog). Cambridge University Press.

Goldstein, A. 2001. *Addiction: From Biology to Drug Policy*, 2nd edn. Oxford University Press.

Goldstein, A., and H. Kalant. 1990. Drug policy: striking the right balance. *Science* 249:1513–21.

Gravelle, J. 1991. Do individual retirement accounts increase savings? *Journal of Economic Perspectives* 5:133–48.

Gross, D., and N. Souleles. 2002. Do liquidity constraints and interest rates matter for consumer behaviors? Evidence from credit card data. *Quarterly Journal of Economics* 117: 149–86.

Gruber, J., and B. Koszegi. 2001. Is addiction "rational"? Theory and evidence. *Quarterly Journal of Economics* 116:1261–303.

———. 2004. A theory of government regulation of addictive bads: tax levels and tax incidence for cigarette excise taxation. *Journal of Public Economics* 88:1959–87.

Gul, F., and W. Pesendorfer. 2001. Temptation and self-control. *Econometrica* 69:1403–35.

———. 2004a. Self-control, revealed preference and consumption choice. *Review of Economic Dynamics* 7:243–264.

———. 2004b. Self-control and the theory of consumption. *Econometrica* 72:119–158.

———. Forthcoming. Harmful addiction. *Review of Economic Studies*.

Hammermesh, D. S. 1984. Consumption during retirement: the missing link in the life cycle. *Review of Economics and Statistics* 66:1–7.

Harbaugh, W. 1998. What do donations buy? A model of philanthropy based on prestige and warm-glow. *Journal of Public Economics* 67:269–84.

Harris, J. E. 1993. *Deadly Choices: Coping with Health Risks in Everyday Life*. New York: Basic Books.

Hausman, J. A., and L. Paquette. 1987. Involuntary early retirement and consumption. In *Work, Health, and Income Among the Elderly* (ed. G. Burtless), pp. 151–75. Washington, DC: Brookings Institution Press.

Holden, S., J. VanDerhei, and C. Quick. 2001. 401(k) plan asset allocation, account balances, and loan activity in 1998. *Perspective* 6(1):1–23.

Hser, Y. I., D. Anglin, and K. Powers. 1993. A 24-year follow-up study of California narcotics addicts. *Archives of General Psychiatry* 50:577–84.

Hser, Y. I., V. Hollman, C. Grella, and M. D. Anglin. 2001. A 33-year follow-up of narcotics addicts. *Archives of General Psychiatry* 58:503–8.

Hurd, M., and K. McGarry. 2002. The predictive validity of subjective probabilities of survival. *Economic Journal* 112:966–85.

Hurd, M., and S. Rohwedder. 2003. The retirement-consumption puzzle: anticipated and actual declines in spending at retirement. NBER Working Paper 9586.

Hyman, S., and R. Malenka. 2001. Addiction and the brain: the neurobiology of compulsion and its persistence. *Nature Reviews Neuroscience* 2:695–703.

Iannacone, L. R. 1986. Addiction and satiation. *Economic Letters* 21:95–99.

Imrohoroglu, S., A. Imrohoroglu, and D. Joines. 2003. Time inconsistent preferences and social security. *Quarterly Journal of Economics* 118:745–84.

Isaac, M., and J. Walker. 1988. Group size effects in public goods provision: the voluntary contributions mechanism. *Quarterly Journal of Economics* 103:179–99.

Jones, S. R. G. 1984. *The Economics of Conformism*. Oxford: Basil Blackwell.

Katona, G. 1975. *Psychological Economics*. Elsevier.

Kelley, A. E. 1999. Neural integrative activities of nucleus accumbens subregions in relation to motivation and learning. *Psychobiology* 27:198–213.

Kingma, R. 1989. An accurate measurement of the crowd-out effect, income effect, and price effect for charitable contributions. *Journal of Political Economy* 97:1197–1207.

Koszegi. 2002. Note: any model features an untestable assumption about preferences. Manuscript, University of California, Berkeley.

Krusell, P., and A. Smith. 2003. Consumption-saving decisions with quasi-geometric discounting. *Econometrica* 71:365–75.

Krusell, P., B. Kuruscu, and A. Smith. 2000. Tax policy with quasi-geometric discounting. *International Economic Journal* 14:1–40.

——. 2001. Temptation and taxation. Mimeo, Princeton University.

——. 2002. Equilibrium welfare and government policy with quasi-geometric discounting. *Journal of Economic Theory* 105:42–72.

Laibson, D. 1994. Self-control and saving. Mimeo, MIT.

——. 1997. Golden eggs and hyperbolic discounting. *Quarterly Journal of Economics* 112:443–77.

——. 2001. A cue-theory of consumption. *Quarterly Journal of Economics* 116:81–120.

Laibson, D., A. Repetto, and J. Tobacman. 2003. A debt puzzle. In *Knowledge, Information, and Expectations in Modern Economics: In Honor of Edmund Phelps* (ed. P. Aghion, R. Frydman, J. Stiglitz, and M. Woodford). Princeton University Press.

——. Forthcoming. Estimating discount functions from lifecycle consumption choices. NBER Working Paper.

Lazear, E. P. 1994. Some thoughts on saving. In *Studies in the Economics of Aging* (ed. D. A. Wise), pp. 143–69. University of Chicago Press and NBER.

Ledyard, J. 1995. Public goods: a survey of experimental research. In *Handbook of Experimental Economics* (ed. J. Kagel and A. Roth), pp. 111–94. Princeton University Press.

List, J. A. 2001. Do explicit warnings eliminate the hypothetical bias in elicitation procedures? Evidence from field auctions for sportscards. *American Economic Review* 91:1498–507.

Loewenstein, G. 1996. Out of control: visceral influences on behavior. *Organizational Behavior and Human Decision Processes* 65:272–92.

——. 1999. A visceral account of addiction. In *Rationality and Addiction* (ed. J. Elster and O.-J. Skog). Cambridge University Press.

Loewenstein, G., and T. O'Donoghue. 2004. Animal spirits: affective and deliberative processes in economic behavior. Manuscript.

Loewenstein, G., and D. Schkade. 1999. Wouldn't it be nice? Predicting future feelings. In *Well-Being: The Foundations of Hedonic Psychology* (ed. D. Kahneman, E. Diener, and N. Schwarz), pp. 85–104. New York: Russell Sage Foundation.

Loewenstein, G., T. O'Donoghue, and M. Rabin. 2003a. Projection bias in predicting future utility. *Quarterly Journal of Economics* 118:1209–48.

Loewenstein, G., D. Read, and R. Baumister (eds). 2003b. *Time and Decision: Economic and Psychological Perspectives on Intertemporal Choice*. New York: Russell Sage Foundation.

Long, J. E. 1990. Marginal tax rates and IRA contributions. *National Tax Journal* 43:143–53.

Lusardi, A. 2000. Saving for retirement: the importance of planning. *Research Dialogue*, No. 66. TIAA-CREF Institute.

———. 2003. Planning and savings for retirement. Mimeo, Dartmouth College.

MacCoun, R., and P. Reuter. 2001. *Drug War Heresies: Learning from Other Vices, Times, and Places*. Cambridge University Press.

Madrian, B., and D. Shea. 2001. The power of suggestion: inertia in 401(k) participation and savings behavior. *Quarterly Journal of Economics* 116:1149–87.

Mariger, R. P. 1987. A life-cycle consumption model with liquidity constraints: theory and empirical results. *Econometrica* 55:533–57.

Masclet, D., C. Noussair, S. Tucker, and M.-C. Villeval. 2003. Monetary and non-monetary punishment in the voluntary contributions mechanisms. *American Economic Review* 93:366–80.

McCabe, K., D. Houser, L. Ryan, V. Smith, and T. Trouard. 2001. A functional imaging study of cooperation in two-person reciprocal exchange. *Proceedings of the National Academy of Sciences* 98:11 832–835.

McCaffrey, E., and J. Slemrod. 2006. Toward an agenda for behavioral public finance. In *Behavioral Public Finance: Toward a New Agenda* (ed. E. J. McCaffrey and J. Slemrod), pp. 304–51. New York: Russell Sage Foundation.

McClure, S., D. I. Laibson, G. Loewenstein, and J. D. Cohen. 2004. Separate neural systems value immediate and delayed monetary rewards. *Science* 306:503–7.

Metcalfe, J., and W. Mischel. 1999. A hot/cool-system analysis of delay of gratification: dynamics of willpower. *Psychological Review* 106:3–19.

Mischel, W. 1974. Processes in delay of gratification. In *Advances in Experimental Social Psychology* (ed. D. Berkowitz), Volume 7, pp. 249–72. Academic Press.

Mischel, W., and B. Moore. 1973. Cognitive appraisals and transformations in delay of gratification. *Journal of Personality and Social Psychology* 28:172–79.

Mischel, W., Y. Shoda, and M. Rodriguez. 1992. Delay of gratification in children. In *Choice Over Time* (ed. G. Loewenstein and J. Elster). New York: Russell Sage Foundation.

Modigliani, F., and R. Brumberg. 1954. Utility analysis and the consumption function: an interpretation of cross-section data. In *Post Keynsian Economics* (ed. K. K. Kurihara). Rutgers University Press.

National Institute on Alcohol Abuse and Alcoholism. 2001. Economic perspectives in alcoholism research. *Alcohol Alert Magazine* No. 51. Bethesda, MD: National Institutes of Health.

National Institute on Drug Abuse. 1998. *The Economic Costs of Alcohol and Drug Abuse in the United States, 1992.* Bethesda, MD: National Institutes of Health.

Nestler, E. J. 2001. Molecular basis of long-term plasticity underlying addiction. *Nature Reviews Neuroscience* 2:119–28.

Nestler, E. J., and R. C. Malenka. 2004. The addicted brain. *Scientific American* 290:78–85.

Norstrom, Th., and O.-J. Skog. 2005. Saturday opening and alcohol retail shops in Sweden: an experiment in two phases. *Addiction* 100:767–76.

O'Brien, C. 1976. Experimental analysis of conditioning factors in human narcotic addiction. *Pharmacological Review* 25:533–43.

——. 1997. A range of research-based pharmacotherapies for addiction. *Science* 278:66–70.

O'Donoghue, T., and M. Rabin. 1999a. Procrastination in preparing for retirement. In *Behavioral Dimensions of Retirement Economics* (ed. H. J. Aaron), pp. 125–56. Washington, DC: Brookings Institution Press.

——. 1999b. Doing it now or later. *American Economic Review* 89:103–24.

——. 2001. Choice and procrastination. *Quarterly Journal of Economics* 116:121–60.

——. 2005. Optimal sin taxes. Manuscript. UCLA Department of Economics.

Office of National Drug Control Policy. 2001a. What American users spend on illegal drugs. Publication No. NCJ-192334. Washington, DC: Executive Office of the President.

——. 2001b. The economic costs of drug abuse in the United States, 1992–1998. Publication No. NCJ-190636. Washington, DC: Executive Office of the President.

O'Neill, B. 1993. Assessing America's financial IQ: realities, consequences, and potential for change. Mimeo, Rutgers Cooperative Extension.

Ornstein, S. I., and D. M. Hanssens. 1985. Alcohol control laws and the consumption of distilled spirits and beer. *Journal of Consumer Research* 12:200–12.

Orphanides, A., and D. Zervos. 1995. Rational addiction with learning and regret. *Journal of Political Economy* 103:739–58.

——. 1998. Myopia and addictive behavior. *Economic Journal* 108:75–91.

Palfrey, T., and J. Prisbrey. 1997. Anomalous behavior in public goods experiments: how much and why? *American Economic Review* 87:829–46.

Paserman, D. 2002. Job search and hyperbolic discounting: structural estimation and policy evaluation. CEPR Discussion Paper 4396.

Phelps, E., and R. Pollack. 1968. On second-best national savings and game equilibrium growth. *Review of Economic Studies* 35:185–99.

Prelec, D., and G. Loewenstein. 1998. The red and the black: mental accounting of savings and debt. *Marketing Science* 17:4–28.

Rabin, M. 2002. A perspective on psychology and economics. *European Economic Review* 46:657–85.

Redish, A. D. 2004. Addiction as a computational process gone awry. *Science* 306:1944–47.

Rilling, J., D. Gutman, T. Zeh, G. Pagnoni, G. Berns, and C. Kilts. 2002. A neural basis for social cooperation. *Neuron* 35:395–405.

Rilling, J. K., A. G. Sanfey, J. A. Aronson, L. E. Nystrom, and J. D. Cohen. 2004. Opposing BOLD responses to reciprocated and unreciprocated altruism in putative reward pathways. *Neuroreport* 15:2539–43.

Robb, A. L., and J. B. Burbidge. 1989. Consumption, income, and retirement. *Canadian Journal of Economics* 22:522–42.

Robbins, T. W., and Everitt, B. J. 1999. Interaction of depaminergic system with mechanisms of associative learning and cognition: implications for drug abuse. *Psychological Science* 10:199–202.

Roberts, R. 1984. A positive model of private charity and public transfers. *Journal of Political Economy* 92:136–48.

Robins, L. 1993. Vietnam veterans' rapid recovery from heroin addiction: a fluke or normal expectation. *Addiction* 88:1041–54.

Robins, L., D. Davis, and D. Goodwin. 1974. Drug use by U.S. Army enlisted men in Vietnam: a follow-up on their return home. *American Journal of Epidemiology* 99:235–49.

Robinson, T., and K. Berridge. 1993. The neural basis of drug craving: an incentive-sensitization theory of addiction. *Brain Research Reviews* 18:247–91.

———. 2000. The psychology and neurobiology of addiction: an incentive sensitization view. *Addiction* (Suppl.) 2:91–117.

———. 2003. Addiction. *Annual Reviews of Psychology* 54:25–53.

Roemer, J. E. 1998. *Equality of Opportunity*. Harvard University Press.

Rose-Ackerman, S. 1996. Altruism, nonprofits, and economic theory. *Journal of Economic Literature* 34:701–28.

Scholz, J. K., A. Seshadri, and S. Khitatrakun. 2004. Are Americans saving adequately for retirement? Mimeo, University of Wisconsin, Madison.

Schultz, W. 1998. Predictive reward signal of dopamine neurons. *Journal of Neurophysiology* 80:1–27.

Schultz, W. 2000. Multiple reward signals in the brain. *Nature Reviews Neuroscience* 1:199–207.

Schultz, W., P. Dayan, and P. R. Montague. 1997. A neural substrate of prediction and reward. 275:1593–99.

Schwarz, N., and F. Strack. 1999. Reports of subjective well-being: judgmental processes and their methodological implications. In *Well-Being: The Foundations of Hedonic Psychology* (ed. D. Kahneman, E. Diener, and N. Schwarz), pp. 61–84. New York: Russell Sage Foundation.

Scitovsky, T. 1976. *The Joyless Economy*. Oxford University Press.

Sefton, M., R. Shupp, and J. Walker. 2002. The effect of rewards and sanctions in the provision of public goods. CEDEX Research Paper, University of Nottingham.

Sen, A. 1992. *Inequality Reexamined*. Harvard University Press.

Shang, J., and R. Croson. 2005. Field experiments in charitable contributions: the impact of social influence on the voluntary provision of public goods. Manuscript, University of Pennsylvania.

Shiv, B., and A. Fedorikhin. 1999. Heart and mind in conflict: the interplay of affect and cognition in consumer decision making. *Journal of Consumer Research* 26:72–89.

Singer, T., S. J. Kiebel, J. S. Winston, R. J. Dolan, and C. D. Frith. 2004. Brain responses to the acquired moral status of faces. *Neuron* 41:653–62.

Steinberg, R. 1987. Voluntary donations and public expenditures in a federalist system. *American Economic Review* 77:24–36.

Stigler, G., and G. Becker. 1977. De gustibus non est disputandum. *American Economic Review* 67:76–90.

Strotz, R. H. 1955/56. Myopia and inconsistency in dynamic utility maximization. *Review of Economic Studies* 23:165–80.

Sugden, R. 2004. The opportunity criterion: consumer sovereignty without the assumption of coherent preferences. *American Economic Review* 94:1014–33.

Summers, L. H. 1986. Summers replies to Galper and Byce on IRAs. *Tax Notes* 31:1014–16.

Sunstein, C., and Thaler, R. 2003. Libertarian paternalism. *American Economic Review* 93:175–79.

Thaler, R., and S. Benartzi. 2004. Save More Tomorrow^{TM}: using behavioral economics to increase employee saving. *Journal of Political Economy* 112(S1):164–187.

Thaler, R., and H. M. Shefrin. 1981. An economic theory of self-control. *Journal of Political Economy* 89:392–406.

Tigerstedt, C., and C. Sutton. 2000. Exclusion and inclusion: Saturday closings and self-service stores. In *Broken Spirits: Power and Ideas in Nordic Alcohol Control* (ed. P. Sulkunen, C. Sutton, C. Tigerstedt, and K. Warpenius), pp. 185–201. Helsinki: Nordic Council for Alcohol and Drug Research.

Trosclair, A., C. Huston, L. Pederson, and I. Dillon. 2002. Cigarette smoking among adults: United States, 2000. *Morbidity and Mortality Weekly Report* 51:642–45.

Tversky, A., and D. Kahneman. 1986. Rational choice and the framing of decisions. *Journal of Business* 59:5251–78.

United States Census Bureau. 2001. *Statistical Abstract of the United States*. Washington, DC: U.S. Government Printing Office.

United States Department of Health and Human Services. 1994. Preventing tobacco use among young people: a report of the Surgeon General. Atlanta, GA: National Center for Chronic Disease Prevention and Health Promotion, Office of Smoking and Health.

Venti, S. F., and D. A. Wise. 1992. *Government Policy and Personal Retirement Saving*. Tax Policy and the Economy, Volume 6, pp. 1–41. MIT Press.

Walstad, W. B., and M. Larsen. 1992. A national survey of American economic literacy. National Council on Economics Education.

Walstad, W. B., and J. C. Soper. 1988. A report card on the economic literacy of U.S. high school students. *American Economic Review* 78:251–56.

Warshawsky, M. 1987. Sensitivity to market incentives: the case of policy loans. *Review of Economics and Statistics* 69:286–95.

Warr, P. 1982. Pareto optimal redistribution and private charity. *Journal of Public Economics* 19:131–38.

Wertenbroch, K. 1998. Consumption and self-control for rationing purchase quantities of virtue and vice. *Marketing Science* 17:317–37.

Wickelgren, I. 1997. Getting the brain's attention. *Science* 278:35–37.

Winston, G. C. 1980. Addiction and backsliding: a theory of compulsive consumption. *Journal of Economic Behavior and Organization* 1:295–324.

Wise, R. 1989. The brain and reward. In *The Neuropharmacological Basis of Reward* (ed. J. M. Liebman and S. J. Cooper), pp. 377–424. Oxford University Press.

Yerak, B. 2001. Program helps gamblers quit. *Detroit News*, December 2, 2001.

CHAPTER TWO

COMMENT BY NICHOLAS STERN

The issue raised in the title, "Behavioral Public Economics: Welfare and Policy Analysis with Nonstandard Decision-Makers," is a special case of a more general question. This more general question concerns how we should do public economics when the actions an individual or household may take do not conform with preferences which may be relevant for policy or welfare analysis, if indeed there are any preferences relevant for policy analysis. This more general question arises very frequently in practical public policy. It occurs in particularly strong forms in many areas of development economics, a subject which, in combination with public economics, has occupied me for much of my professional life. In both developed and developing economies, public policy faces the challenge that preferences are endogenous, in that they depend on the experience of individuals or households, and that the preferences themselves may be influenced, or should be influenced, by public action.

In standard welfare economics, which underpins much of our theory of public policy, and indeed has been very fertile in shaping the way economists think about policy, individuals act consistently with their preferences. Further, those preferences provide the relevant basis for assessing changes in individual well-being for the purposes of constructing social preferences in a multi-individual community. It is clear that one can break this chain from action to social preferences at two points. The first break could be between individual action and individual preferences and the second could be between individual preferences and social welfare. The authors have focused on just one aspect here: individuals have "true" preferences but they make mistakes, so that their actions do not reflect those preferences accurately. The challenge is then to find ways of discovering their preferences in order to suggest policies which might improve their welfare. As with much research, focusing on one particular aspect of a problem is often very valuable in order to fix ideas and get clear results. I would encourage the authors to try to go further in the task they have defined for themselves. They have indeed focused on an important issue and have gone down a route where specific useful results should be available.

However, I think it is also of great value to look at the more general set of issues. First, if we do this we realize just how general and pervasive the problems are, and that the economics profession has largely ignored them. Second, we may see ways forward that do not jump out so strongly when we look at a particular version of the problem. I should emphasize, as the authors indicate, that whilst this may take us into areas including philosophy, psychology, and biology, which may be unfamiliar to many economists, I think that there are many aspects of the economist's training, tool-kit and approach which should imply that they have a great deal to contribute to clear thinking on the subject of how to analyze policy in the context of endogenous, confused, or mistaken preferences.

The authors emphasize a number of areas where such preferences look to be relevant, including drugs, obesity, savings, and sexual behavior. It should be clear that these are of great importance to policy, economic and otherwise, and not merely analytically irritating issues that occur on the margins of our subject. There are many more examples from development (but not only development) relating to attitudes to different ways of living, including discrimination issues involving education, gender, color, caste, ethnicity, or language. And we should recognize the endogeneity of preferences arising from the experiences associated with major life changes such as migration, education or employment.

Let me illustrate with just one observation involving industrialization and urbanization. The economic historian Richard Tawney made the issue of endogenous preferences central in his remarkable book *Land and Labor in China*, written after visiting China in 1930:

> The movement to industrialization is a growing force. Where it directly affects, for better or worse, the livelihood of one, it indirectly modified the habits of ten. Its effect on the mind... is ultimately more important than its visible embodiment in mills and mines.

> (Tawney 1966, p. 17)

Such examples suggest the notion that "true" preferences, and mistakes relative to them, may not be an appropriate way of embodying disquiet as to whether individual choices reveal preferences relevant for social choices. Different ways of looking at the associated policy questions include:

(i) preferences are socially unacceptable; or

(ii) individuals deliberately embark on a course to change preferences not knowing what will happen (e.g., education); or

(iii) individuals seek help in transforming themselves; or

(iv) we know that preferences will be influenced by processes of development and ask how we should take these into account.

Indeed much of the analysis of development is, or should be, about processes of change of this kind.

To illustrate some of the relevant issues let me raise the example of a Pakistani (say) father who is unwilling to send his daughter to school. On what grounds should we engage with him? How should we (and indeed, should we) try to persuade him otherwise? It may be that we think he has an information problem in that he does not know how high the return will be for her, her children and the family. Or it may be that he does not take into account externalities for others in society. Both information and externalities are a standard part of the theory of economic policy and probably both are relevant to our (where "we" is society in general or the policy makers) wish to engage with him on this subject. But, I would suggest, our discussion would and should go beyond this. We would want to try to influence his ideas on the meaning of a good life for his children. We would actively try to change his preferences. And many of us would suggest further that this kind of interchange and persuasion is part of the democratic process of good governance.

If we do want to influence his preferences, then we should ask ourselves what moral authority do we have? There is no easy answer to this, but let us recognize that we do this all the time concerning, for example, education, exercise, savings, or discrimination. Part of the answer is paternalism and a judgement on the merits or demerits of his preferences. Part lies in a notion of rights for his daughter. Part also lies in an understanding of how preferences are and should be formed, i.e., in the process of formation of preferences and its link with democracy. There John Stuart Mill (see Mill 1861) saw the issue clearly—democracy is about developing ideas and changing attitudes through involvement and discussion ("government by discussion"). Jon Elster more recently argued (Elster 1984) that democracy and policy making are less about Arrow-type theories of aggregating preferences and more about forming and changing preferences through interaction. Thus, policy making, in this view, is about process rather than algorithm.

But there is a very different route to understanding welfare and policy that does not go via preferences. If, as Amartya Sen has argued (Sen 1992), we embrace the idea of capabilities (I would also suggest the language of empowerment here), then we avoid the puzzles and problems of mistaken and/or endogenous preferences. This capability or empowerment route will give us only partial orderings, since it may not be clear whether capabilities or empowerment have been augmented. But the same ambiguities will also be true of the preference-based approach in this context.

I therefore encourage Rangel and Bernheim to pursue their line relentlessly. It is surely one of the key approaches and one that has a chance of being worked through successfully. And we do need specific examples that we can analyze directly and formally to advance or fix ideas on this difficult but very important set of issues. But let us also look more widely to endogenous preferences and how we should act, as a matter of policy, to influence preferences in the pursuit of a better economy and society.

REFERENCES

Elster, J. 1984. *Ulysses and Sirens: Studies in Rationality and Irrationality*, revised edn. Cambridge University Press.
Mill, J. S. 1861. Considerations of representative government. In *John Stuart Mill. Utilitarianism: On Liberty and Considerations on Representative Government* (ed. H. B. Acton, 1972). London: J. M. Dent & Sons.

Sen, A. 1992. Minimal liberty. *Economica* 59:139–59.

Tawney, R. H. 1966. *Land and Labor in China* (reprint of 1932 edn). Boston, MA: Beacon Press.

COMMENT BY EMMANUEL SAEZ

This chapter tackles the general issue of welfare measurement and normative policy analysis in models with nonstandard decision makers. In recent years, there has been much interest in developing such nonstandard models, which incorporate insights from psychology. Most of those "behavioral economics" studies have focused on the positive analysis: uncovering empirical situations where behavior departs significantly from the classical rational model and then developing models which can account for such behavior.

Such nonstandard models potentially offer a fertile ground for normative analysis, as there is no presumption that the free-market equilibrium will be efficient in those situations. However, normative analysis in behavioral models has lagged behind positive analysis. The main reason for such a lag is that normative analysis requires measurement of welfare and most nonstandard models raise difficult issues concerning welfare evaluation.

The analysis of Bernheim and Rangel is, to my knowledge, the first comprehensive and systematic effort to review the difficulties that arise in measuring welfare in nonstandard models. The paper first proposes a general overview of the problems of measuring welfare and then turns to the detailed examination of three topics, saving, addiction, and public goods, which have attracted substantial attention of behavioral economists. Each of those topic-specific sections can almost be read independently and constitute interesting discussions of the welfare measurement and optimal public policy issues that have arisen in those contexts. Thus, the structure of the paper suggests it is difficult to make progress in a general model and that the most fruitful route is probably to advance one model at a time.

In this discussion, I would like to make simple remarks on how some of the most basic findings in empirical behavioral economics should force applied public finance economists to rethink their interpretation of findings in empirical public economics, and how such newly interpreted empirical findings should be used to carry out more meaningful normative analysis.

The empirical literature in behavioral economics has uncovered many instances in which elements that should be largely irrelevant for decision-making in the standard model actually have large effects on economic behavior. The most famous example is probably the large effects of default provisions on 401(k) pension contribution decisions (Madrian and Shea 2001). Those elements can be influenced by government policy. For example, in the case of 401(k) pension plans, it is conceivable to issue regulations requesting employers to enroll all employees by default with a reasonable default contribution level and investment allocation (see Orszag (2005) for a recent testimony to the U.S. Congress proposing reforms along those lines). If the goal of the policy maker is to increase savings without forcing anybody to save, it seems clear that using default rules will be less costly than using traditional economic incentives such as exempting the returns on savings from taxation. Behavioral economics has therefore successfully expanded the set of tools that policy makers can contemplate using to influence economic decisions.

More subtle and more disturbing for traditional public economics, nonstandard behavioral effects probably not only affect the level of an economic decision but also the sensitivity of an economic decision with respect to traditional price incentives. For example, Duflo et al. (2005) show that matching incentives for IRA contributions at the time of tax preparation in the context of a field experiment have a much larger effect on take-up rates and contributions than the larger incentive effects created by the "savers' credit" federal income tax program. The larger response for the experimental match seems to be due to its saliency and simplicity relative to the complexity of the federal program. In the context of charitable contributions, in a laboratory experiment, Eckel and Grossman (2003) have shown that a matching subsidy generates significantly more charitable giving than an economically equivalent rebate subsidy: a 100% match on voluntary contributions generates much higher total contributions (inclusive of the match) than an equivalent 50% rebate on voluntary contributions. It is conceivable that such framing effects can also partly explain the substantial heterogeneity that has been found across studies on labor supply elasticities with respect to taxes and transfers. For example, the Earned Income Tax Credit generates significant labor supply participation effects because recipients understand that positive earnings are necessary to benefit from the credit. The Earned Income Tax Credit does not seem to generate negative effects on hours of work conditional on working because individuals might not understand how the phasing out of the credit reduces net wage rates beyond some earnings level.

The results from the standard normative models on optimal charitable giving subsidies or optimal taxation and redistribution depend crucially on such behavioral response parameters: for example, less redistribution is desirable if labor supply is very sensitive to tax rates. If such parameters are actually sensitive to framing effects, then two new areas of research open up.

First, on the positive side, we need to understand how framing effects affect those behavioral parameters. As described above, empirical studies have started to uncover the existence of framing effects. The task of understanding and classifying framing effects empirically into the subtle and overlapping categories of information, attention, suggestion, persuasion, or temptation is enormous. Systematic laboratory or field experiments seem the most promising way to make progress on those tasks.

Second, on the normative side, optimal framing needs to become an integral part of the analysis. Of course, normative analysis raises additional difficult issues. As Bernheim and Rangel point out in great detail, defining a concept of welfare is far from obvious and can easily fall into unsolvable paradoxes, as the simple example they present in their conclusion shows.

Let me propose a shortcut around these issues. This shortcut is definitely not satisfactory conceptually, but might be acceptable in practice in many situations. There are a number of "normative" exercises, which could be of interest to policy makers and which do not need to be tied to properly defined welfare concepts. For example, in the case of savings for retirement, a government could be interested in designing policies to promote retirement savings and evaluate success in terms of the distribution of replacement rates (average net income during retirement over average net income while working). In the case of charitable contributions, the government's goal might be to design programs or subsidies maximizing net charitable contributions, given that an exogenous budget has been allocated for such a purpose. Conceptually, this is clearly a significant step back relative to the unified welfare and positive theory of the standard model. For practical purposes, policy debates tend to take place along such concrete normative criteria rather than along the choice of a social welfare function aggregating preferences across individuals with different tastes and abilities. Therefore, it is likely that policy makers will be more easily convinced about the virtues of behavioral economics lessons than traditional economists.

Thus, I would like to conclude this discussion on a relatively optimistic note. In the medium term, behavioral economics should be seen as a great opportunity to try to reconcile disparate (and hence not very informative) results that have been obtained in many fields in the standard empirical public finance literature. Such findings could be used relatively easily for policy recommendations by focusing on concrete and nonwelfarist objectives. In the long run, as Bernheim and Rangel argue, it is possible that economists will be able to define concepts of welfare in nonstandard situations that will become broadly acceptable in the profession and allow us to use again a new but unified theory of decision-making and welfare measurement.

REFERENCES

Duflo, E., W. Gale, J. Liebman, P. Orszag, and E. Saez. 2005. Saving incentives for low- and middle-income families: evidence from a field experiment with H&R block. NBER Working Paper 11680.

Eckel, C., and P. J. Grossman. 2003. Rebate versus matching: does how we subsidize charitable contributions matter? *Journal of Public Economics* 87:681–701.

Madrian, B., and D. Shea. 2001. The power of suggestion: inertia in 401(k) participation and savings behavior. *Quarterly Journal of Economics* 116:1149–87.

Orszag, P. R. 2005. Improving retirement security. Testimony to the Committee on Ways and Means, U.S. House of Representatives, May 19, 2005.

Psychology and Development Economics

By Sendhil Mullainathan

3.1 INTRODUCTION

Economists often study scarcity, yet their conception of decision-making assumes an abundance of psychological resources. In the standard economic model, people are unbounded in their ability to think through problems. Regardless of complexity, they can costlessly figure out the optimal choice. They are also unbounded in their self-control, and able to costlessly implement and follow through on whatever plans they set out for themselves. Whether they want to save a certain amount of money each year or finish a paper on time, they face no internal barriers in accomplishing these goals. Furthermore, they are unbounded in their attention. They think through every single problem that comes at them and make a deliberative decision about each one. In this and many other ways, the economic model of human behavior ignores the actual bounds on choices (Mullainathan and Thaler 2001). Every decision is thoroughly contemplated, perfectly calculated, and easily executed.

In contrast to the traditional model, a growing body of research interprets economic phenomena with a more modest view of human behavior. In this alternative conception, individuals are bounded in all of the above-mentioned dimensions (and more). Practically, this conception begins with the rich understanding of human behavior that experimental psychologists have developed through numerous laboratory (and some field) experiments. This view, ironically enough, emphasizes the richness of behavior that arises from scarcities and focuses on the bounds on cognitive ability, self-control, attention, and self-interest. Theoretical models are now being constructed that help to incorporate these ideas into economic applications. Perhaps even more compelling is the recent empirical work that suggests the importance of these psychological insights for real behavior in contexts that economists care about. In a variety of areas, from asset pricing to savings behavior to legal decision-making, well-crafted empirical studies are challenging the traditional view of decision-making.

What does this research have to say about economic development? I begin by highlighting some areas where the existing research can be applied directly to development. The bulk of work on savings can be translated into understanding savings institutions and behavior in developing countries. Additionally, the insights about self-control have some direct links to understanding education, and the behavioral approach also appears to add some insight into the large body of research on the diffusion of innovation. The question of how (and when) to evaluate the impact of development policies can also be better understood. Yet, since psychology is only beginning to make inroads into applied areas of economics, beyond these areas few papers explicitly deal with psychology and development. I therefore speculate about additional specific areas where psychology could be useful in the future: poverty traps, conflict, social preferences, corruption, and research on the psychology of the poor.

An important caveat is in order. The attempt to incorporate psychology into development has a dubious history. In some cases, researchers have attempted to label the poor as especially "irrational" (or "myopic") to explain their state. The research I describe here starts from a completely different presumption, that the poor have the same biases as everyone else.[1] It is neither an attempt to blame the poor for their poverty nor an argument that the poor have specific irrationalities. Instead my goal is to understand how problems in development might be driven by general psychological principles that operate for both poor and rich alike. When I speak of self-control, for example, I am speaking of those self-control problems that exist in equal measure around the world (e.g., the difficulty of resisting a tempting snack). These problems may matter more for the poor because of the context in which they live but their core is universal (Bertrand et al. 2004).

3.2 IMMEDIATE BARRIERS TO EDUCATION

The rational-choice model of schooling is straightforward (Becker 1993). Individuals trade off the costs and benefits of schooling to decide how much schooling to get. Benefits come in a variety of forms such as better jobs or better marriage prospects. Costs could be direct financial costs (e.g., fees) as well as any opportunity costs (e.g., foregone labor). In the case of children, of course, parents make the actual choices. They do so to maximize some combination of their own and their children's long-run welfare, with their exact weight depending on their altruism.

This view of education ignores the richness of the hardships faced by parents trying to educate their children in a developing country. Consider an Indian village where a poor father, Suresh, is eager to send his son Laloo to school for the next school year. Suresh recognizes the value of his son's education in allowing Laloo to get a government job, marry better, or simply live more comfortably in a rapidly

---

[1]This perspective has been put forward in Bertrand et al. (2004).

changing world. To ensure that he has money for school fees, textbooks or perhaps a school uniform, Suresh begins to save early. Quickly he encounters some competing demands on the money. Suresh's mother falls ill and needs money to buy some anesthetics to ease her pain. Though his mother insists that her grandson's education is more important, he is torn. Enormous willpower is required to let his mother suffer while Suresh saves money that he knows could ease her pain. Knowing that he is doing what is best in the long run is small consolation in the moment. Suresh overcomes this hurdle and enrolls his son. After some weeks, Laloo starts to show disinterest. As with most children in the world, sitting in a classroom (and not an appealing one at that) is not very engaging, especially since some of his friends are outside playing. In the evenings, exhausted from tiring physical work and overwhelmed by the pressures of everyday life, how will he handle this extra stress? Will Suresh have the mental energy to convince his son of the value of education? Will he have the energy to follow up with the teacher or other students to see whether Laloo has actually been attending school? This fictional example illustrates merely one important tension in third world educational attainment. Even the best of intentions may be very hard to implement in practice, especially in the high-stress environments that the poor inhabit.

These problems are intimately related to how people view future decisions in the present: a topic that psychologists and behavioral economists have studied extensively through experiments. Several experiments have resulted in theoretical principles used to understand an individual's decision-making process, and these principles can provide a framework with which we can understand the difficulties the fictional Suresh faced in his attempts to implement his decision on his son's schooling.

Behavioral economists have recently begun to better understand the devices people may use to make decisions across time by using hyperbolic discounting theory. Generally, people value preferences differently across time and tend to exhibit short-run impatience and long-run patience. Formally, the theory is modeled by discount rates that vary with horizon. People have very a high discount rate for short horizons (decisions about now versus the future) but a very low one for distant horizons. Hyperbolic discounting is present in many facets of life, as evidenced by the following examples.

Consider the following offer: would you rather receive $15 today or $16 in a month's time? More generally, how much money would I need to give you after one month to make you indifferent to receiving $15 today? What about in one year? What about in ten years? Thaler (1981) presented these questions to subjects and found median answers of $20, $50, and $100. While at first blush these answers may seem reasonable, they actually imply huge discount rates that also vary hugely across time: 345% over one month, 120% over a one-year horizon, and 19% over a ten-year horizon.[2] Subjects greatly prefer the present to the future.

These choices also imply that the extent of patience *changes* with the horizon. This is made most clear in the following choice problem:

(i) Would you prefer $100 today or $110 tomorrow?

(ii) Would you prefer $100 thirty days from now or $110 thirty-one days from now?

Many subjects give different answers to these two questions. In the first scenario, they often prefer the immediate reward ($100 today), but in the latter, they often prefer the delayed reward ($110 in thirty-one days).

Such preferences are inconsistent with the standard model. To see this, suppose people have a utility function u and discount the future at a daily rate δ. Then in scenario (i), the value of $100 today is $u(100)$ and the value of $110 tomorrow is $\delta u(110)$. On the other hand, in problem (ii), the value of the two options is $\delta^{30} u(100)$ and $\delta^{31} u(110)$. In simplified form, this is exactly the same trade-off. In other words, with the standard constant discount rate, individuals should choose the same thing in both situations. The inconsistency between the two choices is resolved only if the discount rate is allowed to vary with time.

Differences in preferences for the immediate versus the future can also be seen in the field. Read et al. (1999) ask subjects to pick three rental movies. The subjects either pick one by one for immediate consumption, or they pick all at once for the future. When picking sequentially for immediate consumption, they tend to pick "low-brow" movies. When picking simultaneously for future consumption, they tend to pick "high-brow" movies. Once again, when planning for the future, individuals are more willing to make choices that have long-run benefits (presumably "high-brow" movies) than when choosing in the present.

The difference in choices at different horizons poses a problem for the individual. Consider a concrete example. Suppose I face the chore of house cleaning. This weekend I am very busy and decide to delay it, but my preference for next weekend is that I should start my cleaning. What happens next week though? What was a decision about the distant future (where I exhibited patience) becomes a decision about the present (where I exhibit impatience). My choice may now change. Once again, the option of putting it off seems appealing—as appealing as it did last week when I made the same decision. In other words, there is a conflict between what I plan to do in the future and what I would actually do when the future becomes the present.

---

[2] One reason subjects may show such preferences is that they may doubt that they will actually get the money in the future, leading them to value it at a lower rate. While this may be an effect, the literature on discounting finds similar results even when these issues of trust are dealt with (Frederick et al. 2002).

This conflict is one of the many difficulties parents face in getting their children educated. Returning to our fictional story, Suresh wanted his son Laloo educated and decided today that his future self would put in the effort and money to send Laloo to school. Yet, in the moment, many immediate pressures impinge on his time, money, and energy, making it hard for Suresh to implement his original plan. This view presumes that parents would like to see their children educated but simply cannot find a credible way to stick to that plan.

This behavioral approach improves our understanding of many components of education. It provides an explanation of the gap between parents' stated goals and actual outcomes. The Public Report on Basic Education (PROBE) in India (De and Drèze 1999) finds that many parents are actually quite interested in education. Even in the poorest Indian states with the worst education systems, they find that over 85% of the parents agree that it is important for children to be educated. In the same survey, 57% of parents feel that their sons should study "as far as possible." Another 39% feel that they should get at least a grade-10 or grade-12 education. Clearly, parents in these regions value education. Yet this contrasts with very low educational attainment in these states. This gap is reminiscent of the gap between desired and actual retirement savings in the United States. In one survey, 76% of Americans believed that they should be saving more for retirement (Farkas and Johnson 1997). Though they want to save, many never succeed. As noted earlier, immediate pressures are even more powerful in the education context. Putting aside money to pay for schooling requires making costly immediate sacrifices. Fighting with children who are reluctant to go to school can be especially draining when there are so many other pressures. Walking a young child every day to a distant school requires a constant input of effort in the face of so many pressing tasks. Put another way, if a middle-class American, supported by so many institutions, cannot save as much as they want, how can we expect a Rajasthani parent to consistently and stoically make all the costly immediate sacrifices to implement their goal of educating their children?

This behavioral framework also helps to explain, in part, an interesting phenomenon in many developing countries: sporadic attendance. In contrast to a simple human-capital model, education does not appear to follow a fixed stopping rule in which students go to school consistently until a particular grade. Instead, students go to school for some stretch of time, drop out for some stretch and then begin again. This sporadic attendance, though potentially far from optimal, is a consequence of the dynamically inconsistent valuation of preferences described earlier. When faced with particularly hard-to-resist immediate pressures, individuals will succumb to them. When these pressures ease, it once again becomes easier to implement the original plan of sending their child to school. More specifically, parents who have "slipped off the wagon" may find certain salient moments to refocus their plans for their child's education. One empirical prediction here is that, at the beginning of the school year, attendance should perhaps be higher than at any other time, as many parents are newly inspired and decide to give it another try. As they succumb to immediate pressures, attendance would then decline throughout the year.[3]

One practical application of the behavioral perspective is that programs that make schooling more attractive to students may provide a low-cost way to make it easier for parents to send children to school. For example, a school meals program may make school attendance attractive to children and ease the pressure on parents to monitor their children's attendance (see Vermeesch (2003) for a discussion of such programs). One could even be creative in coming up with these incentive programs. Offering school sports, candy, or other cheap inputs to children may have large effects on attendance. In fact, under this model, such programs could have extremely large benefit–cost ratios: much larger than could be justified by the monetary subsidy alone.

This perspective on schooling matches the complexity of life in developing countries. Of course, immediate pressures are not the only problem. Numerous other factors—from liquidity constraints to teacher attendance—also play a role, but these areas have already been comprehensively studied. The difficulty of self-control, however, has not, and deserves more scrutiny.

3.3 Demand for Commitment, Default Settings, and Savings

The savings dilemma that, in part, drives the shortcomings in educational attainment is a more general issue in developing countries and links directly to behavioral issues that drive similar savings problems in developed nations. The difficulty of sticking with a course of action in the presence of immediate pressures has implications for how individuals save. In the standard economic model of savings, there is no room for such pressures. Instead, people calculate how much money is worth to them in the future, taking into account any difficulties they may have in borrowing and any shocks they may suffer. Based on these calculations, they make a contingency plan of how much to spend in each possible state. They then, as discussed before, implement this plan with no difficulty. Yet, for the poor in many developing countries, implementing such plans is much more easily said than done. They face a variety of temptations that might derail their consumption goals.

---

[3]This last point provides one potential way to distinguish this explanation from a rational model with very large liquidity shocks. Moreover, such a rational model faces difficulties if parents rationally forecast liquidity shocks and if there are scale economies to attending for long continuous periods. In this scenario, parents would build a "buffer stock" early on to insure against such shocks and then send the child to school for one long (and presumably more productive) stretch.

Hyperbolic discounting is again a useful model with which we can understand individuals' actual saving behavior. As alluded to earlier, a key question in this model is whether people are sophisticated or naive in how they deal with their temporal inconsistency. Sophisticated people would recognize the inconsistency and (recursively) form dynamically consistent plans. In other words, they would only make plans which they would follow through. Naive people, on the other hand, would not recognize the intertemporal problem and would make plans today which assume that they will stick with them, only to abandon them when the time comes. There are reasons to believe both views. On the one hand, individuals appear to consciously demand commitment devices, to help them commit to a particular path. On the other, they appear to have unrealistic plans. Perhaps the best fit of the evidence is that individuals partly recognize their time inconsistency.

The practically important component of this view is that the commitment implicit in institutions is crucial to understanding behavior.[4] Institutions can help solve self-control problems by committing people to a particular path of behavior. Just as Ulysses ties himself to his ship's mast to listen to the song of the Sirens but not be lured out to sea by them, people rely on similar—albeit not so dramatic— commitment devices in everyday life. Many refer to their gym membership as a commitment device ("paying that much money upfront every month really gets me to go to the gym"). Another example is Christmas clubs. While they are less common nowadays, they used to be a very powerful commitment tool for saving to buy Christmas gifts.

Suggestive evidence on the power of commitment devices is given in Gruber and Mullainathan (2002), which studies smoking behavior. Rational-choice models of smoking treat it roughly like any other good. Smokers make rational choices about their smoking, understanding the physiology of addiction that nicotine entails. Behavioral models, on the other hand, recognize a self-control problem in the decision to start smoking and in the decision (or rather, attempts) to quit. There is some survey evidence suggestive of the behavioral model. Smokers often report that they would like to quit smoking but are unable to do so. This resembles the temporal pattern above. Looking into the future, smokers would choose to not smoke. But when the future arrives, they end up being unable to resist the lure of a cigarette today (perhaps promising that tomorrow they will quit). To differentiate these theories, we examined the impact of cigarette taxes. Under the rational model, smokers are made worse off with these taxes. This is a standard dead-weight loss argument. Smokers who would like to smoke cannot now do so because of the higher price. In behavioral

---

[4]Commitment devices might also play a role because of *inter*-personal rather than *intra*-personal problems. People may choose commitment as a way to avoid pressure from other family members or outsiders. The distinction between these two is quite important and further work is needed to distinguish between them.

models with hyperbolic discounters, however, taxes could make smokers better off. The very same force (high prices driving smokers to quit) that is bad in the rational model is good in this model. Smokers who wanted to quit, but were unable to due to the inability to commit, are now better off. In the parlance of time-inconsistency models, the taxes serve as a commitment device.

To determine the effect of the cigarette taxes on smokers' welfare, we use self-reported happiness data. While such data are far from perfect, they can be useful in contexts such as this one.[5] Using a panel of individuals in the United States and taking advantage of state variation in cigarette tax increases, we find that happiness of predicted smokers increases when cigarette taxes increase. Relative to the equivalent people in states with no rise in cigarette taxes (and relative to those who tend not to smoke in their own state), these predicted smokers show actual rises in self-reported well-being. In other words, contrary to the rational model and supportive of the behavioral model, cigarette taxes actually make those prone to smoke *better off*. This kind of effect is exactly the one I alluded to in Section 3.1: institutions (cigarette taxes in this case) have the potential to help solve problems within people as well as between people.

There is also evidence on people actively choosing commitment devices. Wertenbroch (1998) argues that people forego quantity discounts on goods they would be tempted to consume (e.g., cookies) in order to avoid temptation. This is a quantification of the often-repeated advice to dieters: don't have big bags of cookies at home. If you must buy tempting foods, buy small portions of it. Trope and Fischbach (2000) show how people strategically use penalties to spur unwanted actions. They examine people scheduled to undertake small, unpleasant medical procedures for which there is a potential time-inconsistency problem. As the date of the procedure nears, people have a strong desire to skip the procedure. Trope and Fishbach show that people are aware of this problem and value a commitment device. They voluntarily agree to pay penalties for not undertaking the procedure, thus binding themselves to follow through with it In fact, they smartly pick these penalties, by picking higher ones for more aversive procedures. Ariely and Wertenbroch (2002) provide even more direct evidence. They examine whether people use deadlines as a self-control device and whether such deadlines actually work. Students in a class at MIT chose their own due dates for three different papers required in the course. The deadlines were binding so, in the absence of self-control problems, the students should clearly choose the latest due date possible for all the papers. They were told there were neither benefits for early due dates nor penalties for later ones, so they could only gain from the optional choice of being able to turn the papers in as late

---

[5] In this context, the variable of interest is relatively clean and thereby the mismeasurement is simply absorbed in the residual. See Bertrand and Mullainathan (2001) for a discussion of these issues.

as possible. In contrast, students chose evenly spaced due dates for the three papers, presumably to give them incentives to get the papers done in a timely manner. Moreover, deadlines appeared to work. In a related study, it is shown that people given evenly spaced deadlines do better than those given a single deadline for all papers.

Savings in developing countries can also be better understood through the behavioral perspective. It provides an alternative view on institutions such as Rotating Savings and Credit Associations (ROSCAs) (Gugerty 2003). In a ROSCA, a group of people meet together at regular intervals. At each meeting, members contribute a prespecified amount. The sum of those funds (the "pot" so to speak) is then given to one of the individuals. Eventually, each person in the ROSCA will get their turn and thus get back their contributions. ROSCAs are immensely popular, but what is their attraction? They often pay no interest. In fact, given the potential for default (those who received the pot early may stop paying in), they may effectively pay a negative interest rate. One reason for their popularity may be that they serve as a commitment device in several ways. By making saving a public act, they allow social pressure from other ROSCA members to commit them to their desired savings level (Ardener and Burman 1995). As some ROSCA participants say, "you can't save alone" (Gugerty 2003). Each ROSCA member has incentives to make sure other members continue to contribute. Given self-control limitations, they also allow individuals to save up to larger amounts than they could normally achieve. Imagine someone who wished to make a durables purchase (or pay school fees) of 1000 rupees. By saving alone and putting aside money each month, they face a growing temptation. When they reach 400 rupees, might not some other purchase or immediate demand appear more attractive? The ROSCA does not allow this temptation to interfere. Individuals get either nothing or the full 1000 as a lump sum. This all-or-nothing property might make it easier to save enough to make large purchases.

It also helps to provide a more nuanced view of an individual's demand for liquidity. In the standard logic, the poor unconditionally value liquidity. After all, liquidity allows people to free up cash in order to attend to immediate needs that arise. If a child gets sick, money is needed to pay for medicine. This is more pertinent for the poor. Shocks that are small for the well-off can be considerable for the poor and force them to dip into real savings. The poor, in these models, however, face a tradeoff. They value liquidity for the reasons cited above, but liquidity for them is also a curse, since it makes access to savings too easy. Consequently, durable goods and illiquid savings vehicles may actually be preferred to liquid savings vehicles. Liquid holdings like cash are far too tempting and spent too readily. On the other hand, by holding their wealth in items such as jewelry, livestock, and grain, individuals may effectively commit themselves to savings and resist immediate consumption pressures. In these models, therefore, there is an optimal amount of liquidity. Even when liquidity is provided at zero cost, they will choose some mix of illiquid and liquid assets.

Another implication of the behavioral perspective is that revealed-preference arguments do not necessarily hold; hence, measuring policy success can be difficult. Observing that people borrow at a given rate (and pay it back) does not necessarily mean that the loan helps them; we must also examine the use of the loan. In some cases, it clearly benefits borrowers by helping them to deal with a liquidity shock. In other cases, the borrower may use the loan to satisfy immediate temptations and end up saddled with debts. This distinction is important for understanding microcredit in developing countries. Often, the metric of success for such programs is whether programs are self-sustainable, but this measure is valid only in the standard model, where revealed preference applies. In this model, profitability implies that people prefer getting these loans even at a nonsubsidized rate; revealed preference then implies their social efficiency. Yet, in the presence of time inconsistency, the relationship between the profitability and social efficiency of microcredit potentially is weak. The key question is the extent to which the loans exaggerate short-run impatience and to which they solve long-run liquidity constraints.[6] Ultimately, one needs a deeper understanding of what drives borrowers. One source for this might be data on loan usage. Are loans being spent on long-run investments (as is often touted) or spent on short-run consumption? Of course, some short-run consumption might well be efficient, but this data, combined with an understanding of the institution, would help us to better understand (and improve) the social efficiency of microcredit.

Policy can also provide cheaper and more efficient commitment devices. Saving grain is an effective, but extremely risky, commitment device. Vermin may eat the grain, or the interest rate earned on the grain could be zero or even negative. Moreover, it is important to recognize that, even if people demand such commitment devices, the free market may not do enough to provide them. The highly regulated financial markets in developing countries may prevent adequate innovation of commitment securities. Monopoly power may also lead to inefficient provision of these commitment devices if a monopolistic financial institution can extract more profits by catering to consumption temptations over the desire for commitment devices. In this context, governments, NGOs and donor institutions can play a large role by promoting such commitment devices.

Ashraf et al. (2006) give a stunning illustration of the role of commitment devices in savings. They offer depositors at a bank in the Philippines the opportunity to participate in "SEED" (Saving for Education, Entrepreneurship, and Downpayment) accounts. These accounts are like deposit accounts, except for the fact

---

[6]To make this contrast stark, note that, in the United States, payday loan companies are a very profitable form of microcredit.

that individuals cannot withdraw deposits at will. Instead, they can only withdraw the money at a prespecified date or once a prespecified savings goal has been reached. This account does not pay extra interest and is illiquid. In most economic models, people should turn down this offer in favor of the regular accounts offered by the bank. Yet banks find that there is a large demand for them. More than 30% of those offered the accounts take them up. They also find these accounts help individuals to save. Six months after the initial deposit, those offered the accounts show substantially greater savings rates. Experiments such as these will contribute to a deeper understanding of savings and greatly improve development policy.

3.4 DEFAULTS AND FINANCIAL INSTITUTIONS

Financial institutions do not simply help savings through their commitment value. A very important set of results in behavioral economics suggests that institutions also affect behavior simply through the defaults they produce. Madrian and Shea (2001) conducted a particularly telling study along these lines. They studied a firm that altered the choice context for employee participation in its retirement plan. When employees joined the firm, they were given a form that they must fill out in order to participate in the savings plan. Though the plan was quite lucrative, participation was low. Standard economic models might suggest that the subsidy ought to be raised. The firm instead changed a very simple feature of its program. Prior to the change, new employees received a form that said something to the effect of:

> Check this box if you would like to participate in a 401(k). Indicate how much you'd like to contribute.

After the change, however, new employees received a form that said something to the effect of:

> Check this box if you would *not* like to have 3% of your pay check put into a 401(k).

By standard reasoning, this change should have little effect on contribution rates. How hard is it to check a box? In practice, the study shows a large effect. When the default option is to not contribute, only 38% of those offered contributed. When the default option was contribution, 86% contributed. Moreover, even several years later, those exposed to the contribution default still show much higher contribution rates.

While we cannot be sure from this data what people are thinking, I would speculate that some combination of procrastination and passivity played a role. Surely many looked at this form and thought, "I'll decide this later." But later never came. Perhaps they were distracted by something more interesting than retirement planning. In any case, whatever the default on the form was, they ended up with it. In fact, as other psychology results tell us, as time went on they may well have justified their "decision" to themselves by saying, "3% is what I wanted anyway" or, in the case of the "not to contribute" default, "that 401(k) plan wasn't so attractive". In this way, their passivity made their decision for them. By making the small active choice to choose later, they ended up making a large decision about thousands of dollars.

These insights can also help us to design new institutions. One example is Save More Tomorrow (SMaRT), a program created by Thaler and Benartzi (2004). The basic idea of Save More Tomorrow is to get people to make one active choice but to have them make it in such a way that if they remain passive afterwards they are still saving. Participants (who have chosen to save) decide on a target savings level and agree to start deductions at a small level from their paycheck *next year*. Each year thereafter, as they receive a raise in their income, their deductions increase until they hit their personal target savings level. They can opt out of the program at any time, but the cleverness of the program is that if they do nothing and remain passive, they will continue to save (and even increase their savings rate).

The results have been stunning. In one firm, for example, more than 75% of those offered the plan participated in it rather than simply trying to save on their own. Of these, less than 20% opted out of the program. As a result, savings rates rose sharply. By the third pay increase (as the default increases cumulated), individuals had more than tripled their savings rates. But perhaps the greatest success has been the diffusion of this product. Many major firms and pension fund providers are thinking of adopting it, and the number of participants in the program will likely soon reach the millions. SMaRT is an excellent example of what psychologically smart institutional design might look like in the future. It does not solve a problem between people but instead helps solve a problem within the person: not saving as much as they would like.[7]

One simple but powerful implication of these results is that behavior should not be confused with disposition (Bertrand et al. 2004). An economist observing the savings behavior of a middle-class American and a rural farmer might be tempted to conclude something about different discount rates. In the standard model, the high savings of the middle-class American surely indicate greater patience. This need not be the case. Such an inference could be just as wrong as inferring that those who defaulted into 401(k) are more patient than those who were not defaulted into it. In other words, the behavioral difference between the farmer and the middle-class American may be a consequence of better institutions facilitating more automatic default savings.

---

[7] In this short space, I cannot do justice to all the psychological tools that the Save More Tomorrow plan relies on. The full discussion in the original paper is well worth reading as an example of how to use psychological tools for better designed policy.

Default behavior has potentially large implications for improving savings in the developing world through bank reform. The lessons learned in the United States could easily be transferred to parts of developing countries. Institutions such as direct deposit of paychecks (into a savings account) could be very powerful in spurring savings. This banking innovation could be a very inexpensive and far-reaching device for improving savings rates of the middle-class in developing countries.

On a more basic level, the evidence on default behavior implies that the introduction of basic banking to rural areas could in and of itself have large impacts on behavior. While deposit accounts are not as powerful a default as direct deposit, a basic deposit account, as opposed to cash in hand, has a psychological element of illiquidity. The person then has to make one active decision (putting the money into the account) but then the act of saving the money becomes a passive one. When cash is available in the household, an individual must take action to save it. When money is in the bank account, one must take action to spend it. In this sense, a bank account may serve as a very basic commitment device. By keeping the money at a (slight) distance, spending it may be a lot less tempting.

3.5 STATUS QUO BIAS AND DIFFUSION OF INNOVATIONS

Another broad area of significance to development is the diffusion of innovation. There is a large literature focusing on the slow rate of adoption of new technologies (Rogers 2003). This literature has been especially important in developing countries, where a long-standing puzzle is why innovations, ranging from the Green Revolution to new medical technologies to fertility practices, appear to diffuse slowly.[8]

Several stylized facts emerge from this largely empirical literature. First, innovations generally follow an S-shaped diffusion, starting off slowly, speeding up suddenly (after a "tipping point") and then slowing down to a steady-state level.[9]

Second, adopters can be classified according to the timing of their adoption. The first adopters, called "innovators," are only weakly connected in a social network sense. The second group of adopters, or "early adopters," is comprised of those who are best connected to the rest of the network. They are often opinion leaders, enjoy high status, and are better educated. Once this subclassification adopts, the rest of the group follows. The final adopters, or "laggards," are socially isolated like the "innovators."

---

[8] See Besley and Case (1994), Foster and Rosenzweig (1996), Munshi (2003), and Conley and Udry (2004) for empirical work in development economics on diffusion of agricultural innovations. Useful summaries of work on fertility are given in Retherford and Palmore (1983) and Montgomery and Casterline (1998).

[9] While much has been made of the shape of this diffusion process, it is unclear why this fact is so surprising. Many processes that start at zero and end at some positive diffusion would have this "S-shape."

Third, diffusion takes place along social network lines. The time-series evidence on adoption clearly supports this view. Slightly more direct evidence can be found in qualitative surveys (and in some quantitative, subjective ones) that ask people what drove their adoption decision. In a few cases, very compelling empirical evidence exists. An early family-planning experiment in Taiwan in 1964 showed social networking effects (Palmore and Freedman 1969). In this randomized experiment, a direct family-planning intervention targeted at a specific group of subjects was shown to have some impact in the targeted group's behavior. But, most interestingly, those who were not directly contacted by the program but were socially connected to the treatment group also showed effects.

A theoretical implication of these findings is that there are multiplier effects in policy interventions. If behavior-changing polices target some people, especially opinion leaders, then the interventions may also have an effect on the broader population. Montgomery and Casterline (1998) illustrate the multiplier effect in their study of a Taiwanese family-planning program. Ignoring diffusion (and hence the multiplier effect), the study finds that program efforts accounted for no more than 5–20% of marital fertility decline. However, taking into account social diffusion increased the estimates of the program effect to account for over 30% of the decline. Multiplier effects have also influenced the shape of policy. In many cases, programs have enlisted specific local groups and institutions. Agricultural extension and doorstep delivery of contraception have both been modified with an eye towards utilizing multiplier effects.

While this work has been quite interesting, the greater incorporation of psychology into this social diffusion literature could increase our understanding in several ways. Much of the slowness of diffusion may come from a phenomenon known as status quo bias (see Samuelson and Zeckhauser 1988) demonstrated by the following example. A group of subjects is given the following choice.

You are a serious reader of the financial pages but until recently have had few funds to invest. You then inherit a large sum of money from your great uncle. You are considering different portfolios. You have the following choices.

(i) Invest in moderate-risk company A. In a year's time the stock has a 0.5 probability of increasing 30% in value, a 0.2 probability of being unchanged, and a 0.3 probability of declining 20% in value.

(ii) Invest in high-risk company B. In a year's time the stock has a 0.4 probability of doubling in value, a 0.3 probability of being unchanged, and a 0.3 probability of declining 40% in value.

(iii) Invest in treasury bills. In a year's time, these will yield a nearly certain return of 9%.

(iv) Invest in municipal bonds. In a year's time, they will yield a tax-free return of 6%.

A second set of subjects is given the same choice but with one small difference: they are told that they are inheriting a portfolio from their uncle in which most of the portfolio is currently invested in moderate-risk company A. The choice now is subtly changed. The problem is now how much of the portfolio to *change* to the other options above. Interestingly, they find a large difference between the two treatments: much more of the money is reinvested in A when subjects choose the status quo. This bias towards the status quo appears to run quite deep and is not just due to some superficial explanations (such as information content of the uncle's investments). Samuelson and Zeckhauser (1988) demonstrate this with a very interesting piece of evidence from the field. In the 1980s, Harvard University added several plans to its existing choice of health plans. This provides an interesting test of status quo bias: how many of the old faculty chose the new plans and how many of the newly joined faculty chose the old plan? They find a stark difference. Existing employees "chose" the older plans at two to four times the rate of the new plans. In other words, incumbent employees make the easiest choice of all: to do nothing. This bias towards the status quo creates a natural slowness of adoption. Not only must the innovation overcome beliefs that it is not worthwhile, but it must also overcome the natural inertia intrinsic in behavior.

There is also a large literature in social psychology showing the power of social pressure towards conformity (see Cialdini and Trost (1998) for a review). Sherif (1937) demonstrated the role of social pressure in a classic psychophysics study. Subjects were seated in a totally dark room facing a pinpoint of light some distance from them. After some time during which nothing happens, the light appears to "move" and then disappear. Shortly thereafter, a new point of light appears. It too moves after some time and then disappears. Interestingly, this movement of the light is a purely psychophysical phenomenon known as the autokinetic effect. The light does not actually move; the brain merely makes it appear to move. The subjects were put in this context for repeated trials (many different resets of the light) and asked to estimate how far it had "moved." When performed alone, these estimates were variable, ranging from an inch to several feet. However, an interesting pattern developed when subjects did this task in groups of two or three. Subjects' estimates invariably began to converge on a particular number. A group norm quickly developed. In one variant, a member of the group was a confederate, someone who worked for the experimenter and gave a specific number. He found that the group quickly converged to the confederate's answers. Others have found that norms manipulated in this way persist for quite some time. Even when subjects are brought in up to a year later, they show adherence to that initial norm. In the context of the Sherif

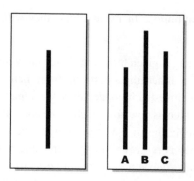

Figure 3.1. Illustration of Asch experiment.

experiment design, Jacobs and Campbell (1961) have shown how norms can be transmitted across "generations" of subjects. Suppose subjects 1 and 2 initially converge to a norm, and then subject 1 is replaced by subject 3 for a sufficient number trials, and then subject 2 is replaced by subject 4. The final group, consisting of totally new subjects 3 and 4, will conform to the norm previously established by subjects 1 and 2.[10]

Asch (1955) expanded these results to an even simpler task. Subjects enter a laboratory and sit with others (confederates) to judge the length of lines such as those in Figure 3.1. The subject hears the judgment of the others and then makes his own. For several trials, this is a very boring task, as it is pretty obvious which line is longer. But then there is a twist. On one of the trials, the first person makes a wrong choice. Then the second person makes the same wrong choice. And so it continues until it is the subject's turn. What Asch found was stunning. Between 50 and 80% of the subjects yielded to the erroneous majority at least once. Of course, as Asch notes, it is not the subjects' perception of the line length that is altered. Many people are simply willing to conform in their behavior.

Similar effects have been found in more naturalistic settings. For example, numerous studies have used high-frequency data to argue for contagion effects in suicides. Media reporting of a suicide often leads to more suicides in areas covered by the newspaper in the days immediately following the reporting (Phillips 1979, 1980). While explanations based on information could be created, a social imitation story is much more plausible for these findings.

These and numerous other experiments highlight the sheer power of social pressure to drive behavior. The traditional economic model acknowledges imitative behavior across networks but explains the phenomenon with an information

---

[10]Camerer and Weber (2003) present an interesting examination of how such norms can arise and evolve over time.

diffusion story. However, some of the social network effects that drive slow diffusion of innovation may also be traced to social pressures and conformity. An important question in this literature is how to empirically disentangle these two effects (information diffusion and social conformity) and to theoretically understand the ways in which they differ.

Even when information diffusion is the explanation of network effects, psychology can be helpful in understanding the impact of information. In particular, most models of diffusion (including the Bayesian model) crucially assume that the most useful information diffuses and has the correct impact on beliefs. This need not be the case. For example, experimental studies have shown that the salience of a piece of data, independent of its information content, affects how it will influence beliefs. Recent experimental work is beginning to examine which data people choose to pass on to their social network. The evidence suggests that emotional factors can have large effects, once again independent of the information content (Heath et al. 2001). These results could be useful in interpreting diffusion, especially in determining which ideas tend to diffuse well (those with salient positive outcomes) and which tend to diffuse poorly (those with nonsalient benefits or with salient costs).

For example, a recent study by Miguel and Kremer (2003) on social learning about deworming pills can be fruitfully interpreted in this light. They selected several schools at random and offered them deworming drugs. Using experimental variation, they estimated that the deworming drugs had extremely large and positive health and education benefits. Miguel and Kremer further exploited this randomization to see the impact on nonselected schools in the following year when they too were offered the opportunity to take the deworming pills. They examined children who had friends in the treatment schools (and hence had friends who had already had experience with the pills). Given the positive benefits of the drugs, social learning models would imply that these children would be much more likely to take the deworming pills. In contrast, Miguel and Kremer find that they are much less likely to take the drug. This "negative" social influence effect can be understood in terms of salience.[11] Deworming pills, while beneficial in the long run, have short-run costs that are particularly salient. Children can have stomach cramps, vomiting and other side effects as the worms work their way out of the system. This asymmetry in salience of the costs and benefits suggests that the costs may well spread more than the benefits (and be more influential on choice). On average, children and parents may hear more stories about the short-term side effects than the long-run benefits.

Slow diffusion may also be a consequence of the self-control bounds, discussed earlier, that hamper efforts to save. People may be interested in adoption but still

---

[11] Miguel and Kremer themselves prefer a standard economic interpretation in which expectations of the deworming pills were even higher than their realized benefits.

have delays in getting the required savings or undertaking the other actions required to adopt. This is made most transparent in recent work by Duflo et al. (2004). They examine the decision by Kenyan farmers to adopt fertilizer. The fertilizer clearly shows large positive productivity benefits, but Duflo et al. find that, even when farmers can see its benefits, they do not necessarily adopt it. Even in cases where they adopt it, they often revert to old practices after a few years. Using a set of innovative financial interventions, Duflo et al. argue that the psychology of financial management plays a role. It appears that although the farmers would like to adopt the fertilizer they are unable to save up enough money to do so. Interventions that help them to overcome this savings problem appear to greatly increase adoption.

As a whole, the literature on diffusion of innovations appears to be going through a period of change. Insights from psychology are helping to uncover new phenomena as well as to cast new light on old ones.

3.6 Self-Serving Bias and Evaluation

Evaluation is one of the important issues facing development practice. When should a particular development program be evaluated? How should it be evaluated? Psychology may help us to gain a better understanding of the social process by which these questions are answered. An often-repeated finding in psychology is that beliefs, and the perceptions that feed into forming them, can be biased. This bias may be the result of prior beliefs, personal affiliations, or a desire for a particular outcome. Hastorf and Cantril (1954) got two groups of students, one from Princeton and one from Dartmouth, to watch film of a Princeton–Dartmouth football game. Each student was asked to count the number of penalties committed by both teams as determined by their personal judgment (and not the official count from game referees). Though both groups watched exactly the same tape, the counts show that they "saw a different game." Dartmouth students saw an equal number of flagrant and mild penalties committed by both teams. Princeton students, on the other hand, counted three times as many flagrant penalties by Dartmouth than flagrant penalties by Princeton and the same number of mild penalties. Clearly, school affiliations influenced the game they "saw."

Babcock and Loewenstein (1997) provide a particularly stunning example of the self-serving bias. Subjects are asked to bargain over how to deal with a particular tort case that is based on a real trial that occurred in Texas. Researchers assign each subject the role of lawyer for the defendant or plaintiff. They read all the case materials and then bargain with each other over a settlement amount. If they fail to settle, the award will be what the judge decided in the actual case (which is unknown to the subjects at the time of bargaining). Interestingly, subjects are paid as a function of the final settlement amount and pay an explicit additional cost if they must go to the judge for a decision. Subjects are also asked to assess (in private) how much they think the judge will award them. Finally, some pairs of subjects read the entire description of the case *before* knowing which role they will play. Others read it afterwards. This order of reading has a large effect. Those who read the case prior to their role assignment settle at a 94% rate and do not require a decision by the judge. But those who read afterwards only settle at a 72% rate. Moreover, as a rule, those who were assigned their roles prior to reading the case details tended to exaggerate how much the judge would favor them. In short, they exhibit quite biased beliefs based on their role. These conflicting beliefs are generated through nothing more than the assigned roles. Even more significant is the fact that this role-playing bias goes against their real-life material interests in one important way: they must pay to go to court, yet their biased beliefs force them to do so much more often. Much like with the football game, these subjects saw very different cases. In some sense, they saw what they "wanted" to see.

These examples of self-serving bias have far-reaching implications for all development policy and underscore the importance of randomized approaches. Implementers of specific policies will largely have this natural, self-serving bias, which may cloud the evaluation of an intervention's success. A useful example of this danger is the study of Cabot's intervention program for delinquent youth in Cambridge and Somerville, Massachusetts (Powers and Whitmer 1951). This intervention combined all the best available tools at the time for helping these delinquent youth, from tutoring and psychiatric attention to interventions in family conflicts. Those involved in the program raved of its success. They all had very positive impressions. What made the program unique, however, was that a truly random assignment procedure was used to assign the students. When these data were examined, contrary to the very positive (and likely heartfelt impressions of the caseworkers), there was little program effect.

Ross and Nisbett (1991) cite another interesting example of self-serving bias: a meta-analysis by Grace et al. (1966), who study all medical research on the "portacaval shunt." This was a popular treatment for cirrhosis of the liver, and fifty-one studies examined the efficacy of this treatment. The doctors and scientists doing these studies all had the same good intention: to see whether this procedure worked. But the studies differed in one important way: fifteen of them used controls without randomization, while four of them used truly randomized strategies. Thirteen of the fifteen nonrandomized studies were "markedly or moderately enthusiastic" about the procedure. Yet only one of the randomized studies was "markedly or moderately enthusiastic."

What is going on here? I believe the good intentions of the doctors and scientists compromise the evaluation. There is always subjectivity in nonrandomized trials: which controls to include, which controls not to include, which specification to run, etc. Such subjectivity gives room for self-serving bias to rear its head. Exactly because the researchers on these topics are well-intentioned and exactly because they hope the procedure works, it is all too easy for them to find a positive result. Much as with the Dartmouth and Princeton students, they saw in some sense what they wanted to see.

These examples highlight the damaging role of self-serving bias in evaluation. Especially in the context of development where most people working on a project would like to see it succeed, it is all too easy for self-serving bias to affect evaluations. Beyond the obvious econometric benefits of randomized evaluation, the reduction of researcher's latent biases is one of randomization's greatest practical benefits. The methodology allows us to escape the dangers of biased perception, of which researchers or field workers are no freer than anyone else in the population. One of the big changes in modern development research is the greater reliance on randomized trials. This will better insulate us from the psychological fallibilities of researchers and policy makers.

3.7 INTERESTING FURTHER DIRECTIONS

3.7.1 *Self-Control and Poverty Traps*

The evidence on self-control bounds suggests that savings can be psychologically difficult. Can these results help in theoretical models of poverty traps? In ongoing work with Abhijit Banerjee, I am investigating this question. Traditional models of poverty traps often rely on investment nonconvexities. If investment projects require, for example, a certain discrete amount to earn extremely large returns, then there can be a reinforcing nature to poverty. With liquidity constraints, the poor may not be able to save enough to avail themselves of investment opportunity.

Self-control problems present the possibility of a different kind of poverty trap. Under the assumption that temptations are concave in income, richer individuals face fewer temptations, proportionally, than poorer ones.[12] Suitably modeled, such temptations could in principle generate poverty traps themselves. The poor suffer from low savings rates since temptations effectively "tax" a greater proportion of income. The rich, on the other hand, while they face and succumb to similar temptations, are not as affected in a proportional sense. This can make poverty an absorbing state. Understanding the theoretical underpinnings and empirical importance of this type of model could be a fruitful area for future work.

---

[12]For example, temptations such as especially tasty desserts are sublinear. The presence of some temptations like those whose cost do not scale with income would create a declining importance of temptations as a proportion of income.

3.7.2 Loss Aversion and Property Rights

Consider the following simple experiment. Half a roomful of students are given mugs and the other half are given nothing (or a small cash payment roughly equivalent to the value of the mugs). The subjects are then placed in a simulated market where a mechanism determines an aggregate price at which the market clears. How many mugs should change hands? Efficiency dictates that market clearing should allocate the mugs to the 50% of the class that values them the most. Since the mugs were initially randomly assigned, trading should have resulted in exactly half the mugs changing hands. Kahneman et al. (1990) have in fact run this experiment. Contrary to the simple prediction, however, they find a stunningly low number of transactions. Roughly 15% of the mugs trade hands. This oddity is explained by a phenomenon called the *endowment effect*, in which those given objects appear to very quickly come to value them more than those not given the object. In fact, those who were given mugs had a reservation price three *times* that of those who were not given the mug.

This phenomenon reflects in part a deeper fact about utility functions: prospect theory, where people's utility functions are defined in large part on changes. In the traditional model of utility, people would value the mug at $u(c + \text{mug}) - u(c)$. Notice the symmetry: both those with and without the mug value it the same (on average). Under prospect theory, utility is defined by a value function that is evaluated locally and in changes. Those who receive the mug consider its loss as a function of $v(- \text{mug}) - v(0)$. Those who do not receive the mug value its gain at $v(\text{mug}) - v(0)$. In this formulation, valuations are asymmetric. The difference in valuation between the two depends on whether $v(\text{mug})$ is bigger or smaller than $-v(- \text{mug})$. The evidence above is consistent with a variety of evidence from other contexts: losses are felt more sharply than equivalent gains. Thus, $v(x) < -v(-x)$. This phenomenon, known as loss aversion, has been seen in many contexts (see Odean (1998) and Genesove and Mayer (2001) for two good examples).

The insight about loss aversion can also help us understand why policy change is so difficult in developing countries. Consider market reforms that transfer resources from one group to another with an efficiency gain. Suppose privatizing a firm will result in gains for customers while resulting in losses for incumbent workers. Prospect theory helps to explain why such reforms are fought so vigorously: the losses are felt far more sharply by the workers. One implication of loss aversion is, at the margin, to pursue strategies that preserve the rents of incumbents rather than ones that try to buy out incumbents. All other things equal, a strategy that offers a buyout for incumbent workers will be far more costly than one that grandfathers them in. The buyout requires the government to compensate them for their loss and this can be much larger than simple utility calculations can suggest. In contrast, a strategy that guarantees incumbent workers a measure of job security would not need to pay this cost.[13] Many situations of institutional change require some form of redistribution. The recognition of loss aversion suggests successful policies may require more consideration of the losses of incumbents.

Loss aversion also reinforces the importance of well-defined property rights. Consider a situation where there is a single good, such as a piece of land L. There are two individuals, A and B, who can engage in force to acquire (or to protect) the land, and engaging in violence may result in acquisition. In the presence of well-defined property rights (say this land belongs to person A), the decision to engage in force is straightforward. If B engages in force, he stands to gain $v(L)$ if his force is successful. A on the other hand stands to lose $v(-L)$ if he does not engage in force. In this case, loss aversion implies that A stands to lose a lot more than B could gain. So with well-defined property rights A would engage in more force than B. Consequently, B may never attempt force. Even in the absence of enforcement, loss aversion may mean that well-defined property rights may deter violence.

Consider now the case of ill-defined property rights. Suppose that both are unsure who owns the land. Specifically, take the case where they both think they own it. This is an approximation to the situation where ownership with probability $\frac{1}{2}$ already gives a partial endowment effect, or to the situation of biased beliefs where both parties may have probability greater than $\frac{1}{2}$ of owning it. In this case, both A and B think they stand to lose $v(-L)$ if they do not fight for the land. In other words, in the absence of well-defined property rights, both parties will put in large amounts of resources to secure what they already think is theirs. This is one of the powerful implications of loss aversion. Defining property rights appropriately prevents two (or more) parties from having an endowment effect on the same object. Conflicting endowments such as this are sure to produce costly attempts at protecting the perceived endowments. Anything from costly territorial activities (fencing and de-fencing) all the way to violence may result.

3.7.3 Social Preferences and Corruption

In many important development contexts, self-interested behavior is very deleterious. Bureaucrats in many countries are corrupt. They enforce regulations sporadically or take bribes. Another stark example is teacher absenteeism. Numerous studies have found that teacher absenteeism is one of the primary problems of education in developing countries. Teachers simply do not show up to school, and as a result, little education can take place. This blatantly selfish behavior stands in contrast to

---

[13]Of course, this is a comparative static only. In any given context, there may be pressing reasons to favor one policy over the other.

some evidence on social preferences that individuals may value the utility of others. I will review this literature and describe how social preferences may be contributing to the problem and may serve as part of the solution.

A very simple game called the ultimatum game has become an excellent tool for studying social preferences (Güth et al. 1982; Thaler 1988). In this game, one player (call him the "proposer") makes the first move and offers a split of a certain amount, say $10. The second player ("responder") decides whether to accept or reject this split. If it is accepted, P and R get the proposed split. If rejected, then both get zero. This game has been run in many, many countries and for stakes that range from a few dollars in the United States to a few months' income in many countries. Yet the pattern of findings is relatively constant.[14] First, responders often reject unfair offers (i.e., away from 50–50 splits). Second, proposers often make very fair offers, close to 50–50 or 60–40. Moreover, proposers' fair offers are not just driven by fear of rejection. They tend to make offers larger than that which a simple (risk-neutral) fear of rejection implies.[15] The ultimatum game illustrates two facts about interpersonal preferences: people care about others and are willing to give up resources to help others, and people react negatively to *perceived* unfair behavior and are willing to give up resources to punish it. The second fact illustrates part of the "dark side" of interpersonal preferences. In simple altruistic models, interpersonal preferences are only a good thing: having one person care in a positive way about another only makes it easier to deal with externalities and so on. The responder's possible "punishment" behavior shows, however, the way in which interpersonal preferences could potentially cause inefficiencies and conflicts.

This possibility is clearest in a classic experiment by Messick and Sentis (1979). They ask subjects to imagine they have completed a job with a partner. They are asked to decide what "fair" pay for their work is. They divide the subjects into two groups, however. One group is told to imagine that they had worked for seven hours on the task while the partner had worked ten. The other group is told to imagine that they had worked for ten hours while the partner had worked seven. Both groups were told that the person who had worked seven hours had been paid $25 and were asked what the ten-hour person should be paid. Those who were told that they had worked seven hours (and paid $25) tended to feel that the ten-hour subject should be paid $30.29. In contrast, those who were told that they had worked ten hours felt they should be paid $35.24. The source of the bias can be seen in the bimodality of the distribution of perceived "fair" wages. One mode was at equal pay ($25 for both), while the other

---

[14]See Henrich et al. (2002), however, for some interesting differences in some tribal cultures.

[15]This is most directly seen in a variant of the ultimatum game, called the dictator game. Here the proposer makes an "offer" but the responder has no choice but to accept it. In this game, the threat of rejection is removed and one continues to find nonzero offers by the proposer, although they are lower than in the ultimatum game.

mode was at equal hourly wage (so the ten-hour worker gets paid approximately $35.70). Interestingly, the difference between the two treatments was mainly in the proportion at each mode. Those who had worked for seven hours showed more subjects at the equal pay level mode, while those who had been told they had worked for ten hours showed more subjects at the equal hourly pay mode. In other words, both groups recognized two compelling norms: equal pay for equal work and equal pay for equal output. Yet their roles determined (in part) which norm they picked. Such conflicts could easily arise even if there is disagreement about measuring input levels (which often are not fully observed). More broadly, when there is not universal agreement about what is fair division, individuals trying to act "fairly" may produce even more conflict than individuals acting in a self-interested manner.

Let us return to the case of teacher absenteeism. PROBE surveyed teachers extensively in many areas of India and noted high absenteeism levels. Its in-depth interviews are illuminating about their attitudes and highlights how teachers often feel unmotivated. Some of this discouragement can be viewed as a perceived failure of reciprocity. As noted earlier, individuals strongly adhere to the norm of reciprocity. Failures of reciprocity (or perceived failures) can result in punitive or self-interested behavior in response. Teachers may feel a strong social preference early on and be motivated to teach and give much more than they need to. After all, from a motive of pure self-interest, they know they can get away with very little teaching. Yet they may be initially motivated to do more, to come to school, to struggle with tougher students and so on. They may view these contributions as a "gift," in large part due to the initial framing of the job (as a "plum job, with good salaries, secure employment and plenty of other time for other activities"). Thus, a young teacher may think, "I am giving a lot to the school." As with any giving, however, the teacher may expect strong reciprocity and see (perhaps in a self-interested way) many outcomes as a lack of reciprocity. For example, PROBE notes that many schools have terrible infrastructure; accordingly, teachers may feel that the government is not reciprocating their "gifts." This may be especially exaggerated by the transfer system in India which moves teachers to various areas, disrupting the lives of teachers. Thus, both the benign neglect of schooling and the active transfers could easily drive teachers to feel that the government does not reciprocate their efforts. They may also come to feel similarly vis-à-vis parents, who they may feel do not care about their children's education.

Even an initially motivated teacher may very quickly feel justified in their growing apathy. They gave it their best and think that their efforts were not reciprocated. Are these inferences justified? Perhaps not. As in the Messick and Sentis study, teachers may very well be making such inferences in a self-interested way. The failure of the context may very well be in it allowing teachers to make such biased attributions of fairness. Alternatively, teachers may very well be justified in these attributions. We simply cannot tell.

At a deeper level, these studies of fairness suggest that the problem of corruption may have interesting social preference wrinkles. People may be more willing to avoid taxes if they feel they are not "fair." This judgment of unfairness could be the result of getting very few government services or having to bribe corrupt middlemen in order to procure government services. Economic models of corruption, by assuming blatant self-interest, ignore the tension corruption generates. If most people, as the evidence suggests, have strong social preferences, then corrupt acts will require self-justification. This resembles anecdotal evidence on corruption experiences. It is very rare that an official simply asks for a bribe. The request is often couched with an explanation for the reason for the bribe. Even though the bribe is clearly a violation of the law, there is usually a story that serves to justify it in the context of the law. For example, a customs officer may point to improper packaging as a reason for an extra payment. These kinds of insights may one day help to better understand the nature of corruption and anti-corruption policies.

3.7.4 *Psychology of the Poor*

The work I have described so far starts with a very simple premise: apply the general insights of psychology to the context of development. This raises the question of whether there are psychological features that are unique to poverty. Are there any judgmental heuristics, for example, that are uniquely applied in some developing countries? Are there cultural differences in some developing countries that may in turn be reflected in their psychology and hence by economic outcomes? These questions all fall under the purview of cultural psychology, a long dormant branch of psychology that is now enjoying resurgence (Matsumoto 2001). For example, recent work suggests that East Asians are more overconfident than European-Americans in making probabilistic estimates and tend to focus less on individuals and more on contexts in making attributions (see Nisbett 2004). Though the formal explanations of such cultural differences are topics of ongoing discussion, laboratory experiments are identifying a seemingly culture-dependent difference in reasoning. Given the large differences in context and affective experiences between rich and poor, might there be equally large differences between these two "cultural" groups as well? There is currently no work that I know of on this, but it seems worth pursuing.[16]

---

[16] In ongoing work with Marianne Bertrand and Eldar Shafir, I have isolated a few suggestive differences between the urban poor and the well-off in decision-making. I should note here that this type of work should not be confused with pejorative work that argues that the poor are "dumber." Instead, this work attempts to highlight more subtle differences in cognitive heuristics used by the poor and the well-off.

3.8 CONCLUDING OBSERVATIONS

Much of recent development economics has stressed the importance of institutions. Property rights must be enforced to give appropriate incentives for investment. Government workers must be given appropriate incentives to ensure high-quality public service provision. Banking may need to be privatized to ensure a well-functioning credit system that in turn allows for better savings and smoother consumption. The common theme here is that institutions must be improved to help to resolve issues between people. They may reduce externalities, solve asymmetries of information, or help to resolve coordination problems. This focus on institutions resolving problems *between* people, rather than them being solved *within* a person is natural to economists. The predominant economic model of human behavior leaves little room for individuals themselves to make mistakes. In fact, economists assume that people are unbounded in their cognitive abilities, unbounded in their willpower and unbounded in their self-interest (Mullainathan and Thaler 2001). Once we admit human complexities, institutional design in development becomes not just about solving problems *between* people. It is also about developing institutions that help any one person deal with their own "problems." I hope the small set of examples I have presented illustrates how a deeper understanding of the psychology of people might eventually improve development economics and policy.

REFERENCES

Asch, S. E. 1955. Opinions and social pressure. *Scientific American* 193:31–35.

Akerlof, G. A. 1991. Procrastination and obedience. *American Economic Review* 81:1–19.

Ardener, S., and S. Burman (eds). 1995. *Money-Go-Rounds: The Importance of Rotating Savings and Credit Associations for Women*. Washington, DC: Berg.

Ariely, D., and K. Wertenbroch. 2002. Procrastination, deadlines and performance: self-control by precommitment. *Psychological Science* 13:219–24.

Ashraf, N., D. Karlan, and W. Yin. 2006. Tying Odysseus to the mast: evidence from a commitment savings product. *Quarterly Journal of Economics* 121:635–72.

Babcock, L., and G. Loewenstein. 1997. Explaining bargaining impasse: the role of self-serving biases. *Journal of Economic Perspectives* 11:109–126.

Becker, G. 1993. *Human Capital*, 3rd edn. University of Chicago Press.

Bertrand, M., S. Mullainathan, and E. Shafir. 2004. A behavioral-economics view of poverty. *American Economic Review* 94:419–423.

Besley, T., and A. Case. 1994. Diffusion as a learning process: evidence from HYV cotton. Working Paper No. 174. Woodrow Wilson School of Public and International Affairs, Princeton University.

Camerer, C., and R. Weber. 2003. Cultural conflict and merger failure: an experimental approach. *Management Science* 49:400–15.

Cialdini, R. B., and M. R. Trost. 1998. Social influence: social norms, conformity, and compliance. In *Handbook of Social Psychology*, Volume 2 (ed. D. T. Gilbert, S. T. Fiske, and G. Lindzey). New York: McGraw-Hill.

Conley, T., and C. Udry. 2004. Learning about a new technology: pineapple in Ghana. Mimeo, Yale University.

De, A., and J. Drèze (eds). 1999. *Public Report on Basic Education in India*. Cambridge University Press.

Duflo, E., M. Kremer, and J. Robinson. 2004. Understanding technology adoption: fertilizer in Western Kenya. Preliminary results from field experiments. Mimeo, MIT and Harvard University.

Farkas, S., and J. Johnson. 1997. *Miles to Go: A Status Report on Americans' Plans for Retirement*. New York: Public Agenda.

Foster, A., and M. Rosenzweig. 1996. learning by doing and learning from others: human capital and technical change in agriculture. *Journal of Political Economy* 104:1176–1209.

Frederick, S., G. Loewenstein, and T. O'Donoghue. 2002. Time discounting and time preference: a critical review. *Journal of Economic Literature* 40:351–401.

Genesove, D., and C. Mayer. 2001. Loss aversion and seller behavior: evidence from the housing market. *Quarterly Journal of Economics* 116:1233–60.

Gruber, J., and S. Mullainathan. 2002. Do cigarette taxes make smokers happier? NBER Working Paper 8872.

Grace, N. D., H. Muench, and T. C. Chalmers. 1966. The present status of shunts for portal hyperextension in cirrhosis. *Gastroenterology* 50:684–91.

Gugerty, M. K. 2003. You can't save alone: testing theories of rotating savings and credit organizations. UCLA International Institute. Mimeo, Harvard University.

Güth, W., R. Schmittberger, and B. Schwarze. 1982. An experimental analysis of ultimatum bargaining. *Journal of Economic Behavior and Organization* 3:367–88.

Hastorf, A., and H. Cantril. 1954. They saw a game: a case study. *Journal of Abnormal and Social Psychology* 49:129–34.

Heath, C., C. Bell, and E. Sternberg. 2001. Emotional selection in memes: the case of urban legends. *Journal of Personality and Social Psychology* 81:1028–41.

Henrich, J., R. Boyd, S. Bowles, C. Camerer, E. Fehr, H. Gintis, and R. McElreath. 2002. Cooperation, reciprocity and punishment: experiments from fifteen small-scale societies. Santa Fe Institute Working Paper 01-01-007.

Kahneman, D., J. L. Knetsch, and R. H. Thaler. 1990. Experimental tests of the endowment effect and the Coase Theorem. *Journal of Political Economy* 98:1325–48.

Jacobs, R. C., and D. T. Campbell. 1961. The perpetuation of an arbitrary tradition through several generations of a laboratory microculture. *Journal of Abnormal and Social Psychology* 34:385–93.

Laibson, D. 1997. Golden eggs and hyperbolic discounting. *Quarterly Journal of Economics* 62:443–78.

Madrian, B. C., and D. F. Shea. 2001. The power of suggestion: inertia in 401(k) participation and savings behavior. *Quarterly Journal of Economics* 116:1149–87.

Matsumoto, D. (ed.). 2001. *The Handbook of Culture and Psychology*. Oxford University Press.

Messick, D. M., and K. P. Sentis. 1979. Fairness and preference. *Journal of Experimental Social Psychology* 15:418–34.

Miguel, E., and M. Kremer. 2003. Networks, social learning, and technology adoption: the case of deworming drugs in Kenya. Mimeo, University of California at Berkeley and Harvard University.

Montgomery, M., and J. Casterline. 1998. Social networks and the diffusion of fertility control. Working Paper 119. (Available at http://www.popcouncil.org/pdfs/wp/119.pdf.)

Mullainathan, S., and R. H. Thaler. 2001. Behavioral economics. *International Encyclopedia of Social Sciences*, 1st edn, pp. 1094–1100. Pergamon.

Munshi, K. 2003. Social learning in a heterogeneous population: technology diffusion in the Indian Green Revolution. Mimeo, Brown University.

Nisbett, R. E. 2004. *The Geography of Thought: How Asians and Westerners Think Differently... and Why*. New York: Free Press.

Odean, T. 1998. Are investors reluctant to realize their losses? *Journal of Finance* 53:1775–98.

O'Donoghue, T., and M. Rabin. 2001. Choice and procrastination. *Quarterly Journal of Economics* 66:121–60.

Palmore, J., and R. Freedman, 1969. Perceptions of contraceptive practice by others: effects on acceptance. In *Family Planning in Taiwan: An Experiment in Social Change* (ed. R. Freedman and J. Takeshita). Princeton University Press.

Phillips, D. P. 1979. Suicide, motor vehicle fatalities, and the mass media: evidence toward a theory of suggestion. *American Journal of Sociology* 84:1150–74.

——. 1980. Airplane accidents, murder, and the mass media: towards a theory of imitation and suggestion. *Social Forces* 58:1001–24.

Powers, E., and H. Whitmer. 1951. *An Experiment in the Prevention of Delinquency*. New York: Columbia.

Read, D., G. Loewenstein, and S. Kalyanaraman. 1999. Mixing virtue and vice: combining the immediacy effect and the diversification heuristic. *Journal of Behavioral Decision Making* 12:257–73.

Retherford, R., and J. Palmore. 1983. Diffusion processes affecting fertility regulation. In *Determinants of Fertility in Developing Countries* (ed. R. A. Bulatao and R. D. Lee), Volume 2. Academic.

Rogers, E. M. 2003. *Diffusion of Innovations*, 5th edn. New York: Free Press.

Ross, L., and R. E. Nisbett. 1991. *The Person and the Situation: Perspectives on Social Psychology*. McGraw-Hill.

Samuelson, W., and R. Zeckhauser. 1988. Status quo bias in decision making. *Journal of Risk and Uncertainty* 1:7–59.

Sherif, M. 1937. An experimental approach to the study of attitudes. *Sociometry* 1:90–98.

Strotz, R. 1955/56. Myopia and inconsistency in dynamic utility maximization. *Review of Economic Studies* 23:165–80.

Thaler, R. 1981. Some empirical evidence on dynamic inconsistency. *Economics Letters* 8:201–7.

——. 1988. The ultimatum game. *Journal of Economic Perspectives* 2:195–206.

Thaler, R., and S. Benatzi. 2004. Save More Tomorrow[TM]: using behavioral economics to increase employee saving. *Journal of Political Economy* 112(S1):164–187.

Trope, Y., and A. Fishbach. 2000. Counteractive self-control in overcoming temptation. *Journal of Personality and Social Psychology* 79:493–506.

Vermeesch, C. 2003. School meals, educational achievement and school competition: evidence from a randomized evaluation. World Bank Working Paper 3523.

Wertenbroch, K. 1998. Consumption self-control by rationing purchase quantities of virtue and vice. *Marketing Science* 17:317–37.

COMMENT BY ANNE CASE

Mullainathan has written an insightful piece summarizing the many and varied ways in which psychology is beginning to help us better understand the process of economic development. The paper is rich with detail and lays out an exciting research agenda where experimental psychology meets development economics.

In my remarks I will focus on a couple of concerns I have about the kinds of commitment devices that Mullainathan discusses in his paper. Mullainathan spends a good deal of time talking about savings behavior in developing countries, and ways in which the results from the experimental psychology literature could be put to use to change savings behavior in developing countries. Reminiscent of Ulysses tying himself to the mast in order not to be lured by the Sirens' song, new experimental work suggests that if people can commit themselves to a savings scheme, they will be more successful in putting aside resources.

I would encourage researchers to take care in identifying whether savings, in the absence of such schemes, are thwarted by *within-person* conflict or by *between-person* conflict over resources. It is not clear in much of the literature cited whether the authors are making this distinction, but such a distinction will surely matter for policy.

Between-person conflicts are especially common in developing countries, where there are often sharing norms that do not allow one to deny resources to kin. To take a couple of examples, in many parts of the developing world, people are expected to feed neighbors and kin who come to the door hungry. In one of my South African field sites the best approach we have found to uncovering whether adults were poor when they were children is to ask, "How often did you go to other people's places to eat when you were young?" Child fostering is also often a responsibility that kin must bear. If my sister is in trouble in Johannesburg, for example, and wants to send her children to me in Durban, I would be expected to take them in.

In our South African sites, we also find that old-age pensions (large cash grants delivered monthly) are used to feed children, pay school fees, and keep body and soul together for all household members, not just pensioners. In our data, we are seeing two types of consumption patterns emerging with respect to the old-age pension. One might be characterized as an "eat it fast" approach, and the other as "make it last." Starting with the latter, we find in some households receiving the pension that consumption is smooth over the course of the month. In contrast, in the "eat it fast" households, the pension is spent quickly at the beginning of the month (on meat, electricity, and luxuries) and by month's end household members have little variety in their diets, no electricity, and no luxury expenditures. The "eat it fast" households may be struggling with the sort of within-individual commitment problems of the kind Mullainathan is focusing on. Alternatively, they may represent between-individual commitment problems in the presence of sharing norms, with pensioners thinking that they had better hurry up and eat their pension before someone else does. Clearly, if everyone else lives in an "eat it fast" household, it would not be possible to maintain a "make it last" household. (A third explanation for "eat it fast" behavior is that consumption memories are durable goods, and pensioners may choose to have large pension-financed parties of a sort that would not have surprised Kahneman and Tversky. Without more information, we cannot know which of these is at work.)

ROSCAs and, for example, the take-up of SEED accounts in the Philippines, which Mullainathan discusses, may represent people guarding against others, not necessarily themselves. The bigger question, perhaps, is whether this is a distinction with a difference. I think it is easy to make a case that there is a difference, and that it may be very important. Offering lock-box savings would not be expected to rip the fabric of society, if the commitment problems were within-individuals. But they may well do so, if they are between kin. The sorts of commitment devices and financial education that would be most helpful will also differ, depending on which tensions are most at play.

Mullainathan also notes that commitment devices, introduced in the form of higher taxes, can bring happiness to smokers. Contrary to the rational model and supportive of the behavioral model, Mullainathan finds that cigarette taxes actually make those prone to smoke *better off*. I think this is fascinating, but I also urge caution. When revealed preference no longer provides a measure of policy success, we find ourselves without a compass. Social choice must rest, then, not only on individuals' utility outcomes but, importantly, on the process by which outcomes are determined. Process takes on a much more important role than it did when we believed individuals were the best purveyors of their own well-being (where, then, the optimal 'process' was to leave them unencumbered to choose their own optimal bundles). The role that society should play in protecting people from themselves is far from clear and far from settled.

Behavioral Law and Economics

By Christine Jolls[1]

4.1 INTRODUCTION

Many topics within economics relate to law. A large body of work in public economics, for instance, examines the effects of legally mandated government programs such as disability and unemployment insurance (Katz and Meyer 1990; Gruber 1994; Cutler and Gruber 1996; Autor and Duggan 2003); work on the labor market examines the effects of many types of antidiscrimination laws (Heckman and Payner 1989; Donohue and Heckman 1991; Acemoglu and Angrist 2001; Jolls 2004); and recent corporate governance research studies the consequences of corporate and securities law on stock returns and volatility (Gompers et al. 2003; Ferrell 2003; Greenstone et al. 2006). But, while all of these topics relate to law in some way, neither "law and economics" nor "behavioral law and economics" embraces them as genuinely central areas of inquiry. Thus an important threshold question for the present work involves how to characterize the domains of both "law and economics" and "behavioral law and economics."

Amid the broad span of economic topics relating to law in some way, a few distinctive features help to demarcate work that is typically regarded as within law and economics. One distinguishing feature is that much of this work focuses on various areas of law that were not much studied by economists prior to the advent of law and economics; these areas include tort law, contract law, property law, and rules governing the litigation process. A second feature of work within law and economics is that it often (controversially) employs the normative criterion of "wealth maximization" (Posner 1979) rather than that of social welfare maximization—not, for the most part, on the view that society should pursue the maximization of wealth rather than social welfare, but instead because law and economics generally favors addressing distributional issues that bear on social welfare solely through the tax system (Shavell 1981). Finally, a third distinguishing feature of much work within

---

[1] Thanks to Peter Diamond for inviting me to participate in the conference that led to this volume; to Peter Diamond, Steven Shavell, Cass Sunstein, and conference participants, especially discussants Ian Ayres and Christoph Engel, for very helpful comments; and to Pat Robertson and David Young for excellent research assistance.

law and economics is its sustained interest in explaining and predicting the content, rather than just the effects, of legal rules. While a large body of work in economics studies the effects of law (as noted above), outside of work associated with law and economics only political economy has generally given central emphasis to analyzing the content of law, and then only from a particular perspective.[2]

Given this rough sketch of "law and economics," what then is "behavioral law and economics"? Behavioral law and economics involves both the development and the incorporation within law and economics of behavioral insights drawn from various fields of psychology. As has been widely recognized since the early work by Allais (1952) and Ellsberg (1961), some of the foundational assumptions of traditional economic analysis may reflect an unrealistic picture of human behavior. Not surprisingly, models based on these assumptions sometimes yield erroneous predictions. Behavioral law and economics attempts to improve the predictive power of law and economics by building in more realistic accounts of actors' behavior.

The present paper describes some of the central attributes and applications of behavioral law and economics to date; it also outlines an emerging focus in behavioral law and economics on prospects for "debiasing" individuals through the structure of legal rules (Jolls and Sunstein 2006a). Through the vehicle of "debiasing through law," behavioral law and economics may open up a new space within law and economics between, on the one hand, unremitting adherence to traditional economic assumptions and, on the other hand, broad structuring or restructuring of legal regimes on the assumption that people are inevitably and permanently bound to deviate from traditional economic assumptions.

The paper proceeds as follows. Section 4.2 traces the development and refinement of one of the central insights of behavioral economics—that people frequently exhibit an endowment effect—both outside and within the field of behavioral law and economics. Section 4.3 moves to a general overview of the features of human decision making that have informed behavioral law and economics, emphasizing points of departure from work in other areas of behavioral economics. Section 4.4 describes a series of illustrative applications of behavioral law and economics analysis. Section 4.5 introduces the concept of debiasing through law, and Section 4.6 concludes.

4.2 THE ENDOWMENT EFFECT IN BEHAVIORAL ECONOMICS AND BEHAVIORAL LAW AND ECONOMICS

Early on, law and economics had a central point of contact with behavioral economics. The point of contact was the foundational debate over the Coase Theorem

---

[2]The three features of law and economics identified in the text are not meant to demarcate the intrinsic essence of the field; instead the claim is that these features characterize much of the existing work generally regarded as law and economics.

and the "endowment effect"—the tendency of people to refuse to give up entitlements they hold even though they would not have bought those entitlements initially
(Thaler 1980, pp. 43–47). This early point of contact between law and economics
and behavioral economics helped to lay the ground for a rich literature down the
road on the endowment effect in both behavioral economics and behavioral law and
economics.

4.2.1 *The Coase Theorem*

An unquestioned centerpiece of law and economics is the Coase Theorem (Coase
1960). This theorem posits that allocating legal rights to one party or another will not
affect outcomes if transaction costs are sufficiently low; thus, for instance, whether
the law gives a factory the right to emit pollution next to a laundry or, instead, says
the laundry has a right to be free of pollution will not matter to the ultimate outcome
(pollution or no pollution) as long as transaction costs are sufficiently low. The reason
for this result is that, with low transaction costs, the parties should be expected to
bargain to the efficient outcome under either legal regime. The Coase Theorem is
central to law and economics because of (among other things) the theorem's claim
about the domain within which normative analysis of legal rules—whether rule A
is preferable to rule B or the reverse—is actually relevant.

The Coase Theorem has also played a central, albeit a rather different, role in the
field of behavioral economics. More than fifteen years ago, Kahneman et al. (1990)
reported the results of a set of experiments designed to provide a careful empirical
assessment of the Coase Theorem. In one round of experiments, each subject was
given an assigned value for a "token" (the amount for which the subject could redeem
the token for cash at the end of the experiment), and half of the subjects were awarded
tokens. When subjects subsequently had the opportunity to trade tokens for money
or (for those not awarded tokens) money for tokens, subjects behaved precisely in
accordance with the Coase Theorem. Exactly half of the tokens changed hands,
as theory would predict (given random assignment of the tokens in relation to the
specified values). The initial allocation of tokens proved irrelevant. These findings
are a striking vindication of the Coase Theorem.

Having thus established that transaction costs in the experimental setting were
sufficiently low to vindicate the Coase Theorem, Kahneman et al. went on to study
subjects' behavior when the good to be traded was not tokens but, rather, Cornell
University mugs that the subjects would retain after the experiment (rather than
redeeming for an assigned amount of cash). In direct contravention of the Coase
Theorem, the initial assignment of entitlements to the mug mattered dramatically;
those initially given mugs rarely sold them, while those not initially given mugs
seldom bought them. Following Thaler (1980, p. 44), Kahneman et al. referred to

this effect as the "endowment effect"—the refusal to give up an entitlement one holds initially even though one would not have been willing to pay to acquire that entitlement had one not held it initially.[3] In the presence of the endowment effect, the Coase Theorem's prediction of equivalent outcomes regardless of the initial entitlement no longer holds. This conclusion has obvious importance for the design of legal rules.

4.2.2 *The Endowment Effect within Law and Economics*

A central task of law and economics is to assess the desirability of actual and proposed legal rules. The endowment effect both preserves a larger scope for such normative economic analysis—because the Coase Theorem and the associated claim of irrelevance of legal rules no longer hold—and profoundly unsettles the bases for such analysis.

The reason that the endowment effect so unsettles the bases for normative economic analysis of law is that in the presence of this effect the value attached to a legal entitlement will sometimes vary depending on the initial assignment of the entitlement. Normative analysis will then often become indeterminant, as multiple rules may maximize the desired objective (whether wealth or social welfare) depending on the starting allocation of entitlements (Kelman 1979, pp. 676–78). As Sunstein and Thaler (2003, p. 1190) recently observed, in the presence of the endowment effect a "cost–benefit study cannot be based on willingness to pay (WTP), because WTP will be a function of the default rule." Thus, the cost–benefit study "must be a more open-ended (and inevitably somewhat subjective) assessment of the welfare consequences."[4] The conventional normative economic analysis feasible without the endowment effect often cannot survive in the presence of this effect.

One possible approach to normative analysis when the value of an entitlement varies depending on the initial assignment of the entitlement is to base legal policy choices not on the joint wealth or welfare of the parties directly in question—because the answer to the question of which rule maximizes their joint wealth or welfare may turn on the initial rule choice—but rather on the third-party effects of the competing rules. Thus, for instance, if it is unclear whether a particular workplace rule is or is not optimal for employers and employees (because employees will value the entitlement granted by the rule at more than its value with the rule in place but less

---

[3]A recent article by Plott and Zeiler (2005), noted below, addresses the role of experimental design on the existence and degree of the endowment effect.

[4]Sunstein and Thaler's discussion is addressed to both the endowment effect and other factors that produce an effect of the law's structure on people's background preferences. The focus of the discussion here is the endowment effect.

than its value otherwise), but the rule will create important benefits for employees' families, then perhaps the rule should be adopted.

An alternative approach to normative analysis with varying entitlement values depending on the initial assignment of the entitlement is to make a judgment about which preferences—the ones with legal rule A or the ones with legal rule B—deserve greater deference. Sunstein and Thaler (2003, pp. 1190–91) offer some support for this view in the context of default terms in employee savings plans. Referring to research showing that employees are much more likely to enroll in a savings plan if enrollment is the default term and employees must affirmatively opt out to be excluded than they are if non-enrollment is the default term and employees must take affirmative steps to enroll, Sunstein and Thaler make the normative argument that the enrollment outcome is "highly likely" to be better under automatic enrollment than under a default term of non-enrollment because it turns out that very few employees drop out if automatically enrolled. They readily acknowledge that "[s]ome readers might think that our reliance on [employees'] behavior as an indication of welfare is inconsistent" with the basic point about indeterminacy of preferences, "[b]ut in fact, there is no inconsistency" because "it is reasonable to think that if, on reflection, workers realized that they had been 'tricked' into saving too much, they might take the effort to opt out." Sunstein and Thaler draw an analogy to rules calling for mandatory cooling-off periods before consumer purchases: "The premise of such rules is that people are more likely to make good choices when they have had time to think carefully and without a salesperson present." In other words, according to Sunstein and Thaler, we have reason to think that the revealed preferences of the automatically enrolled employee, or the consumer at the end of a cooling-off period, are a more appropriate basis for normative judgment than the revealed preferences of the employee who does not choose to enroll under a default term of non-enrollment, or the consumer before the cooling-off period. We will see similar issues in the discussion of bounded willpower in Section 4.3.2 below.

4.2.3 The Importance of Context

Particularly in light of the central relevance of the endowment effect to normative economic analysis of law, it is appropriate to emphasize the important role of context in whether this effect occurs. An early literature in law and economics is responsible for helping to shape understandings of when the endowment effect will and will not occur.

Prior to the Cornell University "mugs experiments" described above, a series of law and economics articles had demonstrated a set of domains in which the Coase Theorem was in fact empirically robust. Hoffman and Spitzer's (1982, 1986) experiments found that in both large and small groups the predictions of the theorem were vindicated. Likewise, Schwab (1988) showed that the ultimate allocation of entitlements did not turn on their initial allocation in the setting he studied.

All of these experiments, however, shared with the tokens experiment discussed above the feature that subjects' value of each possible outcome was directly specified in dollar terms by the experimenter. Thus, the law and economics work from the 1980s showed that if people are told specifically what each outcome is worth to them, they will generally find their way to a value-maximizing outcome, so long as transaction costs are sufficiently low. However, the later "mugs experiments" demonstrated that this result tends to collapse when actors are not instructed as to the value of outcomes to them. Viewed in light of the later work, the law and economics work from the 1980s is best understood as showing some of the important limits on when the endowment effect will be observed and, more generally, the central role of context in influencing the occurrence or nonoccurrence of this effect. The work by Plott and Zeiler (2005) provides an important recent lens on the role of context in determining the existence and degree of the endowment effect.

Within behavioral law and economics, recent research has refined the basic point about the importance of context. Korobkin (1998), for instance, raised the important question of whether the endowment effect would obtain in the allocation to either prospective sellers or prospective buyers of contract law default rights, such as the right of sellers to withhold goods or services after unanticipated natural disasters or other similar events versus the right of buyers to demand goods or services in those circumstances. (For instance, if a theater owner has promised to allow its theater to be used by another party on a specific date, but the theater then burns down before that date, does the theater owner have the right not to provide the theater, or does the other party have the right to collect damages for the harm it suffered because the theater proved unavailable?) Such contact law entitlements do not attach—and indeed are irrelevant—until and unless a contract is ultimately agreed to, and thus Korobkin noted that it was unclear whether the initial allocation of the entitlements through contract law default rules would create the sort of sense of ownership or possession that in turn would generate an endowment effect.

Korobkin's experiments support the operation of the endowment effect in this context. He finds that if contract law allocates an entitlement to party A unless party A agrees to waive it, then a contract between that party and party B is more likely to award party A that entitlement than if contract law initially allocates the entitlement to party B—even with seemingly low transaction costs. Thus, Korobkin concludes, the endowment effect, and not the Coase Theorem, provides the best account of the effects of contract law default rights. The deepening of knowledge about when the endowment effect does and does not occur—across contract settings and elsewhere—will help refine our understanding of the scope of this effect and, as a direct consequence, the validity of and limits on conventional normative economic analysis of law.

4.3 The Modern Domain of Behavioral Law and Economics

Although the endowment effect has played a central role in behavioral law and economics, other features of behavioral economics are important as well. Following Thaler (1996), it is useful for purposes of behavioral law and economics analysis to view human actors as departing from traditional economic assumptions in three distinct ways: human actors exhibit *bounded rationality, bounded willpower*, and *bounded self-interest*. All three concepts are defined in the brief discussion below. As described below, bounded rationality consists in part of "judgment errors," and along with the usual types of such errors discussed in the existing literature in behavioral economics, behavioral law and economics has recently emphasized a separate form of judgment error—implicit bias in how members of racial and other groups are perceived by individuals who consciously disavow any sort of prejudiced attitude; this form of judgment error provides the starting point for the discussion below.

4.3.1 *Bounded Rationality*

Departures from traditional economic assumptions of unbounded rationality may be divided into two main categories, judgment errors and departures from expected utility theory.

4.3.1.1 Judgment Errors

Across a wide range of contexts, actual judgments show systematic differences from unbiased forecasts. Within this category of judgment errors, behavioral law and economics has recently emphasized errors in the form of implicit bias in people's perceptions of racial and other group members.

Implicit Racial and Other Group-Based Bias.   Perhaps the most elementary definition of the word "bias" is that a person believes, either consciously or implicitly, that members of a racial or other group are somehow less worthy than other individuals. An enormous literature in modern social psychology explores the cognitive, motivational, and other aspects of implicit, or unconscious, forms of racial or other group-based bias. This literature, however, has not featured significantly in most fields of behavioral economics. But a clear contrast is behavioral law and economics, which has recently given significant emphasis to the possibility and effects of implicit racial or other group-based bias.

The behavioral law and economics literature in this area has worked against the backdrop of a heavily Beckerian approach to discrimination. Seminal law and economics works on discrimination envision such behavior as in significant part a rational response to discriminatory "tastes" that disfavor association with particular group members (e.g., Posner 1989). The idea of implicit bias, by contrast, suggests that discriminatory behavior often stems not from taste-based preferences that individuals are consciously acting to satisfy, but instead from implicit attitudes afflicting individuals who seriously and sincerely disclaim all forms of prejudice, and who would regard their implicitly biased judgments as "errors." A number of recent works in behavioral law and economics have begun to explore the implications for the analysis of discrimination law of various types of implicit bias (e.g., Gulati and Yelnosky forthcoming; Jolls and Sunstein 2006b).

While social psychologists have identified diverse means of assessing and measuring implicit bias against members of racial and other groups (e.g., Gaertner and McLaughlin 1983; Greenwald et al. 1998), a particular measure, known as the Implicit Association Test (IAT), has had particular influence. In the IAT, individuals are asked to categorize words or pictures into four groups, two of which are racial or other groups (such as "black" and "white"), and the other two of which are the categories "pleasant" and "unpleasant." Groups are paired, so that respondents are instructed to press one key on the computer for either "black" or "unpleasant" and a different key for either "white" or "pleasant" (a stereotype-consistent pairing); or are instructed instead to press one key on the computer for either "black" or "pleasant" and a different key for either "white" or "unpleasant" (a stereotype-inconsistent pairing). Implicit bias is defined as faster categorization when the "black" and "unpleasant" categories are paired than when the "black" and "pleasant" categories are paired. The IAT reveals significant evidence of implicit bias, including among those who assiduously deny any prejudice (Greenwald et al. 1998; Nosek et al. 2002).

An important question raised by the results on the IAT is whether implicit bias as measured by the test is correlated with individuals' actual behavior toward members of other groups. Several studies, including McConnell and Leibold (2001) and Dovidio et al. (2002), have found that scores on the IAT and similar tests show correlations with third parties' ratings of the degree of general friendliness shown by individuals toward members of other groups. Other connections between IAT scores and actual behavior remain an active area of research.

Although implicit racial or other group-based bias is not conventionally grouped with other forms of bounded rationality within behavioral economics, the fit may be more natural than has typically been supposed. Such implicit bias may often result from the way in which the characteristic of race or other group membership operates as a sort of "heuristic"—a form of mental shortcut. (The concept of a heuristic is discussed more fully just below.) Indeed, recent psychology research emphasizes that heuristics often work through a process of "attribute substitution," in which people answer a hard question by substituting an easier one (Kahneman and Frederick

2002). For instance, people might resolve a question of probability not by investigating statistics, but by asking whether a relevant incident comes easily to mind (Tversky and Kahneman 1973). The same process can operate to produce implicit bias against racial or other groups. Section 4.5.1, below, describes an example of how implicit bias has been analyzed within behavioral law and economics.

The "Heuristics and Biases" Literature. Judgment errors may arise not only from implicit bias against racial or other group members, but also from other biases studied within the so-called "heuristics and biases" literature within behavioral economics. Three types of judgment errors from this literature have received particularly sustained attention within behavioral law and economics.

One such judgment error is optimism bias, in which individuals believe that their own probability of facing a bad outcome is lower than it actually is. As a familiar illustration, most people think that their chances of having an auto accident are significantly lower than the average person's chances of experiencing this event (e.g., DeJoy 1989), although of course these beliefs cannot all be correct; if everyone were below "average," then the average would be lower.[5] There is also evidence that people underestimate their absolute as well as relative (to other individuals) probability of negative events such as auto accidents (Arnould and Grabowski 1981, pp. 34–35; Camerer and Kunreuther 1989, p. 566). Optimism bias is probably highly adaptive as a general matter; by thinking that things will turn out well, people may often increase the chance that they will turn out well. Section 4.4.1, below, describes an application of optimism bias in the behavioral law and economics literature.

A second judgment error prominent in behavioral law and economics is self-serving bias. Whenever there is room for disagreement about a matter to be decided by two or more parties—and of course there often is in litigation as well as elsewhere—individuals will tend to interpret information in a direction that serves their own interests. In a compelling field study, Babcock et al. (1996) find that union

---

[5]As described in Jolls (1998), an interesting subtlety here is that if the question is whether one's probability of experiencing a bad event is below the average probability of experiencing that event (as distinguished from the average *person's* probability of experiencing that event), then it is possible for most people to be below average. To illustrate, suppose that for 80% of the population the probability of being involved in an auto accident is 10%, and for 20% it is 60%. Then the average probability of being involved in an auto accident is 20% ($0.1 \times 0.8 + 0.6 \times 0.2 = 0.2$). So for 80% of the population, the probability of being involved in an auto accident (10%) is below the average probability (20%). But the average person has a 10% chance of being involved in an auto accident, and it would be impossible for more than half of the population to have a probability below this. The natural interpretation of most studies of optimism bias would seem to be that they request a comparison with the average person's probability, rather than with the average probability; the average probability would often be quite difficult to compute and not within the grasp of most subjects. Moreover, at least one study has dealt explicitly with the issue raised here and has found significant evidence of optimism bias even using the average probability benchmark (Weinstein 1980, pp. 809–12).

and school board presidents asked to identify "comparable" school districts for purposes of labor negotiations identified different lists of districts depending on their respective self-interests. While the average teacher salary in districts viewed as comparable by union presidents was $27,633, the same average was $26,922 in districts viewed as comparable by school board presidents. As Babcock et al. observe, this difference was more than large enough to produce teacher strikes based on the size of past salary disagreements leading to strikes. Section 4.4.2, below, discusses an application of self-serving bias in the behavioral law and economics literature.

A third judgment error extensively discussed in behavioral law and economics is the hindsight bias, in which decision makers attach excessively high probabilities to events simply because they ended up occurring. In one striking study, neuropsychologists were presented with a list of patient symptoms and then asked to assess the probability that the patient had each of three conditions (alcohol withdrawal, Alzheimer's disease, and brain damage secondary to alcohol abuse). While the mean probabilities for physicians who were not informed of the patient's actual condition were 37%, 26%, and 37%, respectively, for the three conditions, physicians who were informed of the patient's actual condition routinely said they would have attached much higher probabilities to that condition (Arkes et al. 1988). Even when, as in the study, people are specifically instructed to give the probabilities they would have assigned had they been the one making the initial diagnosis, people seem to have difficulty putting aside events they know to have occurred. As highlighted in Section 4.4.5, below, the hindsight bias has clear relevance to the legal system because that system is pervasively in the business of adjudicating likelihoods and foreseeability after an accident or other event has occurred.

4.3.1.2 Departures from Expected Utility Theory

Boundedly rational individuals not only make judgment errors but also deviate from the precepts of expected utility theory. While this theory is a foundational aspect of traditional economic analysis, Kahneman and Tversky's (1979) "prospect theory" offers a leading alternative to expected utility theory. Within behavioral law and economics, the feature of prospect theory that emphasizes the distinction between gains and losses relative to an endowment point has received by far the most attention; the relevant work on the endowment effect was discussed in some detail in Section 4.2 above.

4.3.2 *Bounded Willpower*

We often observe individuals choosing to spend rather than save, consume desserts over salads, and go to the movies instead of the gym despite all of their best intentions (Schelling 1984; Laibson 1997). Why do people fail to follow through on the plans they make? Behavioral economics has emphasized the concept of bounded willpower, which has a long pedigree in economics (Strotz 1955/56). This concept has featured in behavioral law and economics as well, as illustrated in Section 4.4.4, below.

Much work in law and economics is normatively oriented, and this feature of the work brings to the fore a set of normative questions about bounded willpower—much in the way that normative questions have been prominent in law and economics discussions of the endowment effect (Section 4.2.2, above). With respect to bounded willpower, the central normative question concerns how to view a decision to spend rather than save, to consume desserts rather than salads, or to go to the gym rather than the movies. Why should (if they should) the preferences of the self who wishes to save, eat salad, or go to the gym rather than the self who wishes to spend, eat dessert, or watch movies be used as the benchmark in performing normative analysis?

One possible answer, partially reminiscent of a strand of the endowment effect discussion above, is that saving, eating salad, or going to the gym creates desirable third-party effects that are absent with spending, eating dessert, or watching movies. Another possible answer, also with an analogue in the earlier discussion, is that the preferences of the self who wishes to save, eat salad, or go to the gym reflect a considered judgment about the matter in question—the rightness of which, however, it is not possible always to keep before one's mind (Elster 1979, p. 52). Of course, each of these two types of judgments about the relative merits of different preferences may be contentious in at least some settings.

4.3.3 Bounded Self-Interest

In principle, traditional economic analysis is capacious with respect to the range of admissible preferences. Preferences that give significant weight to fairness, for instance, can be included in the analysis (Kaplow and Shavell 2002, pp. 431–34). In practice, however, much of traditional law and economics posits a relatively narrow set of ends that individuals are imagined to pursue.

Contrary to this conventional approach, bounded self-interest within behavioral economics emphasizes that many people care about both giving and receiving fair treatment in a range of settings (Rabin 1993). As Thaler and Dawes (1992, pp. 19–20) observe:

> In the rural areas around Ithaca it is common for farmers to put some fresh produce on a table by the road. There is a cash box on the table, and customers are expected to put money in the box in return for the vegetables they take. The box has just a small slit, so money can only be put in, not taken out. Also, the box is attached to the table, so no one can (easily) make off with the money. We think that the farmers

who use this system have just about the right model of human nature. They feel
that enough people will volunteer to pay for the fresh corn to make it worthwhile
to put it out there.

Of course, a central question raised by bounded self-interest is what counts as
"fair" treatment. Behavioral economics suggests that people will judge outcomes
as unfair if they depart substantially from the terms of a "reference transaction"—a
transaction that defines the benchmark for the parties' interactions (Kahneman et al.
1986a). In the basic version of the well-known ultimatum game, for instance, where
parties divide a sum of money with no reason to think one party is particularly
more deserving than the other, the "reference transaction" is something like an
equal split; substantial departures from this benchmark are viewed as unfair and,
accordingly, are punished by parties who receive offers of such treatment (Güth et al.
1982; Kahneman et al. 1986b). Section 4.5, below, illustrates how this conception
of bounded self-interest has been applied within behavioral law and economics.

4.4 ILLUSTRATIVE APPLICATIONS OF BEHAVIORAL LAW AND ECONOMICS

The present section offers a set of illustrative applications of behavioral law and
economics. The discussion seeks to illustrate what has become essentially "normal
science" within the literature in behavioral law and economics to date: identification
of a departure from unbounded rationality, willpower or self-interest, followed by
either an account of existing law or a proposed legal reform that takes as a fixed
point the identified departure from unbounded rationality, willpower or self-interest.
Section 4.5 shifts the focus to a new approach within behavioral law and economics,
one that emphasizes the potential for responding to some bounds on human behavior
not by taking people's natural tendencies as given and shaping law around them
but, instead, by attempting to reduce or eliminate such human tendencies *through
the legal structure*—the approach of "debiasing through law" (Jolls and Sunstein
2006a).

Recent surveys on behavioral law and economics by Guthrie (2003), Korobkin
(2003), and Rachlinski (2003) have examined existing legally oriented work on
bounded rationality, devoting extensive attention to both judgment errors and departures from expected utility theory.[6] The present section, by contrast, focuses on a
limited number of applications of bounded rationality, willpower and self-interest,
attempting to give a fuller picture of some of the relevant work in these areas.

---

[6]While work on bounded willpower and bounded self-interest within behavioral law and economics
has not recently been surveyed, examples of behavioral law and economics work on bounded willpower
include Weiss (1991), Jolls (1997), and Camerer et al. (2003), and examples of behavioral law and
economics work on bounded self-interest include Jolls (2002) and Bar-Gill and Ben-Shahar (2004).

4.4.1 *"Distributive Legal Rules"* [7]

As noted in Section 4.1, above, one distinctive feature of law and economics is its frequent focus on wealth maximization—giving legal entitlements to those most willing to pay for them, without regard for distributional considerations—rather than social welfare maximization as the criterion for normative analysis. Many law and economics scholars object to "distributive legal rules"—non-wealth-maximizing legal rules chosen for their distributive consequences—because they believe that distributional issues are best left solely to the tax system (Kaplow and Shavell 1994).

A leading law and economics argument in favor of addressing distributional issues through the tax system rather than through nontax legal rules is the argument that any desired distributional consequence can be achieved at lower cost through the tax system than through distributive legal rules. Of course, pursuit of distributional objectives through the tax system is not costless; higher taxes on the wealthy will tend to distort work incentives. But under traditional economic assumptions precisely the same is true of distributive legal rules: "[U]sing legal rules to redistribute income distorts work incentives fully as much as the income tax system—because the distortion is caused by the redistribution itself..." (Kaplow and Shavell 1994, pp. 667–68). Thus, for example, under traditional economic analysis a 30% marginal tax rate, together with a non-wealth-maximizing legal rule that transfers an average of 1% of high earners' income to the poor, creates the same distortion in work incentives as a 31% marginal tax rate coupled with a wealth-maximizing legal rule. However, the former regime also entails costs due to the non-wealth-maximizing legal rule. (For instance, under a distributive legal rule governing accidents, potential defendants may be excessively cautious and thus may be discouraged from engaging in socially valuable activities.) Thus, whatever the desired distributive consequences, under traditional economic analysis they can always be achieved at lower cost by choosing the wealth-maximizing legal rule and adjusting distributive effects through the tax system than by choosing a non-wealth-maximizing rule because of its distributive properties (Shavell 1981).

A basic premise about human behavior underlies this analysis. Work incentives are assumed to be distorted by the same amount as a result of a probabilistic, nontax mode of redistribution, such as the law governing accidents, as they are as a result of a tax. Thus, for example, if high-income individuals face a 0.02 probability of incurring tort liability for an accident, then a distributive legal rule that imposes $500,000 extra in damages (beyond what a wealth-maximizing rule would call for)

---

[7]This subsection is an abridged version of Jolls (1998).

would distort work incentives by the same amount as a tax of $10,000, assuming risk-neutrality.[8]

Why would distributive tort liability and taxes have the same effects on work incentives? "[W]hen an individual... contemplates earning additional income by working harder, his total marginal expected payments [out of that income] equal the sum of his marginal tax payment and the expected marginal cost on account of accidents" (Kaplow and Shavell 1994, p. 671).

The expected costs of the two forms of redistribution are the same, and thus behavior is affected in the same way. At least that is the assumption that traditional economic analysis makes.

Is this assumption valid? From a behavioral economics perspective, it is not clear that an individual would typically experience the same disincentive to work as a result of a more generous (to victims) tort-law regime as would be experienced as a result of a higher level of taxation.[9] The discussion here will highlight one important reason, related to the phenomenon of optimism bias noted in Section 4.3, above, that behavioral law and economics suggests work incentives may be distorted less by distributive tort liability—which operates probabilistically rather than deterministically—than by taxes. Other reasons for different effects of the two regimes, based on different contextual factors across the regimes, are discussed in Jolls (1998).

As just noted, a salient feature of distributive tort liability is the uncertainty of its application to any given actor. The effect of such liability "tends to be limited to those few who become parties to lawsuits" (Kaplow and Shavell 1994, p. 675). While one knows that one will have to pay taxes every year, one knows that one is quite likely not to become involved in an accident. To be sure, the possibility of uncertain or randomized taxation has received some discussion in the public finance literature. Even supporters of this approach, however, suggest that it is unrealistic from a practical perspective (Stiglitz 1987, pp. 1012–13).

Bounded rationality in the form of optimism bias—the tendency to think negative events are less likely to happen to oneself than they actually are—suggests that uncertain events are often processed systematically differently from certain events. Section 4.3.1.1 above referred to the general body of evidence suggesting the prevalence of optimism bias; there are also empirical studies suggesting that people offer unrealistically optimistic assessments in areas directly related to the effects of distributive tort liability. For instance, most people think that they are less likely than

---

[8]Of course, risk-averse actors may choose to purchase insurance against tort liability; see Jolls (1998) for a discussion of the role of insurance in this analysis.

[9]However, as emphasized in Jolls (1998), only empirical evidence that we do not yet have can definitively resolve the question.

the average person to be sued (Weinstein 1980, p. 810). Likewise, people think that they are less likely than the average person to cause an auto accident (Svenson et al. 1985; DeJoy 1989). They also think that their own probability of being caught and penalized for drunk driving is lower than the average driver's probability of being apprehended for such behavior (Guppy 1993).

What does optimism bias with respect to the probability of the negative event of tort liability imply for the distortionary effects of distributive tort liability as opposed to taxes? People will tend to underestimate the probability that they will be hit with liability under distributive tort liability; therefore, their perceived cost of the rule will be lower. As a result, their work incentives will tend to suffer a lesser degree of distortion than under a tax yielding the same amount of revenue for the government. For instance, in the numerical example from above, risk-neutral individuals may not attach an expected cost of $10,000 to a 0.02 (objective) probability of having to pay $500,000 extra in damages under distributive tort liability; they may tend to underestimate the probability that they will incur liability—and thus they may tend to underestimate the expected cost of liability—as a result of optimism bias.[10]

Of course, optimism bias is not the only phenomenon that affects how people assess the likelihood of uncertain events. In some cases people may tend to overestimate rather than underestimate the probability of a negative event because the risk in question is highly salient or otherwise available to them—for instance, contamination from a hazardous waste dump (Kuran and Sunstein 1999, pp. 691–97). However, the overestimation phenomenon seems relatively unlikely to affect the assessment of distributive tort liability, at least insofar as individuals rather than firms are concerned. Consider, for instance, the quintessential event that can expose an individual to tort liability: the auto accident. As noted above, people appear to underestimate the probability that they will be involved in an auto accident (relative to the actual probability); this presumably results from a combination of underestimation of the general probability of an accident (Lichtenstein et al. 1978, p. 564) and further underestimation of people's own probability relative to the average person's (Svenson et al. 1985; DeJoy 1989). The situation would probably be different, of course, for an event such as contamination from a hazardous

---

[10]Note that underestimation of the probability of liability would affect not only the distortion of work incentives from a distributive (and thus, by the definition given above, non-wealth-maximizing) legal rule, but also the determination of what the wealth-maximizing legal rule would be. If potential tortfeasors underestimate the probability of liability, then optimal deterrence would require greater generosity to tort victims than the wealth-maximizing legal rule without underestimation of probabilities would involve. But the newly generous rule would not be "distributive" in the relevant sense, since it would not be sacrificing wealth maximization to achieve distributive goals. The focus of the present discussion, as stated above, is on legal rules that pursue distributive consequences at the expense of wealth maximization.

waste dump, the probability of which might be overestimated due to its availability; but highly available events tend to involve firm, not individual, liability.
It is difficult to come up with examples of events giving rise to individual liability the probability of which is likely to be overestimated rather than (as suggested
above) underestimated. And with underestimation of the probability of liability,
work incentives will typically be distorted less by distributive legal rules than by
taxes.

4.4.2 Discovery Rules in Litigation

Section 4.1, above, noted that an important aspect of work in law and economics
is analysis of various areas of law that were not previously studied by economists.
One such area concerns the rules governing the litigation process. When someone
believes that a law has been violated, how does the legal system go about deciding
the legitimacy of that claim? The U.S. system relies centrally upon an adversary
approach, under which competing sides are represented by legal counsel who argue
in favor of their respective positions.

Of course, maximally effective advocacy for a position often requires one to
obtain information under the control of one's opponent, and thus the U.S. legal
system contains a set of rules governing when and how one side in a legal dispute
may obtain ("discover") information from the other side. Since 1993 these rules
have required opposing parties to disclose significant information even without a
request by the other party (Issacharoff and Loewenstein 1995). Under conventional
economic analysis this approach should tend to increase the convergence of parties'
expectations and, thus, the rate at which they settle disputes out of court (e.g., Shavell
2004, p. 427).

The phenomenon of self-serving bias described in Section 4.3.1.1, above, however, suggests that individuals often interpret information differently depending on
the direction of their own self-interest. Experimental work by Loewenstein et al.
(1993), Babcock et al. (1995), and Loewenstein and Moore (2004) has examined
self-serving bias in the specific context of litigation. In the first paper in the series,
Loewenstein et al. found that parties assigned to the role of plaintiff or defendant
interpreted the very same facts differently depending on their assigned role; subjects assigned to the plaintiff role offered higher estimates of the likely outcome at
trial than subjects assigned to the defendant role even though they both received
identical information about the case. Moreover, the authors found that subjects who
exhibited the highest levels of self-serving bias were also least likely to succeed in
negotiating out-of-court settlements. This work provided opening evidence of the
role of self-serving bias in shaping the effect of information disclosure on the rate
at which legal disputes are settled.

The initial study just described could not rule out the possibility that the relationship between the degree of self-serving bias and the frequency of settlement was non-causal, for it is possible that an unmeasured factor influenced both the degree of self-serving bias and the frequency of settlement. In a follow-up study, however, Babcock et al. (1995) provided strong evidence that the relationship was in fact causal. They found that parties who were not informed of their roles until after reading case materials and offering their estimates of the likely outcome at trial both failed to exhibit statistically significant degrees of self-serving bias *and* settled at significantly greater rates than parties who were informed of their roles before reading the case materials. The timing of exposure to the case materials matters because "[s]elf-serving interpretations are likely to occur at the point when information about roles is assimilated," for the simple reason that it "is easier to process information in a biased way than it is to change an unbiased estimate once it has been made" (Babcock et al. 1995, p. 1339). The recent study by Loewenstein and Moore (2004) underlines the fact that self-serving bias will operate when there is some degree of ambiguity about the proper or best interpretation of a set of information, as will frequently be the case in litigation.

The prospect that litigants will interpret at least some information in a self-serving fashion means that the exchange of information in litigation may cause a divergence rather than convergence of parties' expectations. Relying in part on this argument, Issacharoff and Loewenstein (1995) suggest that mandatory disclosure rules in litigation may be undesirable. As they describe, self-serving bias undermines the conventional wisdom that "a full exchange of the information in the possession of the parties is likely to facilitate settlement by enabling each party to form a more accurate, and generally therefore a more convergent, estimate of the likely outcome of the case" (Posner 1992, p. 557; quoted in Issacharoff and Loewenstein 1995, p. 773).

Consistent with Issacharoff and Loewenstein's argument, a set of amendments in 2000 significantly cut back—although they did not completely eliminate—the mandatory disclosure rules noted above (192 Federal Rules Decisions 340, p. 385).

4.4.3 The "Business Judgment" Rule in Corporate Law

The third distinctive feature of law and economics discussed in Section 4.1, above, concerned the field's interest in explaining and predicting the content of law—what the law allows and what it prohibits. Law and economics has emphasized the idea that laws may be efficient solutions to the problems of organizing society; it has also emphasized—as has the field of political economy—that laws may come about because of the rent-seeking activities of politically powerful actors (Stigler 1971).

131

Behavioral law and economics has extended this conventional account of the content of legal rules in two important ways. The first, which is the focus of the discussion in this subsection, is that in many cases incorporation of insights about bounded rationality, willpower and self-interest is needed for a satisfactory understanding of law's efficiency properties. A law may be efficient in part because of the way in which it accounts for one of the three bounds on human behavior, as the discussion below illustrates. The second extension of the conventional law and economics account of the content of law is the expansion of behavioral law and economics beyond the two familiar categories from the traditional account—the category of law-as-efficiency-enhancing and the category of law-as-the-product-of-conventional-rent-seeking. Section 4.4.5 discusses and illustrates this second extension developed by behavioral law and economics.

A prominent behavioral law and economics work seeking to understand and explain the efficiency of the content of law is Rachlinski (1998). Rachlinski examines a number of areas of law, including corporate law. A central rule of U.S. corporate law is the "business judgment" rule, according to which corporate officers and directors who are informed about a corporation's activities and who approve or acquiesce in these activities have generally fulfilled their duties to the corporation as long as they have a rational belief that such activities are in the interests of the corporation. This highly deferential standard of liability makes it difficult to find legal fault for the decisions of corporate officers and directors.

Rachlinski suggests that the business judgment rule may be corporate law's sensible response to the problem of hindsight bias. As described above, hindsight bias suggests that the sorts of decisions routinely made by the legal system, adjudicating likelihoods and foreseeability after a negative event has materialized, will often be biased toward excessively high estimates—and thus in favor of holding actors responsible—simply because the negative event materialized. But under the business judgment rule, officers and directors will not be held liable for decisions that turn out badly—"even if these decisions seem negligent in hindsight" (Rachlinski 1998, p. 620). Hindsight bias suggests that things will often seem negligent in hindsight, once a negative outcome has materialized and is known, so the business judgment rule insulates officers and directors from the risk of such hindsight-influenced liability determinations. In the absence of the business judgment rule, Rachlinski argues, officers and directors would fail to make the risk-neutral business decisions desired by investors who can limit their overall investment risk through diversification; "[e]nsuring that managers effectively represent this concern and do not avoid business decisions that have a high expected payoff but also carry a high degree of risk is a central problem of corporate governance" (Rachlinski 1998, p. 622). In this respect, hindsight bias can help to explain the efficiency of the content of law governing corporate officers and directors.

4.4.4 *Rules Governing Contract Renegotiation* [11]

The behavioral law and economics applications discussed thus far have involved bounded rationality, but other applications have drawn on the other two bounds on human behavior. This subsection describes an application of the concept of bounded willpower within behavioral law and economics.

As discussed above, an individual with bounded willpower will often have difficulty sticking to even the best-laid plans. With respect to decisions about consumption versus saving, for instance, individuals who earnestly plan to save a substantial amount of next year's salary for retirement may tend, once next year arrives, to save far less than planned. If the failure to stick to the initial plan is understood in advance, then individuals may seek to precommit themselves to their initial plan. An obvious potential means of achieving such precommitment is a contract between the individual suffering from bounded willpower and a bank or other savings institution; but the efficacy of this approach from the standpoint of the individual at the time of contemplating such a contract depends critically on whether contracts are, or can be made, nonrenegotiable. Down the road it will always be in the parties' mutual interest to renegotiate the initial contract, for at later points the individual will be better off if the individual can consume more and save less than the amount the original contract called for, and thus at that point there is a surplus from renegotiation to be divided between the parties. Only if renegotiation is impossible can the parties avoid the effects of bounded willpower and achieve commitment to the initial plan.

The obvious question is then whether contract law allows nonrenegotiable contracts. Certainly the default rule of contract law is that renegotiated agreements are enforceable. The primary exception to enforcement of such agreements concerns renegotiated agreements coerced by one party's threat to breach the original contract if renegotiation does not occur. [12] But in the model discussed here, renegotiation is truly welfare-enhancing—at the time at which it occurs—for both parties relative to the original contract, so the coercion concern does not apply, and thus the default rule would allow enforcement of the renegotiated agreement.

---

[11] This subsection is an abridged version of Jolls (1997).

[12] As Richard Posner explained in a 1990 judicial opinion: "[T]here is often an interval in the life of a contract during which one party is at the mercy of the other. A may have ordered a machine from B that A wants to place in operation on a given date [and] may have made commitments to his customers that it would be costly to renege on. As the date of scheduled delivery approaches, B may be tempted to demand that A agree to renegotiate the contract price, knowing that A will incur heavy expenses if B fails to deliver on time. A can always refuse to renegotiate, relying instead on his right to sue B for breach of contract if B fails to make delivery by the agreed date. But legal remedies are costly and uncertain." (*United States* v. *Stump Home Specialties Manufacturing, Inc.*, 905 F.2d 1117, pp. 1121–22.)

Does contract law allow the parties to supplement the default rules governing renegotiation with additional terms of their own? Perhaps surprisingly, the answer to this question is generally "no." Justice Cardozo's 1919 opinion in *Beatty* v. *Guggenheim Exploration Co.* provides a classic example of the rule and its underlying rationale:

> Those who make a contract, may unmake it. The clause which forbids a change, may be changed like any other.... 'Every such agreement is ended by the new one which contradicts it.'...What is excluded by one act, is restored by another. You may put it out by the door, it is back through the window. Whenever two men contract, no limitation self-imposed can destroy their power to contract again.
>
> (225 N.Y. 380, pp. 387–88 (citations omitted))

While existing contract law thus prohibits enforcement of contractual agreements not to renegotiate, a natural question is whether a contrary rule would be of any effect. Any clause limiting or prohibiting renegotiation will be effective only if some party to the contract has an incentive to enforce the clause. Jolls (1997) provides discussion of circumstances in which this will be the case. Consistent with the discussion here, the law has started to move away from the formalistic principle described above and in some instances now permits parties by contract to remove their future power to renegotiate their original contract *orally* (although written renegotiated agreements are still generally enforceable) (Uniform Commercial Code sec. 2-209).

4.4.5 *The Content of Consumer Protection Law* [13]

A final illustration of behavioral law and economics reveals the way that work in this area has expanded upon the traditional law and economics notion that law's content reflects either efficiency or conventional rent-seeking. The notion that laws emerge from these two considerations would probably strike most citizens as odd. Instead, most members of society—which is to say most of the people who are entitled to elect legislators—believe that the primary purpose of the law is to codify "right" and "wrong." Can this idea be formalized, drawing in part on the notion of bounded self-interest from Section 4.3.3 above?

Consider the case of consumer protection law, which imposes bans on certain market transactions including (in many jurisdictions) "usurious" lending and some forms of price gouging (see, e.g., Uniform Consumer Credit Code sec. 2.201). What accounts for these laws, which impose constraints on gain-producing transactions for ordinary commodities such as television sets and lumber? The bans seem difficult to justify on efficiency grounds; rules prohibiting mutually beneficial exchanges

---

[13]This subsection is an abridged version of Section III of Jolls et al. (1998).

without obvious externalities are not generally thought to have a large claim to efficiency. The laws also do not generally seem well explained in terms of conventional rent seeking by a politically powerful faction.[14]

By contrast, laws banning usurious lending and price gouging when such activities are prevalent are a straightforward prediction of the theory of bounded self-interest described above. (The analysis here assumes that self-interested legislators are responsive to citizens' or other actors' fairness-based demands for the content of law.[15]) In the case of such bans, the transaction in question is a significant departure from the usual terms of trade in the market for the good in question—that is, a significant departure from the "reference transaction." The account above of bounded self-interest suggests that if trades are occurring frequently in a given jurisdiction at terms far from those of the reference transaction, there will be strong pressure for a law banning such trades. Note that the prediction is not that all high prices (ones that make it difficult or impossible for some people to afford things they might want) will be banned; the prediction is that transactions at terms far from the terms on which those transactions generally occur in the marketplace will be banned.

Consider this example:

> A store has been sold out of the popular Cabbage Patch dolls for a month. A week before Christmas a single doll is discovered in a store room. The managers know that many customers would like to buy the doll. They announce over the store's public address system that the doll will be sold by auction to the customer who offers to pay the most.
>
> Kahneman et al. (1986a, p. 735)

Nearly three-quarters of the respondents judged this action to be either somewhat unfair or very unfair, though, of course, an economic analysis would judge the auction the most efficient method of assuring that the doll goes to the person who

---

[14]Although it may be possible to offer efficiency or conventional rent-seeking explanations for certain sorts of laws banning economic transactions (Posner 1995), there does not seem to be a general theory or set of theories that can explain all or even most of these laws on traditional grounds.

[15]Thus, like traditional economic analysis, the behavioral law and economics approach described here views legislators as maximizers interested in their own reelection; legislators interested in their own reelection will be responsive to the preferences and judgments of their constituents and those of powerful interest groups. If constituents believe that a certain practice is unfair, and should be banned, self-interested legislators will respond, even if they do not share these views. Likewise, if a mobilized group holds such views, then legislators' response will be affected, in much the same way as if the group sought legislation to serve a narrowly defined financial self-interest, as posited by the traditional economic account. "Fairness entrepreneurs" may play a role, mobilizing public judgments to serve their (selfish or nonselfish) interests. Of course, it is also possible that legislators themselves act on their own personal conceptions of fairness.

values it most. Although the auction is efficient, it represents a departure from the "reference transaction," under which the doll is sold at its usual price.

As in the doll example, if money is loaned to individuals at a rate of interest significantly greater than the rate at which similarly sized loans are made to other customers, then the lender's behavior may be viewed as unfair. Likewise, because lumber generally tends to sell for a particular price, sales at far higher prices in the wake of (say) a hurricane, which drives demand sky high, are thought unfair. How then should popular items be rationed? Subjects in one study asked whether a football team should allocate its few remaining tickets to a key game through an auction thought that this approach would be unfair, while allocation based on who waited in line longest was the preferred solution (Kahneman et al. 1986b, pp. S287–88). Of course, waiting in line for scarce goods is precisely what happens with laws against price gouging. Thus, pervasive fairness norms appear to shape attitudes (and hence possibly law) on both usury and price gouging. While "[c]onventional economic analyses assume as a matter of course that excess demand for a good creates an opportunity for suppliers to raise prices" and that "[t]he profit-seeking adjustments that clear the market are... as natural as water finding its level—and as ethically neutral," "[t]he lay public does not share this indifference" (Kahneman et al. 1986a, p. 735).

Note that the behavioral law and economics analysis does not imply that these views of fairness are necessarily rational or compelling. Many of those who think "usurious" lenders are "unfair" might not have thought through the implications of their views (for example, that paying an outrageous price for a loan may be better than paying an infinite price, or that a loan to a riskier borrower is a product different in kind from a loan to a safer borrower). Still, if such views are widespread, they may underlie certain patterns in the content of law, such as the legal restrictions on usury and price gouging. The claim here is a positive one about the content of the law we observe, not a prescriptive or normative one about the shape practices or rules should take. As a positive matter, behavioral law and economics predicts that if trades are occurring with some frequency on terms far from those of the reference transaction, then legal rules will often ban trades on such terms.

Of course, further inquiry would be needed to offer a definitive explanation for the full pattern of usury and price gouging laws we observe. Usury seems to be broadly prohibited, so one is not faced with the question of why we observe bans in some states but not others. The same cannot be said of price gouging, which is prohibited only in certain states. Price gouging appears to be prohibited primarily by states that have recently experienced (or whose neighbors have recently experienced) natural disasters; but more in-depth research would be required to determine if this pattern comprehensively bears out.

4.5 Debiasing through Law

The applications described in Section 4.4 illustrate the usual approach in behavioral law and economics work to date: the analysis identifies a departure from unbounded rationality, willpower or self-interest and then offers either a proposed legal reform or an account of existing law that takes as a fixed point the identified departure from unbounded rationality, willpower or self-interest. This approach might be said to focus on designing legal rules and institutions so that legal outcomes do not fall prey to problems of bounded rationality, willpower or self-interest—a strategy of *insulation* of those outcomes from such bounds on human behavior.

A quite different possibility, focused most heavily on the case of judgment errors by boundedly rational actors, is that legal policy may respond best to such errors not by structuring rules and institutions to protect legal outcomes from the effects of the errors (which themselves are taken as a given), but instead by operating directly on the errors and attempting to help people either to reduce or to eliminate them. Legal policy in this category may be termed "debiasing through law"; the law is used to reduce the degree of biased behavior actors exhibit (Jolls and Sunstein 2006a). The primary emphasis is on judgment errors rather than either other aspects of bounded rationality or bounded willpower or self-interest, for the simple reason that those alternative forms of human behavior cannot uncontroversially be viewed as "biases" in need of debiasing. (Recall, for instance, the normative complexities discussed above in connection with both the endowment effect and bounded willpower. And clearly it would not generally be desirable to "debias" boundedly self-interested actors.) As described below, the basic promise of strategies for debiasing through law is that these strategies will often provide a middle ground between unyielding adherence to the assumptions of traditional economics, on the one hand, and the usual behavioral law and economics approach of accepting departures from those assumptions as a given, on the other.

4.5.1 *Debiasing through Substantive and Procedural Law*

The idea of debiasing through law draws on a substantial existing psychology literature on the debiasing of individuals after a demonstration of the existence of a given judgment error (e.g., Fischhoff 1982; Weinstein and Klein 2002). Those who have investigated debiasing in experimental settings, however, have generally not explored the possibility of achieving debiasing through law. A few behavioral law and economics papers have examined the possibility of debiasing through the procedural rules governing adjudication by judges or juries; a well-known example builds on the studies described in Section 4.4.2, above, of self-serving bias in litigation and shows how requiring litigants to consider reasons the adjudicator might rule against them eliminates their self-serving bias (Babcock et al. 1997). However, the potential promise of debiasing through law is far broader, for it is not only the procedures by which law is applied in adjudicative settings but the actual substance of law that may be employed to achieve debiasing.

Consider an example of debiasing through law developed by Jolls (forthcoming), drawing on the work on implicit racial or other group-based bias described in Section 4.3.1.1, above. Might substantive rules governing employment discrimination play a role in debiasing individuals who exhibit such bias? Empirical studies suggest that implicit racial or other group-based bias is profoundly influenced by environmental stimuli. Individuals who view pictures of Tiger Woods and Timothy McVeigh before submitting to testing of implicit racial bias, for example, exhibit substantially less bias than individuals not exposed to the pictures of Woods and McVeigh (Dasgupta and Greenwald 2001). This study and, more broadly, the large social science literature on debiasing in response to implicit racial or other group-based bias (e.g., Macrae et al. 1995; Dasgupta and Asgari 2004) have an intriguing practical counterpart in the ongoing controversies at many universities and the U.S. Capitol over the frequent pattern of largely or exclusively white, male portraits adorning classrooms and ceremonial spaces (Gewertz 2003; Stolberg 2003). In the employment context, it may not be irrelevant to the degree of implicit racial or other group-based bias found in employment decision makers whether, for instance, the walls of the workplace feature sexually explicit depictions of women—the source of frequent sexual harassment lawsuits—or instead feature more positive, affirming images of women. Employment discrimination law's policing of what can and cannot be featured in the workplace environment, described in detail in Jolls (forthcoming), is thus an illustration of debiasing through substantive law.

It is important to emphasize the limits of the domain of this analysis of employment discrimination law as a mechanism for achieving "debiasing" in the sense in which the term is used here. In some cases racial or other group-based bias may reflect genuine tastes rather than, as discussed above, a divergence of implicit attitudes and behavior from non-discriminatory tastes. Of course, the features of employment discrimination law just referenced might still be desirable, and would certainly remain applicable, in the case of consciously discriminatory tastes, but they would no longer illustrate a form of debiasing through law in the sense used here because no form of judgment error would be under correction in the first place.[16]

4.5.2 General Typology of Strategies for Debiasing through Law

The example of debiasing through employment discrimination law and the earlier example from Babcock, Issacharoff and Loewenstein's work of debiasing

---

[16]For further discussion of normative issues in debiasing through law, see Jolls and Sunstein (2006b).

		Type of law	
		Procedural rules governing the adjudicative process	Substantive rules regulating actions taken outside of the adjudicative process
Role of actor	Debiasing actors in their capacity as participants in the adjudicative process	Debiasing through procedural rules	"Hybrid" debiasing
	Debiasing actors in their capacity as decision makers outside of the adjudicative process		Debiasing through substantive law

Figure 4.1. Typology of strategies for debiasing through law.

through restructuring the adjudicative process together illustrate the basic distinction between debiasing through substantive law and debiasing through procedural rules. Figure 4.1 generalizes the point by mapping the terrain of strategies for debiasing through law more fully. The column division marks the line between procedural rules governing the adjudicative process and substantive rules regulating actions taken outside of the adjudicative process. The row division marks the line between debiasing actors in their capacity as participants in the adjudicative process and debiasing actors in their capacity as decision makers outside of the adjudicative process. The upper-left box in this matrix represents the type of debiasing through law on which the prior work on such debiasing has focused: the rules in question are procedural rules governing the adjudicative process, and the actors targeted are individuals in their capacity as participants in the adjudicative process (Babcock et al. 1997; Peters 1999).

Moving counterclockwise, the lower-left box in the matrix is marked with an "X" because procedural rules governing the adjudicative process do not have any obvious role in debiasing actors outside of the adjudicative process—although these rules certainly may affect such actors' behavior in various ways by influencing what would happen in the event of future litigation. The lower-right box in the matrix represents the category of debiasing through law emphasized in Jolls (forthcoming) and Jolls and Sunstein (2006a,b): the rules in question are substantive rules regulating actions taken outside of the adjudicative process, and the actors targeted are decision makers outside of the adjudicative process.

Finally, the upper-right corner of the matrix represents a hybrid category that warrants brief discussion, in part to demarcate it from the category (just discussed) of debiasing through substantive law. In this hybrid category, it is substantive, rather than procedural, law that is structured to achieve debiasing, but the judgment error that this debiasing effort targets is one that arises within, rather than outside of, the adjudicative process. For example, Farnsworth's (2003) work on self-serving bias suggests that such bias on the part of employment discrimination litigants (actors in their capacity as participants in an adjudicative process) might be reduced by restructuring employment discrimination standards (substantive rules regulating action outside of the adjudicative process) to increase the reliance of such standards on objective facts as opposed to subjective or normative judgments. This type of debiasing through law operates through reform of substantive law rather than procedural rules, but the actions to be debiased are those of litigants within the adjudicative process. In the case of debiasing through substantive law, by contrast, both the legal rules through which debiasing occurs and the capacities in which actors are targeted for debiasing are distinct from the context of the adjudicative process.

4.6 Conclusion

In Richard Thaler's view, the ultimate sign of success for behavioral economics will be that what is now behavioral economics will become simply "economics." The same observation applies to behavioral law and economics. Debiasing through law, discussed in Section 4.5, may hasten the speed at which this transition occurs by pointing to a wide range of possibilities for recognizing human limitations while at the same time avoiding the step of paternalistically removing choices from people's hands (Jolls and Sunstein 2006a). Because debiasing through law cannot be applied in every context, however, future work in behavioral law and economics should also seek to refine and strengthen analyses concerned with structuring legal rules in light of the remaining (post-debiasing) departures from traditional economic assumptions of unbounded rationality, willpower and self-interest.

References

Acemoglu, D., and J. D. Angrist. 2001. Consequences of employment protection? The case of the Americans with Disabilities Act. *Journal of Political Economy* 109:915–57.

Allais, M. 1952. *Fondements d'une Théorie Positive des Choix Comportant un Risque et Critique des Postulats et Axiomes de L'Ecole Americaine*. (Translated and edited by M. Allais and O. Hagen, 1979, as "The foundations of a positive theory of choice involving risk and a criticism of the postulates and axioms of the American school." In *Expected Utility Hypotheses and the Allais Paradox: Contemporary Discussions of Decisions Under Uncertainty*, pp. 27–145, with Allais's Rejoinder. Dordrecht: Reidel.)

Arkes, H. R., D. Faust, T. J. Guilmette, and K. Hart. 1988. Eliminating the hindsight bias. *Journal of Applied Psychology* 73:305–7.

Arnould, R. J., and H. Grabowski. 1981. Auto safety regulation: an analysis of market failure. *Bell Journal of Economics* 12:27–48.

Autor, D. H., and M. G. Duggan. 2003. The rise in the disability rolls and the decline in unemployment. *Quarterly Journal of Economics* 118:157–205.

Babcock, L., G. Loewenstein, S. Issacharoff, and C. Camerer. 1995. Biased judgments of fairness in bargaining. *American Economic Review* 85:1337–43.

Babcock, L., X. Wang, and G. Loewenstein. 1996. Choosing the wrong pond: social comparisons in negotiations that reflect a self-serving bias. *Quarterly Journal of Economics* 111:1–19.

Babcock, L., G. Loewenstein, and S. Issacharoff. 1997. Creating convergence: debiasing biased litigants. *Law and Social Inquiry* 22:913–25.

Bar-Gill, O., and O. Ben-Shahar. 2004. Threatening an "irrational" breach of contract. *Supreme Court Economic Review* 11:143–70.

Camerer, C., S. Issacharoff, G. Loewenstein, T. O'Donoghue, and M. Rabin. 2003. Regulation for conservatives: behavioral economics and the case for "asymmetric paternalism". *University of Pennsylvania Law Review* 151:1211–54.

Camerer, C. F., and H. Kunreuther. 1989. Decision processes for low probability events: policy implications. *Journal of Policy Analysis and Management* 8:565–92.

Coase, R. H. 1960. The problem of social cost. *Journal of Law and Economics* 3:1–44.

Cutler, D. M., and J. Gruber. 1996. Does public insurance crowd out private insurance? *Quarterly Journal of Economics* 111:391–430.

Dasgupta, N., and A. G. Greenwald. 2001. On the malleability of automatic attitudes: combating automatic prejudice with images of admired and disliked individuals. *Journal of Personality and Social Psychology* 81:800–14.

Dasgupta, N., and S. Asgari. 2004. Seeing is believing: exposure to counterstereotypic women leaders and its effect on the malleability of automatic gender stereotypes. *Journal of Experimental Social Psychology* 40:642–58.

DeJoy, D. M. 1989. The optimism bias and traffic accident risk perception. *Accident Analysis and Prevention* 21:333–40.

Donohue III, J. J., and J. Heckman. 1991. Continuous versus episodic change: the impact of civil rights policy on the economic status of blacks. *Journal of Economic Literature* 29:1603–43.

Dovidio, J. F., K. Kawakami, and S. L. Gaertner. 2002. Implicit and explicit prejudice and interracial interaction. *Journal of Personality and Social Psychology* 82:62–68.

Ellsberg, D. 1961. Risk, ambiguity, and the Savage axioms. *Quarterly Journal of Economics* 75:643–69.

Elster, J. 1979. *Ulysses and the Sirens: Studies in Rationality and Irrationality*. Cambridge University Press.

Farnsworth, W. 2003. The legal regulation of self-serving bias. *U.C. Davis Law Review* 37:567–603.

Ferrell, A. 2003. Mandated disclosure and stock returns: evidence from the over-the-counter market. Harvard Law and Economics Discussion Paper 453.

Fischhoff, B. 1982. Debiasing. In *Judgment under Uncertainty: Heuristics and Biases* (ed. D. Kahneman, P. Slovic, and A. Tversky), pp. 422–44. Cambridge University Press.

Gaertner, S. L., and J. P. McLaughlin. 1983. Racial stereotypes: associations and ascriptions of positive and negative characteristics. *Social Psychology Quarterly* 46:23–30.

Gewertz, K. 2003. Adding some color to Harvard portraits. *Harvard University Gazette* (May 1), p. 11.

Gompers, P. A., J. L. Ishii, and A. Metrick. 2003. Corporate governance and equity prices. *Quarterly Journal of Economics* 118:107–55.

Greenstone, M., P. Oyer, and A. Vissing-Jorgensen. 2006. Mandated disclosure, stock returns, and the 1964 Securities Acts Amendments. *Quarterly Journal of Economics* 121:399–460.

Greenwald, A. G., D. E. McGhee, and J. L. K. Schwartz. 1998. Measuring individual differences in implicit cognition: the Implicit Association Test. *Journal of Personality and Social Psychology* 74:1464–80.

Gruber, J. 1994. The incidence of mandated maternity benefits. *American Economic Review* 84:622–41.

Gulati, M., and M. Yelnosky. Forthcoming. *Behavioral Analyses of Workplace Discrimination.* Kluwer Academic.

Guppy, A. 1993. Subjective probability of accident and apprehension in relation to self–other bias, age, and reported behavior. *Accident Analysis and Prevention* 25:375–82.

Güth, W., R. Schmittberger, and B. Schwarze. 1982. An experimental analysis of ultimatum bargaining. *Journal of Economic Behavior and Organization* 3:367–88.

Guthrie, C. 2003. Prospect theory, risk preference, and the law. *Northwestern University Law Review* 97:1115–63.

Heckman, J. J., and B. S. Payner. 1989. Determining the impact of federal antidiscrimination policy on the economic status of blacks: a study of South Carolina. *American Economic Review* 79:138–77.

Hoffman, E., and M. L. Spitzer. 1982. The Coase Theorem: some experimental tests. *Journal of Law and Economics* 25:73–98.

——. 1986. Experimental tests of the Coase Theorem with large bargaining groups. *Journal of Legal Studies* 15:149–71.

Issacharoff, S., and G. Loewenstein. 1995. Unintended consequences of mandatory disclosure. *Texas Law Review* 73:753–86.

Jolls, C. 1997. Contracts as bilateral commitments: a new perspective on contract modification. *Journal of Legal Studies* 26:203–37.

——. 1998. Behavioral economics analysis of redistributive legal rules. *Vanderbilt Law Review* 51:1653–77.

——. 2002. Fairness, minimum wage law, and employee benefits. *New York University Law Review* 77:47–70.

——. 2004. Identifying the effects of the Americans with Disabilities Act using state-law variation: preliminary evidence on educational participation effects. *American Economic Review* 94:447–53.

——. Forthcoming. Antidiscrimination law's effects on implicit bias. In *Behavioral Analyses of Workplace Discrimination* (ed. M. Gulati and M. Yelnosky). Kluwer Academic.

Jolls, C., and C. R. Sunstein. 2006a. Debiasing through law. *Journal of Legal Studies* 35:199–241.

——. 2006b. The law of implicit bias. *California Law Review* 94:969–96.

Jolls, C., C. R. Sunstein, and R. Thaler. 1998. A behavioral approach to law and economics. *Stanford Law Review* 50:1471–1550.

Kahneman, D., and S. Frederick. 2002. Representativeness revisited: attribute substitution in intuitive judgment. In *Heuristics and Biases: The Psychology of Intuitive Judgment* (ed. Th. Gilovich, D. Griffin, and D. Kahneman), pp. 49–81. Cambridge University Press.

Kahneman, D., and A. Tversky. 1979. Prospect theory: an analysis of decision under risk. *Econometrica* 47:263–91.

Kahneman, D., J. L. Knetsch, and R. Thaler. 1986a. Fairness as a constraint on profit seeking: entitlements in the market. *American Economic Review* 76:728–41.

——. 1986b. Fairness and the assumptions of economics. *Journal of Business* 59:S285–300.

——. 1990. Experimental tests of the endowment effect and the Coase Theorem. *Journal of Political Economy* 98:1325–48.

Kaplow, L., and S. Shavell. 1994. Why the legal system is less efficient than the income tax in redistributing income. *Journal of Legal Studies* 23:667–81.

——. 2002. *Fairness versus Welfare*. Harvard University Press.

Katz, L. F., and B. D. Meyer. 1990. Unemployment insurance, recall expectations, and unemployment outcomes. *Quarterly Journal of Economics* 105:973–1002.

Kelman, M. 1979. Consumption theory, production theory, and ideology in the Coase Theorem. *Southern California Law Review* 52:669–98.

Korobkin, R. 1998. The status quo bias and contract default rules. *Cornell Law Review* 83:608–87.

——. 2003. The endowment effect and legal analysis. *Northwestern University Law Review* 97:1227–93.

Kuran, T., and C. R. Sunstein. 1999. Availability cascades and risk regulation. *Stanford Law Review* 51:683–768.

Laibson, D. 1997. Golden eggs and hyperbolic discounting. *Quarterly Journal of Economics* 112:443–77.

Lichtenstein, S., P. Slovic, B. Fischhoff, M. Layman, and B. Combs. 1978. Judged frequency of lethal events. *Journal of Experimental Psychology: Human Learning and Memory* 4:551–78.

Loewenstein, G., and D. A. Moore. 2004. When ignorance is bliss: information exchange and inefficiency in bargaining. *Journal of Legal Studies* 33:37–58.

Loewenstein, G., S. Issacharoff, C. Camerer, and L. Babcock. 1993. Self-serving assessments of fairness and pretrial bargaining. *Journal of Legal Studies* 22:135–59.

McConnell, A. R., and J. M. Leibold. 2001. Relations among the implicit association test, discriminatory behavior, and explicit measure of racial attitudes. *Journal of Experimental Social Psychology* 37:435–42.

Macrae, C. N., G. V. Bodenhausen, and A. B. Milne. 1995. The dissection of selection in person perception: inhibitory processes in social stereotyping. *Journal of Personality and Social Psychology* 69:397–407.

Nosek, B. A., M. R. Banaji, and A. G. Greenwald. 2002. Harvesting implicit group attitudes and beliefs from a demonstration website. *Group Dynamics* 6:101–15.

Peters, P. G. 1999. Hindsight bias and tort liability: avoiding premature conclusions. *Arizona State Law Journal* 31:1277–314.

Plott, C. R., and K. Zeiler. 2005. The willingness to pay–willingness to accept gap, "endowment effect," subject misconceptions, and experimental procedures for eliciting valuations. *American Economic Review* 95:530–45.

Posner, E. A. 1995. Contract law in the welfare state: a defense of the unconscionability doctrine, usury laws, and related limitations on the freedom to contract. *Journal of Legal Studies* 24:283–319.

Posner, R. A. 1979. Utilitarianism, economics, and legal theory. *Journal of Legal Studies* 8:103–40.

———. 1989. An economic analysis of sex discrimination laws. *University of Chicago Law Review* 56:1311–35.

———. 1992. *Economic Analysis of Law*, 4th edn. Boston, MA: Little Brown.

Rabin, M. 1993. Incorporating fairness into game theory and economics. *American Economic Review* 83:1281–1302.

Rachlinski, J. J. 1998. A positive psychological theory of judging in hindsight. *University of Chicago Law Review* 65:571–625.

———. 2003. The uncertain psychological case for paternalism. *Northwestern University Law Review* 97:1165–225.

Schelling, T. C. 1984. The intimate contest for self-command. In *Choice and Consequence*. Harvard University Press.

Schwab, S. 1988. A Coasean experiment on contract presumptions. *Journal of Legal Studies* 17:237–68.

Shavell, S. 1981. A note on efficiency vs. distributional equity in legal rulemaking: should distributional equity matter given optimal income taxation? *American Economic Review* 71:414–18.

———. 2004. *Foundations of Economic Analysis of Law*. Cambridge, MA: Belknap Press of Harvard University Press.

Stigler, G. J. 1971. The theory of economic regulation. *Bell Journal of Economics and Management Science* 2:3–21.

Stiglitz, J. E. 1987. Pareto efficient and optimal taxation and the new new welfare economics. In *Handbook of Public Economics* (ed. A. J. Auerbach and M. Feldstein), Volume 2, pp. 991–1042. New York: North-Holland.

Stolberg, S. G. 2003. Face value at the Capitol: Senator wants to "promote some diversity" in congressional artwork. *New York Times*, August 13, Late edn, Section E1, p. 1, col. 2.

Strotz, R. H. 1955/56. Myopia and inconsistency in dynamic utility maximization. *Review of Economic Studies* 23:165–80.

Sunstein, C. R., and R. H. Thaler. 2003. Libertarian paternalism is not an oxymoron. *University of Chicago Law Review* 70:1159–1202.

Svenson, O., B. Fischhoff, and D. MacGregor. 1985. Perceived driving safety and seatbelt usage. *Accident Analysis and Prevention* 17:119–33.

Thaler, R. H. 1980. Toward a positive theory of consumer choice. *Journal of Economic Behavior and Organization* 1:39–60.

———. 1996. Doing economics without *Homo economicus*. In *Foundations of Research in Economics: How Do Economists Do Economics?* (ed. S. G. Medema and W. J. Samuels), pp. 227–37. Northampton, MA: Edward Elgar.

Thaler, R. H., and R. M. Dawes. 1992. Cooperation. In *The Winner's Curse: Paradoxes and Anomalies of Economic Life* (ed. R. H. Thaler), pp. 6–20. Princeton University Press.

Tversky, A., and D. Kahneman. 1973. Availability: a heuristic for judging frequency and probability. *Cognitive Psychology* 5:207–32.

Weinstein, N. D. 1980. Unrealistic optimism about future life events. *Journal of Personality and Social Psychology* 39:806–20.

Weinstein, N. D., and W. M. Klein. 2002. Resistance of personal risk perceptions to debiasing interventions. In *Heuristics and Biases: The Psychology of Intuitive Judgment* (ed. Th. Gilovich, D. Griffin, and D. Kahneman), pp. 313–23. Cambridge University Press.

Weiss, D. M. 1991. Paternalistic pension policy: psychological evidence and economic theory. *University of Chicago Law Review* 58:1275–1319.

COMMENT BY IAN AYRES

This is an excellent paper that is jam-packed with characteristic examples of what has been going on in the field of behavioral law and economics. It also gives insight into Jolls's own approach to this topic, which is natural because she is already such a prominent player in the area.

For the purposes of this comment, I will adopt the role of skeptic to give the reader a taste of the criticisms that are frequently made in law school seminars whenever a behavioral economic analysis is presented. Although Jolls's piece tries to preempt these arguments, it is nevertheless useful to make them explicit.

Before proceeding, however, I wanted to pause to emphasize that this chapter does a very neat thing in connecting two different "bias" literatures. This term is central to the study of bounded rationality and bounded willpower but also to the study of group subordination. By making the link, Professor Jolls forces us to rethink the multiple meanings of bias. Bias does not only mean biased tastes (as in the Beckerian concept of discriminatory preferences) and biased beliefs (as in falsifiably wrong statistical inferences); it can also mean biased associations which are neither tastes nor falsifiable. Keeping track of the type of bias is crucially important in normative analysis, because it is not clear whether education can cure biased association, even though there is at least the hope that it might cure falsifiably wrong beliefs.

For example, in recent research I found that passengers in New Haven tipped black cab drivers approximately one third less than they did white drivers. A substantial portion of this shortfall was caused by passengers' heightened chance of leaving no tip when driving with black drivers, but another portion of the shortfall had a more subtle cause: passengers who rounded their total payment (fare plus tip) to an integer dollar amount were more likely to round up when driving with a white driver and to round down when driving with a black driver. To me, this rounding result may be a close analogue to an Implicit Association Test (IAT) moment. Imagine that just before your cab comes to a stop the fare clicks over to $7. Think fast.

145

What to do you do? Do you leave $8 or $9? Called upon to make a quick decision, even people who think that they are hard-wired percentage tippers may find that unconscious factors influence this rounding decision. Just as people who confront the IAT sorting game often cannot help but treat blacks and whites differently, people who confront the dichotomous rounding game may have trouble purging the influence of race.

But if this is an IAT moment, it is not clear that educating passengers about the problem of discrimination (and thereby making race more salient) is the way to reduce discrimination. Instead, as Professor Tim Wilson suggests, it might be preferable to prime passengers with a debiasing or reframing cue, possibly by putting a picture of Tiger Woods or Michael Jordan in the cab.

Predicting Behavior

One of the most frequent criticisms of behavioral law and economics is that it predicts too much. Instead of "impossibility" theorems, behavioral law and economics has produced tons of interesting "possibility" theorems. But, as with the Bible, one can find scriptural support for just about any proposition. Now, there are many ways for behavioralists to respond to this criticism. Many behavioralists respond by going on the offensive, arguing that nonbehavioral economics does not do such a good job of predicting behavior either. Professor Jolls does not take this tack. Instead she acknowledges the problem, and argues that a prime value of the behavioral approaches is in simply in destabilizing false consensus for nonbehavioral results, calling for more empirical work.

But Professor Jolls goes further, I think, with her example of redistributive legal rules and suggests that behavioral thinking might at times shift the burden of persuasion to nonbehavioralists. She responds to Kaplow and Shavell's arguments that a redistributive car accident rule will have the same income-distortion effect as an analogous progressive tax, with the insight that optimism bias may keep the rich from reacting to a probabilistic redistribution as severely as to a nonprobabilistic tax ("I won't get in an accident"). At seminars, there is a basically a 100% chance that someone would ask, "But are there other cognitive errors that might cut in the other direction?" But Jolls heads them off at the pass. She acknowledges that an availability heuristic might cut the other way. But she goes on to argue, fairly persuasively, that it is not likely to be as powerful a phenomenon in this specific context.

Predicting Content of Law

I am less convinced by Professor Jolls's discussion of the ability of behavioral law and economics to predict the content of legal rules. First, as a descriptive matter, I do not see very many behavioralist articles trying to predict the content of legal rules. Contra to Jolls, I do not see this as a central goal of the behavioral law and economics movement.

And with good reason: Professor Jolls's description of the new behavioral school project still parallels the largely discredited project of the old Chicago school. The meta argument is this: behavioral law and economics can better identify the things that lawmakers want (efficiency, fairness, etc.); the law tends toward these things; so behavioral law and economics will do a better job of identifying legal rules.

But, while George Priest provided a (nonbehavioral) theory for explaining why common judging tends toward efficiency, there is no behavioral theory suggesting why either the common law or statutes would tend the things (like efficiency or fairness) that legislators want. The same bounded rationality and bounded willpower that distorts private decision-making should also distort the decisions of individual public decision makers.

If behavioral law and economics is going to develop an internally consistent theory for predicting the content of legal rules, it should not be a theory of efficient law or fair law, but a theory of framing distortions and the like that predict systematic deviations from either efficiency or public choice theories of the legal production function.

Harnessing Bias

Professor Jolls is on a much stronger footing when discussing her own project with Cass Sunstein on "debiasing through law." Instead of using law to disable bias, Professor Jolls has creatively imagined pragmatic ways that legal rules could reduce various cognitive biases of private decision makers. An example of the disabling bias approach might be the attempts to keep factoring companies from cashing out future cash flows. Bounded willpower problems make people too willing to sacrifice their future inference, so it may be best to simply disable their decision-making power. But another approach is to use law to reduce the bias itself. You might explain to individuals the intertemporal inconsistency of their hyperbolic preferences as a way to discourage early cashouts.

But there is yet another meta approach with regard to bias. And this is to embrace existing biases and harness them for the public good. Indeed, Professor Jolls's own example of redistributive legal rules can be thought of as an example of harnessing bias instead of an attempt to debias. Redistributing wealth via probabilistic tort liability harnesses optimism bias to reduce the distortionary reactions of the wealthy. (Indeed, Professor Jolls's insight suggests that redistribution advocates might consider other cognitively opaque devices for income distribution, including probabilistic taxes, and ex post insurance premia.)

There are many other examples of this harnessing bias. The tit-for-tat strategy in finitely repeated prisoner's dilemma games can be, from a nonbehavioral perspective, strictly irrational. But from a behavioral perspective the strategy is a natural outgrowth of bounded self-interest. The law might want to assiduously avoid reducing this strategy.

Katharine Baker and I are working on an article that might be seen as trying to economize on the preexisting bias of acquaintance rapists. The same misogynist attitudes that might lead a certain class of man not to pay adequate attention to whether a woman has actually consented to sex might also lead to overestimates of the probability that women will bring unsubstantiated claims of coercion. Baker and I try to exploit this latter bias by creating the possibility of criminal liability for first-encounter sex unless a condom is used. From a behavioral perspective, this law might have the biggest impact on men with the largest misogynist bias.

But as Peter Diamond pointed out in discussion, the legal strategy of exploiting bias needs to be carefully justified on independent grounds. It is a form of paternalism that can be used for good or ill. Yale Law School has a loan forgiveness policy that can reimburse graduates in low-paying jobs for a part of their tuition fees. (Although the program's intent is to promote public interest law, its income-based trigger is economically equivalent to a "money-back guarantee" or "failure insurance." It also has the feature of transforming traditional student loans into Tobin loans where the amount paid becomes a function of future income.) A graduate in a low paying-job can have 100% of her loans reimbursed in as little as ten years, but the bulk of the forgiveness comes in the second half of this period: years six to ten. A normative justification for more strongly weighting the back end is that from a life-cycle perspective graduates who dabble in public interest law for a year or two before going to a lucrative firm job are less deserving of loan forgiveness than those who toil in the fields for several years. But from a behavioral perspective, the program exploits the bias of incoming students, who strongly overestimate the probability that they will dedicate their careers to public service. (This is an optimism bias where they are overly optimistic about earning a lower salary!) Professor Diamond notes that exploiting this bias lets Yale Law School engage in more extreme forms of price discrimination that fly below the students' cognitive radar screens. It may also distort student choice between schools. Ultimately, the strategy may still be justified. But the justification for any strategy of exploiting bias will ultimately have to rest on an independent normative analysis of the probable consequences.

COMMENT BY CHRISTOPH ENGEL

Introduction

The evolution of disciplines is path dependent. Had there not been scholars like Guido Calabresi, Richard Posner, or Steven Shavell, there would be no such thing as law and economics (see, for example, Calabresi 1970; Posner 2003; Shavell 1980).

Had there not been scholars like Cass Sunstein, Christine Jolls or Don Langevoort, there would be no such thing as behavioral law and economics (see, for example, Sunstein 2000a; Jolls et al. 1998; Langevoort 1992). Behavioral law and economics is a response to some of the most severe limitations of the law and economics approach. Actually, it is mostly an adaptation of behavioral economics to law. In its core, the approach is thus piggybacking on an unease felt by a growing number of economists with the rigor of the basic assumptions in the rational-choice model. As it turns out, many of the experimental findings generated by behavioral economists are highly relevant for the law as well. Likewise, the models developed by behavioral economists can often be put to good use by lawyers.

Behavioral law and economics thus is indeed a valuable enterprise. But it is not the only way in which the law can open itself up to the scientific study of behavior. The alternative approach is best labeled "law and psychology". On first hearing, this may sound old-fashioned. For more than a century, lawyers have been interested in psychological findings, but topics have been different. Classic questions have been the study of free will (see, for example, Lipkin 1990), criminal behavior (see, for example, Quinsey 1995), or the credibility of witness testimony (see, for example, Sporer et al. 1996). However, the impact of psychological findings and concepts to understanding the law as a governance tool is, optimistically speaking, underdeveloped. This comment contrasts the two approaches.

Behavioral Law and Economics

In the interest of making both approaches comparable, behavioral law and economics may be characterized by the following stylized facts: a descriptive methodology, a normative benchmark, a type of prescriptive advice to policymakers, and an analytical handle on the political process.

Descriptively, behavioral law and economics is an extension of classic law and economics, and of neoclassical economics more generally. Along with these two approaches, it subscribes to methodological individualism (Savage 1954; Becker 1976). Behavior is the independent variable. The research challenge is to explain outcomes, given behavioral dispositions. Usually, some set of restrictions is also taken as given, be that budget constraints, information asymmetries, or institutional intervention. Given these restrictions, actors are assumed to maximize individual utility. Classic law and economics applies this methodology to explaining the effect of legal institutions on outcomes. Behavioral law and economics does the same, but replaces classic *Homo oeconomicus* assumptions with experimental findings. Its standard research objects are systematic deviations from standard rationality, called biases (Kahneman et al. 1982; Kahneman and Tversky 2000). Characteristically, behavioral law and economics is thus interested in optimization under behavioral constraints.

149

Classic law and economics has taken much of its appeal from its normative strand. Scholars in this tradition have thus not only borrowed from the descriptive side of economics, but also from welfare economics. Their aim was to demonstrate the hidden efficiency of legal institutions (prominently Posner 2003). With an interesting twist, behavioral law and economics follows suit. Here, the (often implicit) benchmark is not social, but individual. Any behavior that falls short of the *Homo oeconomicus* assumptions is seen as below standard. This has led to "anti-antipaternalism" (Sunstein 2000b, pp. 2 ff.; Rachlinski 2003), and to "debiasing" (see above). Prescriptively, quite some consumer protection legislation can be justified this way (see, for example, Korobkin 2003). Not so rarely, individual bias is also seen as a social problem, calling for institutional intervention (see, for example, Guthrie 2003).

An additional attractive feature of the rational-choice model is its applicability to political process (Buchanan and Tullock 1962; Brennan and Buchanan 1985). Legally speaking, rule generation and rule application can therefore be explained within the same model (Posner 1993; Mashaw 1997; Engel and Morlok 1998). A logical extension is behavioral public choice (see, for example, Brennan and Hamlin 1998; Hudson and Jones 2002) and the behavioral analysis of law making. A classic example of the latter is the interpretation of politicians as "availability entrepreneurs," surfing on a good scandal to push an issue (Jolls et al. 1998, pp. 1518–21).

There are good epistemic reasons for behavioral law and economics. Two philosophers can be cited in support. Hans Albert demonstrates that ignoring any facts is a necessary precondition for seeing and understanding (Albert 1978). He who tries to see everything will see nothing. Modeling is inescapable. It should therefore not be held against behavioral law and economics that it deliberately ignores many psychological insights about behavior.

Kuhn (1962) shows that science develops by revolutions and explains why. A paradigm is not given up because it has been falsified, or has become implausible, at the margin. Developing a paradigm is a costly social endeavor. A discipline would be foolish to embark on building a new paradigm from scratch as long as the old one still basically worked. Scientists should thus not compare the reality of the current paradigm with the utopia of a fully developed alternative paradigm. Consequently, one should not blame behavioral law and economics for staying too close to neoclassical economics as long as alternative approaches are not viable.

Law and Psychology

Against this backdrop, the alternative approach of law and psychology becomes discernible, as do the significant challenges inherent in it. The presentation follows the same four steps from description to norm, and from prescription to political process.

Not only are economics and psychology different disciplines, but they also differ in the predominant way they define themselves. In its neoclassical mainstream, economics is no longer defined by the economy as an issue area. Rather, the field is defined by its method: methodological individualism. Largely, the self-definition is even narrower. An economist is a person who uses the rational-choice model (Becker 1976). At least this is the part of economics on which law and economics relies. Psychology, however, defines itself by human behavior as its field of observation. Currently, this difference goes along with deemphasizing theoretical work, and predominantly focusing on experimental evidence (but see, for example, Strack and Deutsch 2004; Anderson et al. 2003).

This state of affairs makes it difficult to contrast the economic and the psychological paradigms. Instead, the following observations illustrate the differences by one prominent example: habit-driven decision-making. Most of the time, most people do not engage in careful reasoning before they take a decision. Rather, they rely on ready-made tools, which are often called heuristics (Gigerenzer et al. 1999). They thus do not calculate whether they should sell their cars and use public transport for getting to work. They simply take their cars because they always have. This is not to say that they would never switch to public transport. But a mere change in the opportunity structure, say cheaper tickets for the train, will not in and of itself take people out of their mobility habits, for habits are made to use as little information as possible. Thereby, the human mind is freed from superfluous cognitive effort. Even more radically, habit has no judgmental component at all. There is no weighing of advantages and disadvantages. Actually, there is not even a motivational component, apart from the general drive to respond to a cue. All that happens is matching. The mind checks whether the situation at hand comes close enough to the mental model of a situation for which the habit has been acquired (Engel 2004b).

As with behavioral law and economics, defining a normative benchmark should start at the individual rather than the social level. In principle, there are two options. The first option stays fairly close to rational choice. It takes the cost of generating, transmitting, and processing information into account. This leads to a transaction cost approach (Williamson 1985), and to a variant of optimization under constraints (Stigler 1961). Along the same lines, the scarcity of mental resources could be taken into account.

The second option is more radical. It has been dubbed "ecological rationality" (Gigerenzer et al. 1999, p. 18). It starts from a different definition of reality. Rational choice is most powerful in a certain environment. It still works well if both the problem space and the probabilities of possible events are known ex ante. At the limit, it can be extended to situations where probabilities are unknown (Knight 1921). But

151

rational choice is inappropriate in situations of ignorance, i.e., with open problem space. Such problems are categorically ill-defined. Moreover, rational choice is not the right norm if the problem is well-defined, but overly complex, like a game of chess.[17] In such contexts, aiming for perfection is pointless. Being good enough is what matters (Simon 1955). Consequently, the benchmark cannot be defined in the abstract. It must be taken from the context itself. Specifically, the actor should aim at productively exploiting those features of the context that fit best his personal abilities. Adaptation to a context is hence not ad hoc, but a process. Individual learning history matters.

Turning this into a social norm, i.e., a welfare criterion, is more demanding (see Bernheim and Rangel, Chapter 2, this volume). The classic Pareto criterion is open to individuals who do not know the environment. But it assumes that they would know what they want, were they to know the environment (Pareto 1906). However, in a fundamentally uncertain environment, or in one characterized by prohibitive complexity, desires must be adaptive too. Two things are crucial. If socially relevant information is present in part of the population, it should travel. Conversely, socially detrimental reactions to the environment should stay as local as possible. If the predominant reaction is a heuristic, socially beneficial heuristics should thus spread, and socially detrimental heuristics should be contained. Consequently, communication and learning become decisive for welfare. Moreover, in uncertain or overly complex environments, society permanently faces a trade-off between maintaining viability and remaining open to surprise. In the short run, viability is the main concern. If too many members of society start from different assumptions about reality, the scope for socially beneficial cooperation shrinks dramatically (Engel 2005). However, in the long run, society must be able to replace previously predominant assumptions about reality in the light of patent counter evidence (for a theory of surprises, see Thompson et al. (1990, pp. 69–82)).

If addressees are likely to decide by a heuristic argument, this must also have implications for institutional design. Again, one example must suffice. Heuristics exploit very little information. Rule change is a rare event. Typically, in decision-making by heuristics, the stability of the underlying normative expectations will therefore be taken for granted. Consequently, it is not evident that legal reform changes behavior. The legislator is well advised to see the law is properly learned. This means a number of things. Addressees must be induced to pay attention. Since usually they are not professional lawyers, the technical doctrinal change must be translated into normative expectations a standard addressee is able to understand. Usually, the legislator is interested in long-term behavioral change. If so, it should

---

[17] In statistical jargon, the problem may not be NP-hard. A case in point is the function $y = a^x$.

also provide sufficient opportunities for the addressees to exercise, such that a new habit is built (Engel 2004a).

The importance of heuristics for making new law in Parliament or in the courts is still very much a virgin territory. Two dimensions seem worth exploring. The first dimension is heuristics in the rule-making process itself. In principle, one should expect that heuristics play a remarkable role here, for the degree of perceived complexity and uncertainty could hardly be more pronounced than in policy-making. However, both parliamentary legislation and judicial legal policy-making are embedded in a dense institutional setting. To date, knowledge about the interaction between heuristics and institutions is still fairly limited.

The second dimension is heuristics in addressees as anticipated in rule-making. At first sight, this leads to a rationalistic nightmare. Not all people use heuristics all the time. They keep their ability of rational reasoning. Moreover, heuristics are individual reactions to perceived environment. For both reasons, addressees are likely to exhibit heterogeneity. Seemingly, the complexity of the rule-making task thus explodes. However, there are two benevolent qualifications. Not so rarely, the legislator or the courts can make educated guesses about behavioral dispositions. This is particularly promising if they are interested only in average responses, not in reaching each and every single addressee. For people do not normally build their heuristics from scratch: they learn them by observing their peers (cf. Bandura 1977, 1986). Arguably, one can even push the idea one step further. Since rule-making is an activity under high uncertainty, rule-makers themselves should develop pertinent heuristics for successfully navigating in this environment.

Conclusion

Stylized facts are bound to overly accentuate differences. If one looks at individual contributions in the literature, it will often not be easy to classify them as either behavioral law and economics or law and psychology (a good example is Rachlinski (2003)). The point of this comment, therefore, is as follows: the catchy label "behavioral law and economics" should not lure lawyers into looking exclusively at behavioral economics for insights. Psychology proper is as attractive for the enterprise of laying behavioral foundations for law as governance.

REFERENCES

Albert, H. 1978. *Traktat über rationale Praxis*. Tübingen: Mohr.
Anderson, J. R., D. Bothell, M. D. Byrne, S. Douglass, C. Lebiere, and Y. Qin. 2003. An integrated theory of the mind. Carnegie Mellon University Working Paper. (Available at http://act-r.psy.cmu.edu/papers/403/IntegratedTheory.pdf.)
Bandura, A. 1977. *Social Learning Theory*. Englewood Cliffs, NJ: Prentice-Hall.

——. 1986. *Social Foundations of Thought and Action. A Social Cognitive Theory*. Englewood Cliffs, NJ: Prentice-Hall.

Becker, G. S. 1976. *The Economic Approach to Human Behavior*. University of Chicago Press.

Brennan, G., and J. M. Buchanan. 1985. *The Reason of Rules: Constitutional Political Economy*. Cambridge University Press.

Brennan, G., and A. Hamlin. 1998. Expressive voting and electoral equilibrium. *Public Choice* 95:149–75.

Buchanan, J. M., and G. Tullock. 1962. *The Calculus of Consent: Logical Foundations of Constitutional Democracy*. University of Michigan Press.

Calabresi, G. 1970. *The Costs of Accidents: A Legal and Economic Analysis*. Yale University Press.

Engel, Ch. 2004a. Learning the law. Max Planck Institute for Research on Collective Goods, Bonn, preprint no. 2004/5.

——. 2004b. Social dilemmas, revisited from a heuristics perspective. Max Planck Institute for Research on Collective Goods, Bonn, preprint no. 2004/4.

——. 2005. *Generating Predictability: A Neglected Topic in Institutional Analysis and Institutional Design*. Cambridge University Press.

Engel, Ch., and M. Morlok (eds). 1998. *Öffentliches Recht als ein Gegenstand ökonomischer Forschung: die Begegnung der deutschen Staatsrechtslehre mit der Konstitutionellen Politischen Ökonomie*. Tübingen: Mohr.

Gigerenzer, G., P. M. Todd, and the ABC Research Group. 1999. *Simple Heuristics that Make Us Smart*. Oxford University Press.

Guthrie, C. 2003. Prospect theory, risk preference, and the law. *Northwestern University Law Review* 97:1115–63.

Hudson, J., and P. Jones. 2002. In search of the good Samaritan. Estimating the impact of "altruism" on voters' preferences. *Applied Economics* 34:377–83.

Jolls, C., C. R. Sunstein, and R. Thaler. 1998. A behavioral approach to law and economics. *Stanford Law Review* 50:1471–1550.

Kahneman, D., P. Slovic, and A. Tversky. 1982. *Judgment under Uncertainty: Heuristics and Biases*. Cambridge University Press.

Kahneman, D., and A. Tversky. 2000. *Choices, Values, and Frames*. Cambridge, MA: Russell Sage Foundation and Cambridge University Press.

Knight, F. H. 1921. *Risk, Uncertainty and Profit*. New York: Houghton Mifflin.

Korobkin, R. B. 2003. Bounded rationality, standard form contracts, and unconscionability. *University of Chicago Law Review* 70:1203–95.

Kuhn, T. S. 1962. *The Structure of Scientific Revolutions*. University of Chicago Press.

Langevoort, D. C. 1992. Theories, assumptions and securities regulation: market efficiency revisited. *University of Pennsylvania Law Review* 140:851–920.

Lipkin, R. J. 1990. Free will, responsibility and the promise of forensic psychiatry. *International Journal of Law and Psychiatry* 13:331–57.

Mashaw, J. L. 1997. *Greed, Chaos, and Governance: Using Public Choice to Improve Public Law*. Yale University Press.

Pareto, V. 1906. *Manuale di Economia Politica. Con una Introduzione alla Scienza Sociale*. Milan: Società Editrice Libraria.

Posner, R. A. 1993. What do judges and justices maximize? (The same thing everybody else does.) *Supreme Court Economic Review* 3:1–41.

——. 2003. *Economic Analysis of Law*. New York: Aspen.

Quinsey, V. L. 1995. The prediction and explanation of criminal violence. *International Journal of Law and Psychiatry* 18:117–27.

Rachlinski, J. J. 2003. The uncertain psychological case for paternalism. *Northwestern University Law Review* 97:1165–1225.

Savage, L. J. 1954. *The Foundations of Statistics*. Wiley.

Shavell, S. 1980. Strict liability versus negligence. *Journal of Legal Studies* 9:1–25.

Simon, H. A. 1955. A behavioral model of rational choice. *Quarterly Journal of Economics* 69:99–118.

Sporer, S. L., R. S. Malpass, and G. Kohnken. 1996. *Psychological Issues in Eyewitness Identification*. Mahwah, NJ: Lawrence Erlbaum Associates.

Stigler, G. J. 1961. The economics of information. *Journal of Political Economy* 69:213–25.

Strack, F., and R. Deutsch. 2004. Reflective and impulsive determinants of social behavior. *Personality And Social Psychology Review* 8:220–47.

Sunstein, C. R. (ed.). 2000a. *Behavioral Law and Economics*. Cambridge Series on Judgment and Decision Making. Cambridge University Press.

——. 2000b. Introduction. In *Behavioral Law and Economics* (ed. C. R. Sunstein), pp. 1–10. Cambridge University Press.

Thompson, M., R. Ellis, and A. Wildavsky. 1990. *Cultural Theory*. Boulder, CO: Westview Press.

Williamson, O. E. 1985. *The Economic Institutions of Capitalism. Firms, Markets, Relational Contracting*. New York: The Free Press.

Fairness, Reciprocity, and Wage Rigidity

By Truman F. Bewley[1]

5.1 INTRODUCTION

Most empirical tests of the many competing theories of wage rigidity use publicly available data on pay rates and employment that reveal little about the institutions and motivations that explain wage behavior. In order to learn more, some economists have analyzed unusual sources of data or have conducted surveys and experiments. Management scientists and organizational psychologists have for years been collecting data relevant to wage rigidity. I here report on what I know of these sources of information about the origins of wage rigidity.

5.2 ARE WAGES AND SALARIES DOWNWARDLY RIGID?

It is sensible to check whether wages really are downwardly rigid before considering why this is the case. This question is surprisingly hard to answer, because appropriate data are lacking. It is not even clear what the appropriate definition of the wage should be. A firm's marginal costs depend on the average hourly nominal labor cost per job. Employee welfare depends on total nominal compensation per worker. A third possibility is nominal compensation for an employee with a given job tenure and continuing in the same position with the same employer under fixed working conditions. If the employee is paid by the hour, it is the hourly rate plus the fringe benefits that count. Total compensation is the relevant pay rate for salaried employees, where total compensation is the salary plus fringe benefits and bonuses. This third definition is the one most closely associated with employees' and managers' notions of fairness and hence is most pertinent to the managerial concerns that explain downward wage rigidity. In order to adhere even more closely to the sense of fairness prevailing in business, it might be advisable to include only base pay and exclude variable components, such as bonuses. The three pay rates can change

---

[1] I am grateful to Professor Jennifer Smith of the University of Warwick for comments. An earlier version of this chapter appears in H. Gintis, S. Bowles, R. T. Boyd, and E. Fehr (eds). (forthcoming). *Moral Sentiments and Material Interests: The Foundations of Cooperation in Economic Life*. MIT Press.

independently. For instance, the average hourly labor costs of a job can increase with no change in any worker's pay, if the seniority of workers assigned to the job increases. Similarly, changes in hours worked or in job assignments can change an individual's total pay without changing hourly pay rates or labor costs for any job. There are conceptual ambiguities associated with benefits. For instance, if an increase in the cost of a given medical insurance policy were shared between a firm and its workforce, the firm's nominal labor cost per job would increase, but workers would probably feel that the total value of their medical benefits had decreased.

A wage cut should be defined as a reduction in the wage of the third definition above, the pay of an employee continuing to work under unchanged conditions. Unfortunately, this pay rate is the most difficult to measure, because it requires knowledge of much more than just total pay.

Lebow et al. (2003) is the only study I know of that measures the first definition of wage, the firm's average labor costs. The authors use U.S. Bureau of Labor Statistics data and find that wage costs are somewhat rigid in the downward direction, though there is a considerable amount of wage reduction.

There is a large literature that uses surveys of the income of individual workers to study variation in the third kind of wage. The sources of data are household panel surveys and social security data. The studies include McLaughlin (1994, 1999), Lebow et al. (1995), Card and Hyslop (1997), Kahn (1997), Goux (1997), Altonji and Devereux (2000), Smith (2000, 2002), Beissinger and Knoppik (2001, 2003), and Fehr and Götte (2005). Some of these authors struggled with possible errors in the reporting of earnings. All of the studies suffer from ignorance of changes in hours worked, job assignments, bonuses, or working conditions, so that it is not clear that the data reveal the wage of the third definition. All the studies report large amounts of wage reduction. Goux is able to attribute about 60% of the pay reductions to better working conditions as from a change from night to day shift, a change in occupation, or a change in the annual bonus. She has no information on changes in hours worked. None of the other authors have had such detailed information. The difficulties of the surveys cited are discussed in Kramarz (2001) and Howitt (2002).

Surveys of firms reach conflicting conclusions on wage rigidity. Kaufman (1984), Blinder and Choi (1990), Agell and Lundborg (1999, 2003), Agell and Bennmarker (2002, 2003), and Bewley (1999) simply asked employers whether they had reduced pay. The responses probably apply to the third definition of wage, but one cannot be sure. None of the firms in Kaufman's sample of twenty-six British firms had considered nominal wage cuts during the recession occurring at the time of his study. Blinder and Choi found a high incidence of pay reduction, in five of the nineteen American firms they studied. Agell and Lundborg, on the other hand, found almost no wage cutting; two out of 153 responding Swedish firms had experienced nominal wage cuts during the previous seven years, a period of high unemployment and low inflation. Agell and Bennmarker found that only 1.1% of workers received a pay cut during the deep recession in Sweden in the 1990s. The wage cuts that did occur were for just a few employees. Swedish laws that make it difficult to reduce pay may explain the near absence of wage cutting in the studies by Agell and his coauthors. Although I conducted my survey during a recession and actively sought out firms that had cut pay, I found a low incidence of pay cuts; of 235 businesses studied, 24 had reduced the base pay of some or all employees during the recession of the early 1990s.

Similarly conflicting results appear in surveys of union wage agreements. In *Current Wage Developments* and the *Monthly Labor Review*, the Bureau of Labor Statistics reports on general wage changes for both union and nonunion manufacturing production workers for the years 1959 through 1978. These data show a negligible number of wage reductions: cuts for less than 0.5% of the workers in every year.[2] (The corresponding percentage for my sample was 0.14%.) Conflicting evidence has been found by Mitchell (1985), who uses Bureau of Labor Statistics data to calculate that 13% of all workers covered by major new contracts suffered wage cuts in 1983. Similarly, Fortin (1996) finds that 6% of 1,149 large non-COLA union wage settlements in Canada from 1992 to 1994 involved wage cuts.

Much less ambiguous evidence of downward rigidity in the third kind of wage is contained in the few studies that use company records to learn the histories of job assignments, hours worked, and pay of individual employees. The studies include Baker et al. (1994), Wilson (1997), Altonji and Devereux (2000), Dohmen (2003), and Fehr and Götte (2005). Unfortunately, these authors study only six firms. Baker et al. study one firm. Wilson studies two, one of which is the firm studied by Baker et al. Altonji and Devereux study a third. Dohmen studies a bankrupt Dutch firm, and Fehr and Götte study two Swiss firms. Altonji and Devereux, Dohmen, and Fehr and Götte report data on both hourly and salaried workers. The other two studies have information only on salaried employees. All five studies find a negligible number of pay reductions. Altonji and Devereux find that 2.5% of hourly workers experienced wage cuts, but almost all of these were "associated with changes between full- and part-time status, or with changes in whether performance incentives are part of compensation." These findings are reinforced by a telephone survey that Akerlof et al. (1996) made of 596 people in the Washington, DC, area. The key question was: "Excluding overtime, commissions, and bonuses, has your base rate of pay changed since a year ago today?" A negligible number reported pay reductions. Given the form of the question, this evidence probably pertains to the third definition of wages. Contradicting this evidence are two similar surveys conducted in New Zealand in 1992 and 1993, where 8% and 5%, respectively, of the respondents reported hourly

---

[2]These data are cited in Akerlof et al. (1996, p. 8).

wage reductions (Chapple 1996, Tables 2 and 3). More work should be done: no one has yet conducted a large survey that accurately measures the incidence of cuts in pay according to the third definition.

5.3 EVIDENCE FROM SURVEYS BY ECONOMISTS

There are eight surveys by economists of business managers responsible for compensation policy. The goal of seven of these was to learn the reasons for downward wage rigidity, the studies of Kaufman (1984), Blinder and Choi (1990), two surveys by Agell and Lundborg (1995, 1999, 2003), and single studies by Campbell and Kamlani (1997), Bewley (1999), and by Agell and Bennmarker (2002, 2003). The eighth study, that of Levine (1993), also contains relevant information. Although the findings of the studies differ to some extent, they give a consistent picture of the sources of wage rigidity. I also discuss a paper by Smith (2002), who analyzes a survey of British workers.

I first summarize my own findings, based on interviews with 246 company managers and nineteen labor leaders in the Northeast of the United States during the early 1990s, when unemployment was high because of a recession. I present my findings as reflecting the views of managers, though labor leaders had almost exactly the same opinions on the matters discussed. The primary resistance to wage reduction comes from upper management, not from employees. The main reason for avoiding pay cuts is that they damage morale. Morale has three components. One is identification with the firm and an internalization of its objectives. Another is trust in an implicit exchange with the firm and with other employees; employees know that aid given to the firm or to coworkers will eventually be reciprocated, even if it goes unnoticed. The third component is a mood that is conducive to good work. The mood need not be a happy one, though happiness is important for the performance of some jobs, such as those that involve dealing with customers. The mood could be dislike of an unpleasant job combined with grim focus on achievement or pride in accomplishment. Good morale is not equivalent to happiness or job satisfaction. Workers may be content, simply because they do nothing. Good morale has to do with a willingness voluntarily to make sacrifices for the company and for coworkers.

A general sense of fairness is conducive to good morale; it contributes to an atmosphere of mutual trust. The sense of fairness is created by having supervisors treat workers decently, by having impartial rules for settling disputes and determining promotions and job assignments, and by using reasonable standards for setting the relative pay of different employees. These standards are often elaborate systems and are termed internal pay structures. They fix pay differentials on the basis of such factors as training, experience, tenure at the firm, and productivity. The structures are extremely important, because perceived pay inequity within a firm can cause indignation and disrupt work. The standards of internal equity are somewhat arbitrary and can depend strongly on company tradition.

The pay standards often do not specify that pay be proportional to productivity. Many employers believe that productivity of the workforce as a whole is maximized if pay does not fully reflect productivity, though some individuals might produce more if given stronger financial incentives. There is a division of opinion within business about how sensitive pay should be to productivity. Big income differentials due to differences in productivity can cause resentment, especially if productivity is difficult to measure, which it often is. Many firms, nevertheless, use piece rates when productivity can be measured unambiguously, and, even when piece rates are impractical, ordinary notions of equity require that differences in people's contributions be rewarded financially to some extent. The sensitivity of pay to productivity may be blunted by the influence on pay of other factors, such as longevity with the firm. No matter how sensitive the pay of individuals is to their productivity, firms automatically keep the average pay of broad categories of workers roughly equal to the average value of their marginal product by adjusting the number of workers in each category to the profit-maximizing level.

Managers are concerned about morale because of its impact on labor turnover, on recruitment of new employees, and on productivity. Disgruntled employees are likely to quit as soon as they find another job. A company's best recruiters are its employees, so that it is important not to have them complain about their company. Morale has little impact on productivity in the sense of speed in carrying out routine tasks. Habit and working conditions largely determine this sort of productivity. Managers have in mind the impact of morale on workers' willingness to do the extra thing, to encourage and help each other, to make suggestions, and to work well even when not supervised. Also, workers with bad morale waste time complaining to each other. In considering the impact of morale on productivity, it is important to realize that supervision is so expensive that many employees are not closely supervised and have a significant amount of freedom on the job. Except in some low-level jobs, employers rely on workers' voluntary cooperation and do not simply give orders.

When considering why wage cuts hurt morale, it is necessary to distinguish new from existing employees. The morale of existing employees is hurt by pay cuts, because of an insult effect and a standard-of-living effect. Workers are used to receiving regular pay increases as a reward for good work and loyalty, and so interpret a pay cut as an affront and a breach of implicit reciprocity, even if the pay of all employees is reduced. Individual workers may take a pay cut less personally if everyone's pay falls, but when everyone in a company suffers they stimulate each other's discontent by griping. The standard-of-living effect is the resentment caused by the fall in income; workers blame their employer when they find their lifestyles curtailed. This effect is closely related to what experimental economists call loss aversion.

The arguments just given do not apply to newly hired workers. They probably would hardly care if their firm had a general pay cut just before they were hired. It is possible, however, to reduce the pay of newly hired workers while continuing to give normal pay increases to existing employees; new workers hired after a certain date would simply be paid according to a reduced pay scale. Firms have experimented with such two-tier pay structures, and managers say that new workers hired in the lower tier may be glad at first to have their jobs, but that later their attitude changes after they learn that their pay violates the traditional internal pay structure. They believe they were being treated unfairly, their resentment hurts their morale, and their discontent can spread to the senior workers on the old pay scale.

Resistance to wage reduction and the need for internal pay equity both stem from ideas of fairness that usually refer to some reference wage. The reference wage for pay cuts is the past wage. The reference wage for internal equity is that of other workers at the work place with similar qualifications and a similar job. The fairness of wages has little to do with profits or productivity, though both workers and managers find it appropriate that employees share in the success of their company. Although managers attempt to use reasonable criteria when establishing an internal pay structure, once a structure is established, tradition by itself makes it a standard of fairness.

The explanation of downward pay rigidity just given is closely related to the morale theory proposed by Solow (1979), Akerlof (1982), and Akerlof and Yellen (1988, 1990). They assert that morale and hence productivity increase with the wage and that the trade-off between labor costs and productivity determines a wage that is independent of the unemployment rate. Akerlof (1982) uses his gift-exchange model to explain the link between the wage and morale. According to this model, workers offer more effort than is demanded by the employer in exchange for pay rates in excess of market clearing levels, so that effort increases with the wage level. I do not believe that this theory is fully accurate, because employers say they do not see much connection between effort or morale and wage levels; productivity and morale do not increase when pay levels rise, though they can be hurt by pay reductions or disappointingly small raises. Even generous pay raises do not increase morale or productivity, because workers quickly get used to increases and grow to believe they have a right to them. They soon lose track of any idea that they should offer extra effort in exchange for higher pay. Employers do not think about a trade-off between labor costs and the productivity of existing employees when setting pay, though managers do consider the trade-off between labor costs and the quality of labor that a firm can attract and retain. In the theory of Akerlof, Solow, and Yellen, morale depends on the level of the wage, whereas in the explanation

I have described, wages affect morale only when reduced. What is accurate in the Akerlof–Solow–Yellen theory is the idea that employers avoid cutting pay because doing so would hurt morale. What the theory misses is that employees usually have little notion of a fair or market value for their services and quickly come to believe they are entitled to their existing pay, no matter how high it may be. Workers usually do not use pay rates at other firms as reference wages, for they know too little about them.

Although pay cuts are unusual, they do occur and those that occur usually do not have the harmful effects described by managers when arguing that pay should not be cut. The explanation for this inconsistency is that pay cuts are accepted by the workforce if they prevent a firm from closing or if they save a large number of jobs. Managers were confident they could convince the workforce that a pay cut was necessary, if it were in fact so, and they do not cut pay unless they view the reduction as necessary.

One of the puzzles discussed in the literature on wage rigidity has been why firms lay off workers rather than reduce their pay. I found that most managers believe that the elasticity of their company's demand for labor is so low that pay cuts would not reduce an excess supply of labor within the firm. The elasticity is small, because direct labor is a small fraction of marginal costs and the price elasticity of product demand is far from infinite. Only in firms with a high elasticity of product demand, such as construction companies, is it believed that pay cuts would significantly increase the demand for labor. Many of the pay cuts that occurred were made in such firms or in those that were in danger of closing. Other firms where pay reduction was an alternative to layoff were those that laid off workers simply to save money, not to get rid of excess labor, and there were many such companies. The main argument for preferring layoffs to pay cuts is that layoffs do less damage to morale. Laid off workers suffer, but they are no longer in the firm. In the words of one manager, "Layoffs get the misery out the door." Good management practice is to save up potential layoffs, make a large number all at once, and then to assure workers who remain that there will be no more for some time. Any damage to morale from layoffs is temporary, whereas that from a pay reduction is long-term. Other arguments are that layoffs increase productivity, whereas pay cuts hurt it, and layoffs give management some control over who leaves, whereas the best workers are likely to quit when pay is reduced. The tendency for the best to quit is a concern in many firms, because the leveling effects of internal equity on pay mean that pay for workers within a job category increases less than their contribution to profits. Another consideration is that feasible layoffs often save much more money than feasible pay cuts, which usually cannot be more than about 20% of base pay. Layoffs save the fixed costs of employment, which are often substantial, whereas cuts in pay reduce only its variable part.

Another puzzle appearing in the economics literature is why unemployed workers do not try to take jobs away from employed people by offering to replace them at lower pay. Solow (1990) has proposed that the unemployed do not engage in such undercutting because of a social convention against it. I found that explicit undercutting is impossible for most people, because they do not know exactly what job they are applying for or what its pay is. However, it is not uncommon during periods of high unemployment for job applicants to offer to work for extremely low pay. These offers are not frowned upon, but are almost never accepted, because accepting the offers would violate the internal pay structure and could demoralize the new hire. Low offers may, however, lead to reduced pay during the initial probationary period of employment.

A similar puzzle is why firms do not take advantage of recessions to replace employees with cheaper unemployed ones. Lindbeck and Snower (1988) proposed, with their insider–outsider theory, that firms seldom replace workers because the employees who had not been replaced would harass and refuse to cooperate with and train the new ones, thereby reducing their productivity. I found that the main reasons employers do not replace employees are that the new ones would lack the skills of the existing ones and replacement would demoralize the workforce. The skills would be lost in part because many of them are specific to the firm. Managers agreed that, after replacement, workers who had not been replaced might boycott the new ones, but asserted that other factors took precedence over this possibility as an explanation of why employees were not replaced.

Keynes (1936) proposed that downward wage rigidity is explained by employees' preoccupation with pay differentials with respect to workers in similar jobs at other firms. I found, however, that such external pay differentials are not an issue, except in highly unionized industries. In most companies, employees know so little about pay rates at other firms that they do not know whether they are underpaid. Although labor unions do try to keep their members informed of pay rates at other companies, unions are weak in the United States.

A popular explanation of wage rigidity is the "no shirking" theory of Shapiro and Stiglitz (1984). According to their model, managers induce workers to perform well by firing them if their productivity falls below a prescribed level. Job loss is more costly to the worker the higher is his or her wage, so that higher wages make it possible to insist on greater productivity. According to the theory, managers set the wage so as to optimize the trade-off between wage costs and productivity. This theory does not really explain downward wage rigidity, because it implies that wages should decline when unemployment increases. As unemployment rises, it becomes harder to find a new job, so that firing is more costly to the worker and the theory implies that firms can then obtain the same productivity at lower wages. Despite this drawback, the theory is so popular among economists that I frequently asked managers and labor leaders about it and was almost always told that it did not apply. As was explained in connection with Akerlof's gift-exchange model, employers do not believe there is much connection between pay and morale, except when pay is reduced. Nor do employers obtain cooperation by threatening to fire shirkers. To do so would create a negative atmosphere that could damage morale and encourage rebelliousness. Workers may malinger on the job, but are seldom dismissed for doing so, except during the short probationary period after hiring. Shirking is usually dealt with through discussions and reprimands, and workers are normally fired only because of a pattern of egregious behavior. Managers elicit effort by explaining clearly what is expected, facing employees with their shortcomings in a constructive manner, pointing out the importance of the tasks performed, showing interest and appreciation, and making workers feel they are valued members of the organization. Most employees like to work and to cooperate and want to please their boss.

Despite the inapplicability of the "no shirking" theory, the incentive mechanism posited in it can be effective. For instance, employees do work harder during economic slowdowns, when new jobs are difficult to find and layoffs are imminent, especially if layoffs are made on the basis of performance, that is, if the least productive workers in a job category are laid off first. The increase in effort occurs both because job loss becomes more dangerous during a slowdown and because workers try to avoid layoff by being cooperative and productive. Because layoffs stem from circumstances not controlled by management, they do not generate the hostility that might be generated by systematically firing slackers.[3]

Although firing is not used to incite work effort, financial incentives are thought to be very effective in doing so and are believed not to impair morale. Incentives can even improve morale, because workers find it fair that they be rewarded for their contributions to the company. When incentives are not exaggerated, they contribute to internal equity. Discipline and even firing can do so as well, because workers who make the effort to do their job well and obey company rules can be outraged if they see others get away with flagrant misbehavior. The main purposes of firing are to protect the company from malefactors and incompetents and to maintain internal equity. Dismissals that are managed correctly earn managers respect. What is to be avoided is an atmosphere of retribution that menaces everyone. This assertion appears not to apply, however, to low-level jobs. There was evidence that employers do sometimes use coercion to motivate workers in low-paid jobs that require little training and where employees are easily supervised.

---

[3] In the United States, a legal distinction is made between layoffs and firings. Layoffs occur because of lack of work, whereas workers are fired for wrongdoing.

Another popular explanation of wage rigidity is the adverse selection model of Weiss (1980, 1990). There are two versions, having to do with quits and hiring, respectively. In the quits version, managers prefer layoffs to pay cuts, because the best workers leave if pay is reduced, whereas if managers lay off workers they can select those who leave. According to the hiring version, managers believe that the higher the level of pay that a job applicant is willing to accept, the higher is his or her unobservable quality, and pay offers to new hires are determined by the trade-off between worker quality and pay. Weiss asserts that the relation between pay and job candidate quality is determined by alternative employment in the secondary sector, where quality is perfectly observable. The secondary sector is home production or jobs that have high turnover and are usually part-time. The hiring version of Weiss's adverse selection theory applies to the primary sector, where jobs are long-term and usually full-time. He assumes that real wages in the secondary sector are downwardly rigid because of constant returns to labor in production there. According to the theory, this downward rigidity is then transferred to the primary sector through the impact of adverse selection on hiring pay.

I found strong support for Weiss's theory as it applies to quits, but none as it applies to hiring. Although managers do believe that a pay cut would cause their best employees to quit, I found no evidence that recruiters use pay aspirations as an indicator of job candidate quality. Job recruiters treated the trade-off between pay and worker quality as a basic fact of life, but they did not infer candidate quality from pay demands. Recruiters used the trade-off as a reason for not reducing pay only for skills that were in short supply despite the economic slowdown. For most skills, they believed they could hire all the workers they needed during the recession at lower rates of pay. The secondary sector does not sustain candidates' reservation wages. Hiring pay is more flexible in the secondary than the primary sector: the opposite of the situation predicted by Weiss's theory. Two-tier or multiple-tier wage structures are commonplace in the secondary sector, because the part-time and casual nature of the jobs keeps workers from getting to know each other well and so reduces the need to maintain internal pay equity.

Kaufman's (1984) results support my main findings. He conducted interviews in twenty-six British firms in 1982 during a period of high unemployment. He too found that employers "believed they could find qualified workers at lower wages." He found that employers avoid replacing workers with cheaper ones because of the value of skills and of long-term employment relationships. Employers avoid pay cuts because of concern about productivity. Because supervision is costly, employers rely "heavily on the goodwill of their employees." Workers view wages as "a reward for performing competently" and would regard a wage cut as an "affront." Employers avoid hiring new employees at lower pay rates than existing ones because doing so would create "intolerable frictions," especially with "the newer workers who would eventually become disgruntled about the two-tier wage structure." Managers feel they can cut nominal pay if "severe cutbacks or closure will be necessary unless the nominal wage cuts are enacted."

Blinder and Choi (1990) interviewed managers in nineteen firms, and their findings largely agree with my own. They found little evidence to support Weiss's idea that job candidates' wage demands are useful indicators of productivity. Few of Blinder and Choi's nineteen respondents thought that a higher wage would induce greater work effort, though a majority thought that a wage cut would diminish effort. The majority said effort would decrease because of reduced morale. None mentioned the decreased penalty for being fired. A majority of the respondents believed that higher unemployment would bring greater work effort. All respondents answering the question felt that a wage cut would increase labor turnover, though only one of the five firms that had recently reduced pay had experienced a significant increase in quits. "The reason for the wage cut seemed to matter. . . . Generally, wage reductions made to save the firm from failure or to align wages with those of competitors are viewed as justifiable and fair while those made just to raise profits are not." Managers felt strongly that having a wage policy viewed as unfair "would affect work effort, quits, and the quality of future applicants. . . . Attitudes like this must be strong deterrents to implementing an 'unfair' wage policy though. . . that does not necessarily rule out wage reductions under the right circumstances" (Blinder and Choi 1990, pp. 1008–9). Blinder and Choi found strong support for the idea that worker concern about relative wages is a reason for downward wage rigidity. The question asked, however, did not distinguish between internal and external pay comparisons, so that the support given to Keynes's relative wage theory is ambiguous.

Campbell and Kamlani (1997) surveyed 184 firms, sending questionnaires to managers, who were asked to rate the importance of various statements on a scale from one to four. Most of their findings agree with my own and those of the other surveys. Their respondents attached the greatest importance to the idea that wage cuts would induce the best workers to quit, which is Weiss's adverse selection idea as it applies to quits (Weiss 1990). Campbell and Kamlani found that the best workers are valued because pay does not increase as rapidly as productivity, and employees' skills are often firm specific. Other important management concerns were that a wage cut would increase turnover and hence hiring and training costs and would generate bad feeling that would lead to less work effort. Campbell and Kamlani found less support for the idea that pay cuts would make recruitment more difficult and found no support for the "no shirking" model. Managers did not agree that cutting pay would decrease effort because of a reduced fear of job loss, but did agree that effort would decline because of decreased gratitude and loyalty. Furthermore, good management–worker relations were thought to have a much greater impact on effort than high wages, close supervision, and high unemployment. There was also no

167

support for the insider–outsider theory. Most managers did not believe that if the firm discharged some of its current workers and replaced them with new ones at a lower wage, the old workers who remained would harass and refuse to cooperate with the newly hired ones. The reasons for a pay cut matter; its negative impact on effort would be greater if the firm were profitable than if it were losing money. There is an asymmetry between the impact of wage increases and decreases; the deleterious effect on effort of a decrease would greatly exceed the positive effect of an increase. Similarly, a wage decrease would have a worse impact on effort and morale than having paid the lower wage for a long time.

Agell and Lundborg (1995, 1999, 2003) carried out questionnaire surveys of managers in Swedish manufacturing firms, obtaining responses from 179 firms in 1991 and from 157 of those firms in a follow-up survey in 1998. A large majority of the respondents felt that a nominal wage cut would be strongly resisted by employees and that at least 50% of the firm's jobs would have to be threatened to make a cut acceptable. The respondents gave strong support to Keynes's theory that the desire to preserve external wage relativities explains downward wage rigidity. The inconsistency between this finding and my own is probably explained by the much greater importance of labor unions in Sweden than in the United States. This explanation is supported by the finding of Agell and Bennmarker (2002, 2003) that the importance attributed to external pay comparisons as an explanation of wage rigidity increases with a firm's degree of unionization. Agell and Lundborg found little or no support for the "no shirking" model. Managers did not regard shirking as very common, and "employees who were repeatedly caught shirking were punished by a simple verbal rebuke" (Agell and Lundborg 1999, p. 11). Like Campbell and Kamlani, they found that good management–worker relations were much more important to work effort than high wages, supervision, or unemployment. When managers were asked to list the factors most important to worker motivation, "they answered that their employees ought to be given stimulating work assignments, and to feel involved in decision-making. Some stressed that it was important that all employees felt noticed and trusted, and were provided with continuous feedback and appreciation" (Agell and Lundborg 2003, p. 25, footnote 16). As the authors note, these answers were very similar those I heard from U.S. managers (Agell and Lundborg 1999, p. 13). Managers reported that higher unemployment increased worker effort, and workers seemed to be providing more effort in 1998, when there was high unemployment, than in 1991, when there was little unemployment. These findings on the effect of unemployment confirm those of myself and of Kaufman. Like Blinder and Choi, Agell and Lundborg found little support for Weiss's idea that job candidates' reservation wages are a useful signal of productivity (Agell and Lundborg 1999, Table 6). Agell and Lundborg also found little support for Solow's theory about undercutting. They found, as did I, that offers to work for little pay were not uncommon, though fewer such offers occurred in 1998 than in 1991, perhaps because the much higher unemployment rate in 1998 discouraged job search. Managers usually rejected low offers, because accepting them would create pay inequities within the firm and low bidders were thought to have poor skills (Agell and Lundborg 1995, p. 299). In my survey, I often heard the first explanation, but seldom the second.

The findings of Agell and Bennmarker (2002, 2003) are largely consistent with those of Agell and Lundborg. Agell and Bennmarker also obtained information on the influence of firm size and employee gender on the explanation of wage rigidity—matters that are not germane to this chapter.

Levine (1993) obtained responses to questionnaires on pay policy from 139 compensation managers of large U.S. corporations. The questions focused on the determinants of wages and salaries rather than on the reasons for downward wage rigidity. Nevertheless, he found that the unemployment rate and other measures of excess demand for labor had almost no impact on pay. Also, internal equity considerations take precedence over changes in market pay rates in the determination of relative pay rates for closely related jobs and skills.

In summary, the eight surveys of managers are largely consistent and point to an explanation of wage rigidity based on morale rather than on the work incentives that play a role in the "no shirking" model.

I now turn to the analysis by Smith (2002) of data from the British Household Panel Study of 6,000 employed workers from 1991 to 1999. She uses data on the 70% of workers who did not change employer or job grade during the nine years. The data include monthly income and responses to questions about satisfaction with pay and job. She finds that, in a typical month, about 28% of workers suffered nominal reductions in their monthly income and the pay of about 6% was frozen (in that their monthly nominal income did not change). She studies the association between changes in satisfaction and monthly income and finds that workers who suffered cuts were on average less satisfied than those who enjoyed pay increases, though the difference in satisfaction is not striking. She also finds that those whose pay was frozen were just as satisfied as those whose income declined. She interprets this last finding as evidence against the morale theory of wage rigidity outlined above, because according to that theory pay cuts should cause greater unhappiness than do pay freezes. The theory, of course, may be wrong, but it is not clear what conclusions should be drawn from her analysis, because she probably does not have data on pay cuts and freezes in the sense of the third definition given in the previous section, and this is the definition that is relevant to downward wage rigidity. Monthly incomes can fluctuate for a great many reasons, such as changes in overtime, shifts, job assignments, bonuses, or hours, and she has information on none of these except hours, and she is not sure the data on hours are accurate. Pay raises, freezes, and cuts have to do with the rules by which pay is calculated. A great deal more information is required than total monthly income in order to detect changes in these rules. I find it extremely unlikely that on average 28% of the workforce suffered pay cuts from one month to the next according to the proper definition of pay cut. Another issue is that actual pay cuts often turn out to do little harm to morale, because they are done for a good reason and are accepted by workers as fair. When managers say that pay cuts would hurt morale, they refer to unjustified cuts. Also, job and pay satisfaction are probably not good measures of morale.

A question of interest to macroeconomists is whether downward wage rigidity is real or nominal. In other words, do workers suffer from money illusion? Would they be as offended by a 10% reduction in nominal wages when the consumer price level had declined by 5% as they would be by a wage freeze when inflation was 5%? It is hard to address this issue using surveys without asking hypothetical and hence confusing questions of informants. Most surveys have been done during periods of low inflation, when inflation does not seem relevant. The answers that managers gave Agell and Bennmarker (2002, 2003) to a question similar to the one posed above indicate that managers believe that their workers suffer from money illusion. In my own work, I obtained similar responses on the few times I asked such questions. It is hard to know how to evaluate such findings because of the speculative nature of the questions. Although there is ample evidence that many people do suffer from money illusion (Kahneman et al. 1986; Shafir et al. 1997; Fehr and Tyran 2001), it is not clear that money illusion is a significant factor in downward wage rigidity.

5.4 Evidence from Experimental Economics

Experimental evidence is accumulating that, for the most part, agrees with what managers say about their own choices and about worker motivation. The most important finding is the prevalence of reciprocity. Many people, when placed experimentally in the role of worker or employer, offer extra effort when offered extra pay or offer extra pay after receiving extra effort, even when no *quid pro quo* is required. People also reciprocate bad for bad. In experiments, subjects incur a cost in order to harm others who have hurt them. The general willingness to reciprocate good for good is the essence of good morale. Negative reciprocity is what underlies the insult effect of pay cuts, which is resentment caused by the firm's perceived breach of positive reciprocity; workers expect employers to offer pay increases, not cuts, in exchange for loyalty and effort. The pervasiveness of negative reciprocity probably explains managers' belief that the systematic use of firing would not motivate employees to work well. Another finding is that financial incentives do inspire effort, provided they are framed in a way that avoids an impression of menace. Surveys of the experimental literature are given in Fehr and Gächter (1998b, 2000), Fehr and Falk (2002), and Fehr and Fischbacher (2005).

A series of laboratory experiments demonstrate the importance of reciprocity in mock employment relationships (Fehr et al. 1993, 1998a,b; Kirchler et al. 1996; Gächter and Falk 2002). In these experiments, there are two types of subjects (employers and workers) and two stages of interaction. At the first stage, each employer makes a wage offer, which is either accepted or rejected by some worker. Acceptance leads to employment and to the second stage, where either the worker or the experimenter chooses an effort level. An employer can employ only one worker, and a worker can work for only one employer. An employed worker's payoff is the wage minus a cost, which is increasing in the effort level. The employer's payoff increases in the effort level and, of course, decreases with the wage. Notice that the employer has no way to enforce the worker's effort choice. The two stages are repeated, usually ten to fifteen times. In some experiments, one worker and one employer are paired for all the repetitions. In others, the experimenter changes the pairings after every repetition. In still another version, the pairings are established at each repetition by competitive bidding for workers and jobs. In such market interactions there are more workers than employers, so that market-clearing wages should be little more than the workers' reservation level, which is their cost of effort. Experimenters consistently find that if workers choose the effort level, then the average wage is considerably higher than the reservation level, even when competitive bidding should force wages down to it. Furthermore, the worker's average effort is higher than the minimum allowed and increases with the wage offered. In addition, the wage equals little more than the reservation level, if the experimenter chooses effort and there is competitive bidding with an excess supply of labor. These results hold, even if the employer and worker interact only once. That is, workers offer extra effort in exchange for a higher than minimal wage, even though wages are agreed on before workers choose effort levels and employers never have another opportunity to reward or punish workers. Employers anticipate and exploit workers' reciprocity by offering generous wages.

The experiments show that only some people reciprocate. Others do not do so and behave selfishly. Selfish workers offer the minimum amount of effort. Some employers who would probably otherwise behave selfishly are induced to offer generous wages by the expectation that some workers will react to them by offering liberal amounts of effort. Because wages fall to minimal levels when the experimenter fixes the effort level, we may tentatively conclude that employers' behavior is driven mainly by the expectation of reciprocation, not by a sense of fairness, that is, by a desire to divide evenly the economic surplus generated by the worker–employer interaction.

The tendency to reciprocate may be built into the human psyche. Rilling et al. (2002) used magnetic resonance imaging to study the reactions of the brain to repeated playing of the prisoner's dilemma game and found that experiencing

171

cooperative responses and deciding to cooperate were both accompanied by patterns of brain activity normally associated with pleasure.[4]

All these findings support the explanation of wage rigidity proposed by Akerlof (1982) in his gift-exchange model. I pointed out earlier that this theory does not seem to apply in business contexts because workers quickly grow to believe that they deserve whatever pay they receive. Experiments do not continue for long enough to capture this habituation effect.

What is important about the experiments is that they reveal that a significant fraction of the population reciprocates. In addition, the experimental findings do reflect some of the practices that managers describe. When setting the pay of new hires, recruiters sometimes offer a little more than applicants expect in order to get the relationship with them started off on the right footing and to create excitement about the new job. One of the many reasons recruiters dislike hiring overqualified applicants is that they are likely to be disgruntled because their pay disappoints their expectations.

Fehr and Falk (1999) perform interesting modifications of the experiments of Fehr et al. (1993) and others described above. Fehr and Falk make the bidding for jobs and workers two-sided rather than one-sided in the situation with competitive bidding and an excess supply of workers. That is, workers as well as employers can make wage offers. The authors find that, when the experimenter determines effort, the employers accept only the lowest offers and wages are forced down almost to the reservation level. When the workers choose the effort level, however, the wage is higher, just as in experiments where only employers make offers. Workers make many low offers to try to obtain a job, but these are refused, apparently because the employers hope to incite high effort by paying good wages. The experimental employers' behavior corresponds to that of actual firms, who do usually refuse workers' offers to work for very little.

Burda et al. (1998) have performed experiments involving wage cuts. In their work, an employer and worker are matched for two periods, and the employer makes a wage offer in each of them, which the worker may accept or reject. If the worker rejects the offer, the employer may, after paying a fixed training cost, hire a fictitious worker at a market wage, which the actual worker also receives, as if hired by some other fictitious firm. The market wage is predetermined by the experimenters and declines from the first to the second period. In the experiments, there is little wage rigidity; the wages that employers and employees agree on tend to decline along with the market wage. The employer and worker in effect play two successive ultimatum games, the bargaining position of the worker weakens from the

---

[4]I owe this reference to Angier (2002), who makes the connection with the experimental work of Ernst Fehr.

first to the second game, and as a result the wage declines. There is no reciprocation of effort for income that could give rise to an insult effect, and the standard-of-living effect does not apply, since the workers do not live off their earnings. The experiments, therefore, provide evidence that without these two effects wages would be downwardly flexible.

Experimental evidence supports the view of businesspeople that financial incentives are effective, even when negative, provided they are not presented in a hostile manner. For instance, Nagin et al. (2002) report on a field experiment performed by a telemarketing firm. In this firm, the telemarketers' pay increased with the number of successful solicitations they claimed, and the company monitored these claims by calling back a fraction of the people declared to be successes. The company secretly varied the fraction of bad calls reported to employees while increasing the true callback rate. By analyzing the company's data, the authors found that cheating increased as the fraction of bad calls reported declined, so that workers did respond to variation in the negative incentive.

Laboratory experimental work by Fehr and Gächter (1998a) and Brown et al. (2004a) shows that the possibility of negative rewards does not keep reciprocation from being a powerful incentive. Fehr and Gächter (1998a) performed the two-stage experiments of Fehr et al. (1993) with the modification that at stage one the employer requested an effort level. The authors compared the results with experiments where in a third stage the employer could reward or punish the worker. The amount of the reward or punishment was chosen by the employer and was not announced in advance. The employer incurred a cost that increased with the absolute magnitude of the reward or punishment. Despite the cost, many employers did reward high effort and punish low effort, and workers on average offered more effort and earned lower wages in the three-stage than in the two-stage experiments. Brown et al. (2004a) repeated the two-stage experiments of Fehr et al. (1993) fifteen times under two conditions. Under one, employers and workers could identify each other by a number, and employers could make offers to a particular worker. This arrangement made it possible for an employer and worker to form a long-term relationship. In the other condition, the identifying numbers were reassigned in every period, so that long-term relationships were impossible. When identity numbers remained stable, individual workers and employers did form relationships that were valuable to both, because they established a pattern of exchanging high effort for high wages. Employers could and many did punish workers for low effort by dismissing them, that is, by ceasing to make them offers. Average wages and effort were considerably higher when identity numbers were stable than when they were reassigned, so workers were not discouraged from reciprocating by the threat of dismissal that was made possible by stable identity numbers. When Brown et al. (2004b) repeated the experiments just

173

described while allowing there to be more firms than workers, long-term relationships formed even though workers could quickly obtain work with another firm if they were let go. The fact that the negative incentives were not made explicit in these experiments may have diminished any bad impression they made. Another explanation for the effectiveness of the negative incentives may have to do with the presence of both selfish and reciprocating workers. Although the reciprocating workers might have been offended by the possibility of punishment, selfish ones might have been induced to offer more effort by the prospect of reward and risk of punishment.

Other experiments that imitate the "no shirking" model provide additional evidence that punishments do not necessarily crush reciprocation and discourage effort. These experiments are described in Fehr et al. (1996, 1997, 2001), and Fehr and Gächter (2002). The experiments have the form of the two-stage experiments described in Fehr et al. (1993), except that the employer requests a certain effort level and a worker is fined with a fixed probability if the effort level offered falls short of that demanded by the employer, that is, if the worker shirks. In its offer, the employer specifies a wage, the fine, and the effort level demanded. The "no shirking" model of Shapiro and Stiglitz (1984) also has a probability of being caught shirking, and the fine in the experiment corresponds to being fired. One finding is that the threat of being fined elicits more than the minimum possible level of effort. Also, some reciprocation exists, in that employers obtain effort above the level they demand when they offer generous wages. Probably because employers hope for reciprocation, they often request effort levels that are too high to be enforced by the fine. The average level of actual effort is reduced by a considerable amount of shirking that may reflect reciprocation of the hostility perceived in the possibility of being fined.

The evidence is mixed on the degree to which the specification of fines discourages reciprocity. Fehret al. (2001) and Fehr and Gächter (2002) compare experimental labor relations models imitating the "no shirking" model, as in Fehr et al. (1996), with labor relations models that depend for success solely on reciprocity or trust, as in Fehr et al. (1993). In the trust model, the employer offers a wage and makes a nonbinding effort request, and the worker then offers an effort level. The "no shirking" model is as described in the previous paragraph. The two papers report opposite results. In Fehr and Gächter (2002), the trust model achieves higher actual effort than the "no shirking" model.[5] In Fehr et al. (2001), the "no shirking" model achieves higher effort. I see no way of explaining the discrepancy, as the payoffs are nearly the same in the two experiments and the differences between them do not

---

[5] See Figure 6 in Fehr and Fischbacher (2002).

seem relevant.[6] Fehr and Gächter (2002) go on to make another comparison that shows that the fine may vex workers to some extent. They compare the "no shirking" model with a mathematically equivalent bonus model, in which the punishment is not a fine but the deprivation of a bonus. The bonus model gives rise to greater effort than the "no shirking" model, but less than the trust model.

Further experimental evidence of the harmful effects of negative incentives is given in Fehr and Rockenbach (2003). In their experiments, subjects play a game, in which an investor chooses a quantity of money to give to a respondent and specifies the amount he or she would like the respondent to return. The amount given is tripled by the experimenter, so if the investor gives x, the respondent receives $3x$. The respondent then chooses how much to return to the investor. In another version of the game, the investor, when making the gift to the respondent, may commit to imposing a fine on the respondent if he or she returns less than the amount requested by the investor. On average, respondents were least generous when the fine was imposed, next most generous when there was no possibility of a fine, and most generous when the investor could impose a fine but chose not to do so.

Experiments by Falk and Kosfeld (2004) show that efforts to control people can also diminish their willingness to cooperate. They had two people play a game in which one is an agent and the other a principal. The agent is given 120 units of money and gives x units of it to the principal. The experimenter doubles this quantity, so that the principal receives $2x$. The principal can either oblige the agent to give at least 10 units or do nothing. A majority of agents give less if the principal restricts them in this way, and on average agents give less when so constrained.

Gneezy and Rustichini (2000) provide other evidence on the destructive effects of negative incentives. They made an experiment with a day-care center in which they imposed for the first time a monetary fine on parents for picking up their children late. The introduction of the fine increased parents' lateness, and the lateness did not diminish after the fine was removed. It seems likely that the increase in lateness occurred because parents interpreted the fine as a fee charged for keeping their children longer.

Two papers by Falk et al. (2000, 2003) provide experimental evidence that perceived intentions as well as the desire for a fair division affect reciprocation. Falk et al. (2000) report on experiments with a variant of the game, described above, of Fehr and Rockenbach (2003). On the first move, the investor may take money away from or give money to the respondent, and the respondent may then in turn give or take money away from the investor. In another version of the game, the

---

[6]In Fehr et al. (2001), the employer chooses the type of model used, there is no excess supply of labor, and the experimenter matches one worker to one employer in each period, whereas in Fehr and Gächter (2002) the experimenter chooses the model, there is an excess supply of labor, and the matching of workers to employers is determined by market bidding.

experimenter determines the investor's move according to a random distribution. In both versions, respondents on average react by taking money back if it is taken from them and give money back when it has been given to them. Their responses are, however, of a larger magnitude when the first move is chosen by the investor rather than by the experimenter. This behavior shows that the respondents' behavior was driven to some extent by a desire to even the winnings from the game, but above all by an urge to reciprocate the good or bad intentions of the investor. Falk et al. (2003) reach similar conclusions from experiments with various ultimatum games. Player A can propose one of two possible splits of ten monetary units to a respondent. One possibility is always an (8, 2) split: eight for the proposer and two for the respondent. Alternatives are (5, 5), an even split, or (2, 8), (10, 0), or even (8, 2), which means that there is really no alternative. Respondents reject the (8, 2) split more frequently, the less fair it seems in comparison with the alternative. For instance, (8, 2) is rejected most often if (5, 5) is the alternative, and least often if (10, 0) is the alternative.

These results provide some (but not strong) support for managers' assertions that using firing systematically to stimulate effort would dampen morale and depress productivity. I suspect that the effects managers refer to are difficult to capture experimentally, because firing is a much more severe punishment than can be imposed in the laboratory and it is hard to reproduce in a laboratory the menacing atmosphere that could be created in a work place by frequent firings and by the explicit threat of firing.

5.5 EVIDENCE FROM ORGANIZATIONAL PSYCHOLOGY AND MANAGERIAL SCIENCE

Although early investigations by managerial scientists and organizational psychologists of the relations between pay, morale, and productivity contradicted some of what managers say about these matters, the subject has since evolved and now much of what they say has been corroborated. Recall that managers assert that pay levels have little impact on motivation or performance, but that financial incentives linked to performance can increase productivity considerably. These conclusions have been supported by a large amount of research by management scientists and psychologists, which I do not describe. The relevant literature is reviewed in Vroom (1964, p. 252) and Lawler (1971, p. 133). The management intuitions that did not receive much support in early research had to do with the link between morale and productivity. Morale was measured from questionnaire evidence on job satisfaction and organizational commitment or loyalty, and performance was measured through direct observation or by supervisors' evaluations. There is a huge literature on this subject that has been reviewed by many (Brayfield and Crockett 1955; Herzberg et al. 1957, Chapter 4; Vroom 1964, pp. 181–86; Locke 1976, pp. 1330–34; Iaffaldano and Muchinsky 1985; Mathieu and Zajac 1990). The general conclusion is that the correlations between the measures of morale and performance are positive, but small. The measures of performance include those of both individuals and groups. In a way, these findings confirm what managers say, because most of them assert that good morale is not the same as happiness.

There is a considerable amount of evidence that job satisfaction is negatively related to quitting and absences. The literature on this subject is reviewed in Brayfield and Crockett (1955), Herzberg et al. (1957, pp. 106–7), Vroom (1964, pp. 175–80), Locke (1976, pp. 1331–32), Price (1977, p. 79), Steers and Rhodes (1978), Mobley (1982, pp. 95–105), Staw (1984, pp. 638–45), and Mathieu and Zajac (1990).

There was interesting research in the 1950s which did support management feelings about the importance of morale. The investigators made experimental changes in management practices to determine the relation between attitudes and performance of work groups (Viteles 1953, Chapter 8; Seashore 1954; Whyte et al. 1955, 1961; Likert 1961, Chapter 3). One of the main conclusions was that performance is positively associated with pride in the work group or firm, but is not related to other attitudes.

In response to the failure to find a significant relation between job satisfaction and performance, researchers studied the link between job attitudes and workers' doing things for employers that are outside normal duties. Contact with business may have led scholars to look for such a connection, because managers claim that the impact of good morale on productivity is felt mainly through employees' willingness to do more than the minimum required of them. Investigators have given "doing more than the minimum" various names, such as spontaneous behavior (Katz 1964), pro-social behavior (O'Reilly and Chatman 1986, Brief and Motowidlo 1986), extra-role behavior (O'Reilly and Chatman 1986), and, most commonly, organizational citizenship behavior (Organ 1988). These concepts differ to some extent. Organ (1988) defines five categories of organization citizenship behaviors, altruism (helping other workers), conscientiousness (obeying company rules, being punctual, and showing up for work regularly), sportsmanship (good-humored toleration of inconveniences), courtesy (considerate treatment of fellow workers), and civic virtue (participation in the internal political life of the organization).

An initial question is whether good morale increases organizational citizenship behavior. Organizational psychologists have done most of the research on this topic. They typically start with a number of loosely defined concepts, such as job satisfaction, perceptions of fairness in the work place, and organizational citizenship behavior, and then try to determine how these are related by analyzing responses of a sample of several hundred people to questionnaires. Each concept is usually broken into several components, such as Organ's five categories of organizational citizenship behavior, and a list of questions is associated with each component. Employees answer questions on job satisfaction and perceptions of fairness. Employees or their supervisors answer questions on organizational citizenship behavior. Factor analysis is used to check whether responses to the questions are such that those corresponding to one conceptual component are highly correlated with each other and have less correlation with responses to other questions. The relations among the concepts and their components are then estimated using regression analysis. The advantage of such surveys over laboratory experiments is that they can investigate real-life situations in which there are long-term associations between workers and employers. The subjects in laboratory experiments are usually college students and do not know each other well. A disadvantage is that causation is much harder to establish in surveys than it is in experiments.

The findings of organizational psychologists do not all agree, but their work supports the conclusion that typical measures of morale, such as job satisfaction and organizational commitment, do have a positive relation with organizational citizenship behavior. What is more important is that a perception of fairness within a business organization has a positive relation with both job satisfaction and organizational citizenship behavior and may be the dominant factor affecting both. Furthermore, procedural justice, and especially the interactional aspect of procedural justice, is more closely related to job satisfaction and organizational citizenship behavior than is distributive justice. Distributive justice has to do with the allocation of rewards to employees, whereas procedural justice has to do with the system used to arrive at the allocation. Interactional justice has to do with the consideration, politeness, and respect with which superiors treat subordinates. Another conclusion is that organizational citizenship behavior depends less on the employees' mood than on their conscious perceptions about their jobs. The impact of fairness on organizational citizenship behavior is discussed in Organ and Konovsky (1989), Moorman (1991, 1993), Folger (1993), Moorman et al. (1993), Niehoff and Moorman (1993), Podsakoff and MacKenzie (1993), Organ and Ryan (1995), Konovsky and Organ (1996), and Netemeyer et al. (1997). Moorman (1991) discusses the relative impacts of the various forms of justice. The impact of mood is discussed in Organ and Konovsky (1989), George (1991), and Moorman (1993). The relative impacts of mood and cognitive job satisfaction are discussed in Organ and Konovsky (1989) and Moorman (1993). The impact of job satisfaction and commitment on organizational citizenship behavior is discussed in O'Reilly and Chatman (1986), Puffer (1987), Farh et al. (1990), Moorman (1991), Organ and Lingl (1995), Organ and Ryan (1995), Konovsky and Organ (1996), Netemeyer et al. (1997), and MacKenzie et al. (1998). Good reviews of the impact of fairness on organizational citizenship behavior are Organ (1988, 1990), Schnake (1991), Greenberg (1993), and Organ and Moorman (1993).

Another connection between morale and organizational citizenship behavior is made through studies of the impact of leadership style on subordinates' organizational citizenship behavior. A distinction is made between transactional and transformational leadership. The transactional style asserts itself by means of praise and admonishment, whereas the transformational style inspires people to go beyond their personal interests and think of those of the company or task. The transformational style persuades people to identify with the company, and the transactional style focuses on people's self-interest. The transformational style is intended to create good morale in the sense that businesspeople seem to have in mind. Investigators have found that transformational leadership has a strong positive impact on both in-role job performance and organizational citizenship behavior, that its impact exceeds that of transactional leadership, and that the impact of transformational leadership is due in part to increased trust in the leadership. The relevant studies are by Podsakoff et al. (1990, 1996) and MacKenzie et al. (2001).

An obvious question is whether organizational citizenship behavior increases a company's profitability. Managers apparently think that it does, because there is evidence that supervisors' performance evaluations of subordinates are strongly and positively influenced by organizational citizenship behavior. Papers that establish this connection are MacKenzie et al. (1991, 1993) and Podsakoff et al. (1993). A few studies have measured the impact of organizational citizenship behavior on the performance of work groups in various settings and have found the effects to be positive. These studies include George and Bettenhausen (1990), Podsakoff and MacKenzie (1994, 1997), Walz and Niehoff (1996), and Podsakoff et al. (1997). The observed correlations may be spurious, however, because there is evidence from laboratory experiments that the high performance of a work group may have a positive influence on perceptions within the group of organizational citizenship behavior (Bachrach et al. 2001). The subject is reviewed in Podsakoff et al. (2000).

Some interesting recent work has explored the connection between identification with an organization on the one hand, and quits and performance, especially extra-role performance, on the other hand. Tyler has participated in much of this work. He thinks of identification with a company as internalization of its goals and asserts that identification occurs as a result of judgments about organizational status, which he calls pride, and about status within the organization, which he calls respect. Pride has to do with a favorable view of the organization as a whole, and respect has to do with being treated well within it. Status judgments can be comparative or autonomous, where a comparative judgment relates an organization or person to others and an autonomous judgment is an absolute one. Tyler believes that if people identify with an organization, they will want it to succeed, because its success will strengthen their own self-image. Identification with an organization is, in my opinion, a much better interpretation of what managers mean by good morale than are job satisfaction and even organizational commitment. Tyler and his coauthors find that identification is a dominant explanation of voluntary cooperation with organizations. In the context of business organizations, identification with the company is a much more important explanatory factor than financial rewards received from it. These investigators find that the greatest impact of identification is on organizational citizenship, extra-role, or discretionary behavior as opposed to in-role or mandatory behavior, that is, behavior required by a job description. The primary impact of pride is on rule following or conscientiousness, whereas the primary impact of respect is on helping behavior, that is, assisting coworkers. Autonomous judgments of status have a much bigger effect than comparative ones. Tyler and his coauthors assert that perceptions of fairness and especially procedural justice have an important impact on judgments about the status of an organization and hence on willingness to identify with it. Recall that management scientists cited earlier (Viteles 1953; Seashore 1954; Whyte et al. 1955; Likert 1961) also found a connection between pride in an organization and performance. The work of Tyler and his colleagues is reported in Tyler (1999) and Tyler and Blader (2000, 2001). Abrams et al. (1998) observe a close association between identification with an organization and intentions to quit. Much of the work of Tyler and his coauthors on identification and cooperation with organizations has been done in the context of political, social, and educational institutions, but the recent work just cited has to do with businesses. This interesting work raises the question of why people identify with organizations. Status is an incomplete explanation, since the term status has little independent content and includes all possible reasons for liking an organization. It is interesting that fairness has a strong influence on status and that people are proud of organizations that treat them and others fairly, but researchers have given no explanation of why this is so.

An obvious question is: "What evidence has been collected on the impact of actual pay cuts or pay freezes on morale?" The only works I have found on the subject are by Greenberg (1989, 1990) and Schaubroeck et al. (1994). In the first paper, Greenberg finds from a survey that workers did feel underpaid after a 6% pay cut, but job satisfaction did not decline and employees instead paid more attention to the nonfinancial advantages of their jobs. In the second paper, Greenberg reports that, at another business, theft of company property increased after a 15% pay cut. In this chapter, he conducted an experiment in which he gave employees a good explanation of the pay cut in one plant where the pay cut occurred but not in another. In the plant where the explanation was made, feelings of pay inequity and pilferage were fewer than in the other plant. This evidence supports the assertions managers make that employees tolerate pay cuts more easily if they feel they are justified and that it is possible to persuade workers that cuts are necessary. These conclusions are further reinforced by the work of Schaubroeck et al. (1994), who studied the reactions of salaried employees to a pay freeze. These investigators also conducted an experiment, giving a good explanation to some of the employees and not to others. The explanations of the freeze diminished resentment. For those who did not receive the explanation, job dissatisfaction increased with self-reported economic hardship resulting from the freeze, and there was no such relation for those who did receive the explanation.

5.6 CONCLUSION

Perhaps the outstanding conclusion to be drawn from the works discussed is the importance of fairness to labor performance. It is not easy to judge what fairness means. Fairness certainly does not mean an equal distribution of the benefits from a company's operations, for pay levels within firms are far from egalitarian. Even workers doing the same job may receive very different pay because of many factors, such as longevity with the company, skills acquired, and productivity. Fairness is recognized in business as being inherently ambiguous. For instance, judgments about the fairness of internal pay structures are said to depend strongly on company tradition. Another indication that fairness does not mean equality of gains is the evidence from organizational psychology that procedural and interactive justice are more important to an impression of fairness than is distributive justice. A very significant finding, I believe, is that of Tyler and Blader (2000, 2001): perceptions of procedural justice contribute to pride in an organization.

We do not know why people so urgently desire fairness. Is it because it contributes to an atmosphere of positive reciprocation and people like to exchange favors? Does fairness make people feel more secure? Do people feel that fairness is right and want their surroundings to accord with their moral principles? Do people simply want to have a level playing field on which to compete? It is to be hoped that further empirical work will give more insight into these questions.

A sense of fairness is probably the most important determinant of good company morale. Other important factors are close ties among coworkers and the significance attached to the firm's output. One reason pay cuts can be resented is that they can dissolve the sense of fairness. Workers accept a pay cut that they feel is fair and they see it as fair when it saves a great many jobs.

Another important conclusion is that firms try to gain the cooperation of employees by getting them to identify with the company and to internalize its objectives. As Tyler and Blader (2000, 2001) have emphasized, an atmosphere of fairness makes workers more willing to do these things. For an understanding of wage rigidity and of how organizations obtain cooperation, it would be useful to know why people value fairness, why it promotes identification with a company, and why people identify with organizations at all. That they do so is clear.

CHAPTER FIVE

REFERENCES

Abrams, D., K. Ando, and S. Hinkle. 1998. Psychological attachment to the group: cross-cultural differences in organizational identification and subjective norms as predictors of workers' turnover intentions. *Personality and Social Psychology Bulletin* 24:1027–39.

Agell, J., and H. Bennmarker. 2002. Wage policy and endogenous wage rigidity: a representative view from the inside. CESifo Working Paper 751.

———. 2003. Endogenous wage rigidity. CESifo Working Paper 1081.

Agell, J., and P. Lundborg. 1995. Theories of pay and unemployment: survey evidence from Swedish manufacturing firms. *Scandinavian Journal of Economics* 97:295–307.

———. 1999. Survey evidence on wage rigidity and unemployment: Sweden in the 1990s. Office of Labour Market Policy Evaluation, Uppsala, Sweden, Discussion Paper 1999-2.

———. 2003. Survey evidence on wage rigidity and unemployment: Sweden in the 1990s. *Scandinavian Journal of Economics* 105:15–29.

Akerlof, G. A. 1982. Labor contracts as partial gift exchange. *Quarterly Journal of Economics* 97:543–69.

Akerlof, G. A., and J. Yellen. 1988. Fairness and unemployment. *American Economic Association, Papers and Proceedings* 78:44–49.

———. 1990. The fair wage-effort hypothesis and unemployment. *Quarterly Journal of Economics* 105:255–83.

Akerlof, G. A., W. T. Dickens, and G. Perry. 1996. The macroeconomics of low inflation. *Brookings Papers on Economic Activity* 1:1–59.

Altonji, J. G., and P. J. Devereux. 2000. The extent and consequences of downward nominal wage rigidity. In *Worker Well-Being* (ed. S. W. Polachek), Research in Labor Economics, Volume 19, pp. 383–431. Elsevier.

Angier, N. 2002. Why we're so nice: we're wired to cooperate. *New York Times*, Science Section, July 23.

Bachrach, D. G., E. Bendoly, and P. M. Podsakoff. 2001. Attributions of the "causes" of group performance as an alternative explanation of the relationship between organizational citizenship behavior and organizational performance. *Journal of Applied Psychology* 86:1285–93.

Baker, G., M. Gibbs, and B. Holmström. 1994. The wage policy of a firm. *Quarterly Journal of Economics* 109:921–55.

Beisiinger, T., and Ch. Knoppik. 2001. Downward nominal rigidity in West German earnings. *German Economic Review* 2:385–417.

———. 2003. How rigid are nominal wages? Evidence and implications for Germany. *Scandinavian Journal of Economics* 105:619–41.

Bewley, T. F. 1999. *Why Wages Don't Fall During a Recession*. Harvard University Press.

Blinder, A. S., and D. H. Choi. 1990. A shred of evidence on theories of wage stickiness. *Quarterly Journal of Economics* 105:1003–15.

Brayfield, A. H., and W. H. Crockett. 1955. Employee attitudes and employee performance. *Psychological Bulletin* 52:396–424.

Brief, A. P., and S. J. Motowidlo. 1986. Prosocial organizational behaviors. *Academy of Management Review* 11:710–25.

Brown, M., A. Falk, and E. Fehr. 2004a. Competition and relational contracts. Discussion Paper, University of Zürich, Switzerland.

——. 2004b. Relational contracts and the nature of market interactions. *Econometrica* 72:747–80.

Burda, M., W. Güth, G. Kirchsteiger, and H. Uhlig. 1998. Employment duration and resistance to wage reductions: experimental evidence. Tilburg University, Center for Economic Research, Discussion Paper 9873.

Campbell, C., and K. Kamlani. 1997. The reasons for wage rigidity: evidence from survey of firms. *Quarterly Journal of Economics* 112:759–89.

Card, D., and D. Hyslop. 1997. Does inflation "grease the wheels of the labor market"? In *Reducing Inflation: Motivation and Strategy* (ed. C. D. Romer and D. H. Romer). University of Chicago Press.

Chapple, S. 1996. Money wage rigidity in New Zealand. *Labour Market Bulletin* 1996(2):23–50.

Dohmen, T. J. 2003. Performance, seniority, and wages: formal salary systems and individual earnings profiles. Working Paper, Institute for the Study of Labor (IZA), Bonn, Germany.

Falk, A., and M. Kosfeld. 2004. Trust and motivation. Discussion Paper, University of Zürich, Switzerland.

Falk, A., E. Fehr, and U. Fischbacher. 2000. Testing theories of fairness: intentions matter. Institute for Empirical Research in Economics, University of Zürich, Working Paper 63.

——. 2003. On the nature of fair behavior. *Economic Inquiry* 41:20–36.

Farh, J.-L., P. M. Podsakoff, and D. W. Organ. 1990. Accounting for organizational citizenship behavior: leader fairness and task scope versus satisfaction. *Journal of Management* 16:705–21.

Fehr, E., and A. Falk. 1999. Wage rigidity in a competitive incomplete contract market. *Journal of Political Economy* 107:106–34.

——. 2002. Psychological foundations of incentives. *European Economic Review* 46:687–724.

Fehr, E., and U. Fischbacher. 2002. Why social preferences matter: the impact of non-selfish motives on competition, cooperation and incentives. *The Economic Journal* 112:C1–33.

——. 2005. The economics of strong reciprocity. In *Moral Sentiments and Material Interests: The Foundations of Cooperation in Economic Life* (ed. H. Gintis, S. Bowles, R. T. Boyd, and E. Fehr), Chapter 5. MIT Press.

Fehr, E., and S. Gächter. 1998a. How effective are trust- and reciprocity-based incentives? In *Economics, Values and Organizations* (ed. A. Ben-Ner and L. Putterman), Chapter 13. Cambridge University Press.

——. 1998b. Reciprocity and economics: the economic implications of *Homo reciprocans*. *European Economic Review* 42:845–59.

——. 2000. Fairness and retaliation: the economics of reciprocity. *Journal of Economic Perspectives* 14:159–81.

——. 2002. Do incentive contracts undermine voluntary cooperation? Institute for Empirical Research in Economics, University of Zürich, Working Paper 34.

Fehr, E., and L. Götte. 2005. Robustness and real consequences of nominal wage rigidity? *Journal of Monetary Economics* 52:779–804.

Fehr, E., and B. Rockenbach. 2003. Detrimental effects of incentives on human altruism. *Nature* 422:137–40.

Fehr, E., and J.-R. Tyran. 2001. Does money illusion matter? *American Economic Review* 91:1239–62.

Fehr, E., G. Kirchsteiger, and A. Riedl. 1993. Does fairness prevent market clearing? An experimental investigation. *Quarterly Journal of Economics* 108:437–59.

Fehr, E., G. Kirchsteiger, and A. Riedl. 1996. Involuntary unemployment and non-compensating wage differentials in an experimental labour market. *Economic Journal* 106:106–21.

Fehr, E., S. Gächter, and G. Kirchsteiger. 1997. Reciprocity as a contract enforcement device: experimental evidence. *Econometrica* 65:833–60.

Fehr, E., E. Kirchler, A. Weichbold, and S. Gächter. 1998a. When social norms overpower competition: gift exchange in experimental labor markets. *Journal of Labor Economics* 16:324–51.

Fehr, E., G. Kirchsteiger, and A. Riedl. 1998b. Gift exchange and reciprocity in competitive experimental markets. *European Economic Review* 42:1–34.

Fehr, E., A. Klein, and K. M. Schmidt. 2001. Fairness, incentives and contractual incompleteness. Institute for Empirical Research in Economics, University of Zürich, Working Paper 72.

Folger, R. 1993. Justice, motivation, and performance: beyond role requirements. *Employee Responsibilities and Rights Journal* 6:239–48.

Fortin, P. 1996. The great Canadian slump. *Canadian Journal of Economics* 29:761–87.

Gächter, S., and A. Falk. 2002. Reputation and reciprocity: consequences for the labour relation. *Scandinavian Journal of Economics* 104:1–26.

George, J. M. 1991. State or trait: effects of positive mood on prosocial behaviors at work. *Journal of Applied Psychology* 76:299–307.

George, J. M., and K. Bettenhausen. 1990. Understanding prosocial behavior, sales performance, and turnover: a group-level analysis in a service context. *Journal of Applied Psychology* 75:698–709.

Gneezy, U., and A. Rustichini. 2000. A fine is a price. *Journal of Legal Studies* 29:1–17.

Goux, D. 1997. Les salaires nominaux sont-ils rigides à la baisse? Mimeo, Institut National de la Statistique et des Études Économiques.

Greenberg, J. 1989. Injustice and cognitive reevaluation of the work environment. *Academy of Management Journal* 32:174–84.

———. 1990. Employee theft as a reaction to underpayment inequity: the hidden cost of pay cuts. *Journal of Applied Psychology* 75:561–68.

———. 1993. Justice and organizational citizenship: a commentary on the state of the science. *Employee Responsibilities and Rights Journal* 6:249–56.

Herzberg, F., B. Mausner, R. O. Peterson, and D. Capwell. 1957. *Job Attitudes: Review of Research and Opinion.* Pittsburgh, PA: Psychological Service of Pittsburgh.

Howitt, P. 2002. Looking inside the labor market: a review article. *Journal of Economic Literature* 40:125–38.

Iaffaldano, M. T., and P. M. Muchinsky. 1985. Job satisfaction and job performance: a meta-analysis. *Psychological Bulletin* 97:251–73.

Kahn, S. 1997. Evidence of nominal wage stickiness from microdata. *American Economic Review* 87:993–1008.

Kahneman, D., J. L. Knetsch, and R. H. Thaler. 1986. Fairness as a constraint on profit seeking: entitlements in the market. *American Economic Review* 76:728–41.

Katz, D. 1964. The motivational basis of organizational behavior. *Behavioral Science* 9:131–46.

Kaufman, R. 1984. On wage stickiness in Britain's competitive sector. *British Journal of Industrial Relations* 22:101–12.

Keynes, J. M. 1936. *The General Theory of Employment, Interest, and Money.* London: Macmillan.

Kirchler, E., E. Fehr, and R. Evans. 1996. Social exchange in the labor market: reciprocity and trust versus egoistic money maximization. *Journal of Economic Psychology* 17:313–41.

Konovsky, M. A., and D. W. Organ. 1996. Dispositional and contextual determinants of organizational citizenship behavior. *Journal of Organizational Behavior* 17:253–66.

Kramarz, F. 2001. Rigid wages: what have we learned from microeconomic studies? In *Advances in Macroeconomic Theory* (ed. J. H. Drèze). Oxford University Press.

Lawler III, E. E. 1971. *Pay and Organizational Effectiveness: A Psychological View.* New York: McGraw-Hill.

Lebow, D. E., D. J. Stockton, and W. L. Wascher. 1995. Inflation, nominal wage rigidity, and the efficiency of labor markets. Board of Governors of the Federal Reserve System, Finance and Economic Discussion Series Paper 94-45.

Lebow, D. E., R. E. Saks, and B. A. Wilson. 2003. Downward nominal wage rigidity: evidence from the employment cost index. *Advances in Macroeconomics* 3(1), article 2.

Levine, D. I. 1993. Fairness, markets, and ability to pay: evidence from compensation executives. *American Economic Review* 83:1241–59.

Likert, R. 1961. *New Patterns of Management.* New York: McGraw-Hill.

Lindbeck, A., and D. J. Snower. 1988. Cooperation, harassment, and involuntary unemployment: an insider–outsider approach. *American Economic Review* 78:167–88.

Locke, E. A. 1976. The nature and causes of job satisfaction. In *Handbook of Industrial and Organizational Psychology* (ed. M. D. Dunnette), pp. 1297–356. Chicago: Rand McNally.

MacKenzie, S. B., P. M. Podsakoff, and R. Fetter. 1991. Organizational citizenship behavior and objective productivity as determinants of managerial evaluations of salespersons' performance. *Organizational Behavior and Human Decision Processes* 50:123–50.

———. 1993. The impact of organizational citizenship behavior on evaluations of salesperson performance. *Journal of Marketing* 57:70–80.

MacKenzie, S. B., P. M. Podsakoff, and M. Ahearne. 1998. Some possible antecedents and consequences of in-role and extra-role salesperson performance. *Journal of Marketing* 62:87–98.

MacKenzie, S. B., P. M. Podsakoff, and G. A. Rich. 2001. Transformational and transactional leadership and salesperson performance. *Journal of the Academy of Marketing Science* 29:115–34.

Mathieu, J. E., and D. M. Zajac. 1990. A review and meta-analysis of the antecedents, correlates, and consequences of organizational commitment. *Psychological Bulletin* 108:171–94.

McLaughlin, K. J. 1994. Rigid wages? *Journal of Monetary Economics* 34:383–414.

———. 1999. Are nominal wage changes skewed away from wage cuts? *Federal Reserve Bank of St. Louis Review* 81:117–32.

Mitchell, D. J. B. 1985. Shifting norms in wage determination. *Brookings Papers on Economic Activity* 1985:575–99.

Mobley, W. H. 1982. *Employee Turnover: Causes, Consequences, and Control*. Reading, MA: Addison-Wesley.

Moorman, R. H. 1991. Relationship between organizational justice and organizational citizenship behaviors: do fairness and perceptions influence employee citizenship? *Journal of Applied Psychology* 76:845–55.

——. 1993. The influence of cognitive and affective based job satisfaction measures on the relationship between satisfaction and organizational citizenship behavior. *Human Relations* 46:759–76.

Moorman, R. H., B. P. Niehoff, and D. W. Organ. 1993. Treating employees fairly and organizational citizenship behavior: sorting the effects of jobs satisfaction, organizational commitment, and procedural justice. *Employee Responsibilities and Rights Journal* 6:209–25.

Nagin, D., J. Rebitzer, S. Sanders, and L. Taylor. 2002. Monitoring, motivation, and management: the determinants of opportunistic behavior in a field experiment. *American Economic Review* 92:850–73.

Netemeyer, R. G., J. S. Boles, D. O. McKee, and R. McMurrian. 1997. An investigation into antecedents of organizational citizenship behaviors in a personal selling context. *Journal of Marketing* 61:85–98.

Niehoff, B. P., and R. H. Moorman. 1993. Justice as a mediator of the relationship between methods of monitoring and organizational citizenship behavior. *Academy of Management Journal* 36:527–56.

O'Reilly III, C., and J. Chatman. 1986. Organizational commitment and psychological attachment: the effects of compliance, identification, and internalization on prosocial behavior. *Journal of Applied Psychology* 71:492–99.

Organ, D. W. 1988. *Organizational Citizenship Behavior*. Lexington, MA: Lexington Books.

——. 1990. The motivational basis of organizational citizenship behavior. In *Research in Organizational Behavior* (ed. B. M. Staw and L. L. Cummings), Volume 12, pp. 43–72. Elsevier.

Organ, D. W., and M. Konovsky. 1989. Cognitive versus affective determinants of organizational citizenship behavior. *Journal of Applied Psychology* 74:157–64.

Organ, D. W., and A. Lingl. 1995. Personality, satisfaction, and organizational citizenship behavior. *Journal of Social Psychology* 135:339–50.

Organ, D. W., and R. H. Moorman. 1993. Fairness and organizational citizenship behavior: what are the connections? *Social Justice Research* 6:5–18.

Organ, D. W., and K. Ryan. 1995. A meta-analytic review of attitudinal and dispositional predictors of organizational citizenship behavior. *Personnel Psychology* 48:775–802.

Podsakoff, P. M., and S. B. MacKenzie. 1993. Citizenship behavior and fairness in organizations: issues and directions for future research. *Employee Responsibilities and Rights Journal* 6:257–69.

——. 1994. Organizational citizenship behaviors and sales unit effectiveness. *Journal of Marketing Research* 31:351–63.

——. 1997. Impact of organizational citizenship behavior on organizational performance: a review and suggestions for future research. *Human Performance* 10:133–51.

Podsakoff, P. M., S. B. MacKenzie, R. H. Moorman, and R. Fetter. 1990. Transformational leader behaviors and their effects on followers' trust in leader, satisfaction, and organizational citizenship behaviors. *Leadership Quarterly* 1:107–42.

Podsakoff, P. M., S. B. MacKenzie, and C. Hui. 1993. Organizational citizenship behaviors and managerial evaluations of employee performance: a review and suggestions for future research. In *Research in Personnel and Human Resources Management* (ed. G. R. Ferris), Volume 11, pp. 1–40. Elsevier.

Podsakoff, P. M., S. B. MacKenzie, and W. H. Bommer. 1996. Transformational leader behaviors and substitutes for leadership as determinants of employee satisfaction, commitment, trust, and organizational citizenship behaviors. *Journal of Management* 22:259–98.

Podsakoff, P. M., M. Ahearne, and S. B. MacKenzie. 1997. Organizational citizenship behavior and the quantity and quality of work group performance. *Journal of Applied Psychology* 82:262–70.

Podsakoff, P. M., S. B. MacKenzie, J. B. Paine, and D. G. Bachrach. 2000. Organizational citizenship behaviors: a critical review of the theoretical and empirical literature and suggestions for future research. *Journal of Management* 26:513–63.

Price, J. L. 1977. *The Study of Turnover*. Iowa State University Press.

Puffer, S. M. 1987. Prosocial behavior, noncompliant behavior, and work performance among commission salespeople. *Journal of Applied Psychology* 72:615–21.

Rilling, J. K., D. A. Gutman, T. R. Zeh, G. Pagnoni, G. S. Berns, and C. D. Kits. 2002. A neural basis for social cooperation. *Neuron* 35:395–405.

Schaubroeck, J., D. R. May, and R. W. Brown. 1994. Procedural justice explanations and employee reactions to economic hardship: a field experiment. *Journal of Applied Psychology* 79:455–60.

Schnake, M. 1991. Organizational citizenship: a review, proposed model, and research agenda. *Human Relations* 44:735–59.

Seashore, S. 1954. *Group Cohesiveness in the Industrial Work Group*. University of Michigan Press.

Shafir, E., P. Diamond, and A. Tversky. 1997. Money illusion. *Quarterly Journal of Economics* 112:341–74.

Shapiro, C., and J. E. Stiglitz. 1984. Equilibrium unemployment as a worker discipline device. *American Economic Review* 74:433–44.

Smith, J. C. 2000. Nominal wage rigidity in the United Kingdom. *Economic Journal* 110:C176–95.

——. 2002. Pay cuts and morale: a test of downward nominal rigidity. Warwick Economic Research Paper 649, Department of Economics, University of Warwick, U.K.

Solow, R. M. 1979. Another possible source of wage stickiness. *Journal of Macroeconomics* 1:79–82.

——. 1990. *The Labor Market as a Social Institution*. Cambridge, MA: Basil Blackwell.

Staw, B. M. 1984. Organizational behavior: a review and reformulation of the field's outcome variables. *Annual Review of Psychology* 35:627–66.

Steers, R. M., and S. R. Rhodes. 1978. Major influences on employee attendance: a process model. *Journal of Applied Psychology* 63:391–407.

Tyler, T. R. 1999. Why people cooperate with organizations: an identity-based perspective. *Research in Organizational Behavior* 21:201–46.

Tyler, T. R., and S. L. Blader. 2000. *Cooperation in Groups: Procedural Justice, Social Identity, and Behavioral Engagement*. Philadelphia, PA: Psychology Press.

———. 2001. Identity and cooperative behavior in groups. *Group Processes and Intergroup Relations* 4:207–26.

Viteles, M. S. 1953. *Motivation and Morale in Industry*. New York: W. W. Norton.

Vroom, V. H. 1964. *Work and Motivation*. Wiley.

Walz, S. M., and B. P. Niehoff. 1996. Organizational citizenship behaviors and their relationship with indicators of organizational effectiveness in limited menu restaurants. In *Academy of Management Best Papers Proceedings* (ed. J. B. Keys and L. N. Dosier), pp. 307–11. Statesboro, GA: George Southern University.

Weiss, A. 1980. Job queues and layoffs in labor markets with flexible wages. *Journal of Political Economy* 88:526–38.

———. 1990. *Efficiency Wages: Models of Unemployment, Layoffs, and Wage Dispersion*. Princeton University Press.

Whyte, W. F. et al. 1955. *Money and Motivation: An Analysis of Incentives in Industry*. New York: Harper and Row.

———. 1961. *Men at Work*. Homewood, IL: Corsey Press.

Wilson, B. A. 1997. Movements of wages over the business cycle: an intra-firm view. Board of Governors of the Federal Reserve System (U.S.), Finance and Economics Discussion Series, 1997-1.

COMMENT BY SEPPO HONKAPOHJA

Introduction

Bewley presents a very interesting survey of the recent empirical microresearch on wage formation and on reasons for wage rigidity. Much of this work is behavioral in its underpinnings and the results show how notions of fairness and reciprocity play an important role in wage determination. An important aspect of the reviewed empirical work is that these studies are based not just on published statistics but rather on a variety of approaches including questionnaires, field studies, surveys, and experiments. His own work (see Bewley 1999) of course stands out as a particularly meticulous example of this brand of empirical economics.

I am a consumer and not a producer of this kind of research. I am, however, an interested consumer since questions of wage formation and wage rigidity are central to macroeconomics. My comments focus on what macroeconomics can learn from the microresearch discussed in this chapter. I will also take up an important open issue in the surveyed literature.

Lessons from the Empirical Microresearch

The first lesson from this chapter is that the notion of (downward) wage rigidity is not as simple as it sounds. Different concepts of the wage have been used. It could in principle mean a firm's marginal labor costs or total compensation per worker, or total compensation for employees with given job and work conditions. The empirical work has been ambiguous with respect to the different notions. While the results are not fully clear-cut, there seems to be a fair amount of evidence that basic compensation of employees, excluding bonuses, overtime and the like is subject to considerable downward rigidity.

This is not a surprising answer. In some form it has been used as casual evidence for a long time in much of macroeconomics.[7] Numerous models and reasons for wage rigidity have been developed and discussed in macroeconomics over nearly seven decades since the publication of Keynes's General Theory and the birth of Keynesian economics.

Explicit analysis of the motivations behind wage rigidity is a new and interesting aspect of the research discussed by Bewley. The reasons for rigidity given in this behavioral literature can be seen as tests on the different economic theories of wage rigidity. I personally found this aspect of the paper quite interesting as it provides a novel perspective to the different models of wage rigidity used in modern macroeconomics.

An important observation from the microresearch is that pay cuts are resisted because they damage morale, and it is the management who seems to think this way.[8] There is a second important observation that morale is damaged when wages are cut, while wage levels have less to do with morale. Bewley suggests that "employees usually have little notion of a fair or market value for their services," which leads to an important question about the determinants of the reference point for judging fairness. The related literature has some ideas about this and I will return to this point later.

The observation about wage changes and morale runs counter to some earlier models of labor markets. These were largely based on levels of wages and productivity or morale (see, for example, Akerlof 1982; Akerlof and Yellen 1988; Solow 1990). Correspondingly, Keynes's notion of workers' concern about relative wages in similar jobs in different firms does not seem to get much support from the work of Bewley and others.[9] Interestingly, the model of insiders and outsiders (Lindbeck and Snower 1988) fares somewhat better, as harassment and refusal to cooperate can perhaps be interpreted as consequences of the loss of morale.

---

[7] New Classical Macroeconomics and Real Business Cycle theory is, however, largely based on fully flexible wages and prices.

[8] Note that pay cuts are more easily accepted if they save a large number of jobs or possibly the whole firm.

[9] However, unionization of workers leads to more clear-cut formulation of the workers' notion of market wages.

Bewley's basic observation about pay changes and morale does not provide any support for the model of shirking and wages (Shapiro and Stiglitz 1984). Apparently, cooperation between managers and firms is not obtained by threats of firing of shirkers (or workers with low productivity). This is not to say that incentives are not important. Workers do work harder in times of recession but not because management threatens them. The incentives come directly from a tougher external environment.

Another fairly popular model emphasizing information problems and incentives is the adverse selection model of Weiss (1990). Here the micro evidence is interestingly in agreement with that theory when it concerns quits. Managers prefer layoffs to pay cuts, since using the latter would lead to departure of the best workers. However, the other half of Weiss's model, the connection between high wages and hiring of high-productivity workers, is not supported by the micro studies.

These descriptions are just a few examples of the ideas from Bewley's comprehensive survey. Many macroeconomists have for a long time thought that labor markets and wage determination/rigidity involve large degrees of social interactions and that they are not just relatively anonymous markets of commodity exchange.[10] This recent micro work provides support and makes these notions more precise.

There are important methodological questions in the micro evidence that Bewley reviews. In particular, the idea of interviewing not only about wage determination but also about the respondents' reasoning can be problematic. Observations are somehow more reliable about "facts" than about responses to questions about motivation. Do we know enough about the respondents' incentives during the interviews? Yet, it must be acknowledged that these answers are often fascinating.

Fairness Norms and Multiple Equilibria

I now move away from the micro studies and take up a particular aspect of these models, relating to norms or reference points, which are a central part of the new applied models of fairness in wage setting. Let me conduct my discussion by means of a recent interesting work by Driscoll and Holden (2002, 2004) about fairness and inflation persistence. Driscoll and Holden suggest that inclusion of fairness considerations in a standard model of wage bargaining leads to a range of equilibria and this feature can in turn be useful for explaining inflation persistence in the data.[11]

---

[10]Of course, there is the other main line of macroeconomics, which purports to explain wage formation as part of competitive contracting leading to market efficiency.

[11]The role of inflation versus price level persistence has been discussed a great deal in the recent macro literature. The verdict is still out (see, for example, the most recent papers by Ireland (2001) and Roberts (1997), who argue against inflation persistence).

The Driscoll–Holden model depicts a symmetric economy with many monopolistically competitive firms and worker insiders bargaining over wages. The workers
are concerned about fair treatment and in particular they resent being worse off than
identical workers elsewhere.[12] Moreover, the dissatisfaction from being paid less is
stronger than the satisfaction from being paid more. There is thus a kink in the utility
function of workers at the wage level of other workers in their reference group. This
is a form of loss aversion, which is often employed in the literature on wage norms.
Finally, there are several symmetrical groups of workers in the economy.

In this kind of model, Nash wage bargaining is characterized by the existence
of two thresholds. There is a unique outcome, which is equal to what is perceived
to happen in the reference group when the reference group wage is within the
thresholds. If the reference group wage is either above the upper threshold or below
the lower threshold, then the bargaining outcome is equal to the corresponding
threshold. The thresholds depend on the reference group wage, the economy-wide
average wage, and other macro variables.

Assume for simplicity that there are only two groups in the economy, and that
the aggregate demand function specifies demand as being equal to real balances. A
log-linearized version of the model can be written as follows. The contract wage
x_{Jt} of a group J is determined as[13]

$$x_{Jt} \leqslant x_{Gt}^e + \gamma_0(m_t - p_t) + \gamma_1^+,$$
$$x_{Jt} = x_{Gt}^e,$$
$$x_{Jt} \geqslant x_{Gt}^e + \gamma_0(m_t - p_t) + \gamma_1^-,$$

where $\gamma_1^+ > \gamma_1^-$ are threshold parameters and the log price level is

$$p_t = \mu + \tfrac{1}{2}(x_{Jt} + x_{Gt}^e).$$

The idea is that there are thresholds within which the wage must lie. Note that I
have added the superscript "e" to the reference wage x_{Gt}^e of the other group. This
is to emphasize the reaction function of the workers in response to perceived wages
elsewhere. m_t and p_t are the logs of the money supply and price level, respectively.

Taking account of the definition of the price level we can write the model as

$$x_{Jt} = \begin{cases} \phi(x_{Gt}^e)^+ & \text{if } x_{Gt}^e \geqslant \phi(x_{Gt}^e)^+, \\ x_{Gt}^e & \text{if } x_{Gt}^e \in (\phi(x_{Gt}^e)^-, \phi(x_{Gt}^e)^+), \\ \phi(x_{Gt}^e)^- & \text{if } x_{Gt}^e \leqslant \phi(x_{Gt}^e)^-, \end{cases}$$

[12]This assumption is not supported by Bewley's paper, except when there are unions, as is the case
here.

[13]My notation is somewhat different from that of Driscoll and Holden.

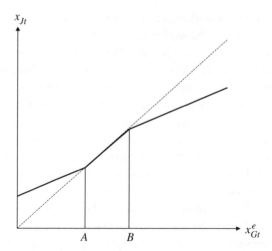

x_{Jt}

A B

x_{Gt}^e

Figure 5.1. Reaction function of a worker group.

where

$$\phi(x_{Gt}^e)^{+/-} = \left(\frac{2 - \gamma_0}{2 + \gamma_0}\right) x_{Gt}^e + \frac{2\gamma_0}{2 + \gamma_0}(m_t - \mu) + \frac{2\gamma_1^{+/-}}{2 + \gamma_0}.$$

Here the notation $\gamma_1^{+/-}$ means γ_1^+ or γ_1^-. Since the economy is symmetric, a rational expectations equilibrium (REE) obtains when $x_{Jt} = x_{Gt}^e$ and it is easy to represent the possible REE by Figure 5.1. There is clearly a whole range of equilibria, represented by the segment (A, B).

Changes in the money supply will move the graph of the best response map. Yet, inside the range (A, B), the REE contract wage may well be unresponsive to money supply variations. This depends on the perceptions of the workers in wage bargaining. Driscoll and Holden assume that workers are just concerned about the wages elsewhere and use past data as a way of generating their perceptions. In this case the whole segment is indeed REE and an interior equilibrium is pinned down by history and it will not respond to current policy variations. On the other hand, the perceptions of workers might be more subtle. In particular, the perceptions could well incorporate money supply variations, especially if systematic patterns in money supply movements are apparent. If this is the case, then monetary policy variations will not leave the contracted wages unaffected, as workers will incorporate such systematic patterns into their wage formation.

I will not pursue the analysis any further; I just wanted to make a basic point: we need to know much more about the determination of fairness reference points and how the environment in which agents operate (in particular, macro variables) affects their reference points.

Conclusion

The recent research on wages and fairness surveyed by Bewley is highly interesting and thought provoking. It has already provided useful evidence on what might be empirically the more interesting models of labor markets as part of the macro economy. There is clearly potential for further theoretical and empirical work concerning the determination of reference points in different economic environments and how these considerations affect range of potential equilibria and the effects of economic policy.

REFERENCES

Akerlof, G. A. 1982. Labor contracts as gift exchange. *Quarterly Journal of Economics* 97:543–69.

Akerlof, G. A., and J. Yellen. 1988. Fairness and unemployment. *American Economic Review* 78:44–49.

Bewley, T. 1999. *Why Wages Don't Fall During a Recession*. Harvard University Press.

Driscoll, J. C., and S. Holden. 2002. Coordination, fair treatment and inflation persistence. Working Paper, Board of Governors of the Federal Reserve System.

———. 2004. Fairness and inflation persistence. *Journal of the European Economic Association* 2:240–50.

Ireland, P. 2001. Sticky-price models of the business cycle: specification and stability. *Journal of Monetary Economics* 47:3–18.

Lindbeck, A., and D. Snower. 1988. Cooperation, harassment and involuntary unemployment: an insider–outsider approach. *American Economic Review* 78:167–88.

Roberts, J. M. 1997. Is inflation sticky? *Journal of Monetary Economics* 39:173–96.

Shapiro, C., and J. E. Stiglitz. 1984. Equilibrium unemployment as a worker discipline device. *American Economic Review* 74:433–44.

Solow, R. A. 1990. *The Labor Market as a Social Institution*. Cambridge, MA: Basil Blackwell.

Weiss, A. 1990. *Efficiency Wages: Models of Unemployment, Layoffs and Wage Dispersion*. Princeton University Press.

Behavioral Economics and Health Economics

By Richard G. Frank[1]

6.1 INTRODUCTION AND BACKGROUND

If one examines the salient economic institutions of the health sector, one might expect that sector to be a breeding ground for applied behavioral economics. Consider a set of economic activities where addictions figure prominently; where consumers have limited information that they must use to make choices in the context of fear, urgency, and trust in an expert; and where the services used are often credence goods (Emons 1997) whose applications are frequently governed by professional norms and habit. In such an economic environment, the methods of behavioral economics might be expected to be prevalent in modifying traditional models to take account of those features that appear to conflict with simple notions of rationality in economic behavior. Yet the application of behavioral economics to issues in health economics has been largely confined to understanding addictive behavior around cigarettes, drugs, and alcohol (see, for example, Becker and Murphy 1988; Gruber and Koszegi 2001; Loewenstein 2001; O'Donoghue and Rabin 1999; Schoenbaum 1997).

6.1.1 *Research Traditions in Health Economics*

Research on addictions has its origins in research on household production and the demand for good health (Becker 1964; Grossman 1972). Decisions about substance abuse involve a set of harmful health choices that appear to represent extreme trade-offs between today's pleasures and tomorrow's health and well-being. A substantial amount of progress has been made in both theoretical analysis and empirical testing of models in this area, and a lively program of research that encompasses behavioral economic concepts is underway.

[1]I gratefully acknowledge financial support from the AHRQ (Grant P0-1HS10803) the Alfred P. Sloan Foundation, an NIH Export Center (Grant P20 MD 000537), and the John D. and Catherine T. MacArthur Foundation. I thank Peter Diamond, Jacob Glazier, Sherry Glied, Bo Koszegi, Tom McGuire, Joe Newhouse, Arnie Epstein, and Paul Cleary for helpful discussion.

In this chapter I draw on a different research tradition, which emanates from the seminal paper by Arrow (1963). The efficiency of health insurance markets, doctor–patient relationships, and the role of nonmarket institutions in promoting efficiency were raised by Arrow and continue to be central issues in the health economics research program. This side of health economics has received far less attention from scholars armed with the tools of behavioral economics than the addictions area. I focus on decision-making about treatment of illness, rationing of health services, and markets for health insurance.

I argue that behavioral economics may be particularly important for modifying neoclassical approaches because, as in many areas of the economy, people appear to make choices about health care that are situation- or context-specific, resulting in cognitive errors and failures to optimize. The health sector is also characterized by institutions and decision-making circumstances that, in addition to making cognitive errors more likely, create friction that impedes market adjustments that may lead to correction of errors over time (Glaeser 2003; Mullainathan and Thaler 2001). These include the stress of decision-making about one's health, professionalism, and a lack of information about medical care. The paper is organized into four sections. This introductory section sets the intellectual context for the review. The second section focuses on physician behavior, which represents a large class of problems in the health sector, where I believe behavioral economics has much to contribute. The third section addresses some puzzles in health economics related to demand behavior and the behavior of health insurance markets. The final section offers some concluding observations and comments on normative issues in health economics.

6.1.2 *Arrow and the Health-Care Challenge for Behavioral Economics*

Arrow's (1963) paper seeks to explain the health sector's institutions as a response to the special features of health care and health insurance. Among the special characteristics are information asymmetry and the significance of medical care in human affairs. The research program stemming from Arrow's work has produced great understanding of health-care delivery. Among the issues at the heart of the research program have been: market failure in health insurance due to moral hazard and adverse selection; the significance of the nonprofit organizational form in health care; and the role of institutions such as professional norms, trust, and morality in medical markets.

Applying traditional economic models that rely on rational utility-maximizing consumers and physicians and efficient market equilibriums has been highly productive both theoretically and empirically, and has contributed to the design of public policy in health care (Culyer and Newhouse 2000). For example, research on hospital payment methods has advanced notably and has been very influential in public policy debates (Newhouse 2003). Yet the application of traditional models has also repeatedly faced puzzles that have served as intellectual impasses. It is in attending to such puzzles that the ideas of behavioral economics may be particularly useful in advancing the analysis of health-care markets and institutions. In the next section I focus on markets for physician services and some puzzles found in those markets. I believe that these issues are representative of broader issues in the economics of the health sector.

6.2 MODELS OF PHYSICIAN BEHAVIOR

Early in his essay, Arrow (1963, p. 949) remarked:

> It is clear from everyday observation that the behavior of sellers of medical care is different from that of businessmen in general.

No area in health economics relies on a vocabulary that is more closely linked to the work of behavioral economics than research on physician behavior. As Pauly (2001) notes, Arrow used words such as "trust" and "morals" to discuss physician behavior. These are words that tend to make economists uncomfortable.

Some of the first econometric studies of health-care markets took aim at the market for physicians' services (Feldstein 1970; Newhouse 1970; Fuchs and Kramer 1972). These studies took the competitive model as their point of departure. Each obtained results showing a positive partial correlation between the physician stock in a market and physician prices: a finding inconsistent with the competitive model. These papers set off a line of research on models of physician behavior that continues to this day. The first reactions to the surprising results were to suspect monopoly in the physicians' market (Newhouse 1970; Frech and Ginsburg 1972). Further analysis found the evidence to be inconsistent with both monopoly and competitive models. Health economists rapidly developed a set of ad hoc explanations grounded in motivations of physicians that departed from profit maximization. Yet, as McGuire (2000) notes, "there is no agreeable alternative" model to that of profit maximization.

Feldstein (1970) sought to explain the apparent departure from simple profit maximization. He argued that physician markets experience persistent excess demand. He proposed that the reason for this is that physicians deliberately set prices below market clearing levels to enable them to choose the most "interesting cases" from among the patient pool. This explanation was not grounded in any evidence about physician motives or the details of medical practice. A second explanation attempted to import an early behavioral economics idea, namely the satisficing model (Simon 1958). Newhouse (1970) and Evans (1974) suggested that physicians might set prices so as to achieve a "target income" in part because maximizing behavior may be seen as socially undesirable. Arrow (1963) first raised this point by observing approvingly that sociologists had argued for a "collectivity orientation" of physicians that would lead them away from profit-maximizing behavior. Evans (1974) proposed that the target income level was set relative to the local income distribution.

Careful analysis of the target income model reveals a variety of shortcomings (McGuire 2000). The basis for establishing the "target" was quite fuzzy. In addition, the "target" is merely an objective. There are numerous ways of hitting the target; the theory does not explain which approach will be taken. A complete model also requires a rule of choice for pursuing the objective. The target income model is typically specified in the context of a monopolistically competitive market structure, where physicians choose a price that will achieve a target income and meets demand. This model setup yields multiple equilibria that are unstable, resulting in dramatic swings in prices in response to small changes in physician supply. In sum the target income model might be viewed as a "false start" in linking behavioral economics and health economics.

A different modeling approach introduced the notion of "physician-induced demand" in the context of a model of utility maximization. Evans (1974) posited that physicians create demand for their own services by exploiting their role as an agent for the incompletely informed patient. That is, physicians are imperfect agents in that they will recommend treatment beyond the "patient's optimum level" in order to gain income. Medical uncertainty and asymmetric information all serve to reinforce this conception of physician behavior. This model treats demand inducement in a manner akin to how advertising is introduced into market models. That is, demand inducement is a shifter in the demand function facing the doctor. The ability to induce demand is also specified as an argument in the physicians' objective function, so that exploiting the agency relation for self-interest reduces physician utility.[2] This device serves to constrain an otherwise unbounded ability to shift demand.

While intuitively appealing, given the importance of the agency relation between physician and patient, little research has been done to understand the forces underlying the ability to induce demand as proposed in these models (McGuire 2000; Reinhardt 1978; Fuchs 1978). Most discussions of demand inducement appeal intuitively to notions of medical ethics and trust between doctors and patients; poor information, fear, and anxiety on the part of patients; and uncertainty in medical choices. The behavioral economics literature has explored how some of these circumstances and others affect decision-making and economic behavior (Rabin 1998). Demand inducement may well result from a number of psychological features

---

[2]Some modeling efforts also assign a pecuniary cost to demand inducement in the context of a profit-maximizing model of physician behavior (Stano 1987).

of doctors and patients operating in health-care markets. There are a number of additional constructs in behavioral economics, such as self-serving behavior, wishful thinking, and the impact of the desire by patients to avoid regret, that might contribute to what appears as demand inducement (Rabin 1998; Thaler 1980). The application of these concepts leads one to consider in greater detail the nature of doctor–patient interactions in the context of models of physician decision-making.

6.2.1 *The Economics of Physician Decision-Making*

Physicians are highly educated and skilled professionals who are motivated to serve their patients in order to improve their health and well-being. They are also frequently in positions in which they face great clinical uncertainty and must persuade patients to pursue one clinical course over others. Physicians have been shown to be creatures of habit in making medical choices, and are slow to adopt new practices and technologies that would improve the quality of care and, in turn, their patients' health (Institute of Medicine 2001). Specifically, a series of studies have shown that, in treating conditions like otitis media, diabetes, depression, and asthma, physicians regularly depart from evidence-based practice (Institute of Medicine 2001, Appendix A). This runs counter to what one might expect from market models that assume either profit maximization or maximization of a physician objective function that might include patient health benefits and income as arguments.

For example, physicians in the United States do not gain financially based on the specific drugs they choose to prescribe for their patients. Therefore one might expect physicians to choose the most cost-effective drugs on behalf of their patients, thereby serving as a "perfect agent." Yet physicians have been observed to be habitual in their choice of pharmaceutical agents, relying on drugs they became familiar with in medical training or learned about through pharmaceutical promotions. This has meant a reluctance to use more effective new drugs or lower cost versions of older drugs (generics) (Hellerstein 1998). Also, physicians have been slow to prescribe drugs that have been widely shown to improve health outcomes, such as beta-blockers for patients following a heart attack (Institute of Medicine 2001).

Health economists attempting to address such puzzles have frequently appealed to the costs of learning about new drugs and procedures. Empirical research on the simplest substitution choices in prescription drugs, that between branded and generic versions of the same drug, show a great heterogeneity in willingness to substitute that is unexplained by factors clearly associated with experience or learning costs (Hellerstein 1998). Thus, simple extensions of the profit or utility-maximizing models have not produced satisfactory explanations of basic clinical choices.

6.2.2 *Models of Maximization, Uncertainty, and Information Asymmetry*

A hallmark of medical decision-making is choice under uncertainty. Arrow's (1963) paper begins with this premise. Microeconomic models of physician decision-making that follow in the tradition of Arrow recognize that there is uncertainty about the effectiveness of any medical technology and there is heterogeneity in patient responses to treatment and preferences about care and how the process of care will unfold. In this section, a simple model of physician behavior is set out that will enable us to examine some potential contributions of behavioral economics to modifying the model. I adopt the model of physician behavior and notation of McGuire (2000) in his review of *Physician Agency*.

A patient is assumed to benefit from the receipt of medical care (m) according to the function $B = B(m)$, where $B' > 0$ and $B'' < 0$. The negative second derivative occurs because of diminishing marginal utility of health status and because the health production function $H = H(m)$ has a negative second derivative. We can therefore restate the benefit function to capture both of these effects as $B(m) = V(H(m))$. Generally, it is assumed that $V'' < 0$, which implies risk aversion.[3] McGuire (2000) introduces uncertainty as a simple additive term to the health production function $H(m)$. In an uncertain medical decision-making context, a patient's benefits from medical care are viewed as expected benefits:

$$E[B(m, u)] = E[V(H(m)) + u], \qquad (6.1)$$

where u is a random error with mean 0 and variance σ_u.[4] One implication pointed to by McGuire (2000) is that if the degree of absolute risk aversion is decreasing in income then the expected benefits of using medical care, m, rises with the level of uncertainty (σ_u). The implication of this observation is that patients will appear to demand "too much" medical care when judged in terms of ex post marginal contributions to health outcomes. The excess use of medical care can be seen as an attempt by uncertain patients to protect themselves against uncertain medical care.

Markets for medical care are characterized not only by uncertainty but also by asymmetric information between physician and patient. Most approaches to paying doctors in medical markets implicitly assume that outcomes are "noncontractible," that is, it is impractical to pay doctors on outcome (Dranove and White 1987).[5] Thus, most health-care markets make use of payment arrangements in which doctors are

---

[3]The application of prospect theory and the use of reference health levels is relevant here. However, an extensive discussion of this point here would distract from the main point which concerns the doctor–patient interaction.

[4]The additive specification of m is a simplification that aides tractability of the model.

[5]It may also be inefficient, because paying on outcomes may heighten existing selection incentives. Nevertheless, there is a growing interest in examining pay-for-performance schemes.

rewarded for performance through retention of patients or by attracting new patients. The vast majority of physician services are paid for either via capitation contracts (per person per year payment) or under fee for service arrangements. In either case, the physician is rewarded for having a higher volume of patients seeking his or her services (Kaiser Family Foundation 2003). Thus, if patients choose doctors or decide to stay with doctors based on performance, then physicians will have an incentive to undertake unobserved actions to improve quality and performance.

Because the health production function is affected by service delivery, physician effort, and other factors, an individual patient's observation of performance does not allow them to easily identify the level of effort supplied by a physician. This agency problem has been a long-standing concern for health economists. Asymmetric information is captured in McGuire's (2000) formulation by restating the benefit function to include physician effort, $B = B(m, e, u)$, where e represents physician effort. It is assumed that e is not observable and is therefore noncontractible. So the patient is assumed to know the relationships in $B(\cdot)$ and to observe m and the outcome of treatment, B_0. A patient is assumed to make Bayesian decisions.[6] Suppose we consider a situation where a physician's effort can be characterized as a simple dichotomous act. For example, a physician can read the literature on treatment for a condition presented by the patient. The Bayesian patient can make an inference about e based on observing m and B_0.[7] The inference can be viewed as a likelihood that a high level of effort was taken, $L_1(B_0, m)$. The likelihood that the proper effort was not taken is $L_0 = 1 - L_1$. The physician's profit-maximization problem with asymmetric information can be described as

$$\pi = n(L_1)R + (p - c)m, \tag{6.2}$$

where n is the number of patients seen by the physician and the term in the second set of brackets is a general statement about revenue and costs that encompasses the continuum of payment arrangements commonly used to pay doctors. These range from a capitation payment, where $R > 0$ and $p = 0$, to fee-for-service payments, where $R = 0$ and $p > 0$. If the patient infers that effort $e = 1$ and believes that the physician will typically undertake the desired effort then observing outcome will provide useful information. In this model incentives for quality care (high level of effort) are created by the demand response $n(\partial n/\partial e)$. It is also important that the payment systems are set up so that physician earnings are affected by the demand response to inferences about effort levels taken by the physician.

---

[6]This is an "as if" assumption that allows this problem to be modeled as a principal agent problem with Bayesian decision makers. As discussed below, this characterization is a focal point for potential contributions or behavioral economics.

[7]The model focuses on effort in this initial formulation. As we discuss below, this model may be easily extended to deal with a larger set of issues such as quality and choice or technology.

The degree of demand response is central to determining the efficiency of health-care markets. The model summarized above, for example, offers an underpinning to the demand inducement model discussed earlier (Dranove 1988). That is, the doctor might misrepresent information to a patient, leading them to believe the marginal product H' of a particular course of treatment is higher than it is in reality. The result is a higher level of demand for m than is efficient. This approach is similar to that taken in the optimal fraud literature and presumes a manipulative physician acting in a calculated self-interested manner even at a possible health cost to the patient. McGuire (2000) and others note that medical treatments frequently involve a sequence of interactions between doctor and patient that may allow a patient to learn about outcomes during the course of treatment. This may permit a patient to respond to physician actions in a manner that rewards effort.

A different modeling tack assumes that quality is an attribute of the physician that is not a matter of choice during a patient encounter. That is, e is a fixed attribute. This type of model has been used as an alternative to those of physician-induced demand (Pauly and Satterthwaite 1981). The implication of this view is that doctors are an experience good that can only be judged by sampling by a consumer or a trusted source of information (friend or family). Thus, in markets where there is a higher concentration of physicians, less may be known about any one physician, which may result in establishing market power for a doctor who is known to a patient. The implication is that an individual physician's demand curve is steeper in markets with more doctors, allowing them to charge higher prices. Such a model is used to explain why prices for physician's services are higher in markets with more physicians without resorting to demand inducement. Why adding a physician to the choice set would necessarily dilute information except in an average sense is unclear. For example, why would I know less about my doctor because other doctors moved into town? The approach illustrates how health economists have gone to considerable lengths to adapt the standard model to stylized facts in the health-care market place.

6.2.3 Behavioral Economics and Models of Physician Behavior: Possible Directions

Behavioral economics has frequently raised questions that go to the heart of the model set out in Equation (6.2), above: $\max \pi = n(L_1)R + (p - c)m$. Patient demand response is key to the transmission of incentives. The model posits that patients will choose a physician based on Bayesian inferences about effort made by the doctor. This requires that patients form a prior about a doctor's willingness to exert effort (an initial impression prior to contact) and engage in an updating process (following an initial contact) that assumes separation between previous judgments about the likelihood that high effort is undertaken and the evaluation of new evidence from, say, a new episode of care (Camerer and Loewenstein 2003). The health sector offers a unique institutional environment within which to view these decisions. When the institutional arrangements are combined with key concepts from behavioral economics a new view of market outcomes in the health sector begins to emerge.

6.2.3.1 Formation of Priors

Consider how people make choices about physicians and the sources of information used to make judgments about the quality of a physician. The methods by which patients obtain information about doctors prior to an initial contact and referrals are obtained play central roles in the formation of priors about doctor quality and willingness to exert effort. Most patients are close to fully insured, carrying cost sharing of 20% or less for physician services. The health sector in recent years has been characterized by expanded public availability of information on provider performance. State governments have published performance data on surgeons and hospitals. Local magazines and newspapers regularly report lists of top-ranking physicians. The Internet has increased the availability of information on hospitals, physicians and their practices. This expansion of information is part of a deliberate strategy to boost consumerism, improve market efficiency and presumably quality in health care (Shaller et al. 2003). Yet recent surveys of consumers show that 70% of people have not seen any information on the quality of providers (Kaiser Family Foundation 2000). These same surveys reveal that 70% of people report that they rely on family and friends and 65% on their usual physician as their most reliable sources of information on other providers of health care and their quality. In addition, patients report that they prefer providers with whom they are familiar. For example, 76% of survey respondents say they would choose a surgeon that they are familiar with over one that was more highly rated by experts such as state government or accrediting organizations.

The implications of these data are that the basis upon which priors about quality and performance are formed is the recounted experience of friends and relatives and to a lesser extent a regular doctor. Patients also put great weight on familiarity with a physician, presumably based on a relatively small number of positive interactions. In the case of choosing a primary care physician the reliance on friends and family is likely to be more important, since the choice suggests that there may be no regular doctor or that the relationship with the regular physician may not be satisfactory. This decision-making context is ripe for the types of situational influences on economic choices that are the focus of behavioral economics.

Tversky and Kahneman (1973) refer to an *availability heuristic* in order to describe the reliance on more vivid or memorable evidence to construct a prior about the probability that a physician is high quality or will exert adequate effort. Akerlof (1991) calls the phenomenon "salience." Given the data cited above, it is likely that personal reports will be relied upon over examination of systematic information collected on health-care qualifications or performance. Personal testimonials on the multidimensional service provided by physicians will be far more available than any systematic data-reporting system. Reliance on reports from family and friends may create distortions in perceived quality because of what is most memorable in personal reports. Consumers of health care have been shown to be good reporters of certain attributes of care and weakly aware of others. For example, patients have been shown to accurately report information on whether a physician was respectful, attentive, clear in explaining clinical issues, and had operated a clean and efficient office. These same patients were found to be inaccurate in reporting of the technical quality of care. That is, they were not accurate in judging whether a physician supplied appropriate evidence-based treatment (Edgman-Levitan and Cleary 1996). It has also been shown that the dimensions of care that consumers understand and can accurately report are not highly correlated with so-called technical aspects of quality care (Cleary and Edgman-Levitan 1997). The implication here is that patients will commonly develop a prior about a primary care physician by relying on reports from family and friends based on observations about some dimensions of medical care and perhaps not on the dimensions that most directly affect their health outcomes. Applying notions of an availability heuristic that focuses on one dimension of physician performance in the formulation of priors on quality expands the conception of demand and demand response in markets for physician services. This offers one promising avenue for better linking of market models to the observed behavior in health care.

The decision-making environment in health care also offers a context where the formation of priors about providers of medical care may be subject to the "law of small numbers" bias (Rabin 1998, 2002). Rabin (2002) explains that when economic agents believe in the "law of small numbers" they overinterpret the extent to which information from observing a small number of events reflects the experience of the "population" from which those events are drawn. In the case of medical markets, priors about a physician may be formed based on reports from friends, family, and physicians. The reports from friends and family will typically be based on a relatively small number of encounters with a medical professional. Referrals from a physician may also be based on a relatively small number of experiences.[8] In fact, health-care consumers regularly report that they have greater confidence in sources

---

[8]Physicians are generally not well trained in statistics and may not be well equipped to make use of the data that might be available to them. For a lively description of physician training and cases of clinical decision-making, see Gawande (2002).

of care that are likely to rely on small numbers than they do in sources that rely on large representative samples such as accreditation agencies and health plan sponsors. National survey data also suggest a high degree of confidence by consumers that they have sufficient information to make the "right" choices about medical procedures and providers. Eighty-one percent of consumers stated they had enough information to make the right choice about a treatment option and 79% said they had enough information to make the right choice of doctor (Kaiser Family Foundation 2000).[9] A key implication of a model that views consumers as believing in the law of small numbers is that priors will reflect too much confidence in an opinion formed about the quality or performance of a health-care provider (Rabin 2002).

6.2.3.2 Updating Priors

The Bayesian consumer is assumed to assess new evidence on the performance of a health-care provider independently of the established priors on the quality of a provider. This feature of the model applies to physician encounters that are repeated, such as those with a primary care physician or a specialist treating a chronic illness. The contrasting case is a specialty surgery, where the physician choice would not involve an updating process. Health-care markets are characterized by a set of institutions and circumstances that might lead consumers to filter information so as to conflict with the Bayesian updating assumption. Arrow (1963) notes that *trust* is a central feature of the doctor–patient relationship. Giving trust this important role stems from the uncertainty and vulnerability of the patient. Trust is offered up as a nonmarket institution that increases efficiency by reducing the disutility and inefficiency from the uncertainty and the anxiety of illness, as well as the agency problems associated with the asymmetry of information between doctor and patient.[10] The health sector is replete with complementary institutions that aim to increase trust between medical providers and patients. These include a code of medical ethics, medical education, professionalism, licensure, and, in the case of hospitals, nonprofit status. Trust is also recognized as an ingredient of treatment affecting the well-being of a patient.

Studies of the prevalence of trust show that patient trust in their doctors remains very high across income, demographic, and health-related social strata (Hall 2001). Some psychological research on the doctor–patient relationship shows a willingness to interpret data showing poor outcomes of treatment as unavoidable events beyond

---

[9]It is worth noting that these data are based on telephone surveys and the questions are general in nature. Patients tend to give somewhat different answers when asked about specific procedures and cases. Nevertheless, evidence form multiple sources suggests the people have confidence in the advice and information they can get on medical matters.

[10]Koszegi (2003) shows how patient anxiety can interfere with a patient obtaining relevant medical information and ultimately result in inefficiently low levels of treatment.

the physician's control (Ben Sira 1980). This raises the question of how patients will use new information to make inferences about the physician effort parameter in the benefit function $B = B(m, e, u)$. Recall that, in the model of doctor–patient interaction set out above, the Bayesian patient estimates the likelihood that appropriate effort will be taken, $L_1(B_0, m)$. Thus, we consider how this likelihood will be formed. The filtering function of the trust relationship is related to what Rabin and Schrag (1999) refer to as *confirmation bias*. For example, does the confidence in a physician generated by a referral from a trusted friend, relative, or physician (the prior) serve as a filter for interpreting new information about a physician? Applying a quasi-Bayesian updating process (i.e., efficiently applying Bayes's rule to biased information) like that proposed by Rabin and Schrag would result in patients misinterpreting certain outcomes as not being a reflection of physician quality or the level of effort exerted. The misinterpretation of physician effort or quality would most likely stem from erroneous interpretation of treatment outcomes or misperception of the nature of the production function for health. Extant literature in health psychology points to patients' perceptions about the production function as being potentially key in confirmatory bias in drawing inferences from poor outcomes by a trusted physician.

Core concepts in behavioral economics seem to fit well with institutions that govern the flow of information and evidence on the manner in which patients use information to make choices. The psychology of forming priors and Bayesian updating, discussed above, points to hypotheses about the nature of demand response to quality signals in markets for medical care. One hypothesis that emerges from applying behavioral concepts to the formation of priors is that the quality signal based on extant market information, or even improved public reporting of quality, may not yield strong demand response to quality signals, as has generally been assumed. The normative implication is that improved information may not result in an efficient quality equilibrium in the market unless some other institution is introduced that overrides the type of patient decision-making we have described (e.g., employers guiding provider choice based on systematic data). Integrating behavioral economics into models of physician behavior would result in different specifications of econometric models of physician services. For example, the degree of demand response might be expected to depend on how patients reach a physician. Those who were referred by family or a physician would be expected to respond differently to quality signals than those referred by a health plan or the local medical society.

6.2.4 *Behavioral Economics and Supply Response in Treatment*

Medicine is, I have found, a strange and in many ways disturbing business. The thing that still startles me is how fundamentally human an endeavor it is.

Gawande (2002)

Embedded in the model of physician behavior set out above is a process by which a physician chooses among a complex set of possibilities to treat a particular patient or type of patient. A physician's choices (assuming profit maximization) depend on her view of the production function, which has also been characterized as a Bayesian learning process (Phelps and Mooney 1993). These models recognize the institutions through which physicians learn after completion of their training. Key sources of learning are peers with whom a physician practices (partners, fellow employees, peers on a hospital staff), continuing medical education courses, pharmaceutical promotion personnel, and medical journals. The application of traditional Bayesian updating models has emphasized local sources of information because they are asserted to be low-cost sources of learning (Phelps 2000). These models have been used to explain the persistent variation across geographic areas in the use of medical procedures that cannot be explained by patient illness characteristics, demographics, or indicators of preferences.

For example, in 1999 Medicare spending was $9,941 per enrollee in Miami, FL, and $4,886 in Minneapolis, MN. The difference cannot be accounted for by health or demographics factors such as age, gender, and race, or differences in medical care prices. Instead, the spending variation is mostly due to more frequent physician visits, diagnostic tests, and hospitalizations and procedures (Wennberg and Cooper 1997). Consistent with this, Phelps (2000) reports coefficients of variation in hospitalization rates across New York State. He shows that coefficients of variation for conditions such as pediatric otitis media, depressive neurosis, and chronic obstructive lung disease were 0.49, 0.42, and 0.35, respectively. These contrast with services where little discretion can be exercised, such as heart attacks, where the coefficient of variation was 0.12.

In the Bayesian updating model of physician choice of treatment technology, the prior about the appropriate use of a particular procedure to treat a specific illness (e.g., cesarean section for deliveries) is formed in medical training (medical school and residency) according to the observed share of total cases of a given illness treated with the procedure. The physician is then assumed to combine new local observations with prior information, giving each case equal weight in order to form the posterior distribution. The result is a weighted average of accumulated observations from medical training and subsequent practice. This model can be used to explain how a "local style" of medical practice can persist and why adoption of new treatments may be slow.

In this model it is assumed that the Bayesian physician overweights information from local sources or that data from medical journals or medical conferences get ignored or are given little weight when assessing the use of medical technologies. Phelps and Mooney (1993) argue that low-cost local sources of information are emphasized. They also note the importance of personal advice from colleagues about how to apply specific medical techniques. This latter point is consistent with the *availability heuristic*, where people tend to overemphasize more vivid personal descriptions of successes and failures than perhaps more representative reports of data from the literature.

Another behavioral construct that is potentially relevant for understanding why local opinions should receive such high weight is the notion of *regret* (Thaler 1980). Physicians commonly must choose from among many competing approaches to treating a particular condition and trusting patients rely centrally on the recommendations of the physician. This makes the physician largely responsible for the consequences of the complex choice. Moreover, these choices are commonly made under considerable time pressure. The typical physician visit is about fifteen minutes. Thus, the potential for regret is high and the physician has incentives to attempt to lower the *responsibility costs* of medical decision-making. One institution that has long been recognized as an important influence on physician behavior is the professional norm (Arrow 1963). In this case the norm might be viewed as the local approach to treatment that a physician can point to as guiding her choices. In the event of a poor outcome, the physician that practices according to local norms can note that they followed standard operating practices, whereas they could more easily be individually tied to a choice if they departed from local practice (Thaler 1980). Giving great weight to local data therefore reduces responsibility costs and might therefore help explain the particular way that Bayesian updating works in medical decision-making. These behavioral influences on decision-making are reinforced by local health plan attempts to affect practice patterns through local profiling of physicians.[11]

This Bayesian physician decision model has been coupled with ideas about how innovations take hold in order to also explain the establishment and persistence of geographic differences in patterns of treatment. The existence of this variation that is unexplained by patient characteristics or outcome implies substantial differences in economic welfare across markets that are not competed away. While not formally acknowledged, ideas from behavioral economics are at least casually invoked in some of this literature. In one example, Phelps (2000) speculates about why different markets might differentially perceive the value of a new medical technique. He proposes that a physician innovator might be exposed to a new technique through the medical literature or by attending a conference. She tries out the new technique on twenty cases and then makes a judgment about whether the new technique is "better" than existing treatment methods. Phelps (2000) notes in passing that the

---

[11] In recent years American health plans have begun to use a limited number of national indicators to set performance norms for profiling. The majority of practice patterns profiled remains based on local practice norms (averages).

physician may not be entirely unbiased because they are invested in the new method. This scenario highlights the potential relevance of the law of small numbers in creating very different views of a particular medical procedure across geographic areas based on a tendency to overinterpret the results from a small trial. It also suggests the potential role for confirmatory bias or filtering of data among physician innovators and adherents of older methods. These ideas can be applied to a Bayesian model of decision-making to help explain the high degree of variation in patterns of treatment across geographic areas and the slow adoption of many new and effective treatment technologies.

The empirical implications of this line of thinking lead to the view that it would be important to include data reflecting a physician's own experiences and those of the immediate community in econometric analyses of physician treatment patterns. These factors may also be important in understanding diffusion of new technologies and reduced use of dominated technologies (sometimes referred to as "exnovation"). Such measures have typically not been included in econometric models of physician behavior.

6.2.5 *An Application*

A recent natural experiment highlights the potential contribution of the ideas set out above. In 1989 the New York State Department of Health initiated a program that would use market forces to improve the quality of care for Coronary Artery Bypass Graft (CABG) surgery. The idea was that, by improving the standardization, reliability, and availability of information on physician- and hospital-specific outcomes, consumers who are largely insured would be better equipped to make choices based on performance. That is, demand response to outcome signals would discipline poorly performing providers of care and would improve quality of care. The State Department of Health developed a very detailed approach to "risk adjustment" of mortality outcomes for both physicians and hospitals, so that outcomes would be standardized for systematic patient mortality risk.[12] Beginning in November 1992, mortality data were released publicly on surgeons performing 200 or more operations per year at one hospital. The Department of Health took great pains to inform the media on issues of quality improvement and interpretation of risk-adjusted mortality rates. The surgeon-specific mortality rates were published in major newspapers, including the *New York Times* and *Newsday*.

Two initial observations were made that pose a puzzle for health economists. The first is that risk-adjusted mortality rates associated with CABG declined from

---

[12]Risk adjustment refers to the statistical standardization of mortality rates so as to account for the severity of illness and the ability of patients to recover from surgery. Details of the risk adjustors used on New York appear in Chassin et al. (1996).

4.17% in 1989 to 2.45% in 1992 (Chassin et al. 1996). The second is that no demand response was observed. There were no significant shifts in patient volume from surgeons and hospitals with relatively high mortality rates to those with low rates (Schneider and Epstein 1998). This was initially thought to be a result of the low awareness of the mortality reports among the public. Subsequent analyses that reexamined patient volume changes at points later in time, when public awareness of the mortality data was higher, show no evidence of significant demand response to the new information.

Little attention from health economists has been accorded the demand response result that represents a challenge to basic models of quality competition in health like the one set out above and like that of Dranove and Satterthwaite (1992). Some facts about doctor–patient roles in decision-making suggest some direction for applying behavioral economics ideas. Data reported above and elsewhere suggest that patients place the greatest weight on recommendations of friends, family, and primary care doctors. The patient appears to become even more reliant on the known professional when making choices about treatments for severe medical conditions. Research on the division of labor in medical decision-making shows that, for medical conditions such as breast cancer and colorectal cancer, the majority of patients prefer the physician to make the treatment decision (78% for colorectal cancer and 52% for breast cancer). In addition, only 20% of the breast cancer patients wanted to be actively involved as opposed to sharing decision-making (Beaver et al. 1999). This research also shows that, when faced with major procedures such as surgery, patients often prefer to be informed but want the physician to make key treatment decisions. In fact, a substantial number of patients report being pushed into more active roles in decision-making than preferred. Such evidence is consistent with the importance of trust in forming priors and the idea of *regret* as a limiting factor in people playing an active "consumer" role. Patients frequently appear not to want to carry the consequences of having made a choice if outcomes are poor.

Economics research has instead focused on selection incentives on the supply side and how the reduction in mortality observed should be interpreted (Dranove et al. 2002). The arguments advanced have been that physicians are risk averse, presumably to a loss of reputation, and as a result will avoid more risky patients. This is possible because of imperfections in the risk-adjustment mechanism. As a result, physicians are less willing to perform surgery on the most severely ill patients. The result is a misleading inference that mortality declined due to improved quality based on the simple morality trends.

The empirical analysis performed by Dranove and coworkers offers evidence consistent with the hypothesized selection behavior. Controlling for selection, they show a reduction in severity of patient illness accompanied by a spending increase.

(It is worth noting that other analyses of the New York experience show that nearly one in five doctors with low performance ratings (bottom quartile) left the practice of cardiac surgery in New York State, which implies an alternative explanation of the observed data (Jha and Epstein 2004).) Dranove et al. (2002) interpret the evidence as pointing to a loss in welfare. To make this interpretation they presume that, prior to the reporting initiative, the sickest patients were being appropriately treated: an assumption not clearly supported by evidence. The analysis therefore asserts a type of reputation-maximizing behavior that dominates concerns about the well-being of the sickest patients. Another interpretation might be that the public reporting of data led physicians to reweight how they use information that comes from sources other than their own or the immediate local experience. This could well generate observations consistent with selection and the observed compression of variance, but might have a less depressing normative conclusion. This might be the case if at baseline physicians were offering CABG to "too many" very sick patients.

6.2.6 Additional Directions: Medical Decision-Making

One prominent theme in health policy that has only begun to receive careful attention from economists is the issue of disparities in treatment and health-care utilization according to race and ethnicity (Institute of Medicine 2002). Balsa and McGuire (2003) suggest a behavioral approach to modification of the type of model of doctor–patient interactions discussed above. They propose a central role for a *stereotyping heuristic* that is used by physicians who face important time constraints and must quickly make assessments of complex clinical circumstances. Such a heuristic can offer an efficient method of making uncertain judgments with limited information. It can also result in important errors. Because personal attributes and health habits are typically important for deciding upon a course of treatment, the use of stereotypes might particularly distort clinical choices. For example, physicians have been shown to hold beliefs that African-American patients are more likely to abuse drugs and less likely to comply with recommended treatments than are otherwise similar (with respect to socioeconomic characteristics) white patients (van Ryn and Burke 2000). The fact that physicians hold such beliefs potentially affects the nature of the efforts that physicians take in administering a particular treatment, because judgments about patient compliance, for example, influence expected outcomes.

A second area of application involves the complexity of the medical practice. American doctors practice in an environment where they treat patients associated with a wide range of insurance arrangements, meaning that the patients face different out-of-pocket prices for differing services and doctors are compensated in a variety of ways. For example, a physician will typically encounter fifteen or more different formulary arrangements that define which prescription drugs are paid for and how.[13] In addition, they will face similar numbers of compensation schemes, bonus arrangements, quality reporting methods, and patient cost-sharing rules. A recent analysis by Glied and Zivin (2002) shows that physician behavior is not consistent with simple maximization models. They examine physician choices about intensity of treatment as measured by duration of visits, test orders, and medications prescribed. Their results show that physicians respond to incentives but not necessarily to the incentives of the marginal patient. They report that the intensity of treatment received by a given patient has as much to do with the payment incentives associated with other patients in the practice as with their own.[14] Similar patients should get similar treatment.[15] If physicians have a collectivity orientation (possibly reinforced by professional norms) as proposed by Arrow (1963), then treating patients similarly may have intrinsic value and may constrain how a physician can respond to heterogeneous incentives in payments. Kahneman et al. (1986) explore how notions of fairness constrain profit-maximizing choices. The notion that there are established standards or entitlements that are internalized by physicians and that these influence the supply responses to heterogeneous incentive arrangements constitutes an extension to the ideas of how fairness constrains profit-seeking.[16]

Another tack that may complement the idea of incorporating fairness into models of physician behavior is that of applying a heuristic in the face of a complex environment in which it is costly to optimize. Fairness in this manner would contribute to the choice of *rules of thumb* in responding to the daunting array of payment arrangements commonly faced by medical practices (Conlisk 1996).

---

[13] A formulary is a list of drugs and a set of rules regarding their use and how a health plan will cover and pay for dispensing of specific drugs.

[14] Doctors appear to alter their "practice styles" as the composition of payment incentives shifts. One behavioral phenomenon not yet discussed concerns the role of fairness. Physicians may put considerable value on treating all their patients according to the same criteria. This idea is intertwined with the ideas of trust noted above. The essential role of patients' trust in their health-care providers and professional norms are seen as efficient nonmarket responses to information asymmetry and contractibility limitations in health-care markets. The importance of establishing a "trust" relationship creates incentives for the provider to not appear to be pursuing obvious optimizing behavior. Arrow (1963, p. 966) observes the following: "To justify this delegation the physician finds himself somewhat limited, just as any agent would in similar circumstances. The safest course to take to avoid not being a true agent is to give the socially prescribed 'best' treatment of the day. Compromise in quality, even for the purpose of saving the patient money, is to risk imputation of failure to live up to the social bond."

[15] This model at first blush conflicts with the discussion of disparities. However, one could assume that rationing would occur based on perceived clinical need and that disparities arise from the application of stereotypes and the perception of different needs by racial group.

[16] It should be noted that these observations relate to an older literature concerning the so-called "norms hypothesis" in medical decision-making.

6.3 HEALTH-CARE DEMAND AND INSURANCE

This chapter has focused primarily on markets for physician services, in part because they serve as an excellent model for a large class of prevalent health sector issues related to the supply and demand for treatment under conditions of asymmetric information and uncertainty. There are also other issues in health economics where traditional models of economic behavior have not resolved some important puzzles and these may lend themselves productively to the application of behavioral economics. I raise several puzzles that relate to demand and health insurance to illustrate the possibilities.

6.3.1 *Demand for Medical Care*

In the discussion of physician behavior, considerable attention was devoted to consumer demand for individual physician services. Here we briefly identify several other issues in the demand for health care where behavioral economics may have a constructive role in aiding the explanation of persistent puzzles. It is commonly observed by health policy analysts concerned with efficiency and quality that there is persistent overuse, underuse and inappropriate use of care (Institute of Medicine 2001). The discussion of physician behavior offered some explanations for what has been termed overuse and inappropriate use of services. The demand-side sources of underuse that are commonly used in the health sector rely primarily on factors such as externalities, as is the case with the demand for vaccines or lack of insurance. The existence of external effects results in inefficiently low levels of demand even when vaccines are made available at a price of zero. The policy response is to install some coercive measures such as requiring childhood immunizations to be documented as a condition of entry into school. Another major source of underuse is the existence of financial obstacles. However, underuse exists in insured populations. In the absence of externalities, understanding the demand side of underuse in the context of a nearly fully insured population is more difficult.

Existing literature on demand for health care offers several directions for studying the issue of underuse of medical care. One line of research incorporates ideas of stigma into the preference function in a fashion that assigns stigma the role of a "price." Research on the demand for mental health services and treatment for HIV-related disorders are cases in point (McGuire 1981; Frank and McGuire 2000). In these models getting treatment serves to reveal a stigmatizing condition, thereby imposing an additional cost on the patient if they get care. Stigma has been used to explain the low rates of treatment among people with mental disorders (e.g., 27% of people with depression and about 50% of people with schizophrenia).

A new approach to understanding demand behavior draws on research in behavioral economics by Caplin and Leahy (2001). Koszegi (2003) makes use of Caplin and Leahy's psychological expected utility model, where mental states that affect utility are influenced by both beliefs and observed outcomes.[17] Information affects beliefs and in turn the mental states that are related to utility. Koszegi uses this framework to show how anxiety might affect the demand for specific information, tests, and treatment. He identifies a trade-off between seeking treatment and obtaining information. Information, for some patients, can create lost utility from anxiety if the news is bad, but having more complete information enables a patient and their doctor to more optimally choose a treatment strategy. Depending on the net contribution of the information to utility, a patient will demand contact with providers and information about their condition. Not having all the available information can cause anxiety in other patients. Applying models of consumer behavior that incorporate anticipatory feelings into quasi-Bayesian updating models about how medical information and associated physician contacts are used and in turn affect demand for services has the potential to address a range of "underuse" problems such as noncompliance with treatment regimens (Loewenstein 1987).

A third direction for studying demand is suggested by observations made by decision scientists who have attempted to study health utility states. They have noted a rather dramatic ability of people to adapt to changing health states. That is, people who develop significant chronic conditions (e.g., diabetes, strokes, limited mobility) tend to rate their well-being at levels similar to that of the general population. The usual specifications of preferences propose inter-temporal and inter-state stability in preferences.[18] These observations suggest a somewhat different process than that studied in hyperbolic discounting (Thaler 1981). Modeling adjustment to health states may contribute to explaining behavior with respect to hospice care, end-of-life care, and the use of advance medical directives.

Unrelated to issues of "under treatment" is a demand-side puzzle that has come to light in recent studies of demand response to different drug formulary designs (see, for example, Huskamp et al. 2004). Those studies estimated demand response to changes in the relative prices, created by implementation of a formulary design change, for different drugs within a therapeutic class (e.g., proton pump inhibitors). Several therapeutic classes were studied. Some classes contained drugs that were found in clinical studies to be highly substitutable in production (they produce comparable clinical benefits and have similar side effect profiles), while others are considered more heterogeneous and less substitutable. Estimated demand responses

---

[17]Another recent application of this approach takes on a normative issue related to the underuse of diagnostic tests related to HIV disease (see the recent paper by Caplin and Eliaz (2003)).

[18]Kahneman (2003) notes some key limits on the ability to interpret self-reported well-being. Nevertheless, a variety of approaches to measuring quality of life and well-being show the same result of adaptation.

across classes were generally quite modest and of similar magnitude across therapeutic classes. In particular, the demand response for proton pump inhibitors (a treatment for gastritis) was small, even though studies of the clinical properties of these drugs indicate that they are highly substitutable in production (Wolfe 2003). Moreover, physicians appear to view these drugs as clinically similar. The implication is that consumers are reluctant to change drugs. Why should consumers be unresponsive to substantial relative demand price differences (100%) given the evidence on the high degree of substitution in production?

The parallels between the observations made in the preceding paragraphs and the theoretical and experimental research on reference levels and status quo bias is striking (Knetsch 1989; Samuelson and Zeckhauser 1988). It appears that the initial choice of products affects preferences even in the context of low transaction costs and high degrees of similarity in product attributes. This may explain why pharmaceutical promotion relies so heavily on providing free samples that are commonly used by physicians to start a patient on a new drug regimen. Models of demand for prescription drugs might therefore profitably incorporate information on the history of individual product use. Such considerations have been allowed for when empirical studies of demand response examine new prescriptions separately from refills. The normative implications are potentially significant in that evidence of such preference structures would potentially constitute a rationale for the design of formularies that override consumer preferences. Closed formularies, which will only pay for drugs on the list of preferred products, represent one mechanism that would override consumer preferences and cause a shift to a new reference or status quo product.[19]

6.3.2 Insurance Design

One puzzle from the health insurance markets that has received some treatment from behavioral economics is that of why insurance plans with close to first-dollar coverage dominate health insurance markets. Economists have long been concerned with the nature of the trade-off between moral hazard and risk spreading (Zeckhauser 1970). The fact that health insurance markets persistently have equilibrium policies with levels of cost sharing that approximate first-dollar coverage is puzzling in that there appears to be a surprisingly high willingness to pay for the least valuable forms of insurance protection.

Thaler (1980) addressed this issue by appealing to the idea of *regret*. He argued that insurance features such as deductibles that force consumers to trade-off medical

---

[19]It is interesting to note that most U.S. private health insurance limits choice to a significant extent and about 30–40% of people have no choice of health plan.

care use for money impose important psychic costs because of the potential for regret. In order to avoid making trade-offs that they might later regret, consumers are posited to demand health insurance designs that allow them to remove themselves from making such choices. The result is an increased willingness of people to pay premiums to obtain first-dollar coverage.

Finally, an issue related to the use of markets to purchase health insurance. A long-standing debate in health policy and health economics involves the trade-off between the efficiency gains from competitive insurance markets and the losses that stem from adverse selection (Cutler and Zeckhauser 2000). The empirical health economics literature offers evidence of both substantial price reductions when competition is intense and large losses from adverse selection (Cutler and Reber 1998). There is a presumption in much of health economics that more choice is better. In fact, the de facto model of health-care delivery in the United States and other nations is that of "managed competition" (Enthoven 1988). The assumption is that consumers find the right health plans and that overall the net gains of wider choice are positive.

At the same time consumers appear to know little about health plans in their choice sets. Recent consumer surveys suggest that only about 36% of consumers believe they understand differences between health plans offered to them (Kaiser Family Foundation 2000). For example, less than 50% of surveyed consumers knew that health maintenance organizations (HMOs) were plans that place greater emphasis on preventive care. In addition, employers that organize markets for health insurance frequently limit the range of consumer choice of health insurance. Nevertheless, U.S. public policy has in recent years encouraged the broadest choices possible in the design of health insurance schemes such as Medicare and the Federal Employees Health Benefit program. Little research has been conducted on the effectiveness of consumer choice in health insurance markets.

General lessons from the behavioral economics literature may lead one to conclude that the analysis of the trade-off from expanding choice among competing health plans may be quite incomplete. Research in behavioral economics shows that, as the number of choices among complicated products expands, consumers appear to consider a decreasing number of the available options, or they attempt to avoid choices altogether by putting off decisions or reverting to a default option (Johnson et al. 1993). It has also been shown that, as decisions become more complex, people adopt increasingly simple rules of thumb to make their choices (Payne et al. 1993). Loewenstein (2000) applies these ideas to the problem of U.S. Social Security reform. He argues that, in that case, the costs of more choice may exceed the benefits. The health insurance market is filled with natural experiments in complex, seemingly high-stakes choices where the choice set varies dramatically. Empirical analysis motivated by the behavioral economics concepts noted here may offer valuable information for better understanding of the net benefits of expanding choice in health insurance.[20]

For example, the U.S. Medicare program offers a rich laboratory for such investigations. There is a great heterogeneity in the number of managed care plan options available to Medicare beneficiaries across the United States. Yet in all markets there is a common default plan, the traditional fee-for-service Medicare plan. Policy makers and researchers have been repeatedly surprised by the low rates of enrollment in Medicare managed care plans given the richer assortment of insurance coverage they frequently offer (e.g., prescription drugs at no additional premium cost). Understanding how the structure of the choice set affects the willingness to depart from the default option would be important for understanding trade-offs in program design choices. Specifically, are Medicare beneficiaries who face larger numbers of choices more likely to choose traditional Medicare over managed care plans? This would be important information for a U.S. Congress that has shown such a strong interest in encouraging enrollment in managed care arrangements for Medicare beneficiaries.[21]

6.4 FINAL OBSERVATIONS

The health sector has long offered a challenging venue for applied economists. Arrow recognized this in the early 1960s. Following the tradition of Arrow, I have focused the discussion here on markets for health services and health insurance. Health economists have become habituated to dealing with institutions and facts that raise questions about the usefulness of applying the neoclassical model to health-care markets. The nature of the doctor–patient interaction in the presence of insurance is at the heart of many of the most challenging problems in health policy and health economics. The first empirical studies in health economics came face to face with the issue of characterizing the doctor–patient interaction, and it remains a central problem in health economics. The application of standard principal–agent models has produced an increasingly sophisticated ability to describe doctor–patient interactions and to develop refutable hypotheses about parameters that affect price, quantity, and quality outcomes. Nevertheless, observed demand and supply responses in markets for physician services are incompletely understood. The case of public reporting of physician performance in CABG surgery offers a vivid example of the limited ability of the standard model to explain market behavior.

---

[20] It should be noted that these issues also apply to choices of specialists, hospitals, and prescription drugs, as well as the assessment of policies such as "any willing provider" statutes.

[21] Obtaining consistent empirical estimates of the impact of greater choice on use of the default option involves dealing with the issue of endogenous entry by health plans.

Behavioral economics offers some concepts and analytical tools that fit well with the institutions of the health sector. The doctor–patient decision-making context of limited information, a noisy health production function, fear, anxiety, insurance coverage, and trust is well suited to the concerns of behavioral economics. I have attempted to highlight how relatively simple models of the doctor–patient interactions can be extended using ideas from behavioral economics to enrich the ability to understand and develop empirical models of health-care markets. The issues identified go to the core concerns of health economics. These include: how information affects equilibrium quality in health-care markets; how physician competition might affect prices and quantities; what produces persistent variations in treatment patterns across markets and the associated welfare losses; and what explains racial and ethnic disparities in health-care use. I have emphasized the role of behavioral economics in extending positive models of health-care markets. Behavioral economics offers direction for addressing long-standing impasses in positive health economics.

There are also important normative implications. Clearly, if doctors and patients make the types of context-specific choices and cognitive errors described here, demand functions can no longer be given the normative interpretations that are common even in health economics (Rice 1998). Critics of the use of standard demand models in health care have clearly and persuasively highlighted the limits to using these for normative model analysis. They have also failed to offer new approaches to understanding such behavior.

One direction pointed to by Thaler and Sunstein (2003) is to use cost–benefit analysis of alternate polices that aim to account for the type of cognitive errors described here. Cost-effectiveness is widely applied in health care to make efficiency judgments about competing medical practices and policies. There are, however, a variety of difficulties in applying these tools in the context of trying to account for consumer preferences for making welfare judgments (Garber 2000).

Another interesting approach is known as case-based decision theory (Gilboa and Schmeidler 2004). In this case the normative analysis is conducted by assessing whether a policy action results in a reduction in the type of decision-making "errors" that serve to undermine the types of expected utility models frequently used in health economics. Thus, policies that reduce distortions in decision-making would be viewed as "welfare-improving." These are new ideas and to date there is no clear path toward a new normative approach that might be applied in fields such as health economics.

The policy implications stemming from the application of behavioral economics in analyzing health-care markets are potentially profound. Two cornerstones of recent U.S. health policy are the presumption that increasing the availability of information to consumers will result in improved quality of care, and that more choice of health plans and providers will inevitably make consumers better off. Examining the basic laboratory and psychological research used in behavioral economics immediately raises challenges to these policy fundamentals. I have attempted to identify some specific areas where these ideas might have particular importance for ongoing policy debates. I expect that a sustained program of research involving the ideas of behavioral economics applied to health-care markets will likely result in at least some intelligent modification of these articles of faith.

REFERENCES

Akerlof, G. 1991. Procrastination and obedience. *American Economic Review* 81:1–19.

Arrow, K. J. 1963. Uncertainty and the welfare economics of medical care. *American Economic Review* 53:941–73.

Balsa, A. J., and T. G. McGuire. 2003. Prejudice, clinical uncertainty and stereotyping as sources of health disparities. *Journal of Health Economics* 22:89–116.

Beaver, K., J. B. Bogg, and K. A. Luker. 1999. Decision-making role preferences and information needs: a comparison of colorectal and breast cancer. *Health Expectations* 2:266–76.

Becker, G. 1964. *Human Capital*. Columbia University Press.

Becker, G., and K. Murphy. 1988. A theory of rational addiction. *Journal of Political Economy* 96:675–700.

Ben Sira, Z. 1980. Affective and instrumental components in the physician–patient relationship: an added dimension of interaction theory. *Journal of Health and Social Behavior* 21:170–80.

Camerer, C. F., and G. Loewenstein. 2003. Behavioral economics: past present and future. In *Advances in Behavioral Economics* (ed. C. Camerer, G. Loewenstein, and M. Rabin). Princeton University Press.

Caplin, A., and K. Eliaz. 2003. AIDS and psychology: a mechanism design approach. *RAND Journal of Economics* 34:631–46.

Caplin, A., and J. Leahy. 2001. Psychological expected utility theory and anticipated feelings. *Quarterly Journal of Economics* 116:55–80.

Chassin, M. R., E. L. Hannan, and B. A. DeBuono. 1996. Benefits and hazards of reporting medical outcomes publicly. *New England Journal of Medicine* 334:394–98.

Cleary, P. D., and S. Edgman-Levitan. 1997. Health care quality: incorporating consumer perspectives. *Journal of the American Medical Association* 278:1608–12.

Conlisk, J. 1996. Why bounded rationality? *Journal of Economic Literature* 34:669–700.

Culyer, A., and J. P. Newhouse. 2000. *The Handbook of Health Economics*. Amsterdam: North-Holland.

Cutler, D. M., and S. J. Reber. 1998. Paying for health insurance: the trade-off between competition and adverse selection. *Quarterly Journal of Economics* 113:433–66.

Cutler, D. M., and R. Zeckhauser. 2000. The anatomy of health insurance. In *The Handbook of Health Economics* (ed. A. Culyer and J. P. Newhouse). Amsterdam: North-Holland.

Dranove, D. 1988. Demand inducement and the physician/patient relationship. *Economic Enquiry* 26:281–98.

Dranove, D., and M. Satterthwaite, 1992. Monopolistic competition when price and quality are not perfectly observable. *RAND Journal of Economics* 23:518–34.

Dranove, D., and W. D. White. 1987. Agency and the organization of health care delivery. *Inquiry* 24:405–15.

Dranove, D., D. Kessler, M. McClellan, and M. Satterthwaite. 2002. Is more information better? The effects of report cards on health care providers. NBER Working Paper 869.

Edgman-Levitan, S., and P. D. Cleary. 1996. What information do consumers want and need? *Health Affairs* 15:42–56.

Emons, W. 1997. Credence goods and fraudulent experts. *RAND Journal of Economics* 28:107–19.

Enthoven, A. C. 1988. *The Theory and Practice of Managed Competition in Health Care Finance*. Amsterdam: North-Holland.

Evans, R. G. 1974. Supplier-induced demand: some empirical evidence and implications. In *The Economics of Health and Medical Care* (ed. M. Perlman). Wiley.

Feldstein, M. S. 1970. The rising price of physicians' services. *Review of Economics and Statistics* 51:121–33.

Frank, R. G., and T. G. McGuire. 2000. Economics and mental health. In *Handbook of Health Economics* (ed. A. Culyer and J. P. Newhouse). Amsterdam: North-Holland.

Frech, H. E., and P. B. Ginsburg. 1972. Physician pricing: monopolistic or competitive comment. *Southern Economic Journal* 38:573–77.

Fuchs, V. R. 1978. The supply of surgeons and the demand for operations. *Journal of Human Resources* 13 (supplement):35–55.

Fuchs, V. R., and M. J. Kramer. 1972. *Determinants of Expenditures for Physician Services in the United States*. Washington, DC: National Center for Health Services Research.

Garber, A. 2000. Advances in cost effectiveness analysis. In *Handbook of Health Economics* (ed. A. Culyer and J. P. Newhouse). Amsterdam: North-Holland.

Gawande, A. 2002. *Complications: A Surgeon's Notes on an Imperfect Science*. New York: Picador.

Gilboa, I., and Schmeidler D. 2004. Case-based decision theory. In *Advances in Behavioral Economics* (ed. C. F. Camerer, G. Loewenstein, and M. Rabin), pp. 659–88. Princeton University Press.

Glaeser, E. L. 2003. Psychology and the market. NBER Working Paper 10203.

Glied, S., and J. G. Zivin. 2002. How do doctors behave when some (but not all) of their patients are in managed care. *Journal of Health Economics* 21:337–53.

Grossman, M. 1972. On the concept of health capital and the demand for health. *Journal of Political Economy* 80:223–55.

Gruber, J., and B. Koszegi. 2001. Is addiction rational? Theory and evidence. *Quarterly Journal of Economics* 116:1261–1303.

Hall, M. A. 2001. Arrow on trust. *Journal of Health Politics, Policy and Law* 26:1131–44.

Hellerstein, J. K. 1998. The importance of the physician in the generic versus trade-name prescription decision. *RAND Journal of Economics* 29:108–36.

Huskamp, H. A., R. G. Frank, K. McGuigan, and Y. Zhang. 2004. The demand response to implementation of a three-tiered formulary. Harvard University Working Paper.

Institute of Medicine. 2001. *Crossing the Quality Chasm.* Washington, DC: NAS Press.

——. 2002. *Unequal Treatment: Confronting Racial and Ethnic Disparities in Health Care.* Washington, DC: NAS Press.

Jha, A. K., and A. M. Epstein. 2004. The predictive accuracy of the New York State bypass surgery reporting system and its impact on volume and surgical practice. Manuscript, Department of Health Policy and Management, Harvard School of Public Health.

Johnson, E. J., J. Hershey, J. Meszaros, and H. Kunreuther. 1993. Framing probability distortions, and insurance decisions. *Journal of Risk and Uncertainty* 7:35–51.

Kahneman, D. 2003. A perspective on judgment and choice: mapping bounded rationality. *American Psychologist* 58:697–720.

Kahneman, D., J. L. Knetsch, and R. H. Thaler. 1986. Fairness as a constraint on profit seeking: entitlements in the market. *American Economic Review* 76:728–41.

Kaiser Family Foundation. 2000. *National Survey on Americans as Health Care Consumers: An Update on the Role of Quality Information. Highlights of a National Survey.* Rockville, MD: Kaiser Family Foundation, and the Agency for Health-care Research and Quality. (Available at http://www.ahrq.gov/qual/kffhigh00.htm.)

——. 2003. Trends and indicators in a changing health care marketplace. Kaiser Family Foundation publications. (Available at http://www.kff.org/insurance/7031/index.cfm.)

Knetsch, J. 1989. The endowment effect and evidence of non-reversible indifference curves. *American Economic Review* 79:1277–84.

Koszegi, B. 2003. Health, anxiety and patient behavior. *Journal of Health Economics* 22: 1073–84.

Loewenstein, G. A. 1987. Anticipation and the valuation of delayed consumption. *Economic Journal* 97:666–84.

——. 2000. Costs and benefits of health and retirement-related choice. In *Social Security and Medicare: Individual vs Collective Risk and Responsibility* (ed. S. Burke, E. Kingson, and U. Reinhardt). Washington, DC: Brookings Institution Press.

——. 2001. A visceral account of addiction. In *Smoking: Risk Perception and Policy* (ed. P. Slovic), pp. 188–215. Thousand Oaks, CA: Sage.

McGuire, T. G. 1981. *Financing Psychotherapy: Costs, Effects and Public Policy.* Cambridge, MA: Ballentine Books.

——. 2000. The economics of physician behavior. In *Handbook of Health Economics* (ed. A. Culyer and J. P. Newhouse). Amsterdam: North-Holland.

Mullainathan, S., and R. H. Thaler. 2001. Behavioral economics. In *International Encyclopedia of Social Sciences*, 1st edn, pp. 1094–1100. New York: Pergamon.

Newhouse, J. P. 1970. A model of physician pricing. *Southern Economics Journal* 37:174–83.

——. 2003. *Pricing the Priceless.* Harvard University Press.

O'Donoghue, T., and M. Rabin. 1999. Addiction and self-control. In *Addiction: Entries and Exits* (ed. J. Elster), pp. 169–206. New York: Russell Sage Foundation.

Pauly, M. V. 2001. Kenneth Arrow and the changing economics of health care: foreword. *Journal of Health Politics, Policy and Law* 26:829–34.

Pauly, M. V., and M. Satterthwaite. 1981. The pricing of primary care physician's services: a test of the role of consumer information. *Bell Journal of Economics* 12:488–506.

Payne, J. W., E. J. Johnson, and J. R. Bettman. 1993. *The Adaptive Decision Maker*. Cambridge University Press.

Phelps, C. E. 2000. Information diffusion and best practice adoption. In *Handbook of Health Economics* (ed. A. Culyer and J. P. Newhouse). Amsterdam: North-Holland.

Phelps, C. E., and C. Mooney. 1993. Variations in medical practice: causes and consequences. In *Competitive Approaches to Health Care Reform* (ed. R. Arnould, R. Rich, and W. White). Washington, DC: Urban Institute Press.

Rabin, M. 1998. Psychology and economics. *Journal of Economic Literature* 36:11–46.

———. 2002. Inference by believers in the law of small numbers. *Quarterly Journal of Economics*.

Rabin, M., and J. Schrag. 1999. First impressions matter: a model of confirmatory bias. *Quarterly Journal of Economics* 114:37–82.

Reinhardt, U. 1978. Comment on monopolistic elements in the market for physician services. In *Competition in the Health Sector* (ed. H. Greenberg), pp. 121–48. Aspen, CO: Aspen Press.

Rice, T. 1998. *Health Economics Reconsidered*. Chicago, IL: Health Administration Press.

Samuelson, W., and R. Zeckhauser. 1988. Status quo bias in decision making. *Journal of Risk and Uncertainty* 1:7–59.

Schneider, E. C., and A. M. Epstein. 1998. Use of public performance reports: a survey of patients undergoing cardiac surgery. *Journal of the American Medical Association* 279:1638–42.

Schoenbaum, M. 1997. Do smokers understand the mortality effects of smoking? Evidence from the health and retirement survey. *American Journal of Public Health* 87:755–59.

Shaller, D., S. Sofaer, S. D. Findlay, J. H. Hibbard, D. Lansky, and S. Delbanco. 2003. Consumers and quality-driven health care: a call to action. *Health Affairs* 22:95–101.

Simon, H. 1958. Theories of decision making in economics and behavioral science. *American Economic Review* 49:253–283.

Stano, M. 1987. A further analysis of the physician inducement controversy. *Journal of Health Economics* 6:229–38.

Thaler, R. H. 1980. Toward a positive theory of consumer choice. *Journal of Economic Behavior and Organization* 1:39–60.

Thaler, R. H., and R. Sunstein. 2003. Libertarian paternalism. *American Economic Review* 93:175–79.

Tversky, A., and D. Kahneman. 1973. Availability: a heuristic for judging frequency and probability. *Cognitive Psychology* 5:207–32.

Van Ryn, M., and J. Burke. 2000. The effect of patient race and socioeconomic status on physicians' perceptions of patients. *Social Science and Medicine* 50:813–28.

Wennberg, J. E., and M. M. Cooper (eds). 1997. *Dartmouth Atlas of Health Care*. Chicago, IL: American Hospital Publishing.

Wolfe, M. W. 2003. Overview and comparison of the proton pump inhibitors for the treatment of acid-related disorders. (Available at http://patients.uptodate.com/topic.asp?file=acidpep/10094.)

Zeckhauser, R. 1970. Medical insurance: a case study in the trade-off between risk spreading and appropriate incentives. *Journal of Economic Theory* 2:10–26.

COMMENT BY JACOB GLAZER [22]

6.4.1 Introduction

There are few, if any, sectors in the economy where the growing paradigm generally termed "behavioral economics" seems to be as relevant and important as the market for health services. Starting with Arrow (1963), many economists have recognized the fact that, in the health services and health insurance market, consumers and providers cannot (on the basis of their behavior) reasonably be described as rational agents acting to maximize their expected utility or profit. Furthermore, motives and considerations such as altruism, trust, and norms, often outside the economists' usual playground, appear to play an important role in the agents' decision-making process. Most of these researchers, however, have implemented their own, often ad hoc, assumptions about how agents behave in these markets and very few have actually relied on models developed and results obtained in related behavioral fields such as psychology, sociology, and, especially, the more recently emerging field of behavioral economics. It is perhaps for this reason that, in spite of the voluminous research addressing this issue and the tremendous effort it has involved, many economists feel that we have not yet come up with a good model (or models) for understanding one of the most important activities in health care: the doctor–patient interaction (see McGuire (2000) for a thorough discussion on this issue).

There is no doubt in my mind that bridging between these two almost parallel lines of research—behavioral economics and heath economics—will take us in the right direction if we wish to get a better understanding of the relationship between doctors and patients. Frank's work is an excellent start in laying down the foundations for that bridge. Frank identifies the main domains in the health-care market in which agents do not seem to behave according to the "cognitive paradigm" and, more importantly in my opinion, he points out some "regularities" in the, so to speak, "boundedly rational" behavior of these agents. Frank goes on to raise many interesting ideas of how models and ideas developed by behavioral economists and other researchers might be applied to obtain a better understanding of how patients and doctors act and interact, and he even suggests possible explanations for some of the puzzling phenomena that have been observed in this market.

In what follows I briefly present my understanding of some the main aspects of the doctor–patient interaction where behavioral economics seems very relevant and potentially very useful. This discussion is based mainly on Frank's presentation (see above) as well as some other readings. In the first part of this essay, I present the main

---

[22] I gratefully acknowledge financial support from the National Institute of Mental Health (R34 MH07142). I would like to thank Richard Frank and Tom McGuire for fruitful discussions.

dimensions on which providers and patients decide and act in the market for health care. In the second part I highlight some of the main observations regarding how agents behave in this market. In the third part I bring the two groups of agents, doctors and patients, together and briefly discuss the phenomenon that many economists view as the main symptom of the market failure in health care: small area variations. The last part is devoted to some thoughts regarding the implications of behavioral health economics for the efficiency of markets and welfare in general.

6.4.2 *What Do Agents Decide On?*

Consumers in the health-care market (often referred to as patients) face a wide set of decisions and actions. Grouping some of these decisions together, we can say that consumers in the health-care market make decisions with respect to

- their health insurance coverage,
- whether or not to seek care,
- which provider to go to,
- what to tell the provider,
- whether or not to comply with the provider's recommendations,
- whether or not to seek a second opinion.

Providers of health care make decisions with respect to

- which diagnostic procedures to perform,
- which treatments to recommend and perform,
- what to tell the patient.

6.4.3 *How Do Agents Decide?*

Health care is an extremely complicated product. Each case is different and may involve multiple decisions with multiple uncertainties. New data and evidence about the effectiveness of different procedures keep arising alongside new technologies. It is no surprise, therefore, that both consumers and producers find decision-making in such an environment very difficult and frustrating and that they often find themselves following a decision-making procedure that might seem suboptimal to an outside observer (a recommended reading for most of the issues discussed here is McCall (1996)).

Casual observation and much empirical evidence have demonstrated that patients often form their beliefs and make their decision on the basis of

- small samples (e.g., a young woman decides to have a mammography just because a friend has been diagnosed with breast cancer),

- uncontrolled experiments (e.g., people who suffer from back pain choose to have acupuncture because many people have taken this treatment before and seem to be doing better),
- extreme cases (e.g., a pregnant woman decides to have amniocentesis after a neighbor has had her baby diagnosed with Down's Syndrome),
- trust (the patient simply follows the doctor's advice, often saying: "you are the doctor"),
- fear of breaking the trust (patients do not seek a second opinion because they do not want to upset their doctor),
- instinct and "faith" ("this medication really works for me").

Similarly, providers of health care often form their beliefs and take actions on the basis of

- small samples (e.g., the doctor stops prescribing a particular medication just because it did not seem to help one or a few of her patients),
- uncontrolled experiments (e.g., a doctor might prefer one treatment over another just because more of her own or her colleagues' patients seem to be doing better on it),
- extreme cases (the death of a patient, for example, may have a dramatic effect on the doctor's decisions in future cases that look similar),
- stereotypes (e.g., the doctor believes that certain groups of patients tend not comply with a physician's recommendations),
- common practice (the doctor does not actually "make a cognitive decision" for each new case she treats, but rather follows some "standard operating procedure" common among her peers or colleagues or even simply something that she has adopted and became familiar with),
- the need to "do something" (sometimes, even when there is really no solution to the patient's problem, the doctor feels that she cannot just send the patient home without a recommendation or prescription),
- the patient's expectations (e.g., sometimes doctors prescribe antibiotics just because this is what the patient has asked for, not because it is supposed to work in his case).

Furthermore, even though deciding on the optimal treatment almost always involves solving a "decision tree," agents (i.e., doctors and patients) often prefer to think about it "one step at a time" (i.e., they do not apply backward induction).

Overall, it seems that agents in the health-care market adopt different decision-making procedures and modes of behavior, depending on the circumstances. I think that health economists have done far too little in trying to understand how exactly

Table 6.1. Highest and lowest rates of performance (per 10,000 people) in different geographical areas, for different medical procedures.

Procedure	Highest rate	Lowest rate
Injection of hemorrhoids	17	0.7
Knee replacement	20	3
Carotid endarterectomy	23	6
Bypass surgery	23	7
Heart catheterization	51	22
Hip replacement	24	8
Appendix removal	5	2
Hernia repair	53	38

the agents' decision-making procedure is determined in the different situations and how it can be affected. This is precisely where ideas from behavioral economics might be most helpful.

There are many different hypotheses that might be useful in understanding doctors' and patients' behavior. Among them are

- costs of collecting the information,
- costs of processing the information,
- rapid technological innovation (see Newhouse 2002),
- distorted incentives (see Newhouse 2002),
- loss aversion,
- availability heuristic (see Tversky and Kahneman 1974),
- anxiety (see Koszegi 2003),
- case-based decision (see Gilboa and Schmeidler 1995),
- statistical discrimination (see Balsa and McGuire 2003).

Though these hypotheses ought to be analyzed and tested, they at least provide a starting point for a theory that will better explain the doctor–patient interaction.

6.4.4 The Main Symptom: Small Area Variations

Even without a full understanding of the reasons behind the agents' behavior, we can talk about some of its consequences. Perhaps the most notable phenomenon in the health-care market and the one that many health economists view as the strongest evidence for market failure in that market is the phenomenon called "small area variations" (SAVs). Numerous researchers have found and documented major differences in the rates of various medical procedures performed and/or outcomes across populations of patients with similar characteristics. This phenomenon is referred to as

Table 6.2. Examples of medical procedures for which excess use has been documented.

Procedure	Proportion of use
Hospitalization	23% inappropriate (27% for women and 18% for men)
Blood transfusion	41% inappropriate
Hysterectomy	35% inappropriate
Bypass surgery	30% equivocal, 4% inappropriate
Pacemakers	36% questionable, 20% definitely unnecessary
Endoscopy	Only 72% were found to be appropriate

small area variations. Table 6.1 presents the highest and lowest rates of performance (per 10,000 people) in different geographical areas, for different medical procedures (McCall 1996, p. 188).

If we think that (ceteris paribus) there exists a particular level of medical severity or need, below which a certain medical procedure should not be performed and above which it should be performed (for example, the level of severity at which marginal social benefit equals marginal social costs), then SAV is a strong indication that in some situations a procedure may be over performed and in some other situations it is under performed.

Indeed, many researchers have studied the question of overuse and underuse of medical services and have found both. Some examples of medical procedures for which excess use has been documented are presented in Table 6.2 (the figures in the right-hand column show the proportion of use found inappropriate, or equivocal, according to a group of medical experts). The source for the data that appears in this table is McCall (1996).

Some other examples where excess use has been reported are angioplasty, cataract operations, back surgery, and prescribing antibiotics.

Perhaps the most extreme and troublesome example of excess use is the rapidly growing multibillion dollar market for services and products that have no scientific basis for their claims and for which there is sometimes even scientific evidence showing that they do not do what they claim they do. Many of these treatments are what we often call "alternative" medicine.

But excess use is not the only problem. Cases of underuse have also been documented. For example, even though hypertension can lead to stroke, heart failure, renal failure, and blindness, between 75 and 90% of patients diagnosed with this disorder fail to take their medication regularly or follow other recommendations. The area where underuse seems the most common is in preventive medicine. People simply tend not to take medication if they do not feel sick.

A better understanding of providers' and consumers' decision-making procedures and preferences can shed some light on the question of how many of the SAVs are

Table 6.3.

Treatment	True probability of success	Beliefs about the probability of success
C	ε	ε
A	0.01	0.25

indeed an inefficiency and what can be dome to improve the functioning of the health-care markets in these cases.

6.4.5 Two Final Thoughts

I would like to end this discussion by raising two thoughts that I find somewhat intriguing.

6.4.5.1 Can Markets Substitute Trust?

Until recently the market for health care was built mainly on trust. Patients did not search for the best available provider whenever they had a medical problem, but rather used the one with which they had become familiar. Patients usually did not know much, and in most cases did not even try to learn much, about their problem and what the available treatments were. And, finally, when their doctor made a recommendation, the patients hardly ever questioned her judgment. Things are very different today. More and more information about providers' performance is becoming public and may assist patients in choosing their provider. Medical information about various diseases and the most recent procedures with which to treat them is easily accessible (e.g., via the Internet) and patients often demand a certain treatment from their doctor. Moreover, if they are unsatisfied with the doctor's treatment, patients are much less reluctant to ask for a second opinion or seek another doctor. The market for health care is becoming more and more like any other market. The advantages of this new market organization are clear: patients can make more educated and overall much better decisions as they have more information to rely on and doctors have much stronger incentives to provide high-quality care, since their quality is being more tightly "monitored" by the consumers and payers. One should remember, however, that, given the complexity and dynamics of the health-care product, market competition and incentive schemes, efficient as they may be, will probably not be sufficient to achieve the highest feasible quality of care and in the end it will still be the doctor's preferences and sense of responsibility that play a major role in the treatment's outcomes. Even under this new market organization, a significant part of the information regarding the suitable and relevant procedures to treat a patient will remain with the doctor, among other things, because of her professional education and experience, and the patient will still have to rely a lot on the doctor's effort and good intentions. An interesting question, I think, is whether the shift of the doctor–patient relationship, from one that is mainly built on trust and where it is common knowledge that the patient expects the doctor to care for him to a relationship that looks more like any other economic transaction, may not diminish the doctor's sense of responsibility for the patient and, hence, her (unobservable) effort and, at the end, the quality of care she provides. Is it not possible that the doctor's preferences will change with the change in the market environment?

The second question that I would like to raise has to do more with the normative aspects of behavioral health economics.

6.4.5.2   Is There a Market Failure in a "Fools' Paradise"?

Patients (and doctors) often make decisions on the basis of unfounded or even wrong beliefs. This type of behavior raises some serious questions regarding the welfare criteria to adopt in such situations. Consider the example in Table 6.3.

In this example there are two treatments: one that I call "C" (for "conventional") and the other that I call "A" (for "alternative"). Based on the scientific evidence, the probability that treatment A will solve the medical problem is estimated at 0.01, whereas the probability that treatment C will solve the same problem is estimated at some $\varepsilon > 0$. The consumer, however, behaves as if he believes that treatment A can solve his medical problem with probability 0.25, whereas for treatment C, he knows the true probability, ε. Everything else being equal, if $\varepsilon < 0.25$, the patient will prefer treatment A over C. Assuming a benevolent central planner, should he inform the patient that his beliefs about treatment A are wrong? Obviously, for ε large enough he should. But how about when ε is small? For $\varepsilon < 0.01$, not only does the patient take the better treatment but he also lives with the belief that the probability of success of the treatment is 0.25. It seems that telling the patient that he is actually wrong about A will not make him better off (unless, of course, there are some other decisions involved). Now, how about the case where ε is greater than but close to 0.01? Will telling the patient that he is actually wrong about A necessarily make him better off in this case? The answer to this question is not at all simple and it illustrates, I believe, one of the many difficulties economists will face in trying to address welfare aspects when the revealed-preferences paradigm is no longer taken for granted.

REFERENCES

Arrow, K. J. 1963. Uncertainty and the welfare economics of medical care. *American Economic Review* 53:941–73.

Balsa, A. J., and T. G. McGuire. 2003. Prejudice, clinical uncertainty and stereotyping as source of health disparities. *Journal of Health Economics* 22:89–116.

Gilboa, I., and D. Schmeidler. 1995. Case-based decision theory. *Quarterly Journal of Economics* 110:605–39.

Koszegi, B. 2003. Health, anxiety and patient behavior. *Journal of Health Economics* 22:1073–84.

McCall, T. B. 1996. *Examining Your Doctor: A Patient's Guide to Avoiding Harmful Medical Care*. New York: Carol Publishing Corporation.

McGuire, G. T. 2000. The economics of physician behavior. In *Handbook of Health Economics* (ed. A Culyer and J. P. Newhouse). Amsterdam: North-Holland.

Newhouse, P. J. 2002. Why is there a quality chasm? *Health Affairs* 21:13–25.

Tversky, A., and D. Kahneman. 1974. Judgment under uncertainty: heuristics and biases. *Science* 185:1124–31.

COMMENT BY BOTOND KOSZEGI

As with any speaker at the conference, Frank had his work cut out for him, having to summarize the state of research in behavioral health economics. He responded with a very nice paper, a tour de force of problems in health economics, with some issues we know a lot about and many puzzles behavioral economics might help resolve. There is theory in here, mostly an outline of the classical model of physician decision-making and a little on patient decision-making. There are many empirical facts on both physician and patient behavior, and thoughtful discussions tying theory and empirical data together. There is speculation about the psychological forces underlying the different types of behavior, and suggestions for future research. I learned a lot from the paper.

In this discussion, I will briefly describe the context of medical decision-making and the paper's topics, and then point out a few directions in which future research will hopefully go. I confine the discussion to treatment of illness and health services, and ignore the quite different health insurance market.

One of the main lessons we have taken to heart from psychology is that behavior is sensitive to the context in which choices are made. Thus, it is worth identifying some general aspects of the context in which medical decision-making occurs. Decisions about health are typically very important for welfare; they involve extreme trade-offs—both the costs and the benefits are often very high—and occur under uncertainty and asymmetric information and knowledge. The consumers of health care are not in a position to make decisions by themselves, but there are experts (doctors) who know much more about the available treatment options and the patient's condition than the patient does, and who offer their advice and services in a market with lots of options and (at least nowadays) lots of information about providers.

Neoclassical economic theory predicts that in these situations, outcomes are going to be pretty close to optimal (under the constraints of medical knowledge and resources). Because the decision is important and the potential costs and benefits are high, patients seek out a lot of information from a variety of sources, exert a lot of effort in their rehabilitation and treatment programs and to maintain their health, carefully follow their drug regimens, and so forth. And because the business is so important and therefore lucrative, doctors work hard to keep their knowledge up to date, and provide the best care to maintain their reputations and patients.

In stark contrast to this economic theory view that health care is an environment that will induce people to make very good choices, psychologists would say that it is in some ways rather conducive to making the worst mistakes. This makes health care an illustrative and important application of behavioral economics. In medical decision-making, a lot of information must be acquired and processed quickly and distilled into major decisions, and—like most of us—both doctors and patients make many mistakes in doing this. Because of the importance of the decisions and the large stakes, and because of uncertainty, patients' decisions must be made under extreme emotions and stress. And patients must make many painful investments that will show returns only far in the future. These are exactly where psychologists predict behavior will deviate greatly from neoclassical economic theory.

With this as a general motivation, one way to categorize the themes in the paper is the following. First, a few key aspects of the health care context fit right in with standard economic concepts and, because of this, classical methods have been extremely helpful in understanding health-care markets. But that is not what the focus is on here, so I proceed to what the bulk of the paper is about.

The paper devotes considerable attention to physician motivations and decision-making mistakes. Physicians appear not to be driven purely by profit-maximization incentives. A number of alternatives have been proposed—many of which Richard's paper has discussed—but none of them very strongly grounded in evidence or anywhere close to satisfactory. Doctors seem to respond to incentives, but more to average, not marginal ones. And doctors are slow to put into practice even widely available information on the effectiveness of treatments and drugs.

The paper then deals with mistakes on the other side of the market, the patient side. Patients often underuse medical care, and are subject to default effects in drug use and insurance provider choices. Like doctors, patients also use information quite poorly, forming their opinion of a physician based on limited information from family and friends, trusting a lot of their treatment and advice to a single doctor they know well, and tending to forgive bad outcomes as inevitable and outside the doctor's control. This is in part understandable, since patients have difficulty judging the technical expertise of a doctor, but it is in part puzzling, because information on doctors and hospitals is easily available.

These points are mostly about individual decision-making on the two sides of the market. What economists are most interested in is how these patterns of behavior feed through the market to produce health outcomes and costs. It seems obvious that the first-order effect of many of the mistakes discussed is to make health outcomes worse. But doctors and patients interact in the market, so psychological effects on their behavior will interact and influence each other. This is a place where economists, with their understanding of equilibrium feedback, can add a lot to the debate, and where a lot of the interesting and complex questions are going to be. With individual decision-making being complicated enough, there is very little research on this so far.

But since I expect and hope that there will be much more in the near future, I devote some space to speculation. One natural question to ask is how patient behavior affects the incentives of doctors to provide good care. To the extent that Frank's paper deals with this question, it comes across as quite pessimistic. Since patients use very limited information and tend to trust and stay with their regular physicians, the argument goes, demand is unresponsive to performance, so doctors have little or no incentives to perform well. I think this is a more complicated issue, and I am not sure whether I agree with the paper's conclusion. True, the fact that patients ask their friends for advice about doctors, and do not look at more reliable publicly available data, implies that most of the time they do not respond to doctor performance. This of course benefits a doctor with mediocre performance. But for the same reason, demand can be quite volatile. If a critical mass of people decides that a doctor is not good enough, this doctor might lose a lot of patients very quickly, as rumors about her performance spread. Once this happens, the same forces that benefited a mediocre doctor before now work against her: it will be very difficult for her to win the patients back. This threat might discipline doctors as much as or more than a competitive market. Of course, at the same time it might also give them incentives to provide good care in the wrong dimensions (e.g., to take steps so that people like them, not necessarily to choose the technically best options).

To model these demand responses, we will certainly need very different market models than those that exist today. The paper does not deal at all with the flip side of this issue: how doctors' motivations and decision-making mistakes affect the behavior of patients. This is an equally rich area for exploration. To begin with, it would be interesting to know to what extent patients are aware that doctors regularly make mistakes, and if they are not, what creates their "faith" in the medical profession.

If they are aware—which is likely to be the case to some extent—further fascinating issues arise. From a classical point of view, it is then even more puzzling why patients often rely on the advice of just one doctor and do not seek out a lot of medical information. But realizing that doctors are imperfect might also make medical decision-making more uncertain and stressful, exacerbating the psychological mechanisms that hinder proper health behavior.

Table 6.4. Prognostic optimism communicated to patients and colleagues
(Christakis 1999, p. 228).

Physician's statement to patient (%)	Physician's statement to colleague (%)			
	Pessimistic	Neither	Optimistic	Total
Pessimistic	36.5	3.0	0.5	39.9
Neither	16.8	2.5	0	19.2
Optimistic	15.3	14.3	11.3	40.9
Total	68.5	19.7	11.8	100

Note: 203 internists received a vignette describing a sixty-six-year-old man with chronic obstructive pulmonary disease and pneumonia necessitating ICU admission. Subjects were queried regarding how much prognostic optimism or pessimism they would communicate to the patient and to a colleague.

There are three things I felt were missing from the paper. First, in terms of the overarching topics emphasized in the paper, there is very little about the psychological aspects of the doctor–patient relationship. The two sides of the market are treated more or less in isolation, and the interaction that occurs (demand response to doctor performance) is very classical. Yet doctors serve an important role in communicating diagnoses and treatment options to patients, in motivating them to follow through in their treatment, in making sure that they practice adequate preventive care, that they perform checkups and have the right lifestyle, and so on. These are all psychologically rich issues. They also cause a lot of frustration for doctors and are very important for patients. In surveys, patients tend to express satisfaction with their doctor's technical expertise, but complain about interaction-type issues such as respect, speaking in understandable, nontechnical terms, and communicating in a sensitive manner.

As an illustration that understanding the doctor–patient relationship requires more than understanding the two sides of the market separately, consider Table 6.4, taken from Christakis (1999). Doctors were given short descriptions of hypothetical medical scenarios, and were asked about how they would behave in each case. Strikingly, doctors are much more likely to communicate optimism about a given case when dealing with the patient than when talking to another doctor. This discrepancy is clearly not about how doctors form their own opinions, and is unlikely to be about demand inducement or other classical concerns. Rather, it is probably about the human side of the doctor–patient relationship.

Second—and this is a general concern regarding behavioral economics—once we start to import insights from psychology, a lot of observed economic behavior will seem grossly overdetermined. That is, there will be multiple reasonable explanations for the same phenomenon. Yet to think about the right policies, having some explanation for a phenomenon is not sufficient; since different models will often have very different policy implications, it is crucial to have the right explanation.

For example, Frank's paper identifies three possible sources of patient underuse of medical care, i.e., that patients do not take advantage of health resources when they should: externalities, stigma, and emotions. If underuse of care is due to externalities (that part of the reason people should get care is to benefit others), the right policy is to subsidize or regulate use (e.g., by requiring immunizations). Subsidies will probably work in the other cases as well, but they will be very expensive and crude policies for the purpose. If underuse is due to stigma (that being known to have certain conditions is stigmatizing) policies should probably aim to ensure complete privacy and assure patients that nobody needs to know about their condition, and to make it really easy for them to get treatment, so that they do not have to deal with the stigmatizing activity for very long. If underuse is due to emotions such as fear of bad news, the best policies will manage the information patients receive and how they receive them. In this and other examples, it will be important to identify possible sources of information (either existing sources or potential ways of collecting the information) that might be used to decide which explanation is the right one to what extent. It is likely that we will need very different sources of information than those traditionally used in economics, even health economics.

One way to keep models and ideas grounded in reality is to make sure that they are well founded on psychological and economic evidence—and I think the paper does a good job in doing this. But some of the work in health economics that is reviewed is much less convincing on this front, treating doctors as people whose motivations and norms of conduct are fundamentally different from everyone else's. To a first approximation, doctors are like other humans.[23] Investigating how the psychological tendencies that are present in all of us play out in the context of a doctor's work is a disciplined way to enrich the modeling of their behavior.

Third, related to all this, a lot of Frank's paper is positive in nature, describing patterns of behavior and their possible causes. It would be interesting to develop some of the normative implications of the analysis: how we can use these insights to improve medical outcomes.

REFERENCE

Christakis, N. A. 1999. *Death Foretold: Prophecy and Prognosis in Medical Care*, 2nd edn. University of Chicago Press.

---

[23] In particular, the fact that they have motives other than profit maximization is not really surprising or special.

Behavioral Economics of Organizations

By Colin F. Camerer and Ulrike Malmendier [1]

7.1 INTRODUCTION

This essay analyzes how behavioral economics can be *applied* to organizations, and how it can be *enriched* by thinking about the economic questions associated with economic organization.

Behavioral economics modifies the standard economic model to account for psychophysical properties of preference and judgment, which create limits on rational calculation, willpower, and greed (see, for example, Rabin 1998; Mullainathan and Thaler 2001; Camerer and Loewenstein 2004). The modified economics theory aims at providing parsimonious and psychologically sound explanations for empirical findings that the standard model has a tough time explaining. From a methodological perspective, behavioral economics is simply a humble approach to economics, which respects the comparative empirical advantages of neighboring social sciences and sees neighboring sciences as trading partners. The empirical regularity and constructs carefully explored by those neighboring fields are presumed to be an important input which should often trump the seduction of mathematically elegant economic theories that are empirically unmotivated.

Thinking about organizations naturally extends the definition of behavioral economics to include how socialization, networks, and identity shape individual behavior in organizations (see, for example, Akerlof and Kranton 2005; Gibbons 2004b). As such, the behavioral economics of organizations involve both a special challenge and opportunity. Consider how behavioral *finance* has developed as an academic discipline, and how behavioral organizational economics *could* develop. Until 1990 or so, finance was arguably the area of economics most hostile to the idea that psychological limits matter for the focus of the field's attention—namely, stock price movements. Since then, there has been a dramatic shift in the amount of careful

---

[1] Ideas from the NBER Organizational Economics conference in March, 2004, particularly Bob Gibbons's presentation, have been useful, as well as discussions with Dirk Jenter, Chip Heath, Sendhil Mullainathan, Andreas Roider, Bengt Holmström's discussion in Helsinki, and Peter Diamond's close reading.

attention paid to behavioral ideas. This is surprising because it has been argued that large stock markets are the ultimate domain in which highly rational traders should limit the influence of those who make mistakes. So why did academic asset pricers start to "misbehave" so fast? One reason was good data, which made it easy to test new behavioral theories against the rational incumbents. Another reason was the availability of a clear benchmark model (market efficiency) to argue with. Good data and a sharp benchmark enabled researchers to create a set of clear anomalies in asset pricing. The situation was reversed in corporate finance. Rational arbitrageurs cannot easily limit suboptimal corporate-finance decisions, since it is hard to short-sell a CEO or CFO. Quite the opposite occurs: top executives may be entrenched and hard to get rid of. Biases and mistakes in decision-making are thus much more likely to have a persistent and large effect in corporate finance than on asset pricing. Nevertheless, behavioral research in corporate finance took off considerably later than that in asset pricing, possibly due to the lack of good data and a clear theoretical benchmark. Obtaining executive-level or even firm-level data on corporate finance decision-making has always been more intricate than obtaining stock price data. At the same time, numerous, conflicting theories have been proposed for virtually all types of corporate finance decisions, whether on mergers, stock issuance, or dividends.

The situation in organizational economics closely resembles that of corporate finance. The lack of rich within-firm panel data sets and cleanly identified exogenous variation is a persistent stumbling block, hampering progress in our understanding of the economics of organizations. On the other hand, if systematic biases are identifiable within the firm, they may have a large and persistent impact on organizational decision-making. If workers misallocate their human capital, nobody can take advantage of their mistakes by "short-selling" their capital. Adjustment to mistakes must come from some other source than simply trading against a mistake. Moreover, biases in organizations give rise to the interesting challenges of how organizations should be designed to repair these mistakes or to exploit them, or how firms organize around them if they represent genuine regret-free preferences rather than errors.[2] Moving away from mistakes due to heuristics, a lot of psychology is involved when workers team up in an organization—social comparison, changes in identity, camaraderie, attribution and diffusion of credit and blame, and so forth. This kind of psychology has played a small role in behavioral economics in recent years, but looms large when thinking about organizations.

Our paper is divided into four parts. Each part poses a broad question and suggests some ideas. Little systematic knowledge has been cumulated on many of these topics.

---

[2]Frank (2005) distinguishes mistakes you regret and those you do not. Properties of preference like social comparison fall into the latter category.

For those topics, the paper should be read as a research agenda rather than a review of what has been learned.

Section 7.2 lays out the basic single-activity risk-incentive conflict model and points out psychological considerations which complicate the model. Section 7.3 notes that the simplest risk-incentive model does not particularly account for the fact that people work together in organizations and discusses the importance of group loyalty, peer effects, and the coordinating role and cognitive economics of culture. Section 7.4 is about top management and governance and special considerations that arise like CEO overconfidence. Section 7.5 asks how patterns in individual judgment and choice aggregate into organizational outcomes when organizations can repair or exploit them. Section 7.6 concludes the chapter.

7.2 Complicating the Single-Agent Risk-Incentive Model

A good place to start is to discuss how psychology complicates the simple risk-incentive model of principal–agent relations that is a workhorse in organizational economics. First we will lay out a simple agency model with one type of activity. In the standard labor economics model, workers face a prevailing wage and decide how much labor to supply at that wage (and consume the remaining hours as leisure). We assume that people like money and, by definition, dislike work and like leisure.

A useful way to critique the standard principal–agent model is to ask when its basic assumptions are violated. The goal is not to heckle the model's shortcomings (which are an inevitable byproduct of simplicity), but to offer empirical facts and build up intuition about how it could be extended in useful ways.

We start with a simple exposition of a standard agency model. Worker i chooses effort e_i, which has cost $c(e_i)$. The productivity of effort also depends on a variable called skill, s_i, so that observed output is $x_i = f(e_i, s_i) + \theta_i$, where θ_i is a random component, additive to skill- and effort-based output ("luck"), with distribution $m(\theta_i)$. (In the simplest analysis, skill is homogeneous or does not matter, so $f(e_i, s_i) = e_i$.) Firms observe output x_i and pay a wage $w(x_i)$. This could be a fixed wage, $w(x_i) = w_i$; a step function or bonus package, $w(x_i) = \{w_i$ for $x_i < t_i; w_i + b_i$ for $x_i \geqslant t_i\}$; a linear wage, $w(x_i) = w_0 + \beta x_i$, etc. In subsequent sections we will assume that $w(x_i)$ is increasing in x_i. Assume also that preferences are separable in effort disutility and utility from wages. Then the agent's expected utility is

$$\text{EU}(e_i) = \int_{\theta_i} u[w(f(e_i, s_i) + \theta_i)] m(\theta_i)\, d\theta_i - c(e_i), \qquad (7.1)$$

where the disutility of effort, $c(e_i)$, satisfies the usual assumptions, is increasing in e_i, and convex. The principal's earnings are $\pi(f(e_i, s_i) + \theta_i) - w(f(e_i, s_i) + \theta_i)$, where $\pi(\cdot)$ is the (gross) revenue of the firm.

Including skill makes this formalism cumbersome, but allows room for behavioral influences that are not traditionally considered. We discuss several ways in which the simple model above can be complicated:

(i) workers do not know the disutility of effort.

(ii) wage preferences depend on reference points (such as previous wages, or wages of others);

(iii) workers care about the procedure that generates wages or other outcomes;

(iv) psychic income matters, and may be tied to psychological factors like perceived appreciation;

(v) financial incentives may "crowd out" intrinsic incentives or affect performance negatively;

(vi) firms may be systematically biased in judging the cause of performance (i.e., disentangling worker effort e_i from luck θ_i).

7.2.1 *Workers Do Not Know the Disutility of Effort $c(e)$*

Labor economics extends a standard assumption from consumer theory—namely, that people have complete and consistent preferences across bundles of goods—to the case of labor and leisure. But young people may have only a vague idea of what work they would like to do when deciding on their first jobs, or on college majors (or even colleges), which partly determine their career paths due to irreversibilities and path-dependence.

A way to investigate the stability of labor-market preferences is to measure how much expressed preferences can be influenced by the way that work is described, or the procedure by which preferences are elicited (e.g., bidding wages or choosing at a fixed wage). For example, Ariely et al. (2004a) asked some subjects whether they would *pay* \$2 to attend a fifteen-minute poetry reading, and asked other subjects whether they would attend if they *were paid* \$2.[3] Later, a third of those who were anchored on paying said they would attend for free, compared to only 8% attendance by those who were anchored on being paid. Of course, students may not have developed clear preferences for whether listening to poetry is labor or leisure.[4] But if a random anchor can even influence the *sign* of $c(e)$, then it is likely that stronger

---

[3]Later experiments link the anchor to digits in a person's social security number and make it clear that the anchor was random, so that no information about $c(e)$ is conveyed by the choice of the anchor.

[4]The ambiguity about $c(e)$ is illustrated by a joke about a couple who are going away on a vacation. They ask their teenage neighbor, Mike, if he could take care of their dog while they are away. The couple explain that their dog needs to be fed, walked, and shown lots of loving care. They ask how much this job is worth to Mike. He ponders for a minute and concludes, "Well, I guess I'd pay you \$10." What's labor for one worker may be leisure for another.

influences affect at least some labor market entry decisions about relative values of $c(e)$.[5]

If employers know about anchoring and marketing influences on $c(e)$, then they will try to generate positive anchors, convincing prospective employees that working in their firm is fun. Little is known about the long-run influence or robustness of constructed-preference effects. Anchors might wear off: after experiencing an actual poetry reading, for example, subjects may quickly develop a consistent hedonic preference which is no longer affected by the initial anchor or subsequent ones, and resembles the complete preference assumed in economic theory. Furthermore, in competitive labor markets, anchors will not affect wages, because wages are determined by the marginal revenue product of workers. But anchoring could affect the *quantity* of labor supplied, even if it does not affect the "price" (i.e., the wage) for a given amount of labor supply. In the poetry example, think of the anchor fee/wage as creating a perception about the cost of effort of listening to poetry. Fixing the wage of poetry (through firm competition), more people will listen to poetry if they came to perceive the cost as low. So anchors can affect quantities even if they do not affect prices.

7.2.2 *Wage Preferences Can Depend on Reference Points $u(w(x_i) - r)$*

In the formalism above the utility of wages, $u[w(x_i)]$, does not depend on any special point of reference. But most systems in the brain have a homeostatic dependence on a set point or point of reference (e.g., hunger depends on what you have eaten recently; sweating and shivering respond to deviations of body temperature from a set point). If reactions to income tap similar psychophysical mechanisms, then people will care a lot about their wages relative to psychologically natural benchmarks, requiring a separate component of utility $u(w(x_i) - r)$ and a theory about what r is and how it changes (see, for example, Bowman et al. 1999; Koszegi and Rabin 2004).

Bewley (Chapter 5, this volume) discusses evidence that workers compare current earnings to previous earnings and dislike wage cuts, in traditional jobs where wages are adjusted periodically, so $r_t = w_{t-1}$. (Firms anticipate this and are reluctant to cut wages.) A similar reference dependence shows up in jobs where wages and hours fluctuate daily. For example, inexperienced New York cab drivers, who can adjust their daily hours, act as if they care about a daily income "target," which leads to

---

[5] For example, law school applications rose for a few years after the hit TV show "LA Law" began in 1986 (see Torry 1996). The show portrayed law as fun and empowering, and law firms as sexy, vibrant places to work. It is farfetched to think students are really Bayesian-updating based on new information about the $c(e)$ for law from a television show, because most pre-law students have a lot of information in the first place, or can gather objective information, and the television show is not meant to be an accurate depiction of the life of a lawyer.

labor supply elasticities that are *negative* (Camerer et al. 1997). Experienced drivers, however, have zero elasticity, which suggests a role for learning or attrition over time. Fehr and Götte (2003) find similar results in a field experiment with bicycle messengers. While randomly determined variation in monthly wages has a strong positive effect on the number of shifts per month, it has a (weaker) negative effect on the revenues within shift. Interestingly, the messengers for whom the nonstandard negative revenue effect is strongest also exert sizable loss aversion in a laboratory experiment.

Another kind of reference dependence is two-tier wage deals, which occur when firms are struggling financially. Senior workers doing the same jobs as entry-level workers are sometimes paid a larger wage, to avoid cutting their wages, while entry-level workers are paid less to save on the wage bill. Social comparison models predict that new workers will be unhappy at being paid less than senior workers beyond the disutility from the lower wage itself.

An important feature of reference dependence is that reference points may reflect failure to adjust for purchasing power. The best-studied example is money illusion. Firms act as if workers care about nominal wages rather than inflation-adjusted real wages, in making intertemporal comparisons (see, for example, Kahneman et al. 1986; Shafir et al. 1997). Baker et al. (1994) found there were hardly any nominal year-to-year wage cuts in a financial services firm, but many real wage cuts in inflationary years. The psychological principle behind money illusion may extend to illusions in comparing purchasing power across cities (leading people to prefer higher-salary jobs in the more expensive cities to lower-paying ones in cheaper cities) and in adjusting annual salaries for work hours (leading to taking high-salary jobs with the highest hours), but we do not know of any formal studies of these illusions.

7.2.3 *Workers Care about the Procedure That Generates Wages or Other Outcomes*

A simplifying principle in economic modeling is "consequentialism" or procedure-neutrality. People care only about outcomes and their economic impact, not about the *procedure* which produced those outcomes.[6]

One procedural preference is the effect of the *source* of income. The separability of income utility and effort disutility in Equation (7.1) implies that people value money equally if they earned it through hard work (effort) and if the money arrived as a windfall. But some experimental evidence suggests that money and goods which are

---

[6]Weaker statements of this principle are that preferences over procedures are weak compared with preferences over outcomes (such as compensation), or that procedural preferences are simply too poorly understood to serve as a basis for managerial policy.

earned are more valuable, or at least are treated differently. Coffee mugs which were "earned" are later sold for more than ones that are randomly allocated (Loewenstein and Issacharoff 1994). A brain imaging study showed that earned money produced a stronger activation in the nucleus accumbens, a brain area associated with predicted reward, than equivalent sums of unearned money (Zink et al. 2004).

These findings suggest that the utility of wages depends positively on effort, as if $U[w(x_i), e_i]$ had a positive cross-partial derivative,

$$\frac{\partial^2 U[w(x_i), e_i]}{\partial w(\cdot) \partial e_i} > 0.$$

When workers solve for optimal effort, extra utility from an "earned-income bonus" is like an increase in performance-based pay (a bonus return to effort), except that the incentive is entirely internal. How such a "pride bonus" interacts with sorting and with optimal wage and promotion policies is an interesting open question.

A broader point is that the process by which wages and other organizational outcomes are determined (particularly terminations) may affect how people value the consequences. In organizational studies this phenomenon is called "procedural justice," and it is argued that it is important empirically (Brockner and Wiesenfeld 1996; Tyler 2001). One component of procedural justice is the desire to have a voice or participate in important decisions that affect you. Another component is consistency of procedures. People dislike not knowing the rules that are being applied to judge them. The taste for clear rules motivates bright-line rules like seniority-based firing policies, and many policies in employment law. Of course, a taste for procedural justice is often hard to distinguish from standard preferences. For example, the desire to "have a voice" could just reflect the attempt to achieve individually favorable rules. Clear rules may simply help workers to optimize their effort allocation and reduce influence costs. Moreover, we may worry that procedural concerns, even if we could identify them, are second-order compared with wages. For example, while people may complain that a coworker was unfairly fired, will they actually quit their own job in protest, or accept a wage cut to get the coworker reinstated? Experiments suggest they might. But we would need more empirical research, tied to economic models, to calibrate the taste for procedural justice by pitting it against money in experiments or field analyses.

One kind of sensitivity to organizational procedures involves control. In a standard extension of the simple agency model above, firms observe a variable, γ_i, which is correlated with the unobserved luck component θ_i. The usual presumption is that effort e_i can be controlled by worker i but the error-correlate filtering variable γ_i cannot. Optimal contracting tells us that if workers dislike variance in wages more than firms do, the firms should use what they observe (γ_i) to filter some of the variance in θ_i and reduce the risk imposed on the worker. Workers will not mind having their wages depend on a variable out of their control if it benefits them by reducing undesirable variance in adjusted wages. This changes if workers have preferences for fairness. Sometimes the value of γ_i will lead the firm to penalize a worker when true effort e_i was high (e.g., firing a successful CEO who was much less successful than industry peers). Workers may think this is unfair.

A common example is benchmarking performance to an outside standard, like industry profits. Risk-averse workers should *like* benchmarking because it buffers them against industry-wide shocks. But evidence for direct benchmarking in executive compensation is surprisingly scarce, even though it is not hard to create simple benchmarks which would reduce compensation variance a lot. It does not appear that wages are even indirectly very sensitive to benchmarks (Antle and Smith 1996; Salanié 2003, p. 470).[7]

7.2.4 *Psychic Income*

The basic risk-incentive model divides the worker's world into efforts they dislike, and rewards they like. It is convenient to talk about wages as rewards because they are easily measured, and do not satiate. But people are motivated by many others types of nonpecuniary "psychic income" as well. For example, Stern (2004) uses multiple offers for postdoc biologists to estimate that those who accept offers at more science-oriented firms earn 25% lower wages in order to be able to publish their research and engage in the scientific community. This is consistent with a "compensating differential," in which workers trade off money wages for other aspects of the job they like (or dislike).

The existence of compensating differentials is not controversial. Behavioral economics suggests, however, that the *source* of these differentials might include emotion, social comparison, and other forces not included in typical analyses which focus on safety and education.

Ariely et al. (2004b) use a simple experimental paradigm to calibrate psychic income for what they call the "meaning" of work. Students proofread pages for a declining wage schedule (the wage for the marginal page fell) and handed finished pages to an experimenter. When their work was "ignored" (simply placed on a stack) or immediately shredded, they finished only about six pages, compared with nine pages when their pages were signed and filed away. Thus, the subjects traded off marginal wages for "meaningful" work which was kept rather than shredded.

In discussing our paper at the conference, Holmström suggested that what workers fundamentally care about is that their efforts are *appreciated*. For example,

---

[7]One form of benchmarking is a tournament structure, which seems to account for some features of internal labor markets with clear career paths (see, for example, Main et al. 1993).

entrepreneurs often talk about their desire to get rich as a *byproduct* of making a good product that many people want to buy. They see riches as an expression of appreciation. The fact that tentative evidence suggests income is more (neurally) valuable if it is earned by one's own effort fits with this idea too.

Of course, agents may strive for appreciation of their work for more standard reasons. In a study of "superstar" CEOs, Malmendier and Tate (2005a) found that CEOs who had won awards (such as "CEO of the Year" or "Top Manager") got a big relative pay boost. This effect goes in the opposite direction of a trade-off between appreciation and pay—the award is appreciation *and* a raise in wages. Their findings may indicate a signaling role of awards, or the ability of CEOs to use awards to justify pay increases in the face of weak governance.

Moreover, any theory rooted in the desire for effort appreciation needs to take into account the fact that paying wages is one way of showing appreciation. But appreciation may also depend on relative wages, which creates a role for social comparison in signaling appreciation. Appreciation might also be cheaply generated by organizational activities such as awards, titles, executive visits, "employee of the month" plaques, etc. The desire for feeling appreciated might also be the underpinning of the desire for procedural justice—for being listened to, holding outcomes constant—that was discussed above. Note that, if employees value appreciation, organizations who figure out how to generate effort-appreciation most cheaply will save on the wage bill and will have a competitive advantage over organizations who express appreciation only through expensive wages.

7.2.5 *Financial Incentives May "Crowd Out" Intrinsic Incentives or Affect Performance Negatively*

Psychologists' synonym for psychic income is "intrinsic motivation"—the satisfaction a worker gets from work for its own sake. An interesting phenomenon documented in psychology is the possibility that extrinsic incentives like money can "crowd out" or extinguish intrinsic motivation. For example, Lepper et al. (1973) had children coloring pictures (with no extrinsic incentive). Then they paid the children a small sum of money for each picture colored. When the wage was later removed, the children colored fewer pictures than they had in the initial phase with no payments. Their interpretation, called "overjustification," is that the children infer something about their own intrinsic motivation from the wages they are paid; when they are paid for coloring, they infer that they must not like to color very much, so when the wage is removed they quit coloring pictures.

Kreps (1997) and Benabou and Tirole (2003) consider crowding-out from an economic point of view. Since incentives often do have positive effects, the challenge is to create a theory which permits both positive effects and negative effects (i.e., "hidden costs" or "crowding out"). In Benabou and Tirole's theory, crowding out occurs when an agent thinks the principal knows more about job difficulty or the agent's abilities than she herself does. Then the agent takes the provision of high-powered incentives as a bad sign. Their theory is much like the original idea in social psychology but more carefully specified and rich with empirical implications (chiefly, that hidden costs should only occur when workers think incentives signal bad news). Benabou and Tirole (2004) discuss the case where incentives interact with prosocial behavior.

Leaving aside crowding out, monetary incentives could also affect performance negatively if high incentives create arousal that inhibits automatic responses or creates distraction (e.g., "choking under pressure"). According to the "Yerkes–Dodson Law" (Yerkes and Dodson 1908), arousal increases performance up to a point at which further arousal degrades performance. Ariely et al. (2003) demonstrate this effect with experiments conducted in India. They allowed their subjects to earn up to six months of wages[8] in various simple games. Surprisingly, the subjects with the highest payment perform worse than those with the moderate and the low payment in almost all games. It is, of course, unclear how relevant this effect is for the economics of organizations, given actual wage-setting and reward policies. Even if the effect were prevalent, wage-setters may account for it and adjust wages appropriately. Moreover, if experience with high-stakes situations decreases arousal, the effect may only apply to inexperienced agents.

7.2.6 *Firms May Be Biased in Judging the Cause of Performance*

In the standard agency model laid out above, agents exert effort which is productive, but principals can only observe agents' output. Observed output depends on unobserved effort and unobserved "luck." The usual assumption is that principals know the relative importance of effort and error in determining output, and also anticipate the agents' reaction to knowing their effort is not clearly observed.

This simple assumption buries a lot of behavioral economics. Separating skill from luck is difficult. As a result, it is quite possible that psychological forces bias principals' judgments of whether output is due to skill or luck. Three important psychological forces suggest that separating hard work from luck will often be biased in predictable ways: hindsight bias; overattributing cause to personal traits rather than situational influences; and overconfidence.

---

[8]The maximum pay amounted to half of the average annual consumer expenditure (per capita) in India.

7.2.6.1 Hindsight Bias

The brain's tremendous ability to sense patterns is manifested by our tendency to rapidly rewrite our memories of the past to fit what we have learned. The problem is that revising our beliefs after an event naturally leads to misremembering how little we knew before the event. Rapid rewriting creates "hindsight bias"—the ex post recollection of the ex ante probability of an event will be biased in the direction of the event's realization. Hindsight bias is on display every day in sports commentary and news coverage. It is surely an important force in organizational life but has not been studied at all.

A simple way to think about hindsight bias in agency models is that the effort an agent exerts narrows down the distribution of some relevant variable v at time t, $\sigma_t(v)$. Suppose the agent's job is to make the best decision given the value of v, which will eventually have a public realization v^*. A principal who creates an ex post "recollection" of the ex ante variance based on the realized v^*, $\hat{E}_t[\sigma_t(v)] = E_{t+1}[\sigma_t(v) \mid v^*]$, will infer too much mass around v^*. Suppose the agent did not choose the optimal action conditional on v^*. Then the principal will (mistakenly) infer that the agent did not exert enough effort to narrow the variance $\sigma_t(v)$ (he "should have known"). If the optimal action conditional on v^* is what the agent actually chose, then the agent gets too little credit because the principal will recall the likelihood of v^* occurring as being obvious (i.e., $\hat{E}_t[\sigma_t(v)]$ will be too closely centered around v^*, and the principal will not be impressed that the agent figured out that v^* would happen).

This sketch of a model becomes more interesting if agents *anticipate* that principals will be hindsight-biased. Agents who anticipate being second-guessed will record as much ex ante evidence as they can (also known as "covering your ass"). Agents may also herd into the same decisions other agents make (see Zwiebel 1995) or seek other ways to avoid anticipated hindsight bias.

It would be very useful to have field evidence distinguishing the effects of hindsight bias from other distortions. One method is to compare behavior of owner-managed firms with similar firms where shareholders and boards can second-guess the managers. Hindsight bias should be lower and risk-taking higher among owner-managed firms.

7.2.6.2 Misattribution of Cause

Social psychologists studying "attribution theory" have found that a typical mistake in attributing cause is to credit and blame individuals more than is deserved, compared to blaming and crediting situational variables.[9] In model terms, this

---

[9] Interestingly, recent studies by Nisbett (2004) suggest that the "fundamental error" of overattributing cause to people, rather than situations, is distinctly Western and is reversed in Asian cultures. Applied to

means inferring more than is justified about the unobserved effort e_i from output $f(e_i, s_i) + \theta_i$ or, alternatively, underestimating the importance of luck $(\text{var}(\theta_i))$. In the context of the firm, attribution is likely to be especially important in evaluating top executives, who make far-reaching decisions with noisy and lagged feedback. They are likely to be both credited and blamed too much for forces beyond their control. Applied to a person's own judgement of his or her efforts, however, attributions tend to be self-serving. For example, Bettman and Weitz (1983) find that, when companies do well, corporate annual reports attribute the success to internal factors and skill. When companies do badly, the reports attribute blame to external factors (regulation, demand shocks, and so forth). Those findings lack, of course, the ultimate proof of distortion. Moreover, even evidently distorted information provision may simply be the rational response to investors' lack of information or to investor credulity. Bertrand and Mullainathan (2001) show that exogenous variation in profits is reflected in executives' compensation. They find that compensation of oil company executives rises with worldwide oil prices, even though oil prices are set by global demand and OPEC output and are not influenced much by one executive's action. At the same time, executives are largely shielded from blame (in the form of lower compensation) when oil prices fall. Indeed, the phenomenon of "negative shielding"—relative insensitivity of compensation to poor performance, compared to stronger sensitivity to good performance—is widely documented in executive compensation (Garvey and Milbourn, forthcoming). It remains unclear from these studies which agents—if any—are misattributing positive outcomes. One possibility is that boards mistakenly give credit for positive outcomes and CEOs rationally exploit or even induce the misattribution of board members. Alternatively, executives themselves attribute positive outcomes to their own skills or effort and bad outcomes to bad luck. If corporate governance is weak, such CEOs may then extract disproportionately higher compensation after exogenously higher profits. Finally, it is possible that no party inside the corporation exhibits misattribution error. CEOs in badly governed firms may overadjust their compensation to good outcomes and underadjust for bad outcomes, exploiting investors' naivety, lack of information, or misattribution of executive credit to skill, and blame to outside forces.

7.2.6.3 Overconfidence

Many studies show that people are often overconfident. We define overconfidence as the tendency to overestimate one's own (relative) abilities and resulting outcomes and overoptimism as overestimation of general prospects. Here we briefly mention

---

agency theory, this suggests that pay-for-performance will be more slowly adopted in Asian-controlled firms and the East–West difference may have something to do with CEO status and pay in the different hemispheres.

overconfidence in the basic agency model. Section 7.4, below, has more discussion of overconfidence of top managers.

What does overconfidence of workers mean in the agency model? There are many ways to model overconfidence and it is an open question what these different types of overconfidence imply in equilibrium, or in practice. One possibility is that people overestimate the output x_i they will generate. For example, they may assume a distribution $\tilde{m}(\theta_i)$ that first-order stochastically dominates the true distribution $m(\theta_i)$: observationally equivalent to overestimating luck. Or they may overestimate the marginal productivity of their effort, $\partial f(e_i, s_i)/\partial e_i$. In either case they may work less hard than if they were not overconfident. Assume for example, that their wage schedule includes a piece rate β. At the correct optimum effort with no overconfidence (and corresponding optimal piece rate), agents misperceive themselves as working too hard because they overestimate expected output and, consequently, underestimate marginal utility. As a result, overconfident agents may cut back on effort. In theory, firms will increase the piece rate β to induce more effort, but for reasonable specifications this compensatory effect will not be strong enough to push wages and effort back to the no-overconfidence point.

A different possibility is that overconfident workers think they are more skilled than they really are (i.e., they overestimate their value of s_i). Whether overconfident workers of this sort work too little or too much will depend on whether effort and skill are complementary, and on the types of contracts firms can offer. For example, if e_i and s_i are complements, the firm can offer a contract that pays a large bonus if a very high output level is achieved (similar to backloaded option packages which are common in biotechnology firms, or highly leveraged venture capital deals offered to founders hungry for capital). Workers who overestimate their skill s_i will perceive the marginal return to effort as higher than it actually is and will work hard to grasp the brass ring. If this is true, we would expect to see extraordinary bonuses being offered by firms, to exploit overconfidence, accompanied by high actual failure rates.

The opposite of overconfidence might be important in worker motivation as well. Psychiatrists discuss an "impostor syndrome" in which workers discount their own success, or attribute it to luck, and feel that others have been fooled into thinking they are talented (see, for example, Kolligian and Sternberg 1991). Self-perceived "impostors" may work harder than others if they think that they have talent but need to work even harder to achieve true success.

More generally, there are important caveats to applying the evidence of widespread overconfidence to organizations. Rather than assuming that agents uniformly overestimate their abilities, researchers need to account for heterogeneity and attempt to evaluate ex ante indicators of overconfidence. For example, some studies show that women are less overconfident than men, which might be important for personnel selection. Seventy- to eighty-year-olds are also less overconfident than younger college students on general knowledge questions, which suggests that age teaches people what they know (see Kovalchik et al. 2005). And depressed people are typically *not* overconfident ("wiser but sadder"), which suggests overconfidence is part of mental health, and probably evolutionarily adaptive (see, for example, Taylor and Brown 1988). Overconfidence depends also on the type of task and its framing. For example, overconfidence about a particular estimate shrivels up when a portfolio of estimates are considered (see Kahneman and Lovallo (1993) on the single-case "inside view" compared to the portfolio "outside view"). Consider the 90%-confidence interval task, where subjects are instructed to give a wide interval for each numerical quantity which is only wrong 10% of the time; typically, five out of ten intervals are too narrow. Subjects typically give too narrow intervals. But when subjects are asked how many out of ten questions they got right, they typically do not say "one out of ten," they say "five out of ten"—which is empirically accurate (Sniezek and Buckley 1992). Overconfidence also shrivels up when the question is posed more narrowly, breaking an outcome into components (Dunning et al. 1989). While drivers are overconfident about overall driving ability, they are less overconfident about specific components like driving in snow, avoiding fender-bender accidents in heavy traffic, and so on. This fact suggests that if the criteria used to judge managerial success become more vague as people rise in a firm's hierarchy, overestimation of future success (and career outcomes) will rise too.

7.3 WORKERS AS MEMBERS OF MULTI-AGENT FIRMS

The basic model above focuses on a single principal–agent relation. It makes little use of the special properties of large organizations with many principals, agents, and hierarchies. Scaling the models up to large firms has a variety of implications for social comparison, group and peer effects, emotional and cognitive firm boundaries, and the coordinating role of culture and leadership in large groups.

7.3.1 *Social Comparison*

In the worker expected utility in (7.1), only the worker's own effort and wage enter into her utility. But in real organizations, people make friends and enemies, and compare themselves to others. Workers may thus sacrifice their own earnings to help their friends and harm their enemies, or to create better social comparisons. This topic, and its importance for contracting and labor economics, is discussed in some detail in Fehr and Gächter (2000).

The influence of social comparison can lead to conflict when different agents choose different comparison sets. In a study of actual teacher strikes in Pennsylvania, it was found (Babcock and Loewenstein 1997) that teachers' unions tend to say that nearby school systems with high wages are most comparable to their own, and school boards say that nearby systems with low wages are most comparable. The gap between the two sides' comparisons is correlated with strike incidence. Experiments also show that the gap between perceptions of fairness predicts strike incidence (Babcock and Loewenstein 1997). Importantly, these perceptions are not merely strategic posturing. The gap disappears if subjects are assigned to a bargaining role *after* reading facts about the case. This implies that the self-serving perceptions of fairness arise from differences in encoding what facts are important.

One might think that social comparison is an inferior good—as people are paid more and more, concern for social comparison becomes relatively less important. But social comparison also appears to enter organizational economics even in the very high compensation of executives. Hall and Murphy (2003) note the effect of the U.S. Securities and Exchange Commission (SEC) regulatory changes in 1992 on CEO pay which required "company compensation committees to describe company pay practices and justify in detail how they determined the pay of the chief executive officer...." Presumably the SEC thought that by requiring clearer disclosure of what CEOs earned, and how earnings were linked to past performance, embarrassment would rein in high payouts unjustified by performance, and might link compensation more closely to performance. But in a world where executives hate being paid less than a peer they think is less deserving, and their perceptions are self-servingly biased, disclosing wages leads to a ratchet effect: information which tells CEOs they are being paid less than others can drive all wages up.[10] Similarly, Belliveau et al. (1996) found that CEO pay was more closely correlated with earnings of members of the board's compensation committee than to pay of other board members. One explanation is that compensation committee members compare the CEO's pay with their own.

Social comparison may also affect the boundaries of the firm. If people naturally compare their own wages to those who work in the same firm, then one of the economic effects of a merger is a shift in the comparison sets of workers in the newly merged company. Some workers will now be underpaid relative to their new colleagues. This creates turnover or influence costs, and those costs should be

---

[10]Hall and Murphy (2003) wrote: "Although the new rules made option grants significantly more transparent—which would lead companies to grant fewer options to the extent that options are used to 'hide' compensation—we believe that the rules on net encouraged *increased* grants" (our italics). They note that the growth in option pay was already underway in the 1980s and conclude, "the new rule constituted an implicit government 'blessing' of stock options as appropriate performance-based pay, and this implicit endorsement may have further fueled the escalation of options" (Hall and Murphy 2003, p. 62). The subsequent growth of option-based packages is also consistent with the idea that self-serving comparison fueled growth in options grants.

accounted for as part of the merger cost. For example, when General Electric (GE) bought the television network NBC, the high salaries of NBC employees angered many successful engineers, who suddenly had an immediate reason to compare their wages with the highly paid "new neighbors." Kole and Lehn (2000) make the same point about the takeover of Piedmont Aviation by U.S. Airways. The choice of the boundary of the firm, therefore, is also a choice of social comparison sets, which has economic consequences of its own.

7.3.2 Peers and Groups

One place in which social preferences have entered labor economics is in the concept of "peer pressure." Peer pressure is often invoked to explain why group-based incentives are surprisingly successful despite the incentive to free ride. For example, Knez and Simester (2001) note that a $65/month bonus for all Continental Airlines employees, for improved on-time-arrival rates, actually worked, even though any one employee's performance has a minuscule effect on the firm's overall on-time performance. They note the important influence of immediate pressure by peers to improve performance (see also Kandel and Lazear 1992). The experimental literature on public goods games with sanctions also shows the power of peer pressure (see, for example, Yamagishi 1988; Fehr and Gächter 2000). When subjects can punish others at a cost to themselves, they often do so, which drives contributions up. Note that not every subject punishes, but enough do so to create higher contributions.

Falk and Ichino (2003) measured peer effects on output in an experiment, exploiting the ability to assign workers to pairs randomly, which avoids the problem of endogenous peer selection that is typical in most (though not all) field data sets. They recruited subjects to stuff letters into envelopes for four hours for a fixed fee (with no performance bonus). Some subjects did the activity by themselves; others did it in the presence of a randomly assigned peer. Random pairing led to closely matched output. The absolute deviation of output within each actual peer group averaged 20.6—much smaller than 99% of simulated absolute deviations within artificial pairs composed of solo subjects. Pairing workers also raised output on average (about 10%). Pairs were more likely to escalate each others' output than to tacitly collude by goofing off. The estimated effect of a one-unit increase in output on the peer's output was 0.14 units, close to the 0.14–0.18 estimated from field data in an Italian firm (Ichino and Maggi 2000).

7.3.3 Group Identification

There is a substantial psychological literature on group identification which could be useful for organizational economics (see Akerlof and Kranton (2005), on the economics of identity). Psychological evidence from "minimal group" experiments suggests that people form group affiliations rapidly, e.g., based on which room they were placed into, or according to their preference for Klee or Kandinsky paintings. Furthermore, these affiliations influence allocations in dictator and public-good-type games—they give more to in-group members and less to out-group members.[11]

Extrapolated to organizations, these findings suggest that workers will help members of their own group—*as they perceive their group and its membership*. In this view, a group is a club of people who all agree to help each other. This introduces an interesting role for management of group boundaries.

To fix ideas, suppose there is a component of effort which is productive for the firm but does not increase an employee's own measured output. Call this "helping" and think of it as a contribution to the firm-wide public good. In order to focus attention on group identification rather than multitasking (Holmström and Milgrom 1991), assume that choosing to help does not cut too deeply into a worker's other productive activities.

In the context of the organization, note first that the firm would most like its own workers to help each other, but to not help competitors' workers. But group affiliations that determine helping probably do not map neatly onto legal boundaries. Friendship, ethnicity and language, geography and architecture (which workers live or work nearby), marital status (who hang out after work together at happy hour, or during their children's play dates), and other distinctions create an archipelago of group affiliations within a firm, and across firms.

To some extent, firms can manage group creation through sorting (selecting "our kind of person" in hiring) and other organizational practices. For example, if helping customers *too much* is bad for the firm, it may use job rotation to keep its workers from becoming too helpful with favored customers. The sociology literature, however, provides numerous examples of firms misestimating group effects, such as Roy's (1952) famous study of a small-parts machine shop in Chicago. In this shop, the management designed task-specific piece rates such that for all the different jobs a certain monetary target could be reached with the same "effort." Roy's study demonstrates that workers were able to mislead management and induce piece rates, for which meeting the target was very easy. The workers imposed strong sanctions on anybody attempting to deviate and to exert more effort.

Evolutionary psychology provides an interesting way to speculate about groups and firms. Psychologists think of some kinds of groups as "essential," which means

---

[11]Group dynamics can also induce the opposite bias, a "black-sheep effect." Unpopular in-group members receive higher punishment than unpopular out-group members (Marques et al. 1988), especially if peer pressure is high. Another important caveat is its susceptibility to the experimental framing (Hertel and Kerr 2001).

that group members share a common essence which is immutable.[12] Gil-White (2001, p. 519), for example, argues that ethnic groups are perceived as a species. They have

> (1) a distinctive morphology... (2) many intercorrelated hidden properties... (3) within-category mating and descent-based membership, and (4) saliently labeled categories in cultural discourse.

If a firm can create a sense among workers that they are like a species—with immutable special properties that are inheritable—it might be able to hijack neural circuitry which is highly evolved to distinguish friend from foe on the basis of species and species-like ethnic characteristics, to create a deep sense of group membership and helping. For example, a body feature which cannot be changed marks a species, so one way to create a species illusion is with tattoos. In fact, Nike founder Phil Knight and many of his employees have tattoos of the Nike "swoosh" logo on their left calves as a sign of camaraderie.

Group loyalty can persist even when workers leave the firm. For example, it is typical for lawyers and consultants to eventually leave their firms and work for one of the firms' clients (whom they worked with originally). While there is a clear difference in the employee's decision rights after switching firms, there may be little difference in emotional attachment to their old group (the law firm) and their new group (the client firm). Many consulting firms keep active lists of "alumni" who have left the firm to work for their clients, and presumably use the residue of group loyalty to keep those clients and to resolve disputes.

7.3.4 Coordination, Culture, and Leadership

Organizational relationships are typically repeated games. As Gibbons (2004a) notes, the folk theorem gives us an embarrassment of riches about how repeated games might be played—there are *too many* equilibria. As Schelling (1960) wrote, predicting what players will do in games with many equilibria by pure mathematics is like trying to prove that a joke is funny without telling it. When there are many equilibria, social considerations like historical traditions and norms, and credibility of leaders who make announcements intended to focus attention on good equilibria, will make a difference.

---

[12]For example, the Aryan Brotherhood gang has a saying "blood in, blood out." This means you must shed someone's blood to gain admission to the group, and can only leave if your own blood is shed. U.S. Marines have a saying, "Once a Marine, always a Marine." Groups like military and police often have de facto inheritance, in the sense that special pride is placed on doing the same job as your father, grandfather, etc., and favoritism may be granted to "descendants" in hiring and promotion.

These issues are highlighted by putting incentive conflicts aside and focusing on organizations as "teams." A team has a common interest, but has to coordinate activity and information to make a commonly beneficial choice (see Radner and Van Zandt 2001). Coordination is often neglected in organizational economics, perhaps because of a belief that it is easy to achieve. Indeed, in small groups a quick e-mail may coordinate activity. But when organizations face time pressure, have rapid turnover, and scale up in size, coordination is challenging.

Experimental studies of coordination games have shown that even in very simple settings, with modest group sizes (2–16) and very clear games, coordination failure is common. Several studies have used a "weak-link" game[13]: players simultaneously choose effort levels (integers from 1–7) and earn an amount which increases in the *minimum* effort, as well as a penalty if their effort is above the minimum. The game is tricky because there is one incentive to choose high numbers, to raise the minimum, and another incentive to choose low numbers, to avoid the penalty from wasted effort. Every effort level is a different equilibrium, but choosing the highest effort is Pareto-dominant.

Many studies show that coordination failure in groups playing simultaneously without communication: they generally fail to reach the Pareto-dominant equilibrium (see, for example, Van Huyck et al. 1990; Camerer 2003, Chapter 7). Efficiency can be achieved when two people play together repeatedly, when groups "grow" slowly, starting with two and adding one player at a time (Weber 2006), or when a small bonus is publicly announced if everyone reaches the efficient choices (Knez and Camerer 1994; Brandts and Cooper 2004). Surprisingly, limited communication does not help much (cf. Cooper et al. 1994). When one "leader" is randomly chosen to talk briefly to the group (usually exhorting everyone to choose "7"), large groups still do not reach efficiency and subjects misattribute credit and blame to the leader.

These studies illustrate how coordination games could be used to study facets such as growth of firms, the attention-getting effect of bonuses, and leader credibility in very simple experimental organizations. They also suggest that efficient coordination is usually not easy, even in simple games with clear strategies and payoffs, so that coordination is likely to be important for success of large organizations, and perhaps underestimated in importance. For example, Heath and Staudenmayer (2000) had experimental subjects divide labor to create parts of a "man" from LEGO blocks; they were scored on how good their composite man looked when assembled from the

---

[13]Weak-link games are n-person "stag hunt games." In organizations, they are models of Leontief production processes that are sensitive to the lowest quality input, like an assembly line that is delayed by the slowest worker, or a recipe which is ruined if it has one bad ingredient (see also Kremer's (1993) "O-ring" theory of production).

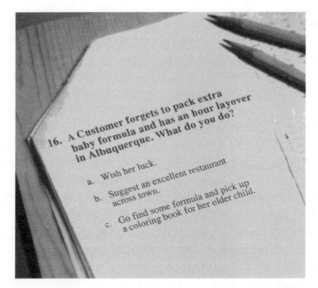

Figure 7.1. A Krepsian quiz at Southwest Airlines.

parts. Appointing a coordinator who made sure the parts being created fit together improved output, but few of the teams spontaneously did so.[14]

7.3.4.1 Culture as Focal Principles and Correlating Devices

Kreps (1990) introduced the idea of an organization's culture as a correlating device (see also Camerer and Vepsäläinen 1988). In this view, cultural rules are meta-principles which tell workers what to do in the face of unforeseen contingencies, in the spirit of Schelling's (1960) focal points in matching games, but extended to meta-principles which prescribe focal points in an ensemble of games.

The idea is illustrated by Figure 7.1, an advertisement from a Southwest Airlines in-flight magazine. This shows a hypothetical quiz given to potential employees about how to react to a customer's problem. A company's culture can be thought of as a set of general recipes which help workers and managers coordinate on the "right" answer in quizzes like this, which correspond to workplace incidents. At Southwest Airlines, the correct answer is get some baby formula for the delayed passenger and pick up a coloring book as well. The example gains force from the fact that it is based on a true story. The point of the ad is that Southwest Airlines is deeply customer-oriented (note that the term "Customer" is capitalized).

---

[14]Large rowing crews use a coxswain—a person who does not row, but sits at the front of the boat and synchronizes timing (and motivates the rowers). The coxswain is a factor of production who helps produce coordination, and whose value presumably outweighs his or her extra body weight (which is typically low).

The idea that culture is a set of principles for generating focal points in specific microgames played by workers and managers is not so different from the way organization theories describe culture. For example, Schein (1983) defines culture as "the *basic assumptions* and *beliefs* that are shared by members of an organization." He later notes that these "assumptions and beliefs are *learned* responses to a group's problems of *survival* in its external environment and its problems of *internal integration*."[15] Shared understanding reduces conflict and, if the culture is visible to outsiders, also encourages efficient assortative matching between workers' attitudes and the attitudes a firm requires.

As important as culture appears to be, it has not been studied very carefully empirically. The biggest obstacle is the lack of empirical measures and exogenous variation. One stream of literature uses psychometric scales to map organizations onto some two-dimensional or multidimensional space (Cameron and Quinn 1999). These studies are not statistically sophisticated and typically treat the whole corporation as one culture, ignoring subcultures. Other studies focus on a dimension of culture, like "strength," and explore its relation to profitability or profit variation (see Kotter and Heskett 1992; Sørensen 2002). Still other studies establish the existence of distinct workplace culture (called "climate" by organizational researchers) and study its consequences for phenomena like turnover (Bartel et al. 2003; Rebitzer 2002).

The lack of a sharp formal framework and clean empirical identification has certainly held back organizational economists interested in culture but progress is being made (see, for example, Hermalin 2001). There is a small emerging literature on "codes"—the language workers use to describe events. Codes have efficiency properties, depend on shared understanding, and can be difficult to change and imitate, like other facets of culture (e.g., corporate values). Crémer et al. (2003) assume that codes are coarse partitions of a large space of events. Coarse partitions are adequate because workers need not communicate exactly which event has occurred. Wernerfelt (2004) offers a similar model.

Codes have been studied experimentally by using a picture-naming paradigm. In these experiments, agents see pictures on a screen. A "manager" must figure out a code to identify predetermined target pictures to workers. Payoffs depend on how rapidly the target pictures can be named without errors. Codes develop rapidly: subjects typically use about 120 characters to describe four picture at first (that is the length of this sentence so far), but use only about five characters per picture after 20–40 practice trials.

---

[15]A useful definition was mentioned by John Roberts in a December 2004 conference at MIT. He diagnoses culture by asking people, "What would a new employee need to know to function effectively in your company?"

One study shows that it is better to have one manager creating code than to rotate code-creation among the subjects (Rick et al. 2004). This suggests that having a single "founder" creating code is better—specialization is better than taking the best code ideas from different workers. However, the single-manager groups have a harder time integrating new employees; the managers are more likely to give up on teaching the new employee, who then makes a lot of costly picture-naming errors.

Two other studies explore how conflict is created when groups "merge." Weber and Camerer (2003) found that when two groups naming the same pictures merged (like a horizontal merger of similar businesses), subjects were too optimistic about how rapidly code could be created in the merged group. Feiler and Camerer (2006) replicated this result with different groups of pictures (like a diversifying merger) and where subjects were endogenously sorted into the merger group through bids for wage premia to join the merged firm. Subjects' guesses about the speed of the merger group and bids in—theoretically incentive-compatible—second-price auctions were too optimistic relative to actual earnings differentials of merged and unmerged groups. It is easy to think of other applications of this sort of code-creation paradigm, as well as expanding its scope to include development of corporate values like reciprocity and camaraderie, expressed by cooperativeness in public goods games.

7.3.4.2   The Cognitive Economics of Organizational Knowledge

Organizations are complicated. Knowledge about how to behave in complicated systems—like the world, or an organization—is often encoded in a form that is very different than the state-space partitions and Bayesian probability that dominate economic theory, and is much simpler and evolutionarily advanced. This suggests that understanding cognitive economy—what kinds of information fits the brain's natural structures for storing, remembering, and reliably repeating information—is important for understanding organizations.

Organization theorists have argued that a narrative or story is a common way of encoding information about what to do in an organization (see, for example, Martin 1982; Heath and Seidel 2004). If the punch line of the story is success or failure, a story is basically an instruction about how to behave. Narratives may be a superior encoding form from the point of view of human memory—if they are better remembered, they will not degrade as much as other kinds of information when passed down from old workers to new ones. If it is fun to tell stories—they often involve humor—they may spread more rapidly and reliably through a firm than boring instructions.[16]

---

[16]Memory appears to be encoded into episodic memory (time-stamped events) and semantic memory

Another element of cognitive economy in organizations is "personification." Much of human perception and judgment is organized around what we know about people and how we summarize our knowledge in the form of traits and thumbnail sketches of people.[17] It is cognitively natural to identify an organization with a charismatic founder or iconic leader, such as Walt Disney, Bill Gates, and Herb Kelleher from Southwest Airlines.

If a leader's behavior and values are thought to exemplify those of the culture, then it may be easier to answer the question, "What does my implicit employment contract require me to do?" by answering the substitute question, "What would Walt do?" (as employees at Disney often did, long after Walt's death). The personality of a corporate icon then becomes an asset that economizes on transaction costs by telling people what to do, in a way their brains can remember and understand more easily than a boring list of rules.

7.3.4.3 Leadership, Simplicity, and Mission Statements

Thinking about coordination and cognitive economy may help explain the nature of leadership and language in companies. A striking feature of corporate talk is that it is highly simplified, but catchy. "Maximize profit" is *not* an inspiring mission statement. Instead, companies have slogans like "Quality is job 1" (Ford), "Just do it" (Nike) "Do no evil" (Google), "Copy EXACTLY!" (Intel, to maximize transfer of wafer-production processes from old plants to new ones) and "Flatter the novice; reward the expert driver" (Mustang cars). The Ritz–Carlton hotel chain supposedly has a rule that up to $2,000 can be spent to solve a guest's problem. The figure $2,000 is useful for two reasons: it is a round number that's memorable; and it is a *surprisingly large* number, a "put your money where your mouth is" signal of the Ritz's commitment to luxury hotel quality.

Why are these stated goals so simple? One explanation is that meta-principles which help workers coordinate on equilibrium workplace norms have to be applied to a broad range of different microgames. The principles have to be made commonly known, and repeated over many years and between many workers without linguistic degradation. Heath and Seidel (2004) suggest some good properties of "language

---

(facts about the world and a distillation of episodic memories). Corporate narratives harness the power of episodic memory. Narratives often involve drama, humor, and emotion as well, which provides added "depth of processing" that enhances their memorability. From a neural point of view these may provide a kind of engineering redundancy because memory is then supported by multiple interconnected systems: Who did it? How did it feel? When did it happen? From the brain's point of view, a story may therefore be simultaneously stored in different locations which are associated, improving retrieval.

[17] Facial recognition is a very special kind of object recognition with dedicated neural circuitry (the facial fusiform area, FFA), which suggests that there may be some cognitive advantages to organizing cultural rules around behavior of a "face of a corporation."

memes": they should be simple, memorable, broadly applicable, and evoke complex emotions. Their hypotheses could easily be tested in experiments on how well various linguistic meta-principles coordinate actions in the face of garbling due to labor turnover and the passage of time.[18]

Van Den Steen (2005) tells a story about leadership which is closer to the meta-principle theory of culture. In his model, managers with "vision" have a clear preference for project types.[19] A strong vision is good because it enables efficient labor-market sorting of other managers who agree with the vision into the firm, and saves time that could be wasted by proposing projects that do not fit.

7.4 TOP MANAGERS AND CORPORATE FINANCE

Behavioral considerations contribute to our understanding of corporate finance from two perspectives: first, recognizing that markets make mistakes which managers exploit; and, second, that managers make mistakes which markets do not fully correct. In this section we assume the perspective most relevant to the economics of organizations and consider the possibility that top managers make mistakes.[20] Managers are most likely to be affected in their judgment when they face decisions in which three conditions hold:

(i) decisions are not frequent and do not deliver clear feedback;

(ii) the manager does not specialize in making those decisions; and

(iii) managers are protected from market pressure and competition.

As for (i), the higher the level of a manager in the hierarchy, the less likely decisions are to be repeated enough to learn from feedback. Large-scale investments, merger agreements, or capital restructuring are relatively rare decisions, and the organizational framework of a company may not be optimized to facilitate them. It is also hard to evaluate outcomes. For example, there is no agreed-upon methodology on how to evaluate the long-run returns to mergers, even in the academic literature (Andrade et al. 2001). Regarding (ii), the level of specialization is likely to decrease the higher up in the hierarchy decisions are made. As Lazear (2004) formulates in the

---

[18]Experiments on slogan quality could use paradigms like the game "telephone." In telephone, people form a circle and speak a phrase very rapidly into the ear of the person to their right, who repeats it rapidly to the person on *their* right, and so on. The goal is for a slogan or cultural principle to make it around the circle with the least degradation. One could also test the durability of shared memory of a slogan by announcing it to a group, then asking group members at future times whether they remember it, and whether they think others remember it. Good cultural principles will be remembered, and expected to be remembered by others, over long spans of time.

[19]This is a stylized version of corporate vision as "a mental image of a possible and desirable future state of the organization" (Bennis and Nanus 1985).

[20]For a survey that covers the first perspective, see Baker et al. (2004).

context of entrepreneurship, the top decision maker in a firm has to be (and typically is) a jack-of-all-trades rather than a specialist. And regarding (iii), we know from many studies of corporate governance and entrenchment that CEOs often manage to protect themselves from market pressure (see, for example, Bebchuk et al. 2002). Sheltered from the discipline of the outside market, they may make significantly less efficient corporate decisions, as Bertrand and Mullainathan (2003) show, exploiting variations in anti-takeover laws.

To push the argument for biased decision-making in corporations even further, the market not only may be unable to "short-sell biased CEOs" and to thereby remedy distorted corporate decision-making, but may actually *value* managerial overconfidence. As Goel and Thakor (2000) and Gervais et al. (2003) point out, diversified shareholders, who would like managers to make risk-neutral choices and to maximize the expected value of their firms, may prefer managers to be overconfident if it balances managers' risk aversion.

If, for all of those reasons, certain managerial biases are unlikely to be eliminated by market pressures or to be remedied by the organizational design, the question is: are top managers likely to exhibit biases in the first place? Shouldn't people successful and smart enough to become the leader of a company—in particular of large companies in the S&P 500—be the very embodiment of the hyper-rational *Homo oeconomicus*? For example, would executive selection processes not ensure that more rational and socially neutral agents rise to the top? Not necessarily. As long as a specific bias is not negatively correlated with the ability to have a successful corporate career, CEOs are not necessarily less likely to deviate from rational decision-making than the average individual. Goel and Thakor (2000) also point out that managers may even be more likely to be promoted to CEOs in a tournament setting if they underestimate project risk, which leads them to take very risky projects with the largest probabilities of very large returns. In the implicit rank-order tournament among potential successors of a CEO, the biased person is thus more likely to have the highest outcome, conditional on success, and is therefore unconditionally more likely to have the highest rank.[21]

Moreover, if superior management skills are correlated with limits on rationality and self-interest then it is conceivable that top managers are even *more* judgmentally biased and social-comparison-minded than average workers. Confidence may be correlated with other kinds of managerial value—like inspiring workers or mesmerizing Wall Street analysts—so sorting may actually *select for* overconfidence rather than filter it out. Mistakes in one type of judgment may be a price one pays for

---

[21] See Van Den Steen (2004) for a related argument about the endogenous generation of overconfidence due to the selection of tasks in which the agent is likely to succeed.

other kinds of managerial skill. Whether this is true is an empirical matter, which cannot be resolved purely by theory.

7.4.1 Overconfidence among Top Managers

Overconfidence and overoptimism, which we may define as overestimation of own skills relative to others, and overestimation of one's own prospects or future outcomes[22] are two patterns that have been widely studied in the academic literature and also discussed often in the business press. One well-established stylized fact is the "better than average" effect. Svenson (1981) first demonstrated that the vast majority of subjects, if asked to assess their driving skills compared to the median person in the group, rate themselves overwhelmingly as "above average." Svenson's finding has been replicated numerous times and with respect to various IQ- or skill-related outcomes other than driving (see, for example, Larwood and Whittaker 1977; Alicke 1985). For example, when asking a sample of entrepreneurs about their chances of success, Cooper et al. (1988) found that 33% attached zero probability to failure, 81% of them between 0 and 30%.

Several additional findings suggest that high-rank executives are particularly likely to overestimate outcomes related to their own actions or skills. First, overconfidence tends to be observed especially in decision makers who have a position of control—or at least have the illusion of control (Weinstein 1980). And who, if not the person on top of the corporate (or divisional) ladder, is the person believed to be the ultimate holder of control? A CEO has the ultimate say about the big strategic decisions and is the one who decides whether or not a large-scale investment goes ahead. Such a position may induce the CEO to believe that he or she can also control the outcome—and thus underestimate the likelihood of a bad outcome (March and Shapira 1987; Langer 1975). Second, personal commitment increases the occurrence of overconfidence (Weinstein 1980). As a quick search in ExecuComp for the option and stock packages of the top four to nine executives of publicly traded companies reveals, a huge portion of their compensation—and presumably of the wealth of many of them—depends on how well the company is doing. Moreover, the value of their human capital is tightly related company returns. If the company is underperforming, this is bad news for their prospects of keeping their job and reduces their outside options. Thus, for compensation and career reasons alone, we would expect top executives to be highly committed to the outcome of their investment,

---

[22]The term "overoptimism" is sometimes used to refer to the overestimation of one's own abilities as well. The labeling suggested above follows the literature on self-serving attribution and allows us to distinguish the overestimation of one's own abilities (such as IQ or managerial skills) and outcomes relating to one's own personal situation from the general overestimation of exogenous outcomes (such as the growth of the U.S. economy).

merger and other corporate decisions. And, finally, a third factor contributing to the occurrence of overconfidence within the top management team is the lack of clear measures or benchmarks for good and bad decisions. Overconfidence has been found to be strongest when it is difficult to compare performance across individuals and when the reference point is abstract (Alicke et al. 1995). Given the amount of noise in stock prices, and the long horizon over which good and bad investments pay off or fail, there is little clear feedback that would shake a CEO's overconfidence.

It is thus not surprising that experimental studies have found that executives are particularly prone to display overconfidence, both in terms of the better-than-average effect and in terms of underestimating risk (Larwood and Whittaker 1977; Moore 1977). Overconfidence, in the form of the better-than-average effect, also affects the attribution of causality. Because individuals expect their behavior to produce success, they are more likely to attribute good outcomes to their actions, but bad outcomes to (bad) luck.[23]

But how important are such biases in real-world corporate decision-making? Roll (1986) was one of the first to link overconfidence to mergers. He proposed a "hubris hypothesis": in corporate takeovers the overconfidence of individual decision makers often results in bidding firms paying too much for their targets. What he had in mind is a type of winner's curse in merger fights. Roll's hubris hypothesis may be best summarized by a famous quote from the 1981 Berkshire Hathaway Annual Report:

> Many managements apparently were overexposed in impressionable childhood years to the story in which the imprisoned handsome prince is released from a toad's body by a kiss from a beautiful princess. Consequently, they are certain their managerial kiss will do wonders for the profitability of Company T[arget]. . . . We've observed many kisses but very few miracles. Nevertheless, many managerial princesses remain serenely confident about the future potency of their kisses—even after their corporate backyards are knee-deep in unresponsive toads.
>
> (Taken from Weston et al. 1998)

Confirming this hypothesis, Malmendier and Tate (2003) find that a firm is indeed significantly more likely to acquire another firm if the CEO is overconfident. In a sample of CEOs from Forbes 500 companies in the 1980s and the first half of the 1990s, Malmendier and Tate find that overconfident CEOs are about 1.7 times as likely to conduct a merger in any given year as their rational counterpart. Here, the measurement of overconfidence is not based on responses to questions, but on actual personal portfolio decisions. The authors point to the high degree of under-diversification, which high-ranking executives face due to their stock-based compensation and the investment of their human capital in their firm, and argue that

---

[23] Miller and Ross (1975) provide a critical review of the abundant psychology literature on self-serving biases.

rational CEOs of Forbes 500 companies should therefore try to diversify their personal portfolios whenever possible. For example, CEOs should exercise their stock options after the vesting period, if the stock price went up by enough, and should sell company stock following a regular (precommitted) schedule.[24] But some CEOs do exactly the opposite, holding options that are well in the money (far above their exercise price) and buying, rather than selling, company stock (half the CEOs who do this lose money). In fact, during recent corporate scandals, while exorbitant pay, forgiven loans, and accounting manipulations grabbed public attention, it was less noticeable that many of the apparently guilty executives truly believed in the potential of their firms and their industry. The former CEO of WorldCom, Bernard Ebbers, lost millions of dollars because his private portfolio was narrowly invested in telecommunication stocks, while doing one merger after another.[25]

Managerial overconfidence thus has the potential to explain the big puzzle implied by $2 trillion spent on acquisitions by U.S. firms between 1998 and 2001, of which $250 billion was *lost* by shareholders of the acquiring companies (Moeller et al. 2003).

The same holds for internal investment projects. While it is hard to measure whether internal investments are generally bad bets (such data are rarely available), it is easy to find examples. Roger Smith, the former CEO of General Motors, became convinced that fully robotized plants, with no human presence, are the future of automobile production. His vision led to massive firings at GM and triggered negative responses from business analysts and engineers alike because they did not believe the technology was advanced enough. Such concerns did not stop a visionary like Smith. The result was plants in which

> the robots often began dismembering each other, smashing cars, spraying paint everywhere or even fitting the wrong equipment.
>
> *(The Economist, August 10, 1991)*

The implications of overconfidence are, however, more subtle than simply "more mergers" and "more investment," as the winner's curse view of Roll would suggest. Managerial overconfidence implies a difference in opinion about the value of the firm between the (overconfident) corporate insider and the outside investor. An overconfident CEO will persistently feel undervalued by the capital market and thus be reluctant to issue equity to finance investment projects or mergers (Heaton 2002;

---

[24]Precommitment allows the avoidance of sending negative signals to the market.

[25]The *New York Times*, March 3, 2004, comments: "Unlike many other telecommunications kingpins of the 1990's, who cashed out hundreds of millions of dollars in inflated stock ahead of unsuspecting investors, Mr. Ebbers apparently believed that he could keep the company afloat one way or another. He kept buying WorldCom shares even as the company's house of cards began to topple."

Malmendier and Tate 2005b). It is just the flip side of traditional Myers–Majluf-type models with asymmetric information (Myers and Majluf 1984). There, the manager has inside information, and good types are reluctant to issue equity since they will be taken for bad types. Here, the overconfident manager thinks he has (positive) inside information, with the same effect on equity issuance. Overconfidence amounts to "perceived asymmetric information." As a result, overconfidence may actually lead to *less* investment or *fewer* mergers whenever the overconfident CEO needs to tap the external capital market. A CEO is expected to overinvest only if a firm has abundant internal resources or extra debt capacity. In other words, the investment decision of an overconfident CEO should be sensitive to the availability of internal cash flow, and such investment–cash-flow sensitivity should be strongest in firms with little internal resources. At the same time, the inclination to undertake bad acquisitions should have highest impact in firms with abundant internal resources.

The data confirm all of the predictions above, including some type of pecking-order financing among overconfident CEOs (Malmendier et al. 2006). Similar evidence has been found for a sample of French start-up firms (Landier and Thesmar 2004). This increasingly robust evidence on managerial overconfidence gives rise to the question of how corporate governance should respond to CEO overconfidence. A large literature in corporate finance analyzes how options and stock grants help to align the interest of the CEO (or other corporate executive) with the interest of shareholders (Murphy 1999). The possibility of executive overconfidence alters basic conclusions about these incentive mechanisms. If we worry that a CEO just may have too positive a view on the value he or she can generate, then options and stocks are not helpful. Overconfident CEOs do not need incentives to maximize the market value of the firm's equity—that is what they perceive to be doing already. In fact, options and stocks may then push them to act as if they were risk-loving and choose investment which are riskier (and lower net present value) than shareholders would prefer. This concern is of particular relevance given that the CEO overestimates the expected value of those gambles to begin with.

If CEOs are overconfident, then other incentive devices may work better than stocks and options. One example is debt (see Hart 1995, Chapter 6). An overconfident CEO in a cash-rich firm tends to undertake too many investment projects, including acquisitions. If cash is tied up for debt repayments and the capacity for senior debt is exhausted, the CEO would need to issue more risky debt or equity to finance projects. Given that overconfident CEOs perceive their firms to be undervalued by the equity market and, consequently, expected returns to their projects will be underestimated by providers of risky debt, the preexisting debt will curtail the tendency to overinvest.

More generally, a mechanism that requires the CEO to get an outsider's approval on an investment project would counterbalance CEO overconfidence. That "outsider" could be a vigilant board. Companies typically specify in their charter that the board has to approve any investment beyond a certain dollar amount. Setting the threshold for board approval low enough seems a sensible strategy—if we believe that the board fulfills its monitoring function. The concern about upward biases in a manager's perception thus gives additional importance to group decision-making, even in the absence of informational constraints.

Of course, while CEO overconfidence can create agency costs, overconfidence may be correlated with valuable charisma, the ability to convince investors of the value of a firm, or the ability to motivate employees. Firms may want to attract overconfident leaders but also restrain their actions in some way. One method is to unbundle the leadership and resource-allocation roles of top managers, so that a confident leader creates inspired workers and optimistic investors, but does not overinvest resources.

7.4.2 *Capital Budgeting*

The last section focused on biases in top managers and whether organizational structures can constrain them. Biases in capital budgeting which occur below the CEO's sphere of influence are also important and might crop up in three ways: a tendency to divide capital equally among divisions; escalation in commitment to bad projects; and empire building (and capital suppression).

7.4.2.1 Corporate Socialism and Partition Dependence

Scharfstein and Stein (2000) show empirically that capital is allocated relatively evenly across divisions of different sizes. They call this pattern "corporate socialism," as if equal allocations are a deliberate attempt to subsidize smaller divisions at the expense of larger ones. Lamont (1997) shows the flip side of such within-company subsidization. After the 1986 oil price shock, oil companies significantly reduced their capital expenditure in non-oil subsidiaries even though the quality of non-oil investment projects did not decrease. Equality-biased allocations might also reflect a cognitive pattern called "partition dependence" or the "$1/n$ heuristic"—the tendency for allocations to be biased toward even allocations, given a particular partition of categories (Bardolet et al. 2005). For example, Fox and Rottenstreich (2003) asked subjects to guess the probabilities that the hottest day in the next week would be Sunday or another day of the week. Many subjects answered (sensibly) that there is a $\frac{1}{7}$ chance that Sunday is hottest, and a $\frac{6}{7}$ chance that the hottest day is a day other than Sunday. Others tend to give beliefs for the chance that Sunday is hottest which lie between $\frac{1}{7}$ and $\frac{1}{2}$. The latter beliefs are influenced by the arbitrary partition of the week into two subsets, into "Sunday" and "non-Sunday." A similar effect is found in both laboratory and field data of investment in 401(k) plans (Benartzi and Thaler 2001). When asked to choose between investing in a stock or bond fund, many subjects choose to invest 50% in each. When asked to choose between two stock funds and a bond fund, many subjects choose to spread allocations equally among the three funds, which creates an aggregate investment that is more heavily weighted ($\frac{2}{3}$) to stocks.[26]

Empirical tests of partition dependence in capital budgeting could study what happens when divisions are combined or split apart, for reasons that are exogenous to changes in the demand for capital across business units (e.g., regulation or tax considerations). Anticipating Section 7.6.2 (on organizational "repairs") organizations that recognize the tendency to allocate capital equally across divisions could deliberately structure divisions to mitigate the bias. A fast-growing product line that is starving for capital might be given its own small division to be sure it gets enough capital.

7.4.2.2 Escalation of Commitment

A common theme in behavioral judgment research is that people and organizations escalate their commitments to losing projects (Bazerman and Neale 1992). Most of this literature is based on experiments in which people make ex ante choices, receive good or bad feedback, and then decide whether to continue a project. Experiments suggest that even when feedback is bad, people continue to invest, throwing "good money" after "bad."

Despite the clear experimental evidence of escalation to commitment to bad projects, there is little convincing field evidence of this pattern. Case studies of projects which failed in retrospect have been related to escalation of commitment (see, for example, Staw and Ross 1993). But these may simply be examples of hindsight bias about especially bad projects. Other field studies analyze whether new managers who take over projects pull the plug on them. But the tendency to do so might just reflect differences in prior beliefs rather than escalation by the managers who initiated the bad projects (see, for example, Barsade et al. 1997; Weber and Camerer 1999). The ideal situation for an empirical analysis would thus be

(i) data on similar types of decisions (such as plant closings) for a set of firms,
(ii) where in a strict subset the decision maker changed for exogenous reasons (like the "sudden deaths" of CEOs in Johnson et al. 1985), and
(iii) where the new decision maker would have originally implemented the investment project as well, had he already held the position.

The constraint to (i) is the poor quality of data on decision-making inside the firm and on the success of individual projects. As for (ii), changes in managerial position

---

[26]Huberman and Jiang (2004) present evidence rejecting the $1/n$ heuristic on the individual level, though it is present in the aggregate.

that are exogenously based on schedule or promotion (rather than promotions which endogenously follow project failure) are most promising. And condition (iii) could be remedied by analyzing decisions with objective criteria which leave little room for differing priors.

Even if data satisfying criteria (i)–(iii) were available, we would need to go one step further and account for endogenous organizational response. Organizational design may limit bad escalation. Budget constraints and milestones are in place precisely to avoid escalation. The bigger the risk of bad escalation, the more extensive should be the implementation of such mechanisms. In fact, they may sometimes produce an opposite bad effect: good projects are terminated prematurely. Heath (1995) points out that sometimes people de-escalate *too quickly*, when a project's losses hit a budget constraint.

A promising place to study escalation and organizational responses are firms with large portfolios of small-scale investments, as in corporate R&D, or consumer product companies which expect a high rate of product failure. These firms need to routinely pull the plug on bad projects. Understanding how they cope with high rates of failure could be useful in understanding how to prevent escalation.

7.4.2.3 Empire Building and Capital Suppression

The tendency of top managers to "build empires"—to create divisions which are too large in an economic sense, benefiting managers at the expense of shareholders—is often discussed as an agency cost within the standard, rational framework. Behavioral economics offers a reinterpretation: when managers grow their firms at the detriment of shareholders, they may do so not (only) because of their desire to reign a larger empire and in full awareness of the resulting value destruction. Rather, they may (also) overestimate how much value will be created under their leadership, as discussed in Section 7.2.6.3 on overconfidence. Or they may feel competitive towards top managers of other firms, without full awareness of the resulting value destruction.

The same psychology, then, could help a better understanding of the reverse tendency—suppression of capital—in business units that are speculative but growing rapidly and have huge potential. As an example of capital suppression, Holmström and Kaplan (2001) note that it is hard to imagine how internal capital allocation could have created the kind of fast-growing technology-based firms that grew rapidly through venture capital financing and initial public offerings (IPOs) in the late 1990s. They suggest that "if Netscape, eBay or Amazon had been invented inside a big company, their potential value would probably have been overlooked" (Holmström and Kaplan 2001, pp. 138–39). They further suggest the barriers to "intrapreneurship" are due to weak internal incentives: "Even if some degree of value had been seen, it would have been difficult or impossible to give management a strong incentive to maximize the value inherent in these ideas."

But what prevents large firms like IBM, Xerox, or Microsoft from simply reproducing the capital allocation mechanisms used by venture capitalists and then selling off its successes to IPO investors (or growing them internally) just as venture capitalists do? Given the interest of larger firms in replicating high-powered incentives for intrapreneurship, it is natural to ask whether there are other barriers that prevent them from allowing very rapid growth of promising business. One barrier might be the psychology of managers of conventional businesses who compete with the rapidly growing new business units. Loss-aversion and social comparison suggest that managers in traditional businesses will be uncomfortable about seeing lots of cash poured into businesses which could outgrow their own.[27] The managerial psychology which creates empire building probably also encourages suppression of growing empires within the firm.

7.5 IMPLICATIONS FOR CORPORATE GOVERNANCE

Our discussion so far considered biases on the side of the managers. We touched upon adjustments in organizational design and corporate governance mechanisms to deal with them. Obviously, limits on rationality and expression of social preferences affect only managers but also the "corporate governors" e.g., board members. The influence of governance forces examination of the conjectures made in the last section. While overconfidence about the firm's projects may be less likely in external board members than in CEOs, partition dependence or escalation of commitment easily affects board decisions as well.

Another very important issue is the selection of board members. Do CEOs look for the most able and knowledgeable people? Or do they install yes-men? The fundamental problem in evaluating board quality is that the literature has yet to come up with a reliable measure of high-quality boards. The analysis of governance rules such as corporate bylaws in Gompers et al. (2003) is certainly a big step forward. But sample limitations (there are still few panel data sets with a long enough time series to analyze changes in corporate governance within firms) and endogenous firm response limit the broader use and long-term reliability. The behavioral perspective may help the quest for better measures of "who speaks up in the boardroom." Monetary incentives may not be all that matters. The ability to speak the language of the CEO and/or the other board members, or even feelings of moral obligation

---

[27] "The hierarchical investment approval process that is characteristic of internal capital markets is another impediment to innovation within firms.... By design, the large corporation is not set up for revolutionary inventions" (Holmström and Kaplan 2001, p. 139).

or social image concerns, may be far better determinants of directors monitoring quality.

7.6 ORGANIZATIONAL REACTIONS: SORTING, REPAIRS, AND EXPLOITATION

A special contribution of *organizational* economics to behavioral economics will come from highlighting the role of selection and endogenous firm response to nonstandard preferences. Given a pool of workers with various skills, cognitive limits and social preferences, organizational output will depend on how workers are sorted, how organizations "repair" mistakes, and whether worker mistakes can be exploited for the good of the firm.

7.6.1 *Sorting*

The starting point is heterogeneity. People are different in skills and tastes. From a behavioral economics point of view, heterogeneity means people might differ in their limits on rational calculation, willpower, and greed, and their familiarity with labor–leisure trade-offs. The impact of these behavioral biases will depend on which kind of people sort into which organizational environment. Lazear et al. (2005) demonstrate how sorting can reverse the impact of behavioral preferences in a simple experimental setting. In a standard dictator game, where subjects decide how much to share with an anonymously matched person, about 75% of people share some positive amount and 25% keep everything for themselves. These proportions reverse if subjects are allowed to sort and decide whether to play the dictator game or to "opt out" and keep the full amount for themselves (without the receiver finding out about the dictator game). Only 30% end up sharing. Interestingly, making the dictator game financially more attractive attracts first and foremost the "sharks," who keep all or most of the amount available to dictators for themselves. The flip side of this result is the selection of agents with "desired" behavioral traits. Firms may design hiring practices to identify "team players" with a sense of fairness. Promotion criteria may select workers who are subject to strong in-groups effects, inducing effort beyond monetary incentives.

Similar reasoning applies to cognitive limits. An organization will be more productive if it matches people who make mistakes with jobs in which the types of mistakes they make are not costly. This means that the organization's overall performance could be partly or largely immunized against mistakes by assortative matching.[28] Put differently, the output of organizational calculation could be more

---

[28] In a magazine interview, Gary Becker opined that division of labor "strongly attenuates if not eliminates any effects" caused by bounded rationality (see Stewart 2005). He conjectures that " 'it doesn't matter if 90 percent of people can't do the complex analysis required to calculate probabilities. The

rational than the averaged decisions of its individuals (or even than the smartest individual). Not much is known, however, about which types of cognitive mistakes are actually eliminated by organizational sorting and aggregation.

7.6.2 *Repairs*

Beyond the selection process, organizations can attempt to "repair" mistakes of individuals and to overcomes biases with organizational practices. Heath et al. (1998) give many illustrative examples. One example is from Microsoft. Software engineers did not believe the many complaints coming from 1-800 customer service phone lines about the difficulty of using software, or disparaged the frustrated users as stupid. To make customer complaints vivid, Microsoft used a room with a one-way mirror. Through the mirror, engineers could watch customers—who looked like normal, reasonably intelligent folks, not Luddite morons—struggling with software. The room replaced statistical information about phone line complaints with a smaller sample of more vivid information, exploiting the way in which the brain automatically privileges firsthand visual information over abstract symbols. The sheepish engineers went back to the drawing boards to try to make their software easier to use for the people on the other side of the mirror.

Another example was conveyed to us by Chris Mayer. In their study of loss-aversion in housing, Genosove and Mayer (2001) found that the nominal purchase price condominium owners in Boston, MA, had paid for their houses influenced their listing prices and the prices at which they sold their houses. In talking about his findings before some investment bankers, one person in the audience said he knew about this effect, and that his firm had taken steps to limit it. His firm combats loss-aversion by forcing a trader to periodically switch his "position" (the portfolio of assets the trader bought and is blamed or credited for) with the position of another trader in the firm. Switching ensures that traders do not make bad trades because of loss-aversion and emotional attachment to their past actions without affecting the firm's net trading position. If attachment to one's trading position is bad, the switch creates a purely behavioral scope economy, which permits firms with many traders to outcompete firms with fewer traders.

Deadlines are another kind of organizational repair. When people procrastinate, methods for enforcing deadlines will help them get work done (O'Donoghue and Rabin 2001). If firms are able to enforce deadlines better than individuals can, the firm has a cost advantage over individual workers who are self-employed. Deadline

---

10 percent of people who can will end up in jobs where it's required'—such as dealing blackjack, Becker's example, or managing mutual funds." (Actually, blackjack dealers' strategies are completely constrained by casino rules and therefore require no skill at probability judgment.)

enforcement can come in the hard form of firing threats, or in the soft form of feeling bad about letting coworkers down, or the in-between form of risking coworkers' wrath if a missed deadline on a joint project leads to mistaken blame.

While we are lacking convincing field data on organizational repairs, these examples suggest the following recipe for studying them. Find a mistake most people make in individual decisions; ask what organizational practice would limit its effect; then investigate whether the practice works. (Ideally, convince a firm to randomly vary the organizational design across similar departments!) Or reverse engineer the recipe: think of a curious organizational practice; ask what economic (Gibbons 2004b) or behavioral problem in individual choice it might be a solution to.

Repairs can also come from the market rather than from an organizational practice. Commenting on the slow speed of industry consolidation, Jensen (1993, pp. 847) wrote:

> In industry after industry with excess capacity, managers fail to recognize that they themselves must downsize; instead they leave the exit to others while they continue to invest.

The reluctance to downsize might stem from emotional reluctance of executives to fire people (though self-interest surely plays a role[29]). An aversion to firings and layoffs is an organizational manifestation of loss-aversion. For most managers this is a kind of effort in the simple agency model sketched above—an activity which they dislike doing but which is good for shareholders.

One solution to the problem of necessary downsizing is sorting—hire managers who do not find firing people effortful (like "Chainsaw Al" Dunlop and "Neutron Jack" Welch). Jensen suggested that the emergence of the leveraged buyout (LBO) organizational form has been a useful mechanism for downsizing (and other changes in governance would help too). An important feature of the LBO is that control shifts to new investors (the LBO partnership), who typically have no emotional attachment to the firm's workers. This element of psychological transfer, and willingness to accept a "loss" from the firm's previous policy, may be central to the success of this kind of restructuring. Of course, the LBO form also offers huge financial incentives to restructure, and to do so rapidly (because of the large debt service burdens). But maybe these large rewards just reflect how emotionally painful downsizing is for most managers.

---

[29]Most studies show that compensation is more strongly tied to firm size than to any other variable. Thus, laying off workers generally reduces the size of an executive's compensation. The suggestion here is that layoffs are effortful beyond these incentive effects.

7.6.3 *Exploiting Worker Biases*

A growing literature on the "behavioral economics of industrial organizations" deals with the interaction of individuals and firms (DellaVigna and Malmendier 2004; Eliaz and Spiegler 2004; Gabaix and Laibson 2005; Heidhues and Koszegi 2005). The baseline assumption in this literature is that consumers make systematic mistakes and firms are rational actors. This is reasonable because experience, specialization, larger resources, sorting, and market competition all work in the direction of enabling organizations to train and choose managers who are expert at exploiting mistakes by consumers—and by their own workers (Glaeser 2004). Rational firms can exploit the biases of individual consumers, for instance by charging high flat rates for services or goods consumers will consume less than they plan to—think of your gym attendance!—by designing contracts with automatic renewal if consumers tend to procrastinate cancelation, or by issuing stock when investor sentiment is high (DellaVigna and Malmendier 2003; Baker and Wurgler 2000).

Similarly, the individual employee in an organization may display biases from which the organization can extract rents. For example, Oyer and Schaefer (2005) analyze why firms give options to medium- or lower-level employees. Given the relatively small size of these grants and the risk premia associated with them, options are unlikely to be an efficient way to provide incentives for these employees. Option grants may, however, allow firms to attract and retain employees. The analysis of Oyer and Schaefer suggests that the benefits of option compensation are particularly high if employees are overly optimistic about the future prospects of the company. Making options part of the compensation package allows firms to identify those (potential) employees who have particularly strong beliefs about the future prospects of the company and to reap the rents from compensating them with overvalued options rather than cash. Such a compensation strategy is profitable if these employees are also more productive, for instance, due to their enthusiasm about the company.[30]

Other elements of organizational design have similar properties. Lazear and Rosen (1981) have shown conditions under which tournaments dominate other forms of

---

[30] As pointed out by Bergman and Jenter (2004), overoptimism about the prospects of the company by itself is not sufficient to explain options as part of the employment contract. Individuals with such beliefs can be compensated equally cheaply in cash—their reservation wage will be lower due to the overvaluation of company stock and options which they can buy with that cash. Or, they may not even work for the company and just buy the stock or options of the company. These constraints, however, do not bite if markets are incomplete. For example, the typical ten-year employee option on a public company's stock is not traded on a public exchange, and even shorter-duration options are not traded for private companies. Employees may also not be able to value options based on observed market prices. In these cases, options may be part of a profit-maximizing compensation contract design, even if employees with optimistic beliefs about a company do not have higher abilities.

labor contracts, especially with sorting among high-ability and low-ability workers. Their argument is strengthened (and more robust) if we introduce heterogeneity in self-confidence among workers. If some workers are overly convinced of their own abilities (and their overconfidence is not negatively correlated with ability), tournaments become a particularly cheap form of compensation. Overconfident individuals will overestimate the expected value of entering the tournament outcome and will be willing to accept lower current compensation.

Option-based compensation and rank-order based promotion are two examples of how firms can reduce their compensation costs at the expense of employees who are too optimistic about the firm's prospects. These examples assume implicitly that the organization itself—or the top management teams of an organization—is not affected by biases observed in individuals further down the hierarchy or outside the organization, but may remedy or even exploit them.

7.7 CONCLUSION

This chapter is about both *applying* behavioral economics to organizations, and *enriching* behavioral economics by asking questions that are specific to the roles of workers and managers in organizations. This chapter is less of a review of what is known than it is a research agenda, with more questions than answers. This conclusion recaps some of the common themes.

The first question is how to complicate the basic agency model. One complication is that agents' preferences (i.e., effort disutility and reservation wages) may be sensitive to how jobs are described or how wage offers and job choices are elicited. Limits on greed and self-interest imply that people often like to help their friends and harm their enemies, and dislike unequal treatment. Precise models of social preference that have been carefully honed on experimental data from simple games would need to be plugged into organizational economics applications. In the laboratory, preferences are often sensitive to reference points, such as previous wages (due perhaps to habit formation) and wages of other workers. There is evidence of such effects from labor practices (e.g., two-tier wage deals in financially distressed firms) and executive compensation. Workers also seem to care about fair or just procedures for determining outcomes. The strength of these preferences in field data and organizational design responses has, however, not been studied thoroughly. Psychological influences on judgments of causality (in agency-theory terms, inferring agent effort from output) are also important. Hindsight bias, overattribution of cause to workers rather than luck, asymmetric attribution (taking credit and exporting blame), diffusion of blame across a large group, and overconfidence about skill may all play important roles, and these have not been studied much in organizational contexts.

Section 7.2 moves from the individual to the organizational level. Organizing requires informal rules for coordinating action. Following Kreps (1990), we take the view that corporate culture is a set of shared meta-focal principles for resolving coordination problems in the face of the cognitive inability to fully specify an employment contract. Having a sharp economic concept like this to work with could provide a basis for useful empirical work on culture. The way the brain organizes information ("cognitive economy") may also explain why culture is often transmitted in the form of stories, personification, and simple slogans (Heath and Seidel 2004). The value of having cultural principles that can be commonly understood, and are immune to errors in language translation, gives a role for leadership and managerial statements that are simple (like corporate mission statements).

In large business organizations (especially U.S. firms), the judgment of top managers (e.g., CEOs) is especially influential. Section 7.3 discusses the fact that top managers are particularly prone to specific biases, such as overconfidence, given their past successes and the noisy feedback on their large-scale decisions. Then they may make mistakes, especially if weak corporate governance does not discipline mistakes. Overconfident managers, for example, will rely too much on internal cash flow when (over)investing, and enter into value-reducing mergers.

If organizations are aware of the mistakes workers and managers make, they can sort around them (via hiring practices and internal matching of workers into jobs where their mistakes are least costly), they can design "organizational repairs," or they can exploit mistakes by workers (e.g., offering backloaded incentives to optimistic workers who are sure they will succeed). Thinking about the optimal design problem in the face of worker error, as suggested in Section 4.4, is both positive economics and potentially normatively useful for managers.

We end the book with an important caveat. Psychology and economics share a basic methodological individualism: psychologists are interested in people, and economists are interested in how economic outcomes arise from the interaction of people (and institutions). Many organizational theorists, however, work at a middle level sometimes called "meso," in which the organization is the unit of analysis. Meso concepts like organizational routines and learning are not rooted in individual behavioral concepts. It is possible that organizational economics could be tied to meso-organizational (or macro-organizational) constructs, but this is not an active area of research.

References

Akerlof, G., and R. Kranton. 2005. Identity and the economics of organizations. *Journal of Economic Perspectives* 19:9–32.
Alicke, M. D. 1985. Global self-evaluation as determined by the desirability and controllability of trait adjectives. *Journal of Personality and Social Psychology* 49:1621–30.

Alicke, M. D., M. L. Klotz, D. L. Breitenbecher, T. J. Yurak, and D. Vredenburg. 1995. Personal contact, individuation, and the better-than-average effect. *Journal of Personality and Social Psychology* 68:804–25.

Andrade, G., M. Mitchell, and E. Stafford. 2001. New evidence and perspectives on mergers. *Journal of Economic Perspectives* 15:103–20.

Antle, R., and A. Smith. 1996. An empirical investigation into the relative performance evaluation of corporate executives. *Journal of Accounting and Economics* 24:1–40.

Ariely, D., U. Gneezy, G. Loewenstein, and N. Mazar. 2003. Large stakes and big mistakes. Federal Reserve Bank of Boston Working Paper 05-11.

Ariely, D., G. Loewenstein, and D. Prelec. 2004a. Tom Sawyer and the myth of fundamental value. MIT Working Paper. (Available at http://sds.hss.cmu.edu/faculty/Loewenstein/downloads/Sawyersubmitted.pdf.)

Ariely, D., E. Kamenica, and D. Prelec. 2004b. Man's search for meaning: the case of Legos. Harvard Business School Working Paper. (Available at http://www.people.fas.harvard.edu/~kamenica/papers/legosFinal.pdf.)

Babcock, L., and G. Loewenstein. 1997. Explaining bargaining impasse: the role of self-serving biases. *Journal of Economic Perspectives* 11:109–26.

Babcock, L., X. Wang, and G. Loewenstein. 1996. Choosing the wrong pond: social comparisons in negotiations that reflect a self-serving bias. *Quarterly Journal of Economics* 111:1–19.

Baker, G., M. Gibbs, and B. Holmström. 1994. The wage policy of a firm. *Quarterly Journal of Economics* 109:921–55.

Baker, M., and J. Wurgler. 2000. The equity share in new issues and aggregate stock returns. *Journal of Finance* 55:2219–57.

Baker, M., R. Ruback, and J. Wurgler. 2004. Behavioral corporate finance: a survey. Harvard Business School Working Paper. (Available at http://www.people.hbs.edu/mbaker/cv/papers/behavioralcorporatefinance.pdf.)

Bardolet, D., C. Fox, and D. Lovallo. 2005. Partition dependence in organizational capital allocation: an experimental investigation. UCLA Anderson School Working Paper.

Barsade, S., K. Koput, and B. Staw. 1997. Escalation and the credit window: a longitudinal study of bank executives' recognition and write-off of problem loans. *Journal of Applied Psychology* 82:130–42.

Bartel, A., R. Freeman, C. Ichniowski, and M. M. Kleiner. 2003. Can a work organization have an attitude problem? The impact of workplaces on employee attitudes and economic outcomes. NBER Working Paper 9987.

Bazerman, M. H., and Neale, M. A. 1992. Nonrational escalation of commitment in negotiation. *European Management Journal* 10:163–68.

Bebchuk, L., J. Fried, and D. Walker. 2002. Managerial power and rent extraction in the design of executive compensation. *University of Chicago Law Review* 69:751–846.

Belliveau, M. A., C. O'Reilly, and J. Wade. 1996. Social capital at the top: effects of social similarity and status on CEO compensation. *Academy of Management Journal* 39:1568–93.

Benabou, R., and J. Tirole. 2003. Intrinsic and extrinsic motivation. *Review of Economic Studies* 70:489–520.

Benabou, R., and J. Tirole. 2004. Incentives and prosocial behavior. Princeton University Working Paper. (Available at http://www.wws.princeton.edu/rbenabou/w11535.pdf.)

Benartzi, S., and R. Thaler. 2001. Naïve diversification strategies in defined contribution saving plans. *American Economic Review* 91:79–98.

Bennis, W., and D. Nanus. 1985. *Leaders: The Strategies for Taking Charge*. New York: Harper and Row.

Bergman, N., and D. Jenter. 2004. Employee sentiment and stock option compensation. MIT Sloan Research Paper 4504-04.

Bertrand, M., and S. Mullainathan. 2001. Are CEOs rewarded for luck? The ones without principals are. *Quarterly Journal of Economics* 116:901–32.

———. 2003. Enjoying the quiet life? Corporate governance and managerial preferences. *Journal of Political Economy* 111:1043–75.

Bettman, J. R., and B. A. Weitz. 1983. Attributions in the board room: causal reasoning in corporate annual reports. *Administrative Science Quarterly* 28:165–83.

Bowman, D., D. Minehard, and M. Rabin. 1999. Loss aversion in a consumption–savings model. *Journal of Economic Behavior and Organization* 38:155–78.

Brandts, J., and D. Cooper. 2004. A change would do you good…. An experimental study on how to overcome coordination failure in organizations. Weatherhead Business School Working Paper. (Available at http://pareto.uab.es/wp/2004/60604.pdf.)

Brockner, J., and B. Wiesenfeld. 1996. An integrative framework for explaining reactions to decisions: interactive effects of outcomes and procedures. *Psychological Bulletin* 120:189–208.

Camerer, C. F. 2003. *Behavioral Game Theory*. New York: Russell Sage Foundation Press and Princeton University Press.

Camerer, C. F., and G. Loewenstein. 2004. Behavioral economics: past, present, future. In *Advances in Behavioral Economics* (ed. C. Camerer, G. Loewenstein, and M. Rabin). New York: Russell Sage Foundation Press and Princeton University Press.

Camerer, C. F., and A. Vepsäläinen. 1988. The efficiency of cultural contracting. *Strategic Management Journal* 9:77–94.

Camerer, C. F., L. Babcock, G. Loewenstein, and R. Thaler. 1997. Labor supply of New York City cab drivers: one day at a time. *Quarterly Journal of Economics* 112:407–42.

Cameron, K. S., and R. E. Quinn. 1999. *Diagnosing and Changing Organizational Culture*. Reading, MA: Addison-Wesley.

Cooper, A. C., C. Y. Woo, and W. C. Dunkelberg. 1988. Entrepreneurs' perceived chances for success. *Journal of Business Venturing* 3:97–108.

Cooper, R., D. DeJong, B. Forsythe, and T. Ross. 1994. Alternative institutions for resolving coordination problems: experimental evidence on forward induction and preplay communication. In *Problems of Coordination in Economic Activity* (ed. J. Friedman). Kluwer.

Crémer, J., L. Garicano, and A. Prat. 2003. Language and the theory of the firm. University of Chicago Graduate School of Business Working Paper. (Available at http://gsbwww.uchicago.edu/fac/luis.garicano/research/index_files/codes.pdf.)

DellaVigna, S., and U. Malmendier. 2003. Overestimating self-control: evidence from the health club industry. Stanford GSB Research Paper 1800.

———. 2004. Contract design and self-control: theory and evidence. *Quarterly Journal of Economics* 119:353–402.

Dunning, D., J. A. Meyerowitz, and A. D. Holzberg. 1989. Ambiguity and self-evaluation: The role of idiosyncratic trait definitions in self-serving assessments of ability. *Journal of Personality and Social Psychology* 57:1082–90.

Eliaz, K., and R. Spiegler. 2004. Contracting with diversely naive agents. CEPR Discussion Paper 4573.

Falk, A., and A. Ichino. 2003. Clean evidence on peer pressure. IZA Discussion Paper 732. (Available at ftp://repec.iza.org/RePEc/Discussionpaper/dp732.pdf.)

Fehr, E., and S. Gächter. 2000. Cooperation and punishment in public goods experiments. *American Economic Review* 90:980–94.

——. 2000. Fairness and retaliation: the economics of reciprocity. *Journal of Economic Perspectives* 14:159–81.

Fehr, E., and L. Götte. 2003. Do workers work more when wages are high? Evidence from a randomized field experiment. IEW Working Paper 125.

Feiler, L., and C. F. Camerer. 2006. Code creation in endogenous merger experiments. Caltech Working Paper. (Available at http://www.hss.caltech.edu/~camerer/codecreation_feb 2006.pdf.)

Fox, C. R., and Y. Rottenstreich. 2003. Partition priming in judgment under uncertainty. *Psychological Science* 14:195–200.

Frank, R. 2005. Departures from rational choice: with and without regret. In *The Law and Economics of Irrational Behavior* (ed. F. Parisi and V. Smith), pp. 13–36. Stanford University Press.

Gabaix, X., and D. Laibson. 2005. Shrouded attributes, consumer myopia, and information suppression in competitive markets. NBER Working Paper 11755.

Garvey, G., and T. Milbourn. Forthcoming. Asymmetric benchmarking in compensation: executives are paid for good luck but not punished for bad. *Journal of Financial Economics*.

Genosove, D., and Ch. Mayer. 2001. Loss aversion and seller behavior: evidence from the housing market. *Quarterly Journal of Economics* 116:1233–60.

Gervais, S., J. B. Heaton, and T. Odean. 2003. Overconfidence, investment policy and stock options. Duke University Working Paper. (Available at http://faculty.haas.berkeley.edu/ odean/papers/Managers/GervaisHeatonOdean0703.pdf.)

Gibbons, R. 2004a. Four formal(izable) theories of the firm? MIT Department of Economics Working Paper 04-34.

——. 2004b. What is economic sociology and should any economists care? *Journal of Economic Perspectives* 19:3–7.

Gil-White, F. J. 2001. Are ethnic groups biological "species" to the human brain? Essentialism in our cognition of some social categories. *Current Anthropology* 42:515–54.

Glaeser, E. 2004. Psychology and the market. *American Economic Review* 94:408–13.

Goel, A. M., and A. V. Thakor. 2000. Rationality, overconfidence, and leadership. University of Michigan Working Paper.

Gompers, P. A., J. L. Ishii, and A. Metrick. 2003. Corporate governance and equity prices. *Quarterly Journal of Economics* 118:107–55.

Hall, B., and K. J. Murphy. 2003. The trouble with stock options. *Journal of Economic Perspectives*. 17:49–70.

Hart, O. 1995. *Firms, Contracts, and Financial Structure*. Oxford University Press.

Heath, C. 1995. Escalation and de-escalation of commitment in response to sunk costs: the role of budgeting in mental accounting. *Organizational Behavior and Human Decision Processes* 62:38–54.

Heath, C., and V. Seidel. 2004. Language as a coordinating mechanism: how linguistic memes help direct appropriate action. Stanford University Working Paper. (Available at http://www.si.umich.edu/ICOS/Linguisticmemes4.2.pdf.)

Heath, C., and N. Staudenmayer. 2000. *Coordination Neglect: How Lay Theories of Organizing Complicate Coordination in Organizations* (ed. B. M. Staw and R. I. Sutton), Research in Organizational Behavior Series, Volume 22, pp. 153–91. Greenwich, CT: JAI Press.

Heath, C., R. P. Larrick, and J. Klayman. 1998. Cognitive repairs: how organizations compensate for the shortcomings of individual learners. *Research in Organizational Behavior* 20:1–37.

Heaton, J. B. 2002. Managerial optimism and corporate finance. *Financial Management* 31:33–45.

Heidhues, P., and B. Koszegi. 2005. The impact of consumer loss aversion on pricing. CEPR Working Paper 4849.

Hermalin, B. 2001. Economics and corporate culture. In *The International Handbook of Organizational Culture and Climate* (ed. C. L. Cooper, S. Cartwright, and P. C. Earley). Wiley.

Hertel, G., and N. Kerr. 2001. Priming in-group favoritism: the impact of normative scripts in the minimal group paradigm. *Journal of Experimental Social Psychology* 37:316–24.

Holmström, B., and S. Kaplan. 2001. Corporate governance and merger activity in the United States: making sense of the 1980s and 1990s. *Journal of Economic Perspectives* 15(2):121–44.

Holmström, B., and P. Milgrom. 1991. Multi-task principal–agent analyses: incentive contracts, asset ownership, and job design. *Journal of Law, Economics, and Organization* (Special Issue) 7:24–52.

Huberman, G., and W. Jiang. 2004. The $1/N$ heuristic in 401(k) plans. EFA 2004 Maastricht Meetings Paper 2036. Mimeo.

Ichino, A., and G. Maggi. 2000. Work environment and individual background: explaining regional shirking differentials in a large Italian firm. *Quarterly Journal of Economics* 115:1057–90.

Jensen, M. 1993. Modern industrial revolution, exit, and the failure of internal control systems. *Journal of Finance* 48:830–80.

Johnson, B., R. Magee, N. Nagarajan, and H. Newman. 1985. An analysis of the stock price reaction to sudden executive deaths: implications for the management labor market. *Journal of Accounting and Economics* 7:151–74.

Kahneman, D., and D. Lovallo. 1993. Timid choices and bold forecasts: a cognitive perspective on risk taking. *Management Science* 39:17–32.

Kahneman, D., J. Knetsch and R. H. Thaler. 1986. Fairness and the assumptions of economics. *Journal of Business* 59:285–301.

Kandel, E., and E. P. Lazear. 1992. Peer pressure and partnerships. *Journal of Political Economy* 100:801–18.

Knez, M., and C. F. Camerer. 1994. Creating "expectational assets" in the laboratory: "weakest-link" coordination games. *Strategic Management Journal* 15:101–19.

Knez, M., and D. Simester. 2001. Firm-wide incentives and mutual monitoring at Continental Airlines. *Journal of Labor Economics* 19:743–72.

Kole, S., and K. Lehn. 2000. Workforce integration and the dissipation of value in mergers: the case of USAir's acquisition of Piedmont Aviation. In *Mergers and Productivity* (ed. S. Kaplan), pp. 239–79. NBER and University of Chicago Press.

Kolligian Jr., J., and R. J. Sternberg. 1991. Perceived fraudulence in young adults: is there an "imposter syndrome"? *Journal of Personality Assessment* 56:308–26.

Koszegi, B., and M. Rabin. 2004. A model of reference-dependent preferences. EconWPA Working Paper 0407001.

Kotter, J., and J. L. Heskett. 1992. *Corporate Culture and Performance*. New York: Free Press.

Kovalchik, S., C. F. Camerer, D. M. Grether, C. R. Plott, and J. M. Allman. 2005. Aging and decision making: a comparison between neurologically healthy elderly and young individuals. *Journal of Economic Behavior and Organization* 8:79–94.

Kremer, M. 1993. The O-ring theory of economic development. *Quarterly Journal of Economics* 108:551–76.

Kreps, D. M. 1990. Corporate culture and economic theory. In *Perspectives on Positive Political Economy* (ed. J. Alt and K. Shepsle). Cambridge University Press.

———. 1997. Intrinsic motivation and extrinsic incentives. *American Economic Review* 87:359–64.

Landier, A., and D. Thesmar. 2004. Financial contracting with optimistic entrepreneurs: theory and evidence. CEPR Discussion Paper 3971.

Lamont, O. 1997. Cash flow and investment: evidence from internal capital markets. *Journal of Finance* 52:83–109.

Langer, E. 1975. The illusion of control. *Journal of Personality and Social Psychology* 32:311–28.

Larwood, L., and W. Whittaker. 1977. Managerial myopia: self-serving biases in organizational planning. *Journal of Applied Psychology* 62:194–99.

Lazear, E. 2004. Balanced skills and entrepreneurship. *American Economic Review* 94:208–11.

Lazear, E., and S. Rosen. 1981. Rank–order tournaments as optimum labor contracts. *Journal of Political Economy* 89:841–65.

Lazear, E., U. Malmendier, and R. Weber. 2005. Sorting in experiments with application to social preferences. NBER Working Paper 12041.

Lepper, M. R., D. Greene, and R. E. Nisbett. 1973. Undermining children's intrinsic interest with extrinsic reward: a test of the "overjustification" hypothesis. *Journal of Personality and Social Psychology* 28:129–37.

Loewenstein, G., and S. Issacharoff. 1994. Source-dependence in the valuation of objects. *Journal of Behavioral Decision Making* 7:157–68.

Main, B., C. O'Reilly, and J. Wade. 1993. Top executive pay: tournament or teamwork? *Journal of Labor Economics* 11:606–28.

Malmendier, U., and G. Tate. 2003. Who makes acquisitions? CEO overconfidence and the market's reaction. Stanford Research Paper 1798.

———. 2005a. Superstar CEOs. 7th Annual Texas Finance Festival Paper. (Available at http://ssrn.com/abstract=709861.)

Malmendier, U., and G. Tate. 2005b. CEO overconfidence and corporate investment. *Journal of Finance* 60:2660–2700.

Malmendier, U., G. Tate, and J. Yan. 2006. Corporate financial policies with overconfident managers. (Available at http://faculty-gsb.stanford.edu/malmendier/personal_page/Papers/cs050206.pdf.)

March, J., and Z. Shapira. 1987. Managerial perspectives on risk and risk taking. *Management Science* 33:1404–19.

Marques, J. M., V. Y. Yzerbyt, and J.-P. Leyens. 1988. The "Black Sheep Effect": extremity of judgements towards ingroup members as a function of group identification. *European Journal of Social Psychology* 18:1–16.

Martin, J. 1982. Stories and scripts in organizational settings. In *Cognitive Social Psychology* (ed. A. Hastorf and A. Isen), pp. 255–305. Elsevier.

Miller, D., and M. Ross. 1975. Self-serving biases in the attribution of causality: fact or fiction? *Psychological Bulletin* 82:213–25.

Moeller, S., F. Schlingemann, and R. Stultz. 2003. Do shareholders of acquiring firms gain from acquisitions? *Research Technology Management* 46:62–66.

Moore, P. G. 1977. The manager's struggle with uncertainty. *Journal of the Royal Statistical Society*A 149:129–65.

Mullainathan, S., and R. H. Thaler. 2001. Behavioral economics. In *International Encyclopedia of Social Sciences*, 1st edn, pp. 1094–1100. New York: Pergamon.

Murphy, K. J. 1999. Executive compensation. In *Handbook of Labor Economics* (ed. O. Ashenfelter and D. Card), Volume 3B, Chapter 38. Amsterdam: North-Holland.

Myers, S., and N. Majluf. 1984. Corporate financing and investment decisions when firms have information that investors do not have. *Journal of Financial Economics* 13:187–221.

Nisbett, R. E. 2004. *The Geography of Thought: How Asians and Westerners Think Differently... and Why*. New York: Free Press.

O'Donoghue, T. D., and M. Rabin. 2001. Choice and procrastination. *Quarterly Journal of Economics* 116:121–60.

Oyer, P., and S. Schaefer. 2005. Why do some firms give stock options to all employees? An empirical examination of alternative theories. *Journal of Financial Economics* 76:99–133.

———. 1998. Psychology and economics. *Journal of Economic Literature* 36:11–46.

Radner, R., and T. Van Zandt. 2001. Real-time decentralized information processing and returns to scale. *Economic Theory* 17:545–75.

Rebitzer, J. 2002. Monitoring, motivation and management: the determinants of opportunistic behavior in a field experiment. *American Economic Review* 92:840–64.

Roll, R. 1986. The hubris hypothesis of corporate takeovers. *Journal of Business* 59:197–217.

Roy, D. 1952. Quota restriction and goldbricking in a machine shop. *American Journal of Sociology* 57:427–42.

Salanié, B. 2003. Testing contract theory. *CESifo Economic Studies* 49:461–77.

Scharfstein, D. S., and J. C. Stein. 2000. The dark side of internal capital markets: divisional rent seeking and inefficient investment. *Journal of Finance* 55:2537–65.

Schein, E. H. 1983. The role of the founder in creating organizational culture. *Organizational Dynamics* 12:13–28.

Schelling, Th. 1960. *The Strategy of Conflict*. Harvard University Press.

Shafir, E., P. Diamond, and A. Tversky. 1997. Money illusion. *Quarterly Journal of Economics* 112:341–74.

Sniezek, J., and T. Buckley. 1992. Confidence depends on the level of aggregation. *Journal of Behavioral Decision Making* 4:263–72.

Sørensen, J. 2002. The strength of corporate culture and the reliability of firm performance. *Administrative Science Quarterly* 47:70–91.

Staw, B., and J. Ross. 1993. Organizational escalation and exit: the case of the Shoreham nuclear power plant. *Academy of Management Journal* 36:701–32.

Stern, S. 2004. Do scientists pay to be scientists? *Management Science* 50:835–53.

Stewart, S. A. 2005. Can behavioral economics save us from ourselves? University of Chicago Magazine. Feature article, February, Volume 97, Issue 3.

Svenson, O. 1981. Are we all less risky and more skillful than our fellow drivers? *Acta Psychologica* 47:143–48.

Taylor, S. E., and J. D. Brown. 1988. Illusion and well-being: a social psychological perspective on mental health. *Psychological Bulletin* 103:193–210.

Torry, S. 1996. The paper chase slows down, here and nationally. *Washington Post*, June 10, 1996. (Available at http://www.washingtonpost.com/wp-adv/classifieds/careerpost/library/lesslaw.htm.)

Tyler, T. R. 2001. Cooperation in organizations. In *Social Identity Processes in Organizational Contexts* (ed. M. A. Hogg and D. J. Terry), pp. 149–66. Philadelphia, PA: Psychology Press.

Van Den Steen, E. 2004. Rational overoptimism (and other biases). *American Economic Review* 94:1141–51.

——. 2005. Organizational beliefs and managerial vision. *Journal of Law, Economics and Organization* 21:256–83.

Van Huyck, J. B., R. C. Battalio, and R. O. Beil. 1990. Tacit coordination games, strategic uncertainty, and coordination failure. *American Economic Review* 80:234–48.

Weber, R. A. 2006. Managing growth to achieve efficient coordination in large groups. *American Economic Review* 96:114–26.

Weber, R. A., and C. F. Camerer. 2003. Cultural conflict and merger failure: an experimental approach. *Management Science* 49:400–15.

——. 1999. The econometrics and behavioral economics of escalation of commitment: a re-examination of Staw and Hoang's NBA data. *Journal of Economic Behavior and Organization* 39:59–82.

Rick, S., R. A. Weber, and C. F. Camerer. 2004. The effects of organizational structure and codes on the performance of laboratory "firms". Carnegie Mellon University Working Paper. (Available at http://ssrn.com/abstract=644346.)

Weinstein, N. 1980. Unrealistic optimism about future life events. *Journal of Personality and Social Psychology* 39:806–20.

Wernerfelt, B. 2004. Organizational languages. *Journal of Economics & Management Strategy* 13:461–472.

Weston, J. F., K. Chung, and J. Sui. 1998. *Takeovers, Restructuring and Corporate Governance*. Upper Saddle River, NJ: Prentice Hall.

Yamagishi, T. 1988. The provision of a sanctioning system in the United States and in Japan. *Social Psychology Quarterly* 51:264–70.

Yerkes, R. M., and J. D. Dodson. 1908. The relation of strength of stimulus to rapidity of habit-formation. *Journal of Comparative Neurology and Psychology* 18:459–82.

Zink, C. F., G. Pagnoni, M. E. Martin-Skurski, J. C. Chappelow, and G. S. Berns. 2004. Human striatal response to monetary reward depends on saliency. *Neuron* 42:509–17.

Zwiebel, J. 1995. Corporate conservatism. *Journal of Political Economy* 103:1–25.

COMMENT BY MICHAEL D. COHEN

Beyond Bounded Rationality [31]

This chapter views organizational phenomena through the lens of behavioral economics. It generates many productive insights. In the course of doing so it shifts between two different conceptual frameworks in a way that reflects an important contest of perspectives playing out at the moment across the social sciences.

The careful reader will notice that two quite different organizing perspectives are employed at different points in the article, each reflecting one side of the contention that is in progress. The first perspective employed might be called "deviations from baseline rationality," while the second organizing principle might be labeled "the economic implications of how the brain works." One sees examples of the former in their discussions of topics such as hindsight bias and partition dependence. Examples of the latter occur in their discussions of the "cognitive economies" achieved by narratives and personification and of the set-point dependencies that may shape the valuation of wages.

In my view, this oscillation among frameworks embodied in the essay accurately mirrors the state of the field. Across the social sciences, the working assumptions about the human mind that have relied on metaphors of computation are contending with metaphors of biological process. The "deviations" perspective exemplifies the older approach, with roots stretching back to Herbert Simon's bounded rationality and his models of heuristic human problem solving that rest in turn on his symbol processing hypotheses. Although Simon and his followers engaged in some bitter contests with orthodox economists, both camps worked with a view centered on a strongly cognitive approach to human decision-making. Both presumed that much of what was important about choice and problem solving was accessible for research

---

[31] The essay by Colin Camerer and Ulrike Malmendier on "Behavioral Economics of Organizations" included in the present volume reflects not only the stimulating presentation at the conference, but also the lively discussion that followed, and it embodies further valuable work done subsequently by the authors. Similarly, this commentary contains material from remarks made at the conference, but also responds both to the following discussions and to the revisions made in the Camerer–Malmender article. By now both documents are well-removed from being transcripts of the original sessions. I have, however, retained the title of the conference remarks, which was chosen with the aim of being somewhat provocative. Despite many changes, that remains my goal, as I believe that a period of important change is underway in this field, and I hope to accelerate it.

via introspection and "thinking aloud" protocols. Both cleanly factored emotional aspects of action, allowing them to enter models of choice or decision only through concepts such as value, utility, goal, or aspiration level. In this approach, models of economic action based on empirical observation are framed as conforming with, or systematically deviating from, behavior expected under conventional assumptions of rationality.

The perspective that might be called "economic implications of how the brain works" is newer. It is being propelled into the foreground by a number of cultural and technical forces, but most notably by the very rapid gains in psychological measurement capability that are discussed below. In this approach the starting point is models of mental processing as understood in psychological research. Economic action is taken to be generated by individuals who are characterized by the memory processes, habitual dispositions, and emotional response patterns found in psychological studies. Economic analysis then tries to elucidate the consequences of such actions.

The defining feature of the "deviations from baseline rationality" approach is that it is organized around observed patterns of economic action that fall short of some plausible standard of efficiency. People are found to exhibit a consistent tendency to act in some way that "leaves money (or utility) on the table." For example, they underestimate the probabilities of events that did not occur (examples of this type are collected as "hindsight bias"). Indeed, from this viewpoint, observed deviations are often characterized as "mistakes." The term implies that psychological processes are being assessed for their adequacy in meeting the demands of economic rationality.

In the second approach, it is the problem of economic research to accurately model action generated by normal psychological processes. Though psychological accuracy would seem to be a valuable goal, the risk of this approach is that psychologically rich models may lose contact with the powerful theoretical machinery developed over the last century that allows economists to infer outcomes for groups from assumptions about individuals.

A research survey such as the Camerer–Malmendier essay tries to look both backward over what is known, and forward toward what should be researched. Since so much of what is known was accumulated in the "deviations" perspective, it is appropriate that it play a large role. However, since the gains are developing so rapidly in contemporary psychology and the new tools becoming available are so powerful, it is natural that much of the forward thinking about what research is promising should bring in the perspective of "how the brain works."[32]

---

[32] Indeed, though it is not mentioned here, Camerer himself is doing intriguing work of this kind, as in his recent collaboration on brain imaging of trust development (King-Casas et al. 2005).

My remarks are therefore divided into two clusters. The first consists of observations on the strengths and limitations of the deviations framework. The second discusses examples that may help to bring out the potential—and the challenges—for economics of taking "how the brain works" as a starting point for analysis of organizational economics.

The "Deviations" Perspective

There are some important advantages to the deviations framework as a way of organizing results from behavioral economics for application to the economics of organization. First and foremost, the underlying behavioral economics literature has often used this framework, and so transfer to application in the economics of organization is most direct when it is maintained.

But additional advantages are also obtained. For example, the deviations approach often suggests extensions of existing formal apparatus. Camerer and Malmendier provide a nice example of this with their addition of a skill term to a more standard equation for effort level in an agency model. Though it is a complication, the extension is not unmanageable, and the authors show that the term may allow theory to accommodate a range of observed deviations from simpler representations. The deviation approach is often able to suggest promising modification of existing formalisms. Indeed the whole apparatus of risk aversion, now taken for granted as standard theory, can be viewed as embodying just such a modification.

The deviations approach likewise suggests areas of direct potential benefit to management or policy. Because people are known from field and laboratory observation to have systematic tendencies to miss potential gains, pointing out a general pattern like hindsight bias can be directly useful to practitioners in avoiding costly errors. Moreover, the naming conventions of the deviations approach result in quite memorable labeling of the principles, with the implication that students can be fairly effectively taught to watch out for problems like "the fundamental attribution error."

And finally, the deviations approach suggests to those who study the economics of organization research questions that are likely to be productive. Camerer and Malmendier illustrate this advantage nicely with their account of known individual deviations that may motivate organizations to develop corrective devices. For example, they suggest that budget constraints and project milestones may be organizational devices that function to limit individual tendencies to escalate bad commitments.

There are, of course, some costs to the deviations framework, along with the benefits.

Earlier I suggested the advantage that a deviations approach facilitates adjusting current theory to observed patterns of "mistake". But the quite distorted psychology this can build into theory may itself become a rhetorical albatross. As the richer model

283

of mind now developing in psychology gains credibility in the general intellectual community, that shift may markedly constrain the freedom of economics to operate credibly in the eyes of policy makers and managers while retaining the strongly stylized representations of economic action that might be the most convenient for formalization. Consumers of economic advice may begin to ask where human habits, skills, identifications, and emotions enter into the analysis.

And within economics itself the strategy of modifying existing theory to accommodate behaviorally observed deviations may gradually undermine the elegant simplicity that has been one of its hallmark attractions. The danger is that theory can become encumbered with a mass of Ptolemaic epicycles and the discipline can be left behind after an eventual Copernican simplification.

Still, we have seen that there are considerable advantages to the deviations approach and therefore good reasons to continue using it, despite some problems. Now we can turn to some examples suggestive of the potential—and challenges—of the alternative. I offer my views on the second perspective, the approach that starts from "how the brain works," not as an economist, and also not as a psychologist, but as an organizational theorist who tries to pay close attention to psychology and economics.

At bottom, the relationship to psychology has been a major feature distinguishing organization theory from organizational economics. Roughly, one might say that many organizational theorists have been closer to the second approach described here, feeling obliged to take psychological (and social psychological) results on their own terms, and build up organization theory with those results as starting points, while economists have asked—and rightly so—how psychological results may be assimilated to the needs and theories of economics. In consequence, organization theory has far less formalized theoretical development than does organizational economics, though it addresses a broader array of significant issues.[33]

The Perspective Starting from "How the Brain Works"

My method for illustrating the possibilities now emerging for the second approach will be to consider a few examples of striking developments in psychology and their possible significance for economists' views of organization. I have focused in

---

[33] I think this distinction raises important choices for economics: the economics of organization that meets the needs of economics' other fields (finance, health, labor, macro, . . .) may not need to take into account the full richness of contemporary psychological research, or the full complexity of what we see going on in real organizing. Or it may. . . . But "real economists" have far more wisdom about this question than I do, and so I will devote myself to extending the portrait of what I believe is going on, leaving for those within economics the problems of judging how much of the development needs to be assimilated, and of how that can be done without losing the inferential power of current theoretical formalizations.

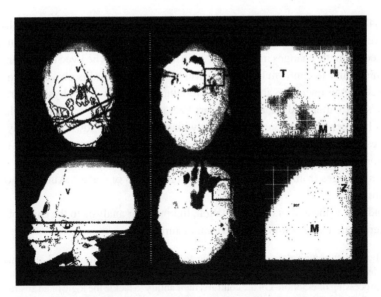

Figure 7.2. Images for analysis of skull of Phineas Gage. Reprinted with permission from Damasio et al. (1994). "The return of Phineas Gage: Clues about the brain from the skull of a famous patient." *Science*, Volume 264, p. 1102. Copyright [1994] AAAS. Reproduced courtesy of Dr Hanna Damasio, the Dana and David Dornsife Cognitive Neuroscience Imaging Center and Brain and Creativity Institute, University of Southern California.

particular on examples involving emotions, since these seem to present some of the deepest challenges.

The first thing to say is that psychology itself is being transformed—as so often happens to a science—in the wake of stunning new possibilities of measurement. The most dramatic and widely noted are various forms of brain imaging—such as positron emission tomography (PET) and functional magnetic resonance imaging (fMRI)—but there are others as well, including improved precision of lesion studies in humans and in animal models; improved chemical detection methods (a few dollars for a simple, reliable saliva assay of important chemicals such as testosterone, cortisol, or progesterone); knockout gene studies in animal models; improved placement of, and recording from, micro-electrodes, now reaching the single brain-cell level; and many more.

The consequences of this measurement gain in psychology are many. Among them is an important increase in our ability to exhibit well-measured counterparts of the previously "soft" observations of clinicians. Thus "hardened," they become more difficult to set aside as we study decision and choice.

A case that dramatizes this change is that of Phineas Gage, a young man of excellent reputation and work habits who was the victim of a construction accident in 1848 that shot a metal rod cleanly through his head. Gage made a full physical recovery from the accident. His intelligence was unaffected. But his physician documented dramatic changes in his character in the dozen years he lived thereafter. Gage lost his ability to conform to social conventions or to honor his own commitments. He became an unemployable and foul-mouthed wanderer. The physician archived Gage's skull after he died, and 155 years later researchers were able to correlate the areas between the entry and exit holes with what is now known from many other studies about lesions affecting the same areas of the brain, the right ventro-medial prefrontal cortex.

Some images from a paper reporting the re-analysis of Gage's skull are shown in Figure 7.2.

And here is the authors' interpretation, linking their analysis to the cases of many modern patients with similar behavioral disturbances:

> For patients with damage comparable to Gage's, their ability to make rational decisions in personal and social matters is invariably compromised and so is their processing of emotion. On the contrary, their ability to tackle the logic of an abstract problem, to perform calculations, and to call up appropriate knowledge and attend to it remains intact. The establishment of such a pattern has led to the hypothesis that emotion and its underlying neural machinery participate in decision-making within the social domain and has raised the possibility that the participation depends on the ventromedial frontal region. This region is reciprocally connected with the subcortical nuclei that control basic biological regulation, emotional processing, and social cognition and behavior, for instance, in amygdala and hypothalamus.
>
> (Damasio et al. 1994)

The case serves to demonstrate two points:

(i) softer clinical observations involving emotions, feelings and social responsibilities can now be aligned with much more precise results from imaging techniques, and lesion studies; and

(ii) fundamental abilities of memory and calculation that have received so much of our attention in work on choice (or decision) are not sufficient to produce minimally effective economic activity.

In normal humans these rational capabilities participate together with emotional responses in a complex choreography that generates thought and action, and that learns from ensuing events—or sometimes does not. In the special cases of injury and disease that have been carefully observed, the choreography breaks down and the breakdown gives us a window onto the fundamental—and often subtle—role of emotion in normal choice activity in social settings.

Another line of research that provides a stimulating example for thinking about organizational settings is work on "mirror neurons." This example is taken from a

Initial endowment: £2,000 facsimile bills

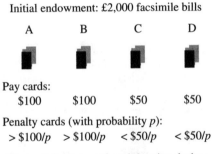

Pay cards:
  $100 $100 $50 $50

Penalty cards (with probability p):
 $> \$100/p$ $> \$100/p$ $< \$50/p$ $< \$50/p$

Figure 7.3. Setup of card-drawing decks.

review by Rizzolatti et al. (2001) of work on such cells. Mirror neurons are active both in motor acts, such as grasping an apple, and in observing the same motor act being carried out by another. Many techniques are involved, but among the most striking is firing data at the individual neuron level recorded from monkeys watching food being placed on a platter and then taking the food off the platter themselves.

The monitored neurons fired both on observing food placement by the experimenter's hand and in the execution of the motor act by the monkey's hand. But when the monkey observed the food being placed using pliers, there was no response from its mirror neurons.

This mirror system is implicated in understanding the actions of others by partially activating the same systems within ourselves that would be involved in carrying out the observed act. And I should add that there is considerable evidence that the mirror neuron systems connect to areas responsible for emotions, such as the amygdala. So, for example, a congenital nerve malformation gives rise to Mobius syndrome. Those suffering it have difficulty moving their facial muscles. These patients also have difficulty learning to understand the emotions expressed in the faces of others.

Results of this kind suggest that emotional responses to experiences of others may be a fundamental predisposition of our normal biological "equipment," that our understanding and evaluation of actions of others arises to some extent through rather detailed mapping onto our own experience, which our body develops special circuitry to carry out. Further work along these lines will presumably have implications for issues such as group identification and altruism.

As a last example, consider an experiment conducted by Bechara and colleagues (1997). In it, subjects, who were either normal or patients with damage to the ventromedial prefrontal cortex, drew cards from one of four decks, beginning with a stock of $2,000 in facsimile bills, and instructed to maximize winnings.

The decks, as indicated in Figure 7.3, contained payoff cards mixed with low-frequency (probability p) penalty cards. In decks A and B, although the payoffs were larger ($100 instead of $50), the penalties were large enough to imply that a

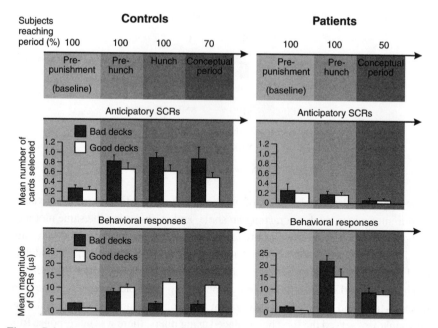

Figure 7.4. Results of card drawing experiment. Reprinted with permission from Bechara et al. 1997. "Deciding advantageously before knowing the advantageous strategy." *Science*, Volume 275, p. 1293. Copyright [1997] AAAS.

draw from the deck was an expected value loss. In decks C and D, with payoffs half the size, the penalties were small enough that they implied expected value gain. No end of play was pre-announced. Play was stopped after 100 trials.

First notice that across the top the data are distinguished for controls on the left and patients on the right. Below those labels this band indicates data separation into phases: prepunishment (before any penalty cards are drawn), pre-hunch phase (after some penalties, but before participants say "I like this deck"), hunch phase (expressed liking *and* anticipatory skin conductance response (SCR)), and conceptual phase (articulating something like "penalties outweigh benefits in $100 decks, but not in $50s").

Skin conductance reveals the subjects' emotional responses as their hands move over the cards. There are a number of things of note:

(i) there is no SCR for any subjects in prepunishment;

(ii) SCR rises for controls in the pre-hunch phase, but stays down for patients, who, in fact, never show significant SCR;

(iii) for controls, the initial preference for bad decks gives way in the pre-hunch phase and becomes very weak in the hunch phase (in fact some control subjects never got the theory but steadily played the C and D decks);

(iv) half the patients were able to state the theory, but they still played A and B more than they played C and D!

Normal subjects are responding emotionally to projected actions even before they can voice a hunch, while patients only have baseline responses, never express hunches, and do not execute the theory even if they do state it correctly. The data thus provide another indication that in the brain a complex process is required to relate evaluations of prior experiences to future actions. That process may affect action before it affects cognition or even without affecting cognition. Conversely, the results for the patients show that a cognitive grasp of the situation may be attained without affecting action.

The examples provided are intended to illustrate how much difference it will make to economic analysis of organization—and other topics in economics—if the shift continues from "deviations" to "how the brain works." The magnitude of the difference can be seen in the concluding remark of the Camerer–Malmendier review:

> Meso concepts like organizational routines and learning are not rooted in individual behavioral concepts. It is possible that organizational economics could be tied to meso-organizational (or macro-organizational) constructs, but this is not an active area of research.

From the deviations perspective on "individual behavioral concepts" this blunt summary is correct. Yet to an organizational theorist it looks odd, since the evolutionary economics community has produced hundreds of papers about firms stemming from the treatment of routine in Nelson and Winter (1982). Moreover, the performance properties of routine action have been linked to "how the brain works" (Cohen and Bacdayan 1994)—in this case to the distinction between procedural and declarative memory (Squire and Kandel 1999). This stark difference suggests that the visibility of research on routine action in organizations, and of many other important aspects of the day-to-day performance of firms, will depend crucially on which of the two contending perspectives future economic researchers have in mind.

REFERENCES

Bechara, A., H. Damasio, D. Tranel, and A. Damasio. 1997. Deciding advantageously before knowing the advantageous strategy. *Science* 275:1293–95.

Cohen, M., and P. Bacdayan. 1994. Organizational routines are stored as procedural memory: evidence from a laboratory study. *Organization Science* 5:554–68.

Damasio, H., T. Graboski, R. Frank, A. Galaburda, and A. Damasio. 1994. The return of Phineas Gage: Clues about the brain from the skull of a famous patient. *Science* 264: 1102–5.

King-Casas, B., D. Tomlin, C. Anen, C. F. Camerer, S. R. Quartz, and P. R. Montague. 2005. Getting to know you: reputation and trust in two-person economic exchange. *Science* 308:78–83.

Nelson, R., and S. Winter. 1982. *An Evolutionary Theory of Economic Change.* Belknap Press of Harvard University Press.

Rizzolatti, G., L. Fogassi, and V. Gallese. 2001. Neurophysiological mechanisms underlying the understanding and imitation of action. *Nature Neuroscience* 2:662–70.

Squire, L., and E. R. Kandel. 1999. *Memory from Mind to Molecules.* New York: Scientific American Library.

Wrap-Up Panel

This chapter consists of commentary from the meeting participants.

8.1 THE PROBLEMATIC CONTENT AND CONTEXT OF DECISIONS: COMMENT BY ELDAR SHAFIR

Good theories are often based on the few things that really matter, and ignore large amounts of detail. What makes a theory successful, however, is our ability to use it to distinguish between detail that can be ignored at low cost and detail that is needed for a successful characterization of the relevant facts. A theory can run into trouble when it dismisses as irrelevant factors that are at the heart of important outcomes.

With regard to modern economic theory as a descriptive enterprise, we have increasingly good evidence for, and some insight into, a variety of behavioral factors that appear to be highly consequential for economic outcomes. Many of these factors, however, are dismissed by the classical theory, explicitly or implicitly, as unimportant detail. The list is long. It includes a variety of cognitive, perceptual, social, cultural, and other factors that appear to play a central role in people's decisions, in ways that are profoundly different from what was envisioned by the progenitors of rational agents. A number of these factors have been discussed in this book, and some are further considered in Tirole's commentary below.

Now, on the descriptive front, it is true that what we have so far consists largely of "a list" of factors, rather than a characterization that is more general or theoretical in nature. And this lack of generalization makes any attempt to incorporate the new behavioral insights into the models quite daunting. It is also at the heart of Tirole's admonition that we resist the temptation to incorporate "stylized facts" into economists' relatively unified, "portable" theory.

As a modeling strategy, that may be exactly right. But for those of us who want an account that is descriptively faithful, some fairly radical revisions to the portable theory seem unavoidable. The problem is deeper than merely choosing which of the stylized facts are in and which are out. The problem we have, if you will, is one not just of content, but also of structure.

The dialogue between economics and psychology presents a classic divergence in disciplinary sensitivities. Whereas the psychologist is happy to focus on the fascinating events happening behind the eyes and between the ears, the economist wants to know what specific behaviors are generated thereby. This tension has had a substantial impact on psychologists who are engaged in the dialogue with economists: their work has veered in the direction of a greater focus on actual outcomes, in real circumstances, with real incentives, and so on. At the same time, economists interested in a behaviorally more sophisticated theory need to take into account some fundamental facts about our mental lives. And by that I do not mean any specific brain processes underlying any particular activity but, rather, a much more general, somewhat mundane, fact about psychology that is critical to decision-making.

Whereas the notion of "construal" is second nature to psychologists, it is far less obvious to the untrained observer and even less so to economists. Economic thinking about optimization concerns itself with things in the world, with alternatives as they really are (or, as they are best understood by a rational actor). The axioms that underlie the normative theory are stated in terms of extensional outcomes, where each option, representing some state of the world, is clearly and uniquely designated, independently of how precisely it may be described or perceived. The problem with this perspective is a terribly trivial but profoundly consequential fact about human nature: people do not actually choose between items in the world— they choose between those items as they are represented in the mind. Decisions are not about objective (extensional) states of the world, but about the mental (intensional) representations of those states (see Tversky and Kahneman 1983). And the mental representation of states of the world is subject to a rich psychology involving perception, embellishment, interpretation, and distortion.

Construal processes are central to many areas of psychology, ranging from auditory and visual perception, memory, language, and self-perception, to judgments, decisions, opinion surveys, and social interaction. In the case of decision-making, as we all know well, nuanced differences in otherwise logically equivalent representations of options can generate significantly different perceptions, trigger different reactions, and yield systematically different choices.

We thus are left with multiple sources of tension. First, there are the "contents" of decision: what attributes enter into people's calculations. These include things such as prosocial behavior, a concern with fairness, or interpersonal comparisons, which turn out to have a more substantial then normatively anticipated impact. Then there is the structure, or context, of decision. This includes unavoidable contextual nuances, ranging from how the options are described (even when providing otherwise identical information), to the process used to elicit preference, the presence or absence of other ("irrelevant") alternatives, the point of reference, and so on.

As a matter of fact, there are additional factors that are somewhere in between context and content. There are features that—unlike fairness, say—people do not profess to care about, and may even be unaware of, but which, once introduced into the context of a decision, nonetheless can have a substantial impact on choice. For example, people gently touched on the shoulder by a waitress at a restaurant tip higher than those who were not touched. And when asked later, all attribute their tipping to the quality of service, with no awareness of the influence of the touch (Crusco and Wetzel 1984; Schwarz 1990; Schwarz and Clore 1983).

We have recently conducted a field experiment in South Africa to assess the relative importance of price and of various subtle psychological features in the decision to take-up a loan offer from a local lender (Bertrand et al. 2005). Some 57,000 incumbent clients of the lender were sent letters offering large short-term loans at randomly chosen interest rates. Consistent with standard economics, those offered higher rates were less likely to take up a loan then those with access to lower rates. In addition, various psychological features on the offer letter, which did not affect offer terms or economic content, were also independently randomized. One of the features consisted of the number of sample loans displayed: the offer letter displayed either one example of a loan size and term, along with the respective monthly repayment, or it displayed multiple (four) examples of loan sizes and terms. In contrast with standard economic prediction, we found higher take-up under the one-example description than under the multiple-example version. The magnitude of this effect was large: the simpler description of the offer had the same positive effect on take-up as dropping the monthly interest on these loans by two percentage points. (In a similar vein, Huberman et al. (2004) found that employees' participation in 401(k) plans drops as the number of fund options proposed by their employer increases.) We also randomized the presence or absence of a smiling woman's picture in the bottom corner of the offer letters. For the men in the sample, the presence of that picture had the same positive effect on take-up as dropping the monthly interest on the loans by 4.5 percentage points! On average, any one psychological manipulation we tried had the same effect as a one-half percentage point change in the monthly interest rate.

Unlike a concern with fairness or even an aversion to losses, nobody would acknowledge or, for that matter, be willing to entertain the possibility that a touch on the shoulder or a picture in the corner of a letter predisposes them to make a substantially different economic decision. Choice behavior is the outcome of a variety of cognitive and affective processes. Some of these we consciously endorse and even insist on; others we have no introspective access to, nor control over (Bargh 1997). And many of both kinds of processes depart in significant ways from economists' unified, "portable" theory.

Tirole correctly observes that (see p. 298, this volume)

> When parents report that they "value" education, when Americans "believe" they should be saving more, or when people "believe" that they perform better than average in a number of dimensions, they may indeed be making mistakes, but they may also be engaging in cheap (although therefore not very effective) reinforcement of their identity or self-image.

Similar remarks may apply to economists' "belief" that their model is "doing just fine, thank you." Perhaps they are not actually making an error, just reaffirming their identity. And meetings such as this may help alleviate the pressure and allow for a more permissive self-image. It is, in fact, quite respectable to be in possession of a theory that is in many ways beautiful, but that nonetheless requires substantial restructuring before it is able to predict our quirky behaviors.

REFERENCES

Bargh, J. A. 1997. The automaticity of everyday life. In *Advances in Social Cognition* (ed. J. R. S. Wyer), Volume 10, pp. 1–61. Mahwah, NJ: Erlbaum.

Bertrand, M., D. Karlan, S. Mullainathan, E. Shafir, and J. Zinman. 2005. What's psychology worth? A field experiment in the consumer credit market. NBER Working Paper 11892.

Crusco, A. H., and C. G. Wetzel. 1984. The Midas touch: the effects of interpersonal touch on restaurant tipping. *Personality and Social Psychology Bulletin* 10:512–17.

Huberman, G., S. S. Iyengar, and W. Jiang. 2004. How much choice is too much: determinants of individual contributions in 401K retirement plans. In *Pension Design and Structure: New Lessons From Behavioral Finance* (ed. O. S. Mitchell and S. P. Utkus), pp. 83–96. Oxford University Press.

Schwarz, N. 1990. Feelings as information: informational and motivational functions of affective states. In *Handbook of Motivation and Cognition: Foundations of Social Behavior* (ed. E. T. Higgins and R. Sorrentino), Volume 2, pp. 527–61. New York: Guildford Press.

Schwarz, N., and G. L. Clore 1983. Mood, misattribution, and judgments of well-being: informative and directive functions of affective states. *Journal of Personality and Social Psychology* 45:513–23.

Tversky, A., and D. Kahneman. 1983. Extensional vs. intuitive reasoning: the conjunction fallacy in probability judgment. *Psychological Review* 91:293–315.

8.2 COMMENT BY JEAN TIROLE

8.2.1 *A Familiar Trade-Off*

Churchill once famously stated that "democracy is the worst form of government except for all those others that have been tried"; economists have long regarded their neoclassical model in a similar light: clearly unsatisfactory, yet superior to alternatives. This unhappy state is of course what makes research and volumes like this so exciting.

The economist's self-view is currently being challenged. Building in particular on work in psychology, the standard model of maximization of present discounted expected utility has been recently amended to allow for

- a broader description of preferences with the introduction of anticipatory feelings and memories, concerns about self-image, social values and even emotions, and the use of reference points and path dependency,
- a broader approach to discounting, as with hyperbolic preferences,
- a broader take on belief formation, including errors in Bayesian updating, imperfect memory, and biases in hedonic forecasts, and
- a challenge to the optimization hypothesis—rules of thumb, mental representations, analogies, and categorization strategies, with an ongoing debate as to whether limited optimization is rational given memory, mental search and time constraints.

As has already been noted in this volume, while other social scientists often do not aim at an overarching theory of decision-making, economists often tend to prefer a relatively unified, "portable" theory that helps explain a wide range of behaviors with a small number of core assumptions. They use a relatively parsimonious framework that has predictive power and normative implications across a broad range of situations. Thaler once rightly remarked that behavioral economics will be successful once it stops being "behavioral" and it becomes just economics. To this purpose, and in my opinion, we sometimes need to resist the temptation to incorporate "stylized facts" about human behavior into reduced forms for economic modeling and should rather build more structural models, "dig deeper," and run experiments to discriminate finely among alternatives in order to perform normative analysis. Our profession has sometimes learned this lesson the hard way, as when, in reaction to the (correct) observation that firms do not maximize profits, the literature of the 1950s and 1960s added objectives into a firm's reduced form payoff function (this literature was abandoned when agency theory built an alternative approach based on the unifying principle of asymmetric information). Understand me well: warning against the use of reduced forms has its limits; after all, we all to some degree always use reduced forms in order to limit complexity, and even reduced forms that are by any measure very sloppy can prove stimulating and ultimately useful (witness IS–LM theory).

8.2.2 *Some Illustrations*

8.2.2.1 Prosocial Behavior

My first illustration may be tainted by recent work with Roland Benabou (Benabou and Tirole, forthcoming), but I will be discussing the challenge to modeling, which

I feel rather confident about, more than the way we address it, for which I am a poor judge. This illustration refers to how economics can take on board prosocial behavior. People frequently engage in activities that are costly to them and mostly benefit others: they vote, volunteer time, help strangers, give to political or charitable organizations, donate blood, join rescue squads, and sometimes even risk or sacrifice their life.

One tractable approach for economists would consist in positing a reduced form in which individuals—or at least a fraction of individuals—have a taste for prosocial behavior in the same way macroeconomists use warm-glow preferences in order to build a tractable model of bequest behavior. One could perhaps also add some situational parameters to account for the wide variations in prosocial contributions across individuals, circumstances, and causes. Even so enriched, the "taste-for-prosocial-behavior-in-the-utility-function" approach may encounter some difficulties.

First, it would be difficult to explain, except in an ad hoc manner, why incentives sometimes crowd out prosocial behavior. In this reduced form, incentives would just add to the natural proclivity of individuals to engage in prosocial behavior.

Second, reduced forms would not offer clues as to why prosocial behaviors are sometimes socially determined.

Third, and quite importantly, the "prosociality" of prosocial behaviors often needs to be questioned. Consider the following.

- We tip taxi drivers in rich countries and fail to give money to starving children in Africa.

- In studies reported in Glazer and Konrad (1996), less than 1% of donations are anonymous.[1]

- People often react with disapproval when someone reveals how generous and disinterested he is.

- In a transportation-related survey of about 1,300 individuals, Johansson-Stenman and Svedsäter (2003) find that people who are asked which attributes are most important to them in a car systematically put environmental performance near the top and social status near the bottom; but when asked about the true preferences of their neighbors or average compatriots, they give dramatically reversed rankings.

- A clever experiment by Dana et al. (2003) reveals that when people know how their choices will affect other people, they often display substantial altruistic behavior; when they are given the opportunity to remain ignorant of how their choices affect others, or of their precise role in the outcome, many choose

---

[1]Anonymous donations are still tax-deductible, so the lack of anonymity is probably due to signaling concerns.

not to know and revert to selfish choices. They exploit the "moral wriggle room." To illustrate this, suppose that an individual plays a "dictator game," i.e., a game in which he chooses between (say) two actions affecting his welfare and that of another, passive individual. A "selfish action," A, gives the highest material payoff, 5, to the dictator. The other action, B, gives him only 4. Suppose that the selfish action yields 0 and action B yields 8 to the passive player. As is well-known, a substantial fraction of dictators in those circumstances would choose action B, sacrificing a bit of material payoff for the psychic payoff associated with a good deed. Suppose, next, that there are two states of nature, and that the dictator's payoff is as above regardless of the state of nature. By contrast, the passive player's preferences across actions depend on the state of nature. In the first state, they are as above. In the second state, action B yields 4 to the passive individual while action A yields her 5. Finally, the dictator is asked whether he wants to know which state of nature prevails. It would seem that the dictator would want to know which state prevails and, provided that she enjoys the psychic payoff from raising the passive individual's payoff from 0 to 8, choose action B in the former case, and action A in the latter case. A substantial fraction of dictators, though, choose not to know and select the selfish action, A, with the "excuse" (in their own eyes at least) that action A may actually benefit the other individual.[2]

- Identification with a group and the concomitant altruistic or even heroic acts are often associated with a hostile or even cruel attitude toward the out-group.

These six observations, and others, suggest that the economists' rendering of prosocial behavior should combine heterogeneity in the individuals' degree of altruism and greed with concerns for social reputation and self-respect. This is in line with (many) psychologists' approach to these issues in terms of the "over-justification effect." For instance, a prominent explanation of the "crowding out effects" of prosocial behavior by incentives alluded to earlier is that the presence of rewards or punishments changes the meaning that people attach to actions (by others or their own) in a detrimental way. My own work with Benabou on prosocial behavior combines heterogeneous social preferences with cognition. That is, prosocial actions are undertaken both because a fraction of individuals are genuinely other-regarding, and because individuals either are in a quest for social esteem or strive to maintain a certain self-view of "what kind of person" they are. In such an environment, incentives then give rise, in economics parlance, to a signal extraction problem, which gives a formal content to the over-justification effect. (This cognitive approach is

---

[2]This evidence on the use of moral wriggle room is the self-signaling counterpart of Anne Case's point on social signaling; namely, that people try to escape social norms of sharing by spending immediately or by investing in illiquid assets.

then used to study various issues such as the form and confidentiality of prosocial behavior, the emergence of multiple social norms enforced by the interplay of honor and shame, and the competition among the recipients of altruism.)

A digression here: when discussing survey evidence on attitudes and beliefs quite generally, we should take social signaling and especially self-signaling more seriously than we currently do. This was pretty clear in the transportation survey just discussed. Similarly, when parents report that they "value" education, when Americans "believe" they should be saving more, or when people "believe" that they perform better than average in a number of dimensions they may indeed be making mistakes, but they may also be engaging in cheap (although therefore not very effective) reinforcement of their identity or self-image.[3]

With prosocial behavior as with any other theme of behavioral economics, social scientists may have to dig deeper in order to find the primitives and to perform a welfare analysis. Other illustrations include three concepts that many at the meeting, including myself, think economists should take on board: fairness, endowment effects, and bounded willpower.

8.2.3 *Fairness*

Why do people turn down unfair offers in ultimatum games; or, as Bewley documented (see Chapter 5, this volume), have their morale reduced when their wage is cut? Is it because of intention-based preferences (an intrinsic preference for reciprocity), social preferences (a preference for certain forms of income distribution—perhaps one that refers to a moral ideal of equal pay for equal work, a rule highly sensitive to adverse selection, or equal pay for equal output, a rule highly sensitive to moral hazard), a preoccupation with self-image (for example, the management of one's self-reputation as someone who does not turn the other cheek), a taste for procedural fairness (also perhaps stemming from a moral ideal associated with organizational efficiency), or a more standard economic explanation, suggested by Holmström at this meeting, in which the victim learns about others' views of himself and project the implications of the signal for the future of the relationship?

I do not know, but two points are worth making: first, different hypotheses have different positive and policy implications. Second, and relating to the first four hypotheses, it would be helpful to understand the origin of the preferences. Ernst Fehr's research agenda should prove very helpful in this respect.

8.2.4 *Loss Aversion and Endowment Effects*

Again, a fascinating and relevant effect (as documented for example, by Bewley (see Chapter 5, this volume) for the quick development, following an increase in

---

[3] Other well-known biases associated with survey evidence include insufficient thinking and the desire to please the experimenter.

pay, of a feeling of entitlement). On the other hand, a key challenge for the theory of loss aversion and endowment effects is that of the determination of the reference point. As Honkapohja noted above (Chapter 5, this volume), empirical observations cannot be interpreted through the lens of an application-specific reference point. Rather, some broad principles are called for. My hunch is that a cognitive approach building on self-signaling and social signaling (and sometimes on informed principal theory) is likely to be relevant. But this is largely unexplored territory at this stage.[4] Furthermore, other approaches, for example, building on neuroscience, are likely to be relevant as well.

Other examples come to mind. For instance, hyperbolic discounting is a tractable reduced form capturing bounded willpower, but one that for some applications will prove rather unsatisfactory. (Incidentally, the classical economists' rendering of bounded willpower—for instance that of Smith, Bohm-Bawerk, or Jevons—was richer than that of behavioral economists.) My guess is that, as for the rest of economics, behavioral economics must build on a back-and-forth interaction between careful and parsimonious modeling combined with structural tests in the field and in the laboratory.

REFERENCES

Benabou, R., and J. Tirole. Forthcoming. Incentives and prosocial behavior. *American Economic Review*.

Dana, J., R. Weber, and J. Kuang. 2003. Exploiting moral wriggle room: behavior inconsistent with a preference for fair outcomes. Carnegie Mellon Behavioral Decision Research Working Paper 349. (Available at http://ssrn.com/abstract=400900.)

Glazer, A., and K. Konrad. 1996. A signaling explanation of charity. *American Economic Review* 86:1019–28.

Johansson-Stenman, O., and H. Svedsäter. 2003. Self image and choice experiments: hypothetical and actual willingness to pay. Göteborg University and London School of Economics, Working Paper 94.

Koszegi, B., and M. Rabin. 2004. A model of reference-dependent preferences. EconWPA Working Paper 0407001.

8.3 COMMENT BY TIMOTHY D. WILSON

It is gratifying to see how ideas in social psychology have been applied to behavioral economics and real-world problems. The two disciplines share a common goal: to understand how people process information and make decisions in ways that impact their lives and the lives of others.

---

[4]An interesting exception is Koszegi and Rabin (2004), which endogenizes the reference point using Koszegi's notion of "personal equilibrium."

It is important, though, to point out differences between the disciplines of social psychology and behavioral economics that have, perhaps, kept them apart. Behavioral economics has largely been concerned with understanding policies and real-world applications, whereas social psychology has focused more on basic research—on what makes people tick. There are also important methodological differences. Psychology is dominated by laboratory experiments, whereas behavioral economics relies more on field studies. There are, of course, many exceptions to these rules in both disciplines, but you are more likely to find a social psychologist doing basic laboratory studies with college students, and more likely to find behavioral economists doing large-scale field studies of important real-world problems.

I think each field can learn from the other and that a lot of progress will be made if we join forces. How might we facilitate such interactions and what form might they take? I suggest that we collaborate on small-scale studies that employ the experimental method in applied settings.

Social psychologists have been reticent to do field research for a number of reasons. One is that it can be difficult to know how the processes we study in laboratory studies, in which we focus on a small number of independent variables, will play out in natural settings. Armchair thinking on how intervention might work is not much help here. We need to take our best shot in small-scale interventions, with randomly assigned control groups, much as argued by Ross and Nisbett (1991).

Admittedly, it is not easy to conduct well-controlled experiments in natural settings. With a little cleverness, however, we can do it, as with the following examples.

Ayres (see p. 145) mentioned a fascinating correlational study he has done in New Haven on tipping taxicab drivers. Taxi passengers gave lower tips to African-American drivers than to white drivers. As with any correlational study, the causal interpretation of this finding is unclear. To make a stronger causal inference, the study could be done experimentally. The driver of the taxi could obscure his face with a hat or hood, making his race unclear. Then, the researcher could randomly assign passengers to race of driver, by changing the picture of the driver that is posted in the back seat. With such an experiment we would know for sure whether the race of the driver is causing people to tip differently (the driver, of course, should not know which picture is posted during any particular ride). This would fall in the domain of social psychology that looks at context effects on people's prejudice attitudes, in particular their uncontrolled prejudiced attitudes.

Second, Mullainathan (see p. 86) described the problem of low school attendance in developing countries. It has been suggested that building in incentives such as feeding kids at school at lunch time might be a way to solve the problem. That could be tried experimentally with a small intervention, in which incentives are offered in some school districts but not in others. There are practical and ethical problems but the power of such designs would probably warrant the experiment.

Third, many universities and businesses are instituting diversity training programs, in which the attendees are asked to undergo some sort of educational exercise to enlighten them about diversity and presumably to change their behavior in more egalitarian direction. Little is known about how these programs affect people. If you ask the organizers how they evaluate whether the program has the intended effects, they often point to the responses of the people who participate in the program. This might have some value, but a much more powerful design would be test these programs experimentally. There is a big industry offering diversity training services but, for obvious reasons, they are not always interested in in-depth evaluation of their effectiveness. However, it would not be difficult to come up with control groups that are randomly assigned to different treatments in order to evaluate their true effects.

Fourth, think of a new drug for cancer. We all agree that it should be tested very carefully for harmful effects before marketing. We seem not to have the same attitude toward psychological interventions. In Canada, for example, the law now requires that cigarette packs have pictures of people with cancer and other scary images to dissuade people from smoking. To my knowledge, this intervention was never experimentally tested to see whether the pictures have any effect, desirable or not. When it comes to psychological interventions, we rely more on common sense about what we think will happen and, unlike testing how a drug will work, see little reason to test these interventions experimentally. I suspect that the pictures on cigarette packs in Canada do have some effect, but that is just my common sense talking, and I think it is important to find out empirically what those effects are.

One often hears from social psychologists that they would like to do more applied research but there are all kinds of practical and institutional barriers. This is one area in which social psychologists should learn more about neighboring fields such as behavioral economics. I have been very impressed with the kind of field studies many economists are conducting, often using experimental designs to study important real-world problems. There is a natural collaboration here. Social psychologists know a lot about social influence and cognitive processing, and many are eager to see how these processes play out in the real world. By partnering with economists who have much more experience studying real-world problems, substantial progress could be made.

8.4 COMMENT BY PETER DIAMOND

I share the hope, expressed above by Tirole, that in time behavioral economics will cease to exist. Currently, a first-year economics graduate student learns statistics, math, micro, and macro. At some point, one of these students interested in behavioral economics studies psychology in some form, taught by an economist or, if the student is lucky, by a psychologist. Integration of the underlying intellectual basis for behavioral analysis into the first-year core is the long-term hope.

In designing this conference we wrestled with the question of planning a conference and a volume that would enhance behavioral economics. This issue was addressed explicitly by Camerer (see Chapter 7), who said that behavioral economics really started with hammering away at anomalies. This is a lot easier to do when relevant data are present. I think it is always important to keep anomalies in mind and I think everybody recognizes that merely hammering at anomalies does not move paradigms all by itself. More than that has to be done.

I hope that the conference and this book can generate an increasing respect towards the potential for psychology in economics. I think this is helped by having all the excitement generated by brain pictures in neuroeconomics. However, to go from these brain images to outcomes is both hard and a long route. But I think that through experiments we can increase awareness of the potential contributions of social sciences to better policy generally. And that will make psychology more acceptable inside economics as well. A primary target for generating excitement for behavioral economics is obviously Congress. Congress votes to provide money for building bridges, but it does not vote on a blueprint for the bridge. Yet when it comes to designing a pension system, Congress lays out the blueprint. If we can get the idea of the importance of experiments more embedded in the public consciousness, i.e., more of the sense that there is real expertise in social science, then maybe Congress will rely more on that expertise, as they do with bridges.

How do we advance behavioral economics beyond the anomalies and generate more respect? I think we need to convince a lot of people, and that means primarily young people, that this is a good research opportunity. That is what this volume is trying to do. So what does it take to make a good research opportunity? A first element is that it has to include the type of work that people like to do. An example is the kind of extremely complex simulations that are perhaps best exemplified by the work of Tom Sargent—this really appeals to a set of people who like to get into the code and have the computer skills to do very complex calculations. If it is not fun for you to do that kind of research, you are not going to get caught up in that style of work. Some people like to do hard theory where they use their math techniques. There were some references in the conference to work by Gul and Pesendorfer, which I think has much potential to help people recognize that there is scope in behavioral economics for doing this kind of work. I say this even though I think the psychology in their work is not well-grounded. We need to recognize that different people like to do different kinds of research and the research endeavor benefits from different people doing different kinds of research.

And here, with some reluctance, I may disagree a little with Tirole. I think that sometimes the insights from reduced-form models are worth having as long as one does not overinterpret them. But this goes with the basic point that the real distinction is not between a good model and a bad model, but between a model that is good for some question and one that is bad for that question.

A second element in having a good research opportunity is that there is an audience. Most people do not write for themselves (although a few do). They want an audience so that they can think they are going to be read, think they are going to be applauded. I think this volume can make it clear that there is a range of areas here with audiences and potential audiences. The way we picked topics was to stay away from the fields that are already well-developed or well-advertised—behavioral finance does not need this kind of advertising and behavioral macro just had all the fuss from a Nobel prize to a practitioner. There was no behavioral industrial organization covered at the conference because there is not yet an audience there.

A third element for a good research opportunity, and the one that gives me the most pause, is the ability to judge the quality of a contribution. Most people do not want to write for an audience if the bulk of the audience is not going to like what is written. A researcher needs a sense of what it takes to do good work. One of the things that bothers me a lot in behavioral economics is that it is much harder to judge what will be well-received than it is in a well-established field, where a researcher can judge whether a potential paper seems more interesting than similar ones that have been published—and so it is easy to see where the subject can go. I feel very nervous when talking to graduate students who are thinking about behavioral research; I think the risk, inherent in doing any research, is larger in behavioral economics than in well-developed fields.

The chapters in this volume can help since they spell out what some researchers like. And of course, the bottom line for the definition of a good research opportunity is from the jobs that follow from research, to which economists pay a lot of attention. It is easier for hot prospects who will end up with jobs in top schools to find a supportive environment than it is for the average job candidate.

Long before coming to the conference, I had the feeling that one should never use the term "preferences" without a modifying adjective, whether it be real preferences, underlying preferences, or choice preferences. Preference, I think, needs to be modified since it is so easy to slip verbally from one interpretation of "preference" to another. One of the things I learned at this conference is that the same should be done with "incentives." We have financial incentives and economic incentives. But we also have other ways of changing behavior that are changes in the nature of incentives. I think we need some terminology here remembering that economists have great interest in incentives as well as in outcomes and in equilibria.

Economics and psychology are different disciplines for the good reason that they try to do different things. Sometimes having different disciplines is important for getting results. Sometimes they create barriers, but barriers that one tries to break down. The participants at the meeting are working at this. I think it is useful to remind fellow economists that we tend to use psychology differently from psychologists. Sometimes the difference is a good idea and sometimes it is not. Another goal of the conference was to show that there is a wide range of psychology that can be useful in economics: that is why we wanted diversity in the type of psychologists in this meeting.

This conference was great fun for us; let us hope it will be good for others.

8.5 GENERAL DISCUSSION

I. Ayres

We should promote the possibility of carrying out experiments about social or economic issues more aggressively to policy makers, and require the testing of laws before they are implemented. An example of an arena where this would be highly desirable is in firearms legislation.

Ch. Engel

An experiment in law is very different from an experiment in medicine because of the Heidelberg Principle: in the case of law, performing the experiment changes the environment.

T. D. Wilson

If you start with a small experiment, this concern about general equilibrium effects is not so serious, and we will still obtain valuable results.

P. Diamond

Politicians may not agree to evaluation through experiments because many politicians would worry that the results of experiments would undermine support for the legislative outcomes they want to push.

From audience: what is the role of evolutionary psychology?

E. Shafir

We do not know much about evolutionary psychology, because there are no fossils. It is good for developing intuitions, but it is not enough for supporting and explaining findings.

T. D. Wilson

Evolutionary psychology is a bit like psychoanalysis. It can explain anything but is very difficult to test. Its value, perhaps, is in generating new hypotheses that can be tested experimentally. I think the number of novel hypotheses it has generated about social behavior, however, is very small.

A. Rangel

I believe in neuroscience and I want to work on this. It is not only about brain imaging, it is about trying to understand which processes are activated. How the brain makes decisions is very relevant to economics. In the case of addiction, we know how particular substances activate processes in the brain. I am surprised that psychologists are even less enthusiastic than economists. Is this because of competition about resources?

I want to come back to animal studies such as the studies on bees that Shafir talked about. There are two kinds of animal studies. Some are about processes, such as monkey studies, and I find those studies valuable. Other studies are about choices, and those are less useful for economics because humans have a much more complex brain circuitry to make choices and hence animal studies are of limited use here.

E. Fehr

I can imagine psychologists in the 1950s saying that social psychology was not useful. I think there is good research and bad research in all fields. There is serious research going on in neuroscience, and it is a legitimate field of inquiry. It has turned out to be very useful for animal and primate research, so it has a potential for understanding human behavior as well. Neuroscience might be hysterical, but it is intrinsically interesting, it will be done, and it might generate very important findings. It is important for economists to play a role, because they ask different questions (in the same way as economists ask different questions to psychologists now).

N. Stern

Can you give examples in neuroscience? This might be easier than in economics. I tried to convince politicians for a long time; and I realized that one good example is worth a thousand regressions.

Politicians have very short time horizons. Therefore, a more promising route to affect policies is to work with government agencies such as the U.S. Department of Education or the World Bank which have much longer time horizons.

S. Mullainathan

This is already well underway. For example, the U.S. Department of Education now requires randomized experiments and careful evaluation before implementing new policies. This is often driven by the person at the head of the institution, and those top administrators are often more open to using randomized trials than [are] elected officials.

There is a tension between psychology and economics: economists like generality, to be able to make predictions, while psychologists are often reluctant to extend their findings beyond the specific context of their study.

T. D. Wilson

This difference is probably not that stark. Psychologists are also willing to make predictions about the real world; it is really about their willingness to go out and test these predictions in the field.

B. Holmström

This is a completely atheoretical conference. One concern that comes up for a theorist is that you listen to examples, and your temptation is to just go with experiments, which will work for a while, but eventually you will have to organize facts using theories (as Tirole emphasized earlier). In this sense, this conference has been disappointing because it has not yet reached the stage of proposing theories.

E. Fehr

There are some domains in behavioral economics where we try to sort theories out: this is the case, for example, with social preferences, where theories are proposed and then tested with experiments. I hope that the cycle between proposing theories and testing those theories with empirical or experimental evidence will be short (weeks), as it is in physics, rather than long (decades) as was the case in economics in the past.

J. Tirole

Everybody uses reduced forms and they are indeed often very useful. For example, although the IS–LM theory in macroeconomics is a very reduced form, it has played a tremendously useful role. Later on, research based on new developments in imperfect competition, costly price readjustments, search theory or for corporate finance ended up capturing aspects of the IS–LM reduced form predictions. Yet, our aim should be to develop unifying theories which are not context dependent, so that they can be used for normative purposes.

E. Shafir

If we want to become behaviorally more sophisticated, I think that, at least at our current level of understanding, we need many different theories and that developing a unifying theory to explain everything is an impossible dream.

Index

401(k), 26, 38, 96, 264, 293

addiction, 40, 91, 195; physiology of,
  91; rational, 41
adverse selection, 166
advertising, 34, 52, 65, 198
Agell, Jonas, 168
Akerlof, George, 162, 189
Allais, Maurice, 116
analysis: normative, 14, 31, 81, 117,
  145, 295
Andreoni, James, 58, 66
Arrow, Kenneth, 196, 223
Asch, Solomon, 100
"as-if" interpretation, 24
attribution theory, 245
availability heuristic, 203
Ayres, Ian, 145, 300

Becker, Gary, 42, 195
behavior: dynamically inconsistent, 30;
  prosocial, 296
behavioral anomalies, 12
Benabou, Roland, 37, 243, 295
Benartzi, Schlomo, 96
Bernheim, Douglas, 7, 10, 23, 43, 67,
  81, 152
Bertrand, Marianne, 246
Bewley, Truman, 158, 188, 239, 298
bias: "law of small numbers", 204;
  group-based, 121, 138; hindsight,
  124, 132, 245; implicit, 122;
  optimism, 123; racial, 121, 138;
  self-serving, 102, 123, 130
Blader, Steven, 181
Blinder, Alan, 167
Bolton, Gary, 13
bounded rationality, 121, 145, 223, 281
Brumberg, Richard, 20

Camerer, Colin, 3, 13, 64, 240, 256, 283
Campbell, Carl, 167
Case, Anne, 113
Choi, Don, 167
Choi, James, 24, 26
choice: dynamically inconsistent, 27;
  inefficient, 26
Christakis, Nicholas, 233
citizenship: organizational, 177
Coase Theorem, 117
cognitive: ability, 110; economics, 256;
  economy, 281; error, 5, 146, 196;
  heuristics, 109; mechanism, 48;
  process, 28, 47; therapy, 44
coherent preference, 11
commitment, 90–91, 133, 260, 265;
  device, 92, 113–14; problem, 114
consumer protection law, 134
consumption, 23
context, 120
contract: law, 120; renegotiation, 133
coordination failure, 253
corporate finance, 258
corporate law, 131
corruption, 106
counter-cue, 52
cue, 28, 146
cue-conditioning, 49
cue-triggered mistakes, 32, 49
cue-triggered present-bias, 53
cue-triggered recidivism, 43
culture, 252

debiasing, 116, 137, 146
default, 82, 90, 95, 118, 133, 231;
  option, 26, 38, 217; plan, 217
development economics, 78, 85